W9-BNU-117

A Rhetoric of Argument

Second Edition

JEANNE FAHNESTOCK

University of Maryland

MARIE SECOR

Pennsylvania State University

McGraw-Hill Publishing Company

New York   St. Louis   San Francisco   Auckland   Bogotá   Caracas
Hamburg   Lisbon   London   Madrid   Mexico   Milan   Montreal
New Delhi   Oklahoma City   Paris   San Juan   São Paulo
Singapore   Sydney   Tokyo   Toronto

For
Anna, Laura,
Peter and
Derek

This book was developed by STEVE PENSINGER, Inc.

A Rhetoric of Argument

Copyright © 1990, 1982 by McGraw-Hill, Inc. All rights reserved.
Printed in the United States of America. Except as permitted under the
United States Copyright Act of 1976, no part of this publication may be
reproduced or distributed in any form or by any means, or stored in a data
base or retrieval system, without the prior written permission of the
publisher.

3 4 5 6 7 8 9 0 DOH DOH 8 9 4 3 2 1 0 9

ISBN 0-07-557734-8

This book was set in Palatino by ComCom, Inc.
The editors were Steven Pensinger and Tom Holton;
the designer was Wanda Siedlecka;
the production supervisor was Valerie A. Sawyer.
R. R. Donnelley & Sons Company was printer and binder.

Library of Congress Cataloging-in-Publication Data

Fahnestock, Jeanne, (date).
     A rhetoric of argument / Jeanne Fahnestock, Marie Secor—2nd
ed.
          p.   cm.
     Includes index.
     ISBN 0-07-557734-8
     1. English language—Rhetoric.   2. Logic.   I. Secor, Marie, (date).
     II. Title.
PE1431.F3   1990
808'.042—dc20   89-8305

Contents

PART FOUR WHAT SHOULD WE DO ABOUT IT? 263

PART FIVE WHAT EVERY ARGUMENT NEEDS 305

Foreword

Argument has been recognized as a kind of discourse ever since Aristotle lectured and Cicero wrote. For centuries teachers have offered guidance to speakers and writers in composing various kinds of argument: One well-known division of arguments recognizes "forensic" arguments, designed to establish the truth or falsity of allegations about people's conduct and the rightness of judgments about their behavior; "deliberative" arguments, designed to establish the desirability of taking or not taking particular actions; and "epideictic" arguments, designed to demonstrate that someone deserves honor and praise. All of these forms of argument have in common the desire to induce belief, change attitudes, and bring about action by means of discourse.

In some sense, all discourse (oral and written) is argument. When we speak or write (even to ourselves in diaries and journals), we seek to draw attention to what we say. Since attention usually is paid only to discourse that listeners or readers find worth heeding, we try to lead our audience to believe that what we say is justifiable—that there are data to support it or good reasons for saying it, and that we are reliable people who can be trusted to locate the data and the reasons and to set them forth fairly. For example, a friendly letter to our relatives, whether about the most mundane details of our life or about a frightening emergency, asks them to believe in the accuracy of what is being reported and, presumably, in the continued sanity and affection of the writer. In asking readers or listeners to pay attention, *any* writer or speaker implicitly promises discourse that will not only be credible but will also offer some benefit to the audience: In short, he or she is engaged in argument.

But when we speak of argument as a form of writing, we usually are not thinking of letters to relatives. Rather we are thinking of a kind of discourse in which the writer is making an outright claim on readers' judgment or belief—and may also be making a request for action. We are thinking of discourse in which the writer alleges that specific events took place, that those events had particular causes or consequences, that the events are open to certain judgments or evaluations, that specific generalizations are tenable, and/or that definite actions should be taken—in circumstances where readers may be in doubt or may be unwilling to believe what the writer claims. In short, a situation calls for *argument* if what the writer will assert is *in doubt.* If readers are neutral and cannot be expected to believe immediately, unquestioningly, what is said, or if they may well disagree with—that is, disbelieve—what the writer says, then argument is called for. It is about argument in this sense, the sense in which Aristotle and Cicero conceived it, that Jeanne Fahnestock and Marie Secor are writing in *A Rhetoric of Argument.*

Argument in this sense pervades our lives. We are asked to buy products, to give money, to participate in campaigns, to cast votes. Because success in inducing readers or listeners to believe, and act upon, an argument often brings benefits to the arguer, it is clearly in the arguer's interest to argue as imaginatively and as cogently as circumstances permit. But because, as we know, the benefit to be gained from successful argument is sometimes great enough to lead an arguer to be overly zealous in making the case, readers have to be on guard against possible distortion. Furthermore, on many questions inviting judgment or action, the data permit reasonable people to reach different conclusions; therefore, a liberal education in a democratic society, many teachers assert, should equip people to recognize how an argument is built. We must be on guard against acting upon arguments that, in benefiting the arguer, may bring discomfort to us. We must be wary of believing too easily, judging too hastily, acting too quickly on problematic issues.

Perhaps for these reasons, most chapters about argument in texts on writing, and large parts of many textbooks on argument alone, emphasize warnings about where arguments *fail.* They guide their users in searching for what may reduce the credibility of arguments. They list by name large numbers of fallacies, illustrating each and showing how each affects the argument it enters. They point out how to locate hidden premises, or assumptions, underlying the argument, so that readers can see the implications of denying the premises or of adopting others. They offer rudimentary introductions to propositional logic, sometimes with diagrams showing interlocking circles to illustrate which propositions are, and which are not, valid. Sometimes they explore the distinctions between "contraries" and "contradictories" in an effort to help students recognize the impact on an argument of its author's failure to differentiate the two. They provide guidelines for the *deconstruction* of arguments, so that readers can maintain the upper hand and avoid being taken in. In this approach, indeed, many texts on writing seem internally inconsistent: When discussing most kinds of writing, the texts tell writers how to address readers, while in discussing argument, they show writers—considered for the moment as readers—how to test, and resist, others' writing. Despite the importance to students, professional people, and citizens of being able to build arguments that avoid fallacious appeals, many such books about writing offer at best sketchy advice on *constructing* an argument.

In *A Rhetoric of Argument,* Fahnestock and Secor go a long way toward filling the large vacuum left by these other books. While continuing to offer help for readers in identifying the weakness of others' arguments and in constructing refutations of those arguments, they focus attention principally on the task that a writer faces in building an argument. They recognize and demonstrate that many subjects are not matters for argument in the narrower sense in which we use the term here. They recognize that effective argument requires an urgent occasion--a reason why the writer/speaker is moved to come before the reader/listener. They contend that the construction of an argument begins with determining the issue—the question about which readers may not immediately believe what the writer asserts—and continues with the identification of the kind of proposition being argued. While recognizing that the writer's characterization of self and the role or stance he/she takes in addressing the reader will affect the audience's response, Fahnestock and Secor assert that the writer's first responsibility is to define the issue and to recognize the kind of proposition that must be discussed to advance the argument successfully.

Secor and Fahnestock's division of arguments into classes is lucid, neat, and elegant. An argument, they contend, may take the form of claiming that an object or event belongs to a specific "class" (and has the perties of members of that class), or that an object or event has particular features. Or it may take the form of a *statement about causes or effects.* Other apparently distinct kinds of argument are in effect versions or combinations of these two kinds, they believe. An *evaluation* is either a claim that its subject must meet specific standards in order to be said to belong to its group, or it is a statement about the effects of that subject, about whether it produces "desired" or undesirable results. Or an evaluation can be both. A *proposal,* an assertion that some action should be taken, is a special form of causal statement—one which predicts that certain recommended actions will improve the current state of affairs. Almost alone among texts on argument, *A Rhetoric of Argument* focuses on the importance of such prediction and connects it to causal analysis. (A prediction differs from an analysis of the causes of ongoing or completed events, of course, in being about *probable* future events.) For each kind of argument, Fahnestock and Secor tell what sorts of support are required, what the writer must demonstrate in order to provide that support, what data writers can offer to accomplish those demonstrations, and how writers can overcome difficulties in the construction of their arguments. Fahnestock and Secor also guide writers in anticipating the objections and points of disagreement that readers may bring forward, and suggest how writers may respond, as they argue, to those possible objections. The authors illustrate various kinds of argument, and tactics for arguing, by analyzing representative passages of academic and popular discourse, and by offering readers an abundance of passages that readers can study on their own. Finally, the authors help their students to experience, through numerous exercises drawn from a variety of fields, the wide-ranging applicability of their teaching about argument.

It is by teaching the invention of arguments and the construction of written argument, in fact, that Fahnestock and Secor offer their best advice about reading and assessing arguments. By demonstrating what is needed for effective argument, the authors help their students to recognize when argument is not effective. By highlighting how words work—how they may act upon a reader—the authors invite students to recognize where vagueness, ambiguity, obscurity, and evasiveness in words and syntax can weaken the credibility of argument. In so doing, they help their students toward alert *evaluative thinking* (a term I would offer as a replacement for "critical" thinking) about the arguments of others—and about their own. They help students learn to pay thoughtful attention to what other writers, and they themselves, say.

Probably at least half of the assignments in most writing courses invite argument. Intuitively we recognize, in designing such assignments, the importance of helping students learn to argue successfully—to win the assent, or at least the respect, of their readers for the assertions and recommendations they advance. Such teaching prepares students not only for writing in academic disciplines, but for their participation in civic and professional worlds beyond the campus, where, in diverse settings, they will need to use words to encourage beliefs and to bring about desired actions. That is why all students—all readers—can profit from *A Rhetoric of Argument:* it can help us become well-informed, fair-minded, attentive, perceptive, and thus skillful participants in the dialogues by which defensible beliefs are reached and wise actions are decided upon.

—RICHARD L. LARSON

Acknowledgments

We wish to express our gratitude to those colleagues who have helped and encouraged us during the years of thought and work on this book. For the stimulation of her knowledge, conversation, and company, Wilma R. Ebbitt, who brought the course in written argument into being at Penn State, deserves special thanks. Betsy Brown gave us the support of her expertise and humor, and readings of the manuscript by Douglas Park, John Harwood, and Paul Klemp at different stages of progress proved very helpful.

For his advice and criticism we wish to thank in particular Richard L. Larson of Lehman College, City University of New York, who helped us shape and refine the book and gave us confidence in our approach. We also benefited greatly from the comments of John Auchard, University of Maryland; Robert Connors, Louisiana State University; Lester Faigley, University of Texas; Donovan Ochs, University of Iowa; Richard Hootman, University of Iowa; Robert Esch, University of Texas at El Paso; Donald McQuade, Queen's College, City University of New York; and George Yoos, St. Cloud University.

We owe a debt as well to Richard Garretson for his professional friendship, support, and guidance in the development of this book, and to David C. Follmer, Irene Pavitt, Christine Pellicano, Elaine Romano, and Susan Israel of Random House for seeing it through to completion. Donna Williams and Nancy Royer also aided us materially with their patient typing and preparation of drafts.

For help in producing the second edition of *A Rhetoric of Argument* we wish to thank the following people at Random House/McGraw-Hill: Steven Pensinger, Tom Holton, our copy editor Debra Manette, our front matter editor Caroline Izzo, and our permissions editor Barbara Hale. In addition, we would like to thank our colleagues, who provided helpful suggestions for improving the first edition: Dorothy Bankston, Louisiana State University; Kate Begnal, Utah State University; Robert E. Land, University of California—Irvine, and Jeanette Morgan, University of Houston.

Finally, we wish to thank our husbands, Stephen Fahnestock and Robert Secor, who have done so much over the years to strengthen our skills of argument.

Permissions Acknowledgments

Instructor's Introduction:
What Kind of Argument Text Is This?

This book represents an approach to teaching written argument that we learned the hard way, after making many mistakes. If you look through it, you will find little of the usual paraphernalia of logic—no square of opposition, no Venn diagrams, no classification of syllogisms, no chapters on induction and deduction. The absence of this material is deliberate, but it is not missing because we reject it as a legitimate area of study. Rather, we left it out because the more we taught argument to composition classes, the less we used these materials in logic text form. When we began teaching argument, we spent days on syllogisms, fallacies, and the rules for validity; but eventually we found the bridge between formal analysis and the actual structuring of written arguments shaky. A student who was a whiz at detecting an undistributed middle could not necessarily construct an extended persuasive argument. So instead we have allowed the formal material of logic to sink below the surface and to inform the advice we give here about constructing sound arguments.

In our composition course in argument, we worked from an assumption about topic choice: From the beginning, we were reluctant to assign students specific topics for three reasons. First, we distrusted our ability to think of topics that would interest students. Second, we found that their work improved when they wrote on subjects that interested them rather than on subjects we thought they would find interesting. Third, we feared that students assigned specific topics would simply try to second-guess the instructor's opinion on the issue instead of thinking through their own.

We found, despite our initial misgivings, that students had little trouble coming up with arguable topics from their own experiences, their reading, their other courses, even their favorite sports, pastimes, and people. With only the prodding of a few examples, students came to the next class meeting with a list of things they were individually ready to argue for. Their statements of position spontaneously took the form of single sentences: "Campus police should not carry guns." "The math department's multiple-choice tests are ridiculous." "The university should give students free textbooks." "The dorm reservation system is unfair." "Fast food is stomach pollution." "My roommate is the cause of my being on academic probation this year." We found, in fact, that students can easily generate the one-sentence thesis, the seed crystal of argument. Of course, this preliminary thesis is not sacrosanct. Students modify, qualify, and complicate as they develop their arguments and discover what they can actually support, and much of our class time is spent working through tentative theses to show how they might be developed and adapted for potentially interested audiences.

However, not all our students' preliminary theses were arguable in the first place. We found, in the beginning of the course, that we had to back up and teach an awareness of what an audience will view as an arguable statement or an inarguable one that asserts a fact or matter of taste. Distinguishing the arguable from the inarguable makes good theoretical sense as well, for students must learn to use facts and reject unsupportable opinion in their arguments. Therefore, this book begins with an extended discussion of what is and is not arguable, a more complex problem than most of us start out realizing.

For a while we allowed our students to write on their miscellaneous theses, directing them only with general advice about inference, inductive and deductive structures, fallacies to avoid, and pro and con analyses of issues. We soon grew dissatisfied, however, as we realized that this general advice failed to give students the kind of specific guidance they needed. When we took a closer look at the theses they wanted to argue for, we saw the need to classify them. We sifted through hundreds of thesis statements from students, from published writing, and from our own imaginations, expressed in all the untidy phrasings of everyday language. We kept asking these questions: "How would you support such a statement?" "What would an argument for this thesis look like?"

The answers grouped themselves into piles and the piles into heaps under four headings, each representing a question that the thesis statement answers: "What is it?" "How did it get that way?" "Is it good or bad?" "What should we do about it?" Students were quick to grasp the simplicity and completeness of this four-part division, and, of course, it is not completely new. The classical stases of Cicero, Quintilian, and Hermogenes describe a similar taxonomy of arguments, though the number of basic questions varies slightly from one thinker to another. Basically, we believe that all modes of discourse can be subsumed under argumentation. Thus, this book on argument includes chapters on causal analysis and comparison, which are traditionally considered forms of exposition.

Not only do the four types of arguments answer different questions, but in two cases the answers require different methods of argument. That is why this division is teachable: It translates into specific advice for constructing arguments. Answers to the first question—"What is it?"—can always be put into the form of a statement that links its subject to a category or quality. More complicated answers to this basic question about reality, like comparisons, eventually break down into such statements. The support for these is always some combination of definition and evidence.

Traditional logic helps us with arguments about the nature of things but has less to tell us about the second category, causal arguments answering the question "How did it get that way?" Here we turned to John Stuart Mill, whose methods of causal inquiry can also be used as structural principles for generating causal argument. But for purposes outside the controlled conditions of the laboratory, Mill's methods are too elaborate and formal; arguers frequently use less formal devices, such as "causal chains," for convincing an audience of a causal connection. And as a heuristic for invention in causal argument, we devised sets of causes out of familiar causal terminology. We also found that no tactic of causal argument is convincing without an assumption or demonstration of agency, the smallest link between cause and effect. Agency in causal argument and definition in arguments about the nature of things function as warrants as they are defined in the Toulmin model of argumentation; we find it useful to distinguish among types of warrants.

Answers to the third and fourth questions—"Is it good or bad?" and "What should we do about it?"—require nothing conceptually new, only a thoughtful arrangement of causal and definition arguments. We explore different subjects and methods of evaluation, using both definition and causal arguments, and offer students an ideal outline of a full specific proposal argument, which they can then adapt for their own purposes and the needs of different subjects and audiences. In this section we also encourage students to consider the ethical grounds of their evaluations and proposals as well as the more obvious practical consequences.

Just as ethical assumptions underlie proposals, so also does an ethical assumption inform this book's proposal for teaching written argument. We believe that a course in written argument should produce not only clearly organized writing but also clear-minded citizens; it should improve the student's ability to think. Therefore, our purpose has been to avoid, on the one hand, formulas for argument that the student can fill in thoughtlessly and, on the other, the kind of vagueness that high-mindedly admonishes students to "think clearly, be creative and logical." Instead, we have tried to give specific directions for the construction of arguments without doing the students' thinking for them. For example, rather than order students to "analyze the problem before making a proposal," we suggest that they think about the causes that have brought the situation about, its bad consequences, and its ethical wrongness. Such suggestions are stimuli for invention, not cookie cutters of thought.

Since this book is a rhetoric, considerations of audience begin, end, and permeate it. In the beginning of the book, we define an arguable thesis in terms of audience; without support an audience can share, a writer has no argument. In Parts I through IV we constantly remind our readers to ask themselves how an audience will respond to their propositions to begin with, whether they need to articulate their assumptions about agency or definition, and what they must do to refute objections their audience may raise. Finally, in Part V we discuss some of the finer adjustments in language and structure needed to accommodate an argument to a particular audience.

Altogether then, this book provides a thorough guide to written argument. Since it begins with the simplest structures and builds to the more complex, it can be used from front to back as a text on argumentation. But since it is also divided into extended discussions of different types of arguments, it can be consulted as a reference by writers with a particular thesis to support. Although this book does not cover the general topics of grammar or sentence effectiveness or paragraph coherence, it does discuss word and example choice and calls attention to the affective power of certain words and phrases. Its primary purpose is to help students think about argument as structured discourse directed at particular audiences, and the discussions filled with examples are meant to stimulate topic choice. The instructor can then help students apply the advice to their own particular topics.

1 | Motives for Argument

Suppose you are an avid reader of science-fiction novels. You are working your way through Isaac Asimov, Robert Heinlein, Arthur C. Clarke, Ray Bradbury, Frank Herbert, and Ursula K. Le Guin, and hanging around the sci-fi racks in bookstores is one of your favorite recreations. But you have a friend who has expressed this preposterous opinion: "Science fiction stinks; I can't stand to read it."

Although some people might shrug and say, "That's her business," you don't want to leave this friend in darkness. You genuinely believe that she is missing out on some enjoyable, thought-provoking reading. But can you convince her? Is there anything you can say to change her mind?

The first thing you might do is ask your friend, "Why don't you like it? What bothers you?" If she confesses she has never read any science fiction because she just doesn't like "that sort of thing," then she has presented no reasons you can argue against. Obviously she does have reasons, but she does not or cannot articulate them to herself; the origins of such preconceptions, prejudices, or mind-sets are perhaps beyond recall. You can only urge your friend to give science fiction a try. Perhaps you can tell her why you like it, if you know and if you can get her to listen long enough.

Argument can go no further here; in fact, we can hardly call an exchange at this level argument. One side demonstrates its taste to the other, while the other side simply shrugs its shoulders. Many of our conversations disengage this way, because they have no reason to continue. No minds are changed, nothing happens because nothing is at stake. The only result is that both sides have the satisfaction of declaring a preference.

When we feel that there is no common ground on an issue or that no serious consequence is at stake, we do not usually argue.

PRACTICAL CONSEQUENCES

But when something is at stake, we do argue. Consequences, what is at stake, can take different forms. In its most basic form, a consequence is a concrete and immediate result. People can be blocked, they can lose something, and they can be hurt, even physically injured. If your friend's opinion about science fiction could harm you in any way—if, for example, she threatened to burn all your science-fiction books because she didn't think they were worth reading—you would still be arguing. Or, to give another example, suppose your father thinks that the college you want to attend is nothing but a football factory; if he can withhold your funding, he is worth arguing with over this issue.

Sometimes practical consequences are not so immediate, nor do they concern only two opposed sides arguing with each other. What happens in a profession or workplace, for example, ultimately matters to everyone involved in the enterprise, so arguments within special groups deeply engage their members. And of course what the government does about welfare, nuclear energy, social security, or tax reform is eventually a matter of consequence to every citizen and therefore subject to public argument.

When you argue for a desired consequence, it is by no means always necessary to address your argument to an audience that disagrees with you. In fact, most arguments are actually addressed to the uncommitted or to those who are already friendly toward or in mild agreement with the arguer's point. The arguer's purpose then is to bring certain things to the attention of the unfocused, or to heat up the lukewarm so that they are ready to take action. An audience can be anywhere on a spectrum from the totally opposed to the totally committed, and any argument that nudges them even a little in the direction of agreement is successful. Even lessening the disdain for your position in the minds of a totally opposed audience can be a positive outcome. If nothing else, you have justified your position, showing your audience that you have reasons for your convictions. Martin Luther certainly changed no minds when he made his famous "Here I stand" speech before the prelates of the Catholic Church, but at least he earned respect for himself, and his speech was persuasive when related to other less entrenched audiences.

Arguments addressed to favorably inclined audiences can have other practical consequences aside from such immediate ones as creating enough votes for a new community park or starting a letter campaign. They can also create a group cohesiveness, a solidarity among those who find themselves agreeing with the appeals cast at them. The person who articulates the reasons that hold the group together may of course become its leader. But more important is the fact that the argument that meets with agreement has created a human community ready to act together.

TRUTH WITHOUT APPARENT CONSEQUENCES

Many arguments, such as those surrounding government policies, arise from matters of practical, immediate, or long-range consequence to those who argue about them. But not all. We have all sat up late into the night arguing inconclusively about matters like the following, which affect neither the bread on our tables nor the money in our pockets: "Is football a better sport than baseball?" "Did the universe originate 20 billion years ago in a big bang, or did it always exist?" "Was George Washington really a great man or just the first president?" "Why were the Beatles so popular?" "Would Germany have won World War II if it had not been fighting on two fronts?" Even if one side wins such an argument, nothing immediate or tangible changes or could change. World War II is over, the current president will not be affected by our view of George Washington, and we cannot do a thing about the universe. But we argue about such matters because we want to hold views that are most nearly correct and we want others to share our views. Thus, we could say that a *kind* of consequence is at stake—our own intellectual integrity. We should care that the positions we hold are well thought out and that they could be held by other careful thinkers.

And we should also consider the consequences that might follow from the establishment of any particular point. We argue about isolated points that someday may link up in a chain of consequences that affects our lives. For example, we may conclude the argument about George Washington with the evaluation that he was a supremely tactful administrator, and that conclusion may somehow, someday, influence our choice of a committee leader. Similarly, abstract argument about the nature of light can lead to a concrete consequence like the laser. The present-day investigation of the origin and composition of our solar system, a matter of much argument, has no readily apparent consequences for us now. The layman cannot imagine any practical result from deciding whether there is volcanic activity on Io. But someday the practical consequences will be there when people explore, colonize, or mine other planets. Meanwhile we argue, and in doing so we come to recognize more accurately what we can know, and to what degree of certainty, by the extent to which we can convince others to agree with us.

ARGUMENT FROM EGO

We have to admit one more motive for argument, one that probably inspires more spoken than written controversy. That motive is quite simply ego. We often defend our positions the way a bird defends its territory—fiercely, automatically, without stopping to think. We often fail to see when ego is involved in any position we hold. After all, if we hold it, we undoubtedly have good reasons. Ego also forces us to defend positions just because someone else holds the opposite, and we cannot see that our attitude toward our audience or opponent is crippling our judgment.

To convince yourself that you may argue from ego, imagine the following situation. You and a friend are discussing (you wouldn't even call it arguing) whether Tim Raines or Don Mattingly is a better all-around baseball player. You are supporting Raines for his speed and on-base percentage. Your friend points out that Mattingly has the better batting average and is generally a more consistent and promising player. You are just on the point of agreeing with your friend, when a third party swaggers up and begins to sing Mattingly's praises in a loud, intrusive voice. It's All-Star Charlie, the perfect mind in the perfect body, who in the past defeated you for class president, stole your girlfriend, and beat you out for a Merit Scholarship. All your life he's been three points ahead of you. He's a walking baseball encyclopedia to boot, and cites Raines's and Mattingly's averages for the last three years, the number of triples they've hit against left-handed pitchers, their slugging percentages—all supporting the superiority of Mattingly. Suddenly you are seized by the blinding conviction that Tim Raines is the most underrated player in the history of baseball, and you passionately defend the player whom a moment ago you were ready to abandon. You have no new points to make, only a new certainty that your few facts outweigh your new opponent's many and that right is on your side.

Obviously, ego is involved in this example. All of us find it difficult to "give points" to people we resist, for whatever reasons we resist them, deep-seated or trivial, temporary or long-standing.

The tensions of ego are less obvious in written argument because the act of writing distances and creates the possibility of many readers. Writing usually represents cool second thoughts rather than heated first impulses. You never see the glare in your opponents' eyes when you address a written argument to them. Though ego filters into the written exchanges of wounding critic and wounded artist, or scholars and scientists with opposing points of view, heated arguments inspired solely by ego are rare in print.

2 || What We Do Not Argue About

FACTS

1. You say your living room is 22 feet long. Your mother says it's 25. Would you argue about it? No, you'd pull out a tape measure and find out.
2. You say your great-grandfather came over from Europe in 1900. Your cousin says 1903. Would you argue? Not for long. You'd go ask your oldest aunt, who remembers all the family history.
3. You say bronze is an alloy of tin and copper. Your friend says copper and lead. The argument should go no further than the nearest encyclopedia or dictionary.

Why does common sense tell you not to waste breath arguing over choices like those in the examples above? Because only one side or answer can be right, and the right answer can be found and verified. We call such discoverable answers *facts*.

A fact is a statement that can be verified, and once we accept its verification we must say yes to it. If we can agree on a means of verification, we can also agree with satisfaction that a statement is a fact, or at least that it could be a fact if we had appropriate verification. For example, a friend informs you that the author Washington Irving was a bachelor. This statement is either a fact or it is not. You could be miles away from the nearest library, with no means of verification at hand, and still recognize such a statement as a potential fact.

Most people in the same culture share a similar sense of what can or cannot be a fact. Let's look at some statements to test that sense and see if we can agree on what could and could not be a fact.

1. An American football field is 100 yards long.
2. Abraham Lincoln died on April 15, 1865.
3. Cats are mammals.
4. There are 437 jelly beans in Anna's jar.
5. I passed medieval history last term.
6. My car just hit a telephone pole.

Obviously, all of these statements could be facts. They have to do with time, size, quantity, and clear-cut, acceptable classifications or identifications. These measures are the means by which we create reality, the concepts we share for organizing the world.

We can also recognize a statement as a potential fact in another way. If we turned these statements into questions (Is an American football field 100 yards long?), each question could have only one right answer. Lincoln could not have died on two different days; and if we assume that cats are animals, they can belong to only one of the five classes of vertebrates. The jelly beans in Anna's jar must add up to one definite number; we know that a student cannot both pass and fail the same course; and we all know what a telephone pole is.

Let's take a look at another list.

1. There are 8,963,672,811 beetles in the world.
2. The United States should send an astronaut to Mars.
3. "Happy Birthday" is the most frequently sung song in English.
4. Woody Allen is the greatest comedian who ever lived.
5. Women are more intuitive than men.
6. It is wrong to eat animals.

For various reasons, none of these statements can be a fact. Formulated as questions, some of them have only one right answer, but there is no way to find out what that answer is. The number of beetles in the world is finite, but no one has devised a way to count them all. So we recognize a statement like "There are 8,963,672,811 beetles in the world" as a claim of impossible certainty. It cannot be a fact. (Of course, the number of beetles in the world can be estimated, but when a statement is an estimate, its wording should reveal that.) What other statement in the list above cannot be a fact because what it is talking about cannot be counted? (Hint: Who knows what you sing in the shower?)

The complete set of some things, like beetles and songs, cannot be counted even though we know what they are; other things cannot be measured because we may disagree or be uncertain about what they are. Consider the statement "Women are more intuitive than men." What is "intuitive"? It is an abstraction, a word that names no clear, single object or action. Even if we could give a rough definition of a word like *intuitive*, could a person's intuition be measured accurately? When accuracy is not possible, we have no fact. Therefore, it cannot be a *fact* that "Women are more intuitive than men," although some people might want to argue for the probability of this statement by establishing a sharable definition of "intuitive" and a plausible test by which we can recognize "intuition" in the behavior of men and women.

A recommendation like "The United States should send an astronaut to Mars" is obviously not a fact. You will learn that this kind of statement, with a recommending verb like *should* in it, is best labeled a *proposal*, something to be argued for. Even if you took a poll and found that all 280 million (estimate!) Americans agreed that we should send an astronaut to Mars, this proposal would still not be a fact. The only *fact* would be that 280 million people agreed with this recommendation. The recommendation itself still has no one right answer; a spectrum of responses, beyond a simple yes or no, is possible. Thus, argument is possible. Imagine the variety of responses to the question "Should we send an astronaut to Mars?"

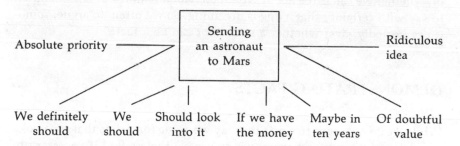

Whenever the response to a statement can be diagrammed this way, we do not have a fact.

You will learn to call a statement like "It is wrong to eat animals" an *evaluation*. Even if you are a committed vegetarian who wants others to share your conviction, you can recognize that this statement could never be a fact. Apply the test: Is a spectrum of responses possible? Yes. Then the statement cannot be fact.

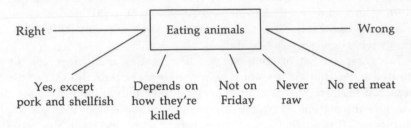

Let's summarize what makes a statement a fact.

1. It must deal with something we agree to measure or label in a certain way. Thus, we can make factual statements only about things we can measure in time and space, or things we can identify without ambiguity.
2. We can respond to a fact statement only with a yes or no, accepting it with a *yes* if it is verified or rejecting it with a *no* if it is not. If we can answer "maybe" or "probably," we have an arguable statement.

You may think our definition of "fact" very narrow. It is. To say that we do not argue about facts, as we have defined them, is only to say that once we agree that a statement is a fact, argument ceases. But determining whether a statement is a fact may give rise to a great deal of controversy. When people disagree about the label for something or about how it can be measured, the dispute may concern whether a statement can be accorded the status of fact. Whether or not dogs dream, for instance, depends on whether we can agree about what behavioral manifestations enable us to say with certainty that a dog is dreaming. So we often do argue, sometimes heatedly, over whether a statement can be a fact.

DEMONSTRATING FACTS

While we do not argue for facts the way we argue for claims that can evoke more than yes or no responses, we may nevertheless find it necessary to lay out the steps we followed in order to infer a fact. We call this process not argument but *demonstration*. The goal of demonstration is not an audience's increased adherence but its unqualified assent. We can claim some success for an argument if it does no more than make our opposition less sure of itself. We can claim no success for a demonstration if it does not clearly and unambiguously convince our audience. Arguments support but demonstrations prove. It is all or nothing in demonstration. We can even put the difference in stronger terms. Someone who persistently disagrees with our arguments may seem pigheaded or stubborn, but someone who persistently disagrees with the clear demonstration of a matter of fact will begin to seem insane. That is the category our society maintains for people who do not share the majority's sense of reality.

Here is a simple example of a demonstration. You know your friend has two brothers and one sister. So you infer that there are four children in your friend's family: One plus one plus two equals four. That's a fairly airtight demonstration of a matter of fact. Everyday examples of factual demonstrations abound: If I had 250 dollars in my checking account and wrote a check for 350 dollars, my account is overdrawn; if I am at the shopping mall in the afternoon, I cannot be home at the same time; if my library book was due on June 10 and it is now June 20, it is overdue; if I cannot leave work until 4:00 and it takes me at least half an hour to drive to my dentist, I will be late for a 4:15 appointment. You can readily expand this list of tidy little demonstrations by which we try to manage our daily lives.

The same process of convincing demonstration rather than probable argument is the goal, though perhaps rarely the achievement, of courtroom procedures. The defense may try to prove that the defendant was somewhere else when the crime was committed. A person cannot be in two places at once. Or the body in question could not be John Doe because John Doe was six feet tall and the skeletal remains of the body found are five feet six. If the defense could really marshal demonstrations of such clarity, it is unlikely the case would come to trial in the first place.

Mathematics is certainly concerned with demonstration, the proof of conclusions according to the fixed axioms of a mathematical system such as Euclidean or Riemannian geometry. Many people mistakenly believe that all scientific argument is likewise really demonstration, but while scientific argument may aspire to the force of demonstration, whether or not it succeeds can be a matter of audience. Take as an example the establishing of "facts" in archaeology or prehistory. Suppose that a team of archaeologists digging at the mouth of a cave in Pennsylvania comes upon a ring of charcoal at a certain stratigraphically defined level. Are these the remains of a human hearth? Suppose that carbon dating places the charcoal at fourteen thousand years ago, plus or minus two thousand years, making this cave the oldest site of human occupation in North America. Surely the discovery of a ring of charcoal at the mouth of a cave must prove human presence and carbon dating must prove the time. The inference seems inescapable. But suppose that other archaeologists believe that such charcoal rings can be produced by natural means, such as lightning strikes. If another explanation is possible, and it usually is in sciences like archaeology, then the argument for the presence of humans on the basis of the presence of a charcoal hearth remains just that, an argument, not a demonstration. Scientists themselves are usually modest about their claims and hedge them in as probabilities, even when no colleague has produced a plausible counterexplanation. But nonspecialists, perhaps reading about the archaeologists' "find" in the newspaper, would take the discovery as proof of the fact of early habitation.

The appeal of demonstration then is strong, so strong that we could say that all argument aspires to the status of demonstration. Ideally an arguer would like to appear to be establishing a matter of fact rather than supporting a probability. And such an appearance can be created with carefully chosen language, especially for naive or less resistant audiences. Researchers have found that just the use of the label *fact* can confer higher credibility on a statement; readers or listeners feel they have touched bedrock with phrases like "it is a fact that." Furthermore, our society has a preference for "information," and a great deal of the argument addressed to general audiences these days masquerades as "information," the mere transport of matters of fact from source to audience. We hope that after reading this book you will be much more sparing in your use of the label *fact*.

EXERCISE

Examine the following statements very carefully. Which of them could be facts and which could not? In which sentences does the definition of a critical word determine whether the statement could be a fact?

1. The New York Yankees are the best baseball team in the world.
2. Franklin D. Roosevelt was a popular president.
3. Jelly Roll Morton's real name was Ferdinand La Menthe.
4. Smoking causes cancer.
5. The four strings on a cello are C, G, D, and A.
6. The amount of knowledge has doubled twice in the last century.
7. Ninety percent of all the scientists who ever lived are still alive.
8. Armadillos always give birth to four young of the same sex.
9. Oak furniture is the heaviest.
10. If you sit on cold concrete, you will get piles.
11. The kumquat tree grows to a height of 15 feet.
12. The writings of Dionysius the Areopagite had an important influence on both the Eastern and Western churches until the sixteenth century, when their authenticity was challenged.

13. Classical music was composed from roughly 1750 to 1820.

14. The piano replaced the harpsichord as the most popular keyboard instrument in the nineteenth century.

15. Primo Carnera was the biggest man ever to win the world's heavyweight championship (6 feet 5 inches, 220 pounds).

16. The Nambiquara of the northwest Mato Grosso section of Brazil are the only people who lack any system of numbers. (They do, however, have a verb that means "they are two alike.")

17. Winslow Homer didn't begin to paint seriously until 1862.

18. The oldest museum in the world is the Ashmolean Museum in Oxford, England, built in 1679.

19. Chopin is often called "the poet of the keyboard."

20. The invasion of Russia was Napoleon's biggest mistake.

21. A mouse eats one-quarter to one-half of its body weight in food every day.

22. The most frequently sung songs in English are "Happy Birthday," "For He's a Jolly Good Fellow," and "Auld Lang Syne."

23. Novel reading was widespread in middle- and upper-class households by the middle of the nineteenth century.

24. Flight 226 will depart for Albuquerque at 7:06 P.M.

FOR YOU TO ANALYZE

The following are short excerpts from newspaper and magazine articles. Carefully distinguish the statements that are or could be facts from those that could not. Don't be fooled by the punctuation of sentences; a fact can be less than a whole sentence.

Recent fossil discoveries in Australia have pushed the date of man's arrival on the island continent substantially further into the past and have added a hitherto unknown element to the gene pool of the Australian aborigine. Twenty years ago the aborigines were thought to have reached Australia only a few thousand years ahead of the Europeans. This view was overturned in the 1960's by the discovery at Kow Swamp in the eastern Australia state of Victoria of a skull that was between 10,000 and 15,000 years old and aborigine in physical type. Since then fossil aborigine remains as much as 20,000 years old have been found at sites along the Murray River in Victoria. Human fossils have now been found buried in the sands of a dry-lake region in western New South Wales only 50 miles north of the Murray River. They appear to be more than twice as old as the Kow Swamp skull.

—"Aboriginal Aborigines"
Scientific American

Ocean City, Md., detectives investigating the deadly fire at The Beach-comber Motel have turned up several suspects, and Mayor Roland (Fish) Powell said yesterday that "it's very possible" the fire was caused by a dangerous game called fireballing.

Police have determined that the fire that engulfed the top floor of the 24-year-old motel early last Sunday began in a vacant unit, said police Det. Vicki Martin. Two Pennsylvania students were killed and 17 other persons were injured in the fire.

The federal Bureau of Alcohol, Tobacco and Firearms continues to study samples of the curtains and carpet taken from the room to determine the cause. Local detectives suspect it was students playing the bizarre game of fireballing, which involves spitting out a mouthful of grain alcohol and lighting the spray with a lighter or match, said Powell, a former fire chief. The game was popularized by the movie *Revenge of the Nerds, Part II.*

"It's very possible" the game led to the fire, Powell said yesterday after conversations with detectives. "There is talk [about fireballing]."

"I'm not an investigating officer and I don't read their reports, but there is a strong possibility it was fireballing," he said.

Detectives played down Powell's remarks, saying they are looking at all possibilities, including cigarettes.

Seventy-five guests, most of them students celebrating the end of the school year, were awakened by the fire, which was noticed at 3:19 A.M. by a patrol officer. Seventeen persons were injured, one seriously, in the blaze, which broke out on the top floor. Four guests leaped from the third floor to a trash dumpster below, and a 1-year-old child was tossed into the waiting arms of police officers.

—"Suspects Emerge in Fire Probe"
Washington Post

MATTERS OF PERSONAL TASTE

That Word *Opinion*

If you pay careful attention to everyday conversation, you will notice phrases that serve as "stop signs" to argument: "That's just your opinion." "That's a matter of opinion." "You're entitled to your own opinion." "Well, that's my opinion." In each case the word *opinion* seems to mean "something that cannot be argued about." We all have many reasons for not wanting to argue: The time may be wrong; the person may not be someone we want to argue with; or we may not feel entirely sure of our ground. For many such social and practical motives, we often disengage from argument with one of these "opinion" phrases. The motives do not concern us here, but the use of the word *opinion* does.

We often use the word *opinion,* as in the phrases above, to suggest not that the situation is inappropriate for argument, but that certain subjects are taboo or that argument itself is impolite. The problem is that the word *opinion*, in the sense of "something not to be argued about," is often used loosely. We label as matters of opinion, not to be argued, many subjects that can and indeed should be argued. For example, most of us have been schooled in politeness and told "never argue about politics and religion." In certain social situations, this advice is wise, but we should not take it as a total ban on thinking, writing, and arguing about these topics. There is a difference between the subject and the situation.

Only one kind of statement deserves the label *opinion* in the sense of "something that cannot be argued about." Once we identify it we will at the same time have defined argument. To be brief, we cannot argue for anything whose grounds of support are wholly personal. For example, how could a statement such as "I like vegetable soup" be supported? The soup lover can give all kinds of reasons: "because I like vegetables," "because I like soup," "because it reminds me of winter afternoons and my mother," "because it is nutritious." But all these reasons amount to explanation for a preference, not argument. And most of them are obviously personal, the kind of statements that only an "I" can make. Although such statements of personal preference often supply us with conversation, we do not argue about them, undoubtedly because we sense the pointlessness.

If you cannot demonstrate any sharable, impersonal grounds for a statement, you do not have a subject for argument. You have an opinion. You can explain the grounds for your opinion with more opinions, and then you have an excursion in self-examination, of interest mainly to yourself and those who care to listen, but still no argument. Now we have defined *opinion* as we shall use the term in this book:

> An opinion is a statement of preference
> whose grounds are wholly personal.

That is a deliberately boxed-in, restricted definition. Next time someone tries to weasel out of an argument by claiming "It's just a matter of opinion," you can at least argue about whether the topic fits that definition.

Now that we have defined *opinion*, a definition of a matter for argument falls in our laps:

> An arguable statement can evoke degrees of adherence, and its grounds
> of support do not depend on the individual who holds them.

These definitions make the distinction between an opinion and an arguable statement look clear, but our habitually imprecise use of language often makes the sorting out of arguable and inarguable statements a challenge. We must not be fooled by the casual wording of a statement. *Whether a statement is arguable is determined by the grounds of its support, not by its wording.* Let us look at some language problems that fool us into thinking that we either do or do not have an arguable statement.

An Arguable Statement That Masquerades as Personal

We often tack a personal label onto statements as though we were identifying them as our own property: "I think," "I believe," "It is my opinion," and the ever-popular "I feel."

1. I *believe that* college football should have a play-off system.
2. I *think* that most lawyers are honest.
3. *In my opinion* downtown was a mess after the homecoming parade.
4. I *feel* the United States should curtail the development of nuclear-power plants.

These look like the vegetable soup example, statements of personal preference. We often add personal qualifiers in order to soften or tone down statements that we want to assert only casually, that we do not expect to be challenged on. But references to self can mask the arguable nature of such statements in some circumstances. Suppose you were the author of the last statement in the list above; you could claim, "Well, that certainly is my opinion, and I'm entitled to it." But if you were asked to give the grounds for your position on nuclear power, are you likely to say "Because I do not care for radiation" or "Nuclear fission is not to my taste"? Of course not. Instead you would produce as grounds the dangers of radiation, the likelihood and consequences of a reactor accident, and the problems of nuclear-waste disposal. These grounds actually support a more direct argumentative statement: "The United States should curtail the development of nuclear-power plants." Policies concerning nuclear power should not rest on personal grounds.

A Personal Statement That Masquerades as Arguable

The pronoun "I" appears in none of the following statements.

1. Red is a terrific color.
2. Variegated peanut butter ice cream is the pits.
3. St. Laurent's "Opium" is the most exquisite of perfumes.

Imagine asking the holder of any of these positions for grounds of support; then the pronoun *I* would almost certainly appear. Most people would not try to argue objectively for the exquisiteness of a perfume. Instead they would come up with statements like the following: " 'Opium' is a sweet and heavy scent, and I like sweet, heavy perfumes." "It reminds me of summer nights in a greenhouse." "My boyfriend bought me my first bottle." You get the idea. The test of an opinion is whether the grounds of support are purely personal, not whether the pronoun *I* or a statement of preference is attached to the sentence.

Discovering Arguable Grounds

Suppose you make the claim "I don't like having to declare a major." That certainly looks like a statement of personal taste, mere opinion. You may repeat the claim emphatically to anyone who will listen, expressing your frustration with the system you find yourself in. But suppose you discover in the *Student Handbook* a little-known provision allowing students who have maintained a certain grade average the option of making a case for an independent degree program that need not meet the requirements of any specific major or college. Such students earn a Bachelor of Philosophy degree.

You now have a chance to act, to change your circumstances *if* you can convince a particular audience, a board made up of administrators and representative faculty members, to agree to your personally designed course of study. But in order to persuade them, you will have to find sharable reasons and not just personal likes and dislikes. Suppose you begin by listing all the reasons you can think of for not wanting to declare a major.

1. I'm not just interested in one thing: I like botany, English history, mechanical drawing, acting, and finance.
2. I don't know why the college should dictate what courses I have to take. Who's paying for this education anyway?
3. I know lots of former graduates who don't work in the field they graduated in.
4. If I had to take twelve courses in the same area I'd be bored to death.
5. No one in this school can predict what knowledge will be necessary ten years from now, or what new careers will evolve.
6. I didn't come here to be trained for a career.
7. I liked it better in high school where I didn't have to be so narrow.
8. I don't know what I want to do with my life yet.

Having survived in the world and school for several years, you immediately recognize that this list would not convince an official board to give you permission to design your own degree program. Most of these statements look like personal preferences supporting your dislike of the need to major in something. You are not arguing to convince someone else when you simply demonstrate that you do not like what you do not like.

But one of these reasons looks unlike the others: number 3, "I know lots of former graduates who don't work in the fields they graduated in." Here you glimpse a reason that might be acceptable to the community you are addressing. For one thing there are generally acknowledgable facts involved here. You know of several cases—well, four—and there may be statistical evidence of a lack of connection between college major and ultimate career. You might be able to bring your audience to acknowledge that since an inevitable connection does not exist between major and career, then perhaps it is not necessary to insist on a major in your case. Promising. If you can find something your audience will agree to—like facts about majors and careers—then you have a better chance of persuading them in your favor. You will spend some time in the library seeing if college counselors have studied the destinations of college graduates. Even if most people stay in careers defined by their college majors, any evidence of a minority who take off in other directions provides an argument for granting an exception.

Armed with your new insight, you reexamine your raw list looking for other potentially sharable reasons. Your feeling of uncertainty about an ultimate goal or career in life again looks like a personal idiosyncracy but here lurks not a fact perhaps but a sharable value. Your school, like many others, values preparing students for productive lives, but even more, it values learning or education as its own end. If you can cast your personal preference as a value that coincides with the predictable values of your audience, you have a reason that might be persuasive to them.

The second reason on your list also looks very unpromising: "I don't know why the school should dictate what courses I have to take. Who's paying for this education anyway?" It amounts to a direct challenge to your school's power to design courses of study. But once again it contains a sharable point, this time a partial definition of what a university or college is. It is not exactly a business, but it does have "consumers" or "customers" that it has to please. And there is a principle of fairness, again a value, involved in giving consumers what they are paying for. You realize that phrasing will be critical here, but the point you will want to get across is that the school has a responsibility, by its very nature, to meet the educational goals of the individual student halfway, to be able to bend to those who want something slightly different for their tuition dollars. Aha! Here you suddenly find a fact at your disposal as well, the fact that your school did create the provision for an independently designed Bachelor of Philosophy degree in the first place.

By now you realize that the act of arguing involves converting what seem mere personal and idiosyncratic preferences into socially acknowledgeable facts and socially sharable values. Another promising value in the academic community, though not as strong perhaps as others, is a tolerance for diversity, for "interdisciplinary" work (there's a word you recognize as likely to trigger approbation in your audience).

The *Student Handbook*'s explanation of the Bachelor of Philosophy option stipulates that candidates must have maintained a certain grade-point average. The facts on your transcript support your penchant for interdisciplinary work and your success at it. But more is needed than a record of good grades in a wide variety of courses. You realize that you must construct a positive image of your "course hopping" and of yourself as a person with certain values and aspirations, not someone who, as reason number 4 on your list suggests, is easily bored by sustained work in one area. Here you come to a sensitive area: Should you lie about yourself in order to please the prejudices of college authorities? No. But you need not go out of your way to talk about every negative reaction you have ever had to a course or instructor. Much better to make a virtue out of exactly what you are, a person with very diverse tastes and talents, a generalist in a world of specialists. You realize that a decision in your favor will have a great deal to do with how your audience perceives your character. In order to build a positive character for yourself in the eyes of your audience, it may be wise simply to describe positive experiences in the most diverse of your courses, like the botany course in which you made a special catalog of the flora in the fields north of campus or the history course in which you researched the nineteenth-century town from which some of your ancestors emigrated. Thinking over these courses, and talking them over with friends who also took them, you realize that what you have really learned in the variety of courses you have taken is a diversity of research methods and an appreciation of how knowledge is constructed in various fields. There is surely a positive value in an educational program that can produce such an awareness; that is a value you can definitely make explicit to your audience.

You began with a personal statement of what you didn't like, made apparently in anger. But with the chance of addressing a real audience and actually changing your situation, you were forced to examine the reasons and motives behind your feelings. The list you made was far from promising; your "reasons" looked like more declarations of feelings. But in order to persuade others you had to produce reasons that were sharable, that did not depend on the tastes and preferences of the individual holding them. By a process of thinking through your preferences and talking them over with others and by continually keeping a lively idea of your audience and what might convince them in mind, you were able to turn your likes and dislikes into acceptable, sharable reasons that as far as possible approximated the standards of fact and value that your audience probably holds. Hard work at drafting, phrasing, and revising faces you, but you now have a chance of changing things in your favor that you did not have before.

This example of working from an emotional statement to a shaped argument demonstrates that the mere wording of a claim will not inevitably tell you if you have a matter of taste or a matter of argument. You have to do some digging in the ground behind the statement. If you can unearth a reason that you can share with your audience, you have a subject for argument. But anything depending solely on your own taste can only be explained, not argued for. You will be surprised to find how many respectable subjects for argument lurk behind your opinions if the audience and occasion arise to explore them. In our analysis of "I don't like having to declare a major," we have taken you through an example of the stages of invention in coming up with an argument. Now we can summarize the steps in this process.

1. You began with a statement of conviction. Its apparent genesis was, if anything, emotion rather than thought.
2. Then, prompted by a specific audience and situation, you looked to see what reasons you could find for that conviction. The list you came up with did not look promising. All but one of the reasons were more emotional claims.
3. But that one led to a new, less personal formulation of your original conviction.
4. Once you had an arguable statement and one supporting statement (in fact you would not have had the arguable statement without the support), you looked over those other reasons again and found sharable grounds for some of them. In that way you found even more support for your original arguable statement.

WHAT, THEN, IS ARGUMENT?

While we have been discussing what argument is not, we have been indirectly suggesting what it is. Now it is time to restate our definitions explicitly. Every argument has four essential elements:

1. A thesis statement, a claim, a proposition to be supported, which deals with a matter of probability, not a fact or a matter of taste.
2. An audience to be convinced of the thesis statement.

3. Exigence, the need to make an argument at a certain time, in a circumstance, or for a purpose.
4. Grounds, reasons, or, as they are sometimes formally called, *premises* that support the thesis.

The Thesis Statement

Every argument, no matter how long or how complicated, has a single, overriding thesis. That single thesis may be qualified, elaborated, complicated, or hedged all around, yet the arguer must always be able to answer the question "What is your point?" Whether in the form of a letter to the editor, a term paper, a scholarly article, a book review, or the book itself, all arguments can be summed up in a single statement that the whole discourse is designed to support. Edward Gibbon's multivolume *Decline and Fall of the Roman Empire*, John Stuart Mill's eloquent essay *On Liberty*, Sigmund Freud's *Civilization and Its Discontents*, E. D. Hirsch's *Cultural Literacy*— even these long, involved arguments can be comprehended as support for a single claim. Actually, long and complex arguments such as these are collections of smaller arguments for subsidiary theses that combine to support the main thesis. Whether the unit of argument is a paragraph or a book, that basic element, the thesis statement, must be discoverable.

If you state a fact and verify it, you are demonstrating its truth, but you are not arguing. If you declare a personal taste and account for it, you are sharing an opinion, but you are not arguing. Argument concerns itself with neither fact nor taste, but with that vast middle territory of statements that are more or less probable. It is, for example, a fact that lakes are inland bodies of water; it is a matter of taste whether any individual likes to vacation by a lake; but it is a matter of argument whether the shore of a particular lake should be zoned for commercial or for recreational development. This last issue has no one right answer; with good intent and the same facts at their disposal, reasonable people might argue on either side. But even the side that wins this argument has not established a truth, only the probable wisdom of a particular choice.

Audience

Now imagine yourself an orator standing on a deserted shore declaiming a thesis to the lake itself: "This lake should remain free and wild forever." Nice thesis, but no argument. An argument needs a human audience, someone to convince. Thus, the second essential element of argument is an audience that the arguer wants to have an effect on, whether to make them believe something, to increase their belief in something, or to urge them to act on that belief. Of course it is possible to argue with oneself, but only by temporarily splitting the self into two personalities, the one waiting to be convinced by the other.

The particular audience of an argument influences how you argue—coolly or with passion, tentatively or with strong conviction, elliptically or in great detail. Imagine arguing the thesis "The south shore of Mendona Lake should become a nature preserve" with different audiences: The federal agency that might fund the nature preserve; the local real-estate developers; the conservation club of a neighboring big city; the people who live near the lake; the readers of *National Geographic.* The local audience will require much less basic information about the lake than the readers of *National Geographic*; the conservation club will be more open to your argument than the real-estate developers whose immediate interests are at stake. Thus, different audiences require significant differences in the support, organization, and wording of your argument.

Exigence

All real arguments have another requirement, something so obvious it is invisible. In our example of arguing to preserve the lake, we have to imagine our speaker standing up at a town meeting in order to capture the full picture of a complete argument. This narrative detail is far from trivial. In order for a real argument to occur there must be some forum and occasion, like a town meeting, some push in the time and circumstances and some purpose for making claims and supporting them. The combination of all these factors has been called the *exigence.* An argument has exigence when it speaks to its time, situation, and audience. Imagine a very imperfect stranger stopping you in the street and forcefully detaining you for a harangue on the merits of plastic toothpicks, an argument totally without exigence in persons, time, situation, and purpose, and you will appreciate the necessity of exigence in argument.

In speaking situations where the factors of time and place are powerful and inescapable, exigence is easy to understand. But in writing situations exigence is harder to grasp. The "now" of the writer is never the "now" of the reader; the writer can rarely count on the reader's background information or sense of urgency over an issue and can never make moment-to-moment adjustments to the perplexities and gleams that cross a reader's face. Plato distrusted writing for these reasons and made Socrates complain, ". . . once a thing is committed to writing it circulates equally among those who understand the subject and those who have no business with it; a writing cannot distinguish between suitable and unsuitable readers. And if it is unfairly abused it always needs its parent to come to its rescue; it is quite incapable of defending or helping itself."

To compensate for this inherent disconnection from its audience, a written argument must frequently create its own exigence. It must give its readers a reason for reading, an answer to the fatal question "So what?" In other words, rather than sorting out the suitable from the unsuitable readers, an argument with exigence tries to *create* suitable readers. Obviously an arguer faces varying degrees of challenge in creating exigence for an audience. The PTA president will use a mailing list to reach a potentially interested audience and will use appeals to an upcoming school fair to give a further push. A writer for a mass-circulation audience has a much more challenging job to commit the merely curious, but actually journalists have developed a closet full of standard devices to create exigence.

Support

Now imagine standing up at a town meeting called on the lake and saying, "This lake should remain free and wild forever," and then sitting down. Audience, thesis, and exigence this time, but still no argument. The fourth necessary element of argument is a *premise,* a reason for an audience to be convinced of the thesis statement. As an arguer you should follow the thesis with at least one "because" statement: "This lake should remain free and wild forever, *because* only then will our children and grandchildren be able to enjoy it." Finally, you have an argument, a thesis, and a supporting statement addressed to an audience whose attention has been captured by the importance of the issue. You could make a much longer argument by introducing more supporting statements for the thesis or by supporting the supporting statements themselves, but at least one premise, one statement that gives the audience a reason to adhere to the thesis, is necessary.

These two elements (thesis and premise) should be explicit. But notice that you have also, strange as it may seem, been working with something that is not stated. You and your audience would not agree that "this lake should remain free and wild forever" because "only then will our children and grandchildren be able to enjoy it" unless you also agreed that "the lake is only enjoyable if it is free and wild." If for some reason you sensed that your audience might not adhere to that unspoken proposition, you would have to bring it out and argue for it as well.

An unspoken premise is called an *assumption.* When you argue you can leave out or assume whatever you feel confident your audience already knows or believes. In fact, you cannot argue at all without some assumptions, which are the common ground, the shared preconceptions and beliefs of arguer and audience. Although an arguer will assume more or less, depending on the audience, every argument leaves something out.

Thesis, audience, exigence, and support, then, are the inextricable elements in every argument. Of these four, audience is the most variable, indeed infinitely variable, since we can have as many audiences as there are people either singly or in endless combinations. Put the same people in a different situation and you have a different audience. The kind of support an argument requires depends on its thesis, but the degree of support depends on audience and is therefore quite variable. You can also create innumerable theses because there are innumerable subjects for argument, but in a sense the thesis statement is the least variable of the four elements, because any arguable thesis can be classified into one of four major categories, according to what kind of fundamental question it answers. These fundamental questions constitute the organizational principle of this book: "What is it?" "How did it get that way?" "Is it good or bad?" "What should we do about it?"

This system of classifying theses gives you the best outline for learning argument, not just because the number four is easier to comprehend than infinity, but because the nature of the thesis determines much of the content of an argument. The *kind* of support varies according to the thesis, though, once again, the *degree* varies according to audience. This book will constantly remind you to consider audience, but it teaches argument by concentrating on thesis and support.

EXERCISE

Here are some apparently personal statements of conviction and the reasons behind them. Can you discover impersonal premises in any of the reasons?

1. The Blue Ridge Mountains are a wonderful vacation spot.
   a. The mountains and lakes are beautiful.
   b. There is a magnificent Holiday Inn just off the interstate.
   c. They have honeymoon resorts with heart-shaped beds.
   d. I played tennis and golf, went horseback riding, and danced the evening away.
2. I do not like Senator Griffenbottom.
   a. He is a Republican/Democrat.
   b. He is a lawyer.
   c. I can't stand politicians who get nose jobs.
   d. His wife drinks.
3. I find AM rock repulsive.
   a. It teaches thirteen-year-olds bad morals.
   b. The music is monotonous.
   c. It's a manufactured product, plastic music for plastic people.
   d. The lyrics are illiterate.

4. Watching sports on television is an incredible waste of time.
   a. I have better things to do.
   b. Joe Garagiola/John Madden/_____ is uninformed.
   c. I'm tired of commercials for shaving cream, beer, and deodorant.
   d. Televised sports have ruined too many of my weekends.

FOR YOU TO WRITE .

1. Write a paragraph of *rant.* That is, carry on in strong language about something you dislike intensely. Here's a start: "One thing that really makes me furious is _____." Now imagine trying to convince someone else to share your loathing. Is there anything in your rant that you could convert into an argument? That is, can you find sharable rather than purely personal grounds for support?

   Take one such point and write another paragraph convincing an impartial audience that the object of your rant deserves their loathing too.

2. Do the same for a *boast,* a paragraph of extravagant self-praise. Then try to convince an audience of strangers such as the readers of a job application that your high opinion of yourself is justified.

Part One
WHAT IS IT?

3 | Claims About the Nature of Things

Recognizing the existence of things, and naming, categorizing, or describing them are basic activities we all perform all of the time. The following series of sentences represents these activities. You should recognize that the first three, given verification of course, are simply statements of fact. The fourth and fifth, however, are arguable.

1. That is a cat.
2. A cat is a mammal.
3. There are no cats native to Antarctica.
4. That cat is malnourished.
5. Cats are never really domesticated.

Notice that these statements are simple sentences with three parts: a subject, a linking verb, and something said about the subject. For convenience, we can borrow the grammarian's term and call what is said about the subject the *complement*. We can also think of the linking verb and the complement together as the *predicate*.

Subject	Predicate	
	Linking verb	*Complement*
A cat	is	a mammal
That cat	is	malnourished

Even if you do not understand the meaning of one of its terms, you can recognize a similarly constructed sentence like "Football is a homoerotic ritual" as a statement defining or describing its subject. You should also recognize this claim as arguable to most audiences. It is by no means a fact, although a fact could take the same grammatical form:

1. Football is a game played with eleven men on a team.
2. Football is played in the Astrodome.

Fact number 1 is a partial definition of football. Fact number 2 describes an event that can easily be verified.

All the examples given so far are claims about the nature of things. Such claims take in a large territory, including facts and arguable statements, but leaving out questions, commands, wishes, and exclamations. "My dog has fleas" is a claim about a state of affairs, but "Get off my lap" or "Would you like to get off my lap?" or "Would that you were off my lap" or "Alas!" are not.

Claims about the nature of things connect a subject to a predicate in one of the following ways: The subject is included in the predicate ("Housework is a form of exercise"), has something to do with the predicate ("Love is often an illusion"), or is completely separated from the predicate ("No Mercury astronauts were scientists").

You Make More Claims Than You Think

Claims about the nature of things do not always come neatly packaged in subject-linking verb-predicate form like the examples given above. In common speech and writing we use many other verbs and sentence patterns to assert an all-in, all-out, or partial connection between subjects and predicates. For example, if you vigorously assert that "Pre-med majors cheat," you are actually classifying. The claim "Pre-med majors cheat" can be transformed into "Pre-med majors are cheaters." Strictly speaking, you are claiming that pre-med majors belong to the class of cheaters.

Here are some more examples of ordinary sentences, with translations into subject–linking verb–complement form so that you can see the claims being made more clearly:

The United States has no population problem.	⟶	The United States is not a nation with a population problem. (exclusion)
My roommate eats compulsively.	⟶	My roommate is a compulsive eater. (inclusion)
The space program does not receive enough tax support.	⟶	The space program is undersupported. (inclusion)
Obstetricians often overcharge.	⟶	Some obstetricians are overchargers. (partial inclusion)
American dance companies always go in the red.	⟶	No American dance companies are financial successes. (exclusion)

As you can see, some of these transformations result in awkward wording. We certainly do not recommend that you turn every assertion about a class into subject–linking verb–complement form. That would make for boring, flabby writing. It is usually much more effective to say "Pre-med majors cheat" than to write daintily "Pre-med majors are not honest persons." But learning to recognize a claim about the nature of things when you encounter one will help enormously when you get ready to set up an argument for it. And the best way to recognize such a claim is to be able to set it up mentally in subject–linking verb–complement form.

EXERCISE

Transform the following sentences into subject–linking verb–complement form.

1. Neo-Victorian architecture has taken over in the suburbs.
2. Eastern European countries funnel high technology to the Soviet Union.
3. Menus often lie about the meals they describe.
4. Right now, the United States has the technology to build space colonies.
5. Bigfoot doesn't exist.

THE BASIC TACTIC: SUPPORT BY EXAMPLES

An arguable claim about the nature of things can often be thought of as a generalization that summarizes a collection of particular instances. Thus you can support such a claim by bringing one or more of those particulars to your reader's attention. Suppose you want to support a simple assertion like "My roommate is a slob." Your subject is identified by his relation to you, and *slob* has a widely understood meaning. You can go right to examples.

1. There's a half-eaten Big Mac in his desk drawer.
2. A pile of unsorted socks has been sitting on the foot of his bed for three weeks.
3. He hasn't showered since the beginning of the term three weeks ago.

Maybe *slob* is too mild a word?

Kinds of Examples

Particular Examples

The examples used to support "My roommate is a slob" are particular. They describe situations, events, or objects connected with one time, one place, and, in this case, one person. They are as close as language can come to real experience. Such particular examples are effective in argument for just that reason: They create a sharable reality for other eyes and help readers to an awareness of what inspired your claim in the first place.

Iterative Examples

We can ascend one level of generality, as it were, from the particular example to the iterative example. The iterative example presents an event in words that suggest that the event happens often or repeats itself. Wording the example in the present tense is one way to achieve this effect:

I brush my teeth after breakfast.

Putting in a word that suggests repetition is another way to create an iterative example:

She often hums "O Sole Mio" while making pizza.

There are many other possible indicators of iterative examples. They include use of the plural ("Confederate soldiers sang 'Aura Lee' to their sweethearts"), mention of an unidentified observer ("Anyone on the Champs Elysées can see the hookers leaning on lampposts"), and use of a singular subject that stands for a group ("The young New Yorker spends Saturdays at Bloomingdale's buying leather accessories").

At its best, the iterative example suggests repeated instances while it creates a specific image. Since a well-written iterative example gives the reader something to see or sense, it can work as well as a particular example.

In the following paragraph the support (with one exception for you to find) is entirely in vivid, iterative examples.

> My mother is a workaholic. Eight years ago our family decided we needed extra money so Mom took a teaching job at the local high school. The only problem with this was, Who was going to do her other work? The answer, Mom. Mom's day starts at six o'clock in the morning. After feeding the livestock on the family farm, she retreats to the house to cook the family breakfast. Then without doing the dishes it's off to school. At four in the afternoon the school is empty except for the Home Ec. room, where Mom prepares for the next day of classes. Upon arriving home she cooks a delicious full-course meal. Without stopping to clean up supper she heads to her garden where she works till dark. Finally she tackles a sink full of dishes and usually a couple of loads of wash. And when I went to bed she was hunched over her sewing machine mending my pants.

Hypothetical Examples

A hypothetical example is fictional, imaginary. The arguer makes it up and therefore has the luxury of creating details and events and outcomes that support a claim perfectly. Often the wording of a hypothetical example will give it away, or the arguer will say specifically that the example represents an approximation of several individual instances. As such, a hypothetical example can be like the "averaging of data" that goes on in science and social science.

However, a hypothetical example is deceptive and basically dishonest if the arguer conceals its nature and allows readers to believe that the particulars existed or occurred exactly as constructed. A hypothetical example is obviously only deceptive when it is used in an argument characterizing a particular thing or state of affairs. An arguer who wants to characterize the nature of something or convince an audience that a certain state of affairs exists can always support a claim with fabricated examples. An arguer intent on proving the existence of Bigfoot or flying saucers could happily invent close encounters.

But there are legitimate uses of hypothetical examples, and we can recognize them if we distinguish among types of claims as the main sections of this book do. Hypothetical examples are often used to set up an ideal definition; they are effective in causal arguments to convey how a causal process works; they can be used in evaluation arguments to construct "what if" situations that clarify the values involved in a real case; and they can be used in proposal arguments to create scenarios of desirable or undesirable outcomes. But they should definitely not be used as unqualified supporting evidence in an argument whose purpose is to characterize the world as accurately as possible.

Typicality, or "It's Not the Number of Examples That Counts"

How many examples does it take to support a claim about the nature of things? Could one ever be enough? Or does it take three or four or ten? Actually, no magic number of examples adds up to sufficient support. It's not the quantity of examples but how you convince an audience of their typicality that counts. No matter how many specific or iterative instances you use, if they do not fairly represent what you are claiming, your argument is insufficiently supported. A high-school student body should not be characterized as "sports crazy" if only 300 out of 3,000 students regularly attend sporting events.

In Chapter 4, where we examine the exact wording of some sample claims, we will have more to say about the choice of examples for support. For now, the main point to keep in mind is that behind every example brought in to support a claim, there must be an assumption, or declaration or even defense of its typicality.

If typicality is strong enough, even one example will suffice. Consider the paleontologist who came to the conclusion that some dinosaurs exhibited parenting behavior, a claim that contradicted a prevailing belief that dinosaurs simply laid their eggs and abandoned them. He had discovered one eggshell-littered nest containing the remains of fifteen baby dinosaurs. Since the teeth of these infant hadrosaurs were worn, he reasoned that food had been brought to them. He then drew the conclusion that a whole species of dinosaurs cared for their young on the basis of only one example, one nest of one dinosaur (*New York Times,* February 12, 1980). He could do so with confidence because we assume great uniformity of behavior among animals in matters related to their survival; what one animal does in natural circumstances, other animals of the same species will also do. But an assumption of typicality this strong cannot be used in generalizing about human behavior. The behavior of one person is rarely seen as typical of all humans, nor is one act always representative of a person's character. One half-eaten Big Mac does not make a slob.

"Examples" That Are Not Examples

Writing with particular examples would seem to be natural since experience is always specific. But oddly enough, detailed, specific writing doesn't come easily. We tend to float away from the particular, past the iterative, on the way to the general. When we try to turn the process around in written argument and support the general statement with specific examples, we often come only part of the way down, producing as "examples" statements that are really lower-level generalizations. Here is a sample paragraph that supports its characterization with more characterizations instead of examples.

> My friend is irresponsible. She never does anything on time, whether it is a homework assignment or arriving at a place for a meeting. Moreover, she doesn't regret being late or feel she should offer any apologies. She doesn't take care of her possessions, but expects others to do it for her and is upset when they don't. She doesn't concern herself with plans, and often doesn't carry out her part in them. She goes places without the money needed for the trip and relies on others to see she returns. Often she leaves without telling anyone where she's going or when she'll return.

We can see this paragraph as a series of claims, some of which support others. If we diagrammed it, showing which supports which, our diagram might look as follows:

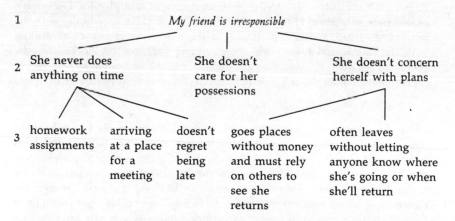

The statements in this diagram fall into a three-tiered hierarchy. At level 1 is the most general claim being supported. The claims on level 2

amount to a definition of *irresponsible,* a term that certainly needs clarification that writer and reader can share. To be "irresponsible," according to this little argument, is never to do anything on time, not to care for one's possessions, and not to concern oneself with plans. At level 3 are some suggestions of iterative examples. We know that a sentence like "She goes places without the money needed for the trip" must be sitting on top of one or more specific events, like that time your friend took the bus to the mall, didn't have the fare back, and had to borrow from another friend; or the time she went to lunch with you and didn't have enough money to cover her part of the check. Particular events like these led to the generalizations at level 2 that culminated in the overall claim "My friend is irresponsible." These particular events are missing from the paragraph. It is certainly not "wrong" without details; it does suggest behavior that most people would consider "irresponsible." But at least some of those particular events should be there for two reasons. First, the writing would be more lively and therefore more readable, and, second, most readers would find the argument more convincing if they could share with the writer the actual evidence, the real events that inspired the characterization.

FOR YOU TO ANALYZE

Examine the following paragraphs. Do the writers get down to examples? Are the examples iterative or particular?

My brother is a mathematical genius. He was awarded the New York State Regents Scholarship with excellence in mathematics and physics. During his second term at Michigan State University, he was working specifically with the head of the mathematics department on the derivation of equations dealing with the fourth dimension. While on summer vacation, he worked for the Hewlett-Packard Corporation as an inventor of new computer and calculator programming, under the direction of many doctorates in physics and mathematics.

My sister Laura is a compulsive clothes buyer. Whenever she hears the word *shopping,* she is always willing to go. Her five charge accounts at the local boutiques along with her VISA card enable her to purchase clothing and accessories at her every whim. If you were to tour her townhouse, you would notice her four large closets, one for each season of the year. Looking through the closets, you would notice the arrangement according to color from the lightest yellows to the blacks. You would also notice numerous tags hanging from the articles which haven't been worn yet.

My roommate is an understanding person. She is always around and eager to help when one needs someone to talk to. She is patient with those that others cannot be patient with. She does little things for people out of the goodness of her heart. She is the type of girl that others gravitate toward because of her sympathetic attitude. I don't believe she even knows the definition of a fair-weather friend.

Occasionally, if examples in a series are obviously connected, it is not necessary to state the generalization they support. Readers will formulate it for themselves. Read through the following paragraphs and supply the missing claims.

Outdoor magazines, including the Japanese edition of *Field and Stream,* are hot. More than 2,000 camping and sports-equipment stores have opened, 10 times the number of a decade ago, and they're doing a land-office business in rugged wilderness gear: hiking boots, fishing rods, safari jackets, cowboy hats. The *Japan Sports Industry News* estimates sales of outdoor goods will total $1.5 billion this year, nearly twice as much as four years ago. And that doesn't include sales of such things as vacation homes and log houses (boom industries in themselves), or macho four-wheel-drive vehicles (sales of which have nearly tripled over the last six years).

—"Japan: The Call of the Wild,"
Newsweek

"We just feel it's time for a change."
Larry Bowa has heard those fateful words, and as of Saturday, he was no longer manager of the San Diego Padres. Chuck Tanner got the word on the evening of May 22, and now *he* is no longer managing the Atlanta Braves. A similar firing line was given to Mike Keenan of the NHL Philadelphia Flyers on May 11, Jacques Martin of the St. Louis Blues on May 17 and John Wetzel of the NBA Phoenix Suns on May 3. In addition, Jean Perron of the Montreal Canadiens resigned under pressure on May 16, and K.C. Jones confirmed on May 22 that he would not coach the Boston Celtics next season.

—"Another One Bites the Dust," *Sports
Illustrated*

Here are the generalizations missing from the above paragraphs. How similar to the originals were the ones you made up?

1. Countless Japanese, it seems, are closet Marlboro men.
2. These changes turned the merry month of May into a sort of Canned Festival for skippers.

FOR YOU TO WRITE

Write a paragraph in which you support a generalization about a person you know with both iterative and particular examples. Its thesis sentence should follow the formula "My ———— (a relative, friend, boss, etc.) is a ————." Your purpose is to convince someone who doesn't know the person to share your characterization.

4 | Analyzing Statements About the Nature of Things

Let's say you have formulated an arguable claim about the nature of something. How can you get a sense of what you need to do to support it for your audience? A useful method of attack is to take it apart, to look at the subject by itself, the predicate by itself, and then the relationship between them. Generally, subjects vary in level of abstraction and in number, and predicates vary in how much definition an audience needs. Thus, you can get a sense of what you have to do to support your claim by looking at subjects and predicates separately.

SUBJECTS

Once you have your claim in subject–linking verb–complement form, you can easily identify the subject. Subjects range from the individual (my cat Fido), through the many (the cats in my neighborhood), to the all (every cat), and from the concrete (Susan) to the abstract (humanity). Sometimes your audience will immediately recognize your subject (the White House). Other times, however, you will need to clarify, define, or even defend what you mean (Manicheism).

The following scheme covers possible classifications that your subject could fall into. Match your subject to a category to find out the special problems it generates.

Single Subjects

A claim with a single subject makes an assertion about a single thing. ("My Chippendale sofa is probably a fake"), a single individual ("Whoever copied this manuscript was an apprentice scribe"), or a single entity ("The Supreme Court is always constructionist").

A single subject must be identified for any audience that would not recognize it immediately. Individual people are often subjects for generalizations because we like to categorize; we understand people by placing them in preexisting categories. Obviously, anyone who reads your argument should understand what individual you are writing about. So unless your subject is a famous person, you may have to identify him or her in a sentence or phrase: "Lindsay, my roommate, is a liar." "Affirmed, the horse that won the Triple Crown in 1978, was overtrained."

Abstractions

An abstraction is something you cannot put your hands on easily. Ask anyone to show you freedom, business, the national interest, or an energy crisis. Someone explaining "energy crisis," for example, might point to a block-long line at a gas station. But others might show you their fuel bills over the last few winters or their new wood stoves. And that is just the point: An abstraction is an umbrella that can shelter a number of different examples. Here are some claims with abstractions as subjects:

1. Organized athletics is expanding.
2. Papal infallibility is a much-contested doctrine.
3. Representative government is time-consuming.
4. Socialism has never existed in pure form.
5. Happiness is everyone's goal.

Let us go through these claims one at a time and examine the problems that their abstract subjects introduce. At this point we will concentrate on the subjects and ignore what is said about them in the predicates.

"Organized athletics" is a large umbrella term, potentially covering everything but a chance meeting of five people in a playground who get up a spontaneous game of touch football. It can include sports from Little League baseball to the World Cup soccer playoffs, from intramurals to the

Olympics. If you really want to say something convincing about organized athletics in general, you should draw your examples from several categories or levels of participation. However, you might find it more convenient, as well as more honest, to replace the large abstraction with a more modest term that fits your examples better. For instance, if your examples are limited to intramurals, perhaps your proposition should read "Intramural sports are expanding." "Intramural sports" is still an abstraction, standing for a number of sports like football, baseball, and volleyball, but at least it is not an umbrella that will carry you away in the wind.

"Papal infallibility" is a technical term. It does not mean that everything the pope says is infallible. Some people misunderstand it that way, which is precisely why the term needs to be defined for any audience except one familiar with Roman Catholic dogma. Here is an authoritative definition: According to the Vatican Council of 1870, the pope is infallible only when he speaks *ex cathedra* ("from the throne"), defining matters of faith and morals. All such technical abstractions, whether they come from religion, nuclear physics, or plumbing, will have to be defined for all but specialized audiences.

"Representative government" is a term with enormous problems lurking behind it. Let's just take the word *government* first. When you read the word *government* your first response may be to think of national government, but the term can refer to an ordering system at any level, from committee meeting to town meeting to union local meeting. If the word *representative* is used to modify *government*, it means that the governing system is operated by deputies, or agents of the governed. According to that broad definition, virtually all nations have some form of "representative government."

Obviously, too many particulars can fit under the umbrella "representative government," so you have to decide how you are going to use the term. You might decide to use no examples and generalize about the nature of representative government: "The very nature of representative government is such that it requires constant dialogue between represented and representative; this back and forth process is time-consuming." But with no examples you risk being accused of not talking about the real world.

You can carefully select examples from all levels of representative government: a PTA committee, a corporate board, a city council, a state legislature, the French *Parlement*, the United Nations General Assembly. Here you risk boring your reader with needless repetition.

You can let your sense of the length appropriate to your audience stop you at an arbitrary number of examples: two from your experience of student government, one from a newspaper article on delay in state assembly committees. Here you risk the charge of insufficient support unless you can convince your reader that your examples are compellingly typical.

You may discover a natural coherence in the examples that come to mind. First, they may all have to do with the United States Congress's waste of time. In that case, you can go back and revise your thesis. It might now read "The United States Congress wastes time."

Or you can keep the more generally worded thesis by asserting that all the examples from this level (in this case national government) are typical of every other level.

The point is that when you are working with an abstraction as broad as "representative government," you have to select a strategy for talking about it specifically. Fortunately, a good sense of your audience will constrain your selection. You can build on what your audience understands by "representative government" and use examples it is likely to be familiar with.

The word *socialism* poses similar problems. What is socialism? Do you mean Fabian socialism? Proudhon's socialism? Utopian socialism? The kind of government practiced in Sweden? In Great Britain? In the United States? You must settle on a definition of this term, which has many possible meanings. Naturally, you will choose a definition that helps your argument by emphasizing the attributes of socialism essential to your case. For a claim like "Socialism has never existed in pure form," you will define "socialism" in such a way that no actual socialist government will measure up as an instance of "pure" socialism.

"Happiness" is an enormous abstraction. Everyone, from Aristotle to Freud, has agreed that happiness is desirable, but any particular person will have his or her own definition of what constitutes happiness. Nevertheless, if you want to argue about a grand philosophical abstraction like happiness, you will have to construct a suitably broad definition, and you will be in good company if you try: "Happiness is the ultimate good" (St. Augustine). "Happiness is the health, beauty, and well being of the soul" (Socrates). "Happiness is the absence of neurosis" (Sigmund Freud). "Happiness is virtue." "Happiness is peace of mind."

As the subjects of arguable propositions, all these abstractions, from "organized athletics" to "happiness," require definition. Before you can go on to say something about them in an argument, you have to stake out an area of reality.

Plural Subjects

Subjects with Definite Numbers

The subject of a claim about the nature of things can certainly be more than a single individual or idea. It can be a set with a definite number of members, and the claim can assert something about all of them.

1. This year's Eland and Biarritz are designed in the German tradition.
2. Three of the basic courses offered in chemistry are aimed at students who have taken AP high-school chemistry.
3. Eighteen states are overrepresented in Congress.
4. The seven liberal arts are still the core of education.

If the definite number is small, your argument must consider each member of the set individually. In example 1 above, a reader would expect both car models to be discussed separately. Why else did you specify them? The three chemistry courses you are characterizing demand separate attention, and most readers would think it strange if you talked about six of the liberal arts and left out the seventh. The common-sense rule is that when you have a subject with a small, definite number of members, mention each of them.

However, a large definite number in the subject, as in example 3 above, gives rise to different problems. In a brief argument you would not be able to give each unit separate attention, so you must adopt a strategy for covering them all. You can at least name all the members to satisfy your reader's curiosity, but you might seize on two or three of the set, discuss them in detail, and treat them as typical, standing for the whole set. What is true about those few must hold for the rest. If, for example, you were arguing for claim 3 above in a brief essay, you might discuss only three states individually—Delaware, Wyoming, and Alaska—assuring your readers that those three states were typical of the eighteen. However, if you were arguing in the House of Representatives, where action could be taken against these eighteen states, you would certainly have to argue each case individually. Too much is at stake, so no shortcuts would be acceptable.

Another tactic at your disposal is to classify your set into smaller groups, each of which you would treat as complete and separate. The set of eighteen states, for example, might be divided into three groups: the old, tiny colonies; the big, empty westerns; and the noncontiguous newcomers. You would name all the members in each group, but when you came up with the attributes that link the members to the predicate, "overrepresented," you would talk about the group as a unit.

Subjects with Indefinite Numbers

When we argue about the nature of things we often refer to *some but not all* of a group. We use an indefinite plural like *some* or *many* when we know that the predicate doesn't hold for all the possible members of the subject, but we don't know or can't know how many it does hold for. For instance, we may know that it would be incorrect to say "All students at Middle Northwestern State need guidance counseling," yet we cannot say that precisely 837 or 1,437 need guidance counseling. So we settle on a rough approximation like "Many students at Middle Northwestern State need guidance counseling." We have the following indefinite number markers at our disposal to suggest shades of proportion, ranging from a few isolated members of a set to nearly all:

a couple	many
a few	a lot
several	a large proportion
few	most
a number	not all
some	

We can also use adverbs as indefinite quantifiers:

rarely	frequently
occasionally	often
sometimes	always

Oddly enough, these indefinite markers can be ordered in relation to one another almost like numbers. Let's consider separately the most common markers and what an argument for a proposition modified by one of them means.

A FEW This term is just a step away from a specified number. It stands for a small number and is used in written argument when a specific number is inaccessible, inappropriate, or unnecessary. We usually do not formulate claims with precise numbers in anything but scientific or technical writing.

FEW Can you sense a difference between these two propositions?

1. *Few* newspapers in this country are organs of political ideology.
2. *A few* newspapers in this country are organs of political ideology.

The second, with "a few" modifying the subject, requires in support a series of examples of newspapers that fit the predicate. You would make a case for perhaps two or three or four separate newspapers. But the first statement has a completely different meaning and would require quite different support. When you write "Few newspapers in this country are organs of political ideology," you say, in effect, "Isn't it surprising that most are not?" In fact, you may not even mention, let alone demonstrate, your claim that a few are organs of political points of view; your attention may be devoted to the "most" that are not.

We might even say that *few* and *most* are corollaries; a claim about "few" may imply the opposite claim about "most."

1. Few clergymen are criminals. / Most are law abiding.
2. Few young people know what to do with their lives. / Most are in a state of career confusion.
3. Few women reach executive positions. / Most remain on the lower rungs of the corporate ladder.

In an actual argument you can support one or the other or both of these pairs of propositions, depending on which your audience needs to hear about and which you have the evidence for.

SOME

1. Some of the homeless are unemployable.
2. Some meteorites are really pieces of Mars.
3. Some supermarkets are really discount department stores.
4. Some bodybuilders are narcissists.

Some is a safe adjective in argument. You can use it when you have a number of examples that fit your case but no way or need to assess what proportion of the whole that number represents. For instance, you may know of four or five homeless people who have been looking for jobs for years. You assume your sample is representative, but have no idea what proportion of all the homeless it represents. If you pursue your research, you might find an estimate of how many homeless there are in an area, but you still would not know what proportion of them fit your category "unemployable." So you stay with the safe word *some*.

MANY *Many* means more than *some* and thus makes a stronger claim. *Many* is still indefinite, but it suggests more examples, and therefore a greater proportion of the whole, than *some* does. Notice the difference between the following two assertions. (These are arguable because people disagree about what constitutes integration and even about what is or is not a suburb.)

1. *Some* suburbs around Chicago are integrated.
2. *Many* suburbs around Chicago are integrated.

Most readers would interpret the second statement as a stronger claim than the first.

How is that bolder claim of "many" supported in an argument? Do you need six examples instead of three, ten instead of five? Actually, a "many" argument may use the same number of examples as a "some" argument. But there is a greater assumption of typicality behind these examples and, thus, the reader is asked to take a bigger leap between example and proposition in the "many" argument.

MOST   In written argument, *most* usually stands for more than half, often much more than half. In fact, a "most" proposition may even be a cautious "all." For example, if you claim that "Most chows [a kind of dog] are vicious," you may not know a single example to the contrary, and yet you hesitate to say "All chows are vicious." Someone, you admit, may own a sweet-tempered chow, although you doubt it. Thus, prefacing your proposition with *most* is a way of protecting yourself against overstatement. A statement about "all" chows could be disproved by one contrary example, but a statement about "most" chows could survive an exception. The "most" statement may be more honest as well, for our experience rarely takes in all the possible members of a set.

What does a "most" statement require in the way of examples? Once again, you may use the same number of examples you used for a "some" or "many" argument. But the difference in a "most" argument is your stronger assumption that your examples are typical of the whole. For example, you have no reason to believe that the chows that bit you were in any way unusual; they had different kinds of owners and led different kinds of lives in different places, so you use them as "typical" examples to support a proposition about "most" chows.

How do you argue the "typicality" of your examples? A new tactic is called for in a "most" argument—an appeal to the essence or defining characteristics of a thing. (Here we anticipate the distinctive tactic of the "all" argument coming up.) Let's take the chow argument as an example. Chows are a breed of dog, and we assume that members of a breed share similar characteristics, both physical and temperamental. Therefore, it follows that any individual chow will approximate the type of the breed, and if chows are characteristically vicious, then examples of vicious chows are believably typical. Why, then, don't you say "All chows are vicious"? Because you know that any individual can vary more or less from the type.

You may speculate that when Aunt Sylvia's chow becomes arthritic and toothless, it may also become benign.

ALL

1. All generalizations are false, including this one.
2. All unions are labor monopolies.
3. All pit bulls are vicious.
4. All the stockholders are supporters of the new president.
5. All Woody Allen movies are funny.
6. Every snowflake is different.

An "all" statement is called a *universal* because it makes an assertion about all the members of a set—every single one, no exceptions. You may think that to argue for such a statement requires a complete counting and accounting for every member of a set. That is, if you wanted to make any kind of statement about "all" U.S. senators, you would have to investigate all 100. And you may also think that your argument would be convincing only if you piled up more examples than you would use to support any other kind of statement.

Actually, that is not so. It is true that if you have a very small set, readily accessible, you must examine each member in order to make a generalization about "all." For example, if you claim that "All the committee members are bigots," and the committee has only six members, you certainly must account for each. You may also use some of the grouping techniques that we talked about under "definite numbers."

But *all* is not reserved for small countable groups. You can use it even when you don't know how large a set you are talking about because you have a different technique of argument at your disposal. No piling up of examples will suffice, nor any extended description of one typical example. Instead, you must define your subject in such a way that what you say about it in the predicate is one of its necessary attributes, not just an accidental or temporary property. That is, the subject by its very nature must include the predicate. If you can make that connection, if you can define the subject so that it is convincingly bound with the predicate, then the connection must hold for all the set's members. The number of examples then becomes irrelevant, although you should never omit them; they are used as illustration, added touches for clarification and persuasion.

Let's see how support for an "all" statement worked for a proposition that the Federal Aviation Administration acted on in 1979: "All DC-10's [a kind of wide-bodied jet] are unsafe." On Wednesday, June 6, 1979, the

FAA suspended the design certificate of the DC-10 and grounded all 138 in use in the United States. How the FAA came around to making this universal claim, a conclusion called "extreme and unwarranted" by the plane's builders, is a fascinating example of the technique required to support an "all" statement.

The FAA began to investigate DC-10's after one dropped an engine at take-off in Chicago, causing a crash that killed more than 270 people. There were 138 DC-10's in use at the time—a large but by no means unmanageable number, considering the resources of the FAA. The FAA did in fact inspect every single American DC-10. But total investigation did not lead to the generalization "All DC-10's are unsafe." In fact, after that initial inspection the planes were allowed to fly again. Not until continued inspection of the planes revealed cracks in several engine mounts that had had no cracks just a few days before were the planes grounded. With the evidence of cracks in only a few planes, the FAA felt that it had evidence of a basic flaw in the structure of all the planes, specifically in the engine mounts. Since the FAA assumed that all DC-10's were essentially the same, that flaw, and its potential consequences, had to exist in all of them. Therefore, the FAA concluded that all DC-10's were unsafe *by their very nature.* The FAA decided that the flawed engine mount was a design defect and therefore a "necessary attribute" of all DC-10's, not just the accidental attribute of a few that might have been improperly built or serviced.

Look again at the process that went on here. Inspection of all 138 planes yielded no conclusion. Yet when cracks that should not have been there appeared in just a few planes, cracks that resembled one in the engine mount of the plane that crashed, FAA officials believed a universal conclusion was justified based on evidence about the very nature of the plane. Since "unsafe" means that the possibility of an accident exists, and all DC-10's seemed to have a design defect that made an accident likely, an argument joining "all DC-10's" and "unsafe" was possible.

HOW DO UNIVERSALS APPEAR IN WRITTEN ARGUMENT?

Formal universals seldom appear in ordinary writing, perhaps because our natural caution prevents us from thumping down with an *all.* But that does not mean that we never argue for universals. We certainly do, but we are likely to phrase them inconspicuously, without using *all.* Often we use a collective noun or a plural noun with no quantifier in front of it, so our universals look like the following:

1. Coastal wetlands are a renewable resource.
2. Man is a beast to man.
3. Farmers are landscape architects.
4. Ballet dancers are athletes.

Whenever we generalize without specifying *some, most, few,* or *many,* we imply *all.* The naked subject stands for the entire set, and this sort of tacit universal is common in both speech and writing. We are likely to slip into a tacit universal when we want emphasis or when not much is at stake in an argument. Most of us probably would not recognize our own state of uncertainty about exactly how strong our claim is unless someone challenged us. Then we would either admit exceptions ("Well, I don't mean *all*") or stand our ground and make the necessary definition argument.

The thesis of an argument is often expressed as a tacit universal, but as a writer you should not be confused about what you mean. If you really mean *all,* you must be prepared to support your proposition in the way described above if it might be challenged. If you do not, you may need to take account of qualifications and exceptions.

SET MAKING IN THE SUBJECT

Another way of constructing a universal statement also avoids the word *all.* Instead of making a grandiose claim, the creative arguer puts together a carefully limited subject that can be treated as a universal. This set-making faculty comes naturally; it is not a dishonest evasion of an *all,* but a sensible narrowing down of the subject of an argument. You probably make statements in this form every day:

1. People who run more than ten miles a day are running away from something.
2. Movies made of vignettes are not popular.
3. Neighborhoods made up of old apartment houses and small stores are inhabited by recent immigrants.
4. Television news programs that originate in small towns are bloodthirsty.

Here the problems of arguing for a universal are partially solved because you have created a more limited, manageable set in the subject. In most cases, as in all the examples above, you do not even need to define the subject further. The narrowing down of the subject is the definition and you can go right to supporting evidence. But remember that whenever you have a universal, you must convincingly link the predicate with the subject.

EXERCISES

Here is a list of tacit universals. Decide how you would argue for them, whether you would treat them as true universals or qualify them in any way.

1. Politicians lie about their pasts.
2. Violinists love their instruments.
3. Aubrey Beardsley's drawings are decadent.
4. Horror movies are sexist.
5. Walt Disney movies are all-American.
6. TV talk shows fulfill their stations' public interest broadcasting requirements.
7. Dogs are sensitive to their owners' feelings.

FOR YOU TO WRITE

1. We assume that you are in a class of about twenty students. Settle on a topic that is a current controversy. (Or each student in the class can take a different controversial topic.) Now interview three of your fellow students, formulate a suitably modified claim (e.g., with *few, some, many, most*) that characterizes your entire class's attitude toward this issue, and write a paragraph supporting it. How confident are you in making this generalization? Now interview seven more for a total of ten, half the class. Will the wording of your claim change now that it is based on a bigger sample? Next interview the rest of your class, so that you know the attitude of every individual. Now write another paragraph. How does it differ from the first?

2. Write sets of paragraphs supporting similar claims to various degrees. For example: "Some college students like classical music." "Many college students like country and western music." "Most college students like rock music." Or, "Some current movies are _____." "Many current movies are _____." "Most current movies are _____." Or, "Some students are _____ (interested in, indifferent to, well informed about) foreign affairs."

"Many students are _____ foreign affairs." "Most students are _____ foreign affairs." Or, "Blind dates are occasionally _____." "Blind dates are often _____." "Blind dates are usually _____."

PREDICATES

The predicate is what we say about the subject, but we cannot categorize predicates the way we can subjects. In general, predicates function differently in the statements they appear in according to the audience addressed; they make the difference between a fact and a highly controversial statement. Although the gradations between fact and arguable statement are often too fine for classification, you can get an idea of the relative differences if you think of statements on a continuum, a gradient from the factual to the very arguable.

Fact

1. *All senators are members of Congress.*

A member of Congress sits in either the Senate or the House of Representatives. So, by definition, senators belong to the larger class of members of Congress.

2. *Nematodes are parasites.*

Parasites are organisms that live off host organisms, usually to the host's detriment. Nematodes live off mammals; they are, therefore, parasites.

3. *The brontosaurus is extinct.*

Has one been seen lately? The word *extinct* is readily understood and 4 billion people verify the extinction of the brontosaurus every day. The support obviously depends on *lack* of physical evidence.

4. *Some tropical fish are live bearers.*

If you had an audience that was interested, you could go on to inform them of what they might be unaware of, perhaps by listing individual live-bearing species.

Arguable

5. *My roommate is sloppy.*

This characterization can be supported by examples alone because most people agree on what constitutes sloppy behavior. The definition of *sloppy* can, in fact, be taken for granted and not even explicitly stated. You wouldn't even argue this one in words if you could take your audience to your room.

6. *The eastern mountain lion is extinct.*

This claim would not be arguable if the absence of physical evidence were as clear-cut as it is for the brontosaurus. But experts disagree about whether the rare photograph of a whiskered, catlike face in the bushes or the plaster cast of a footprint are signs of the mountain lion's continued existence in the eastern United States. As long as there is disagreement over evidence, there is argument.

7. *George Washington was an innovative president.*

Although this statement is arguable, you probably wouldn't get an argument about it. This is the kind of statement we readily give nodding acceptance to, perhaps because we have heard it so often. However, the term *innovative* has no fixed meaning, and it might be possible to find one ornery historian who defines "innovative" in such a way as to exclude Washington.

8. *Many community colleges are their towns' only real educational institutions.*

Arguable because of that term in the predicate. What is a *real* educational institution as opposed to other kinds? You might begin to argue for this proposition by first defining a "real educational institution" as one where voluntary rather than coerced education goes on. No one is required by law to go to a community college so it is the only place for "real" education in many towns. The word *real* is a favorite, and it always signals an appeal to an ideal definition. Undoubtedly, in completing an argument for this proposition, you would include one extended or several briefer examples to show these "real educational institutions" in action.

9. *Calvin Coolidge was an innovative president.*

This one is arguable, and much more so than the proposition about Washington. There will be some resistance to this claim from the average American reader who is not used to hearing positive characterizations of Coolidge—or is not used to hearing about Coolidge at all. The ornery historian who supports this one will have to construct a definition of "innovative" that fits the facts about Coolidge's administration.

10. *Most senators' spouses are members of Congress too.*

Obviously, this proposition is not meant to be taken literally, as is the claim "All senators are members of Congress." You cannot be a member of Congress if you haven't been elected one. But it does have a point. To say that the spouses of senators are "members of Congress" is a figurative way of describing their campaigning, speech making, and lobbying at cocktail parties. This claim will need a number of examples of active spouses, and the few inactive ones might be mentioned to dramatize the involvement of the majority.

Very Arguable

11. *"Slave life was a largely successful struggle for spiritual as well as physical survival."*

This claim comes from a *New York Times* book review. It presents a positive definition of slavery, one designed to replace the more common understanding of slavery as an unrelieved horror. It is qualified by the *largely*, but still makes a sweeping claim for slave life as both spiritual and physical survival. What are physical and spiritual survival? What are their signs? A thorough argument for this one, with careful definitions and well-documented examples, took a whole book.

12. *High-school athletic programs are parasitic.*

Unlike the fact about nematodes, this proposition with a similar predicate invites a new look at a familiar phenomenon. This imaginative linking—who would think of an athletic program as a parasite?—can lead to a new insight. If we think of the essential nature of a parasite as an organism that bleeds its host of vitality, we can see how a high-school athletic program can metaphorically drain the school system that feeds it.

13. *All lies, under all circumstances, are morally wrong.*

Very arguable and very difficult. This is a universal claim, and an emphasized one at that, which allows for no exceptions. Furthermore, it is a statement that few people would go along with. If you were arguing for this one, you could not hope to deal with all the possible situations where someone might think lying justified. You might attempt to categorize these situations and refute them, but ultimately your argument will not be supported by examples. It will have to rest on a pure ethical definition that disdains consequence.

We have ordered the continuum above with a general contemporary American audience in mind. With a more specific audience in mind, we might have ordered it a bit differently, putting 7 before 6, or whatever. But you get the idea: Given the same audience, propositions differ in their arguability depending on the nature of the claim they make. Our concluding advice is that you put any proposition you want to argue for on an imaginary continuum and assess its arguability. Given your audience, your claim, the available support, and what's at stake (the exigence), will you have an uphill battle?

EXERCISES

Rank these propositions in order of arguability for an audience of your classmates. Would an older person rank them differently for an audience of his or her peers?

1. Many women are workaholics.
2. Women are inferior to men in their ability to reason abstractly.
3. Women who work have maladjusted children.
4. Some women are mathematical geniuses.
5. Women instinctively love children.

Now rank these.

1. Some men are mathematical geniuses.
2. Men are superior to women in their ability to reason abstractly.
3. Men instinctively love children.
4. Men who work have maladjusted children.
5. Many men are workaholics.

Here are some subjects. What can you say about them?

1. People who build solar houses are _____.
2. Men who wear earrings are _____.
3. High-school girls who chew gum are _____.
4. Baseball bats made of aluminum are _____.
5. High schools that give awards for academic excellence are _____.

Assess the resistance an audience of your classmates would raise to the following statements. Does arguability depend on how the predicate is defined?

1. Few Iranians have TV sets.
2. Few Merit scholarships actually provide financial aid.
3. The mass of men lead lives of quiet desperation.
   —Henry David Thoreau
4. The business of America is business.
5. The moon landing was a hoax.
6. Most small businesses are begun by recent immigrants.
7. Some apparitions are real.
8. UFOs land on earth frequently.

9. Local television news programs are violent.

10. A true university is a collection of books.

FOR YOU TO WRITE

1. Formulate two characterizations of the same subject. With an audience of fellow students in mind, decide which of the two is more arguable, which needs more support. Write a short argument supporting each.

2. From the exercises above choose a claim you disagree with. Write an argument supporting its negative.

Examples: Women do *not* instinctively love children.

The mass of men do *not* lead lives of quiet desperation.

5 | The Essential Definition

If you look back at the continuum of claims in Chapter 4, you will notice that definition becomes critical just when the propositions become really arguable, from example 8 on. And that's just the point: The more definition the predicate needs—and how much always depends on your audience—the more arguable the proposition.

Earlier, we talked about subjects needing definition or explanation before an argument could proceed. That's a sort of ground clearing before the major construction can get under way. But when we talk about predicates needing definition, we are talking about a foundation absolutely necessary to the building of an argument supporting a claim about the nature of things.

Let's demonstrate this point with the following simple little argument.

> My roommate is a slob. His bedspread hangs two inches lower at the foot of his bed than at the head. His desk blotter is off center, and what's more, there's an ink stain on the upper right-hand corner. One of the books on his shelf has a piece of paper sticking out of it, and the spare thumbtacks on his bulletin board don't line up evenly across the bottom. Even more disgusting, he does his laundry only twice a week, and he actually failed to brush his teeth after lunch today.

Does this series of examples convince you of the claim that "My roommate is a slob"? Obviously, the person who wrote this paragraph has a definition of *slob* in mind that is nothing like the commonly accepted definition. It might pass in a military academy, but nowhere else. If the writer of this quirky paragraph were backed into a corner and asked for his definition of *slob,* he might straighten his collar and declare, "A slob is anyone who does not meet my high standards of order and cleanliness." But even if he puts this definition into his argument, at the head of his examples, few readers would be convinced that the roommate is a slob according to the common meaning of the word. This writer's definition is too personal, too idiosyncratic. He does not have an argument so much as a demonstration of his own taste. Our "slob" example has two morals:

1. If the definition of your predicate is at all critical to your argument, put it in.
2. Never state or even imply a definition that your audience could not share without first arguing for that definition itself.

WHEN THE DEFINITION DOES NOT HAVE TO APPEAR

When your audience readily accepts the definition of the key predicate in your argument, you will not need to make that definition explicit. Your audience's inclination to agree will probably not be damaged by the omission. But then again there is usually not much at stake in arguments where explicit definition is unnecessary. Such readily acceptable claims are not likely to require an extended written argument. They are the stuff of conversation, or perhaps of paragraphs in longer arguments.

1. Adrian is a liar.
2. My uncle is a cheapskate.
3. Weightlifting is a strenuous activity.
4. Driving on interstates is nerve wracking.

Arguments for these simple claims could go right to examples because all the predicates have relatively obvious meanings to most audiences. A "liar" is someone who intends an untruth; a "cheapskate" won't spend his or her money; a "strenuous activity" is one that would make most people tired; and a "nerve wracking" experience is upsetting and trying. These one-line definitions need not even appear in your argument, although it would not hurt if they did.

Although you can argue for such claims without explicitly defining the predicate, the predicate is in a sense defined by the examples, both specific and iterative, you use, or by any words with meanings related to or synonymous with the predicate. For instance, if you are writing about driving on interstates, your paragraph might look like the following.

> Driving on an interstate is nerve wracking. When you miss an exit
> iterative ⎰ on an interstate, you drive 20 miles or more to the next one, wasting both
>   ⎱ time and gas. That happened to me once on the way to Pittsburgh. I
> *panicked* when I had to read a map, make a quick decision, and drive at
> 55 in heavy traffic at the same time. I knew I wanted Exit 35, but I was
> *confused* by a sign proclaiming two exit 35's, one north and one south.
>   ⎰ *Undecided,* I took a wild guess and was wrong. And, how often, when
> iterative ⎨ driving on an interstate, have you looked in your rearview mirror and
>   ⎱ seen the enormous grill of a semi-trailer tailgating you down a hill at 65?

The absence of an explicit definition of *nerve wracking* would not bother most readers here because the examples so clearly define the term as most people use it. What makes this paragraph an argument, although an unchallenging one, rather than a statement of personal feeling, are the iterative examples. They are worded "at" readers, reminding them of their own similar experiences that confirm the writer's claim. Furthermore, words like *panicked, confused,* and *undecided* clearly refer to the predicate term, constantly pointing the evidence back to *nerve wracking*.

Remember that you can leave out explicit definition only when your evidence fits the most common meaning of the predicate term. You could not include an example like the following in the "nerve wracking" paragraph.

> When you drive on the interstate, you go mile after weary mile, staring at
> lane markers, while the landscape repeats itself again and again, like the back-
> ground in a cartoon.

This example does not fit most people's definition of *nerve wracking*. Perhaps it does better for *monotonous*. If you could explain how monotony can be nerve wracking, you might be able to fit it in, but you would have to make that explanation an explicit part of your argument.

Examples of other predicate terms that might not need definition are words like *educational, creative,* and *neurotic*. While such words are baggy monsters with large areas of meaning, they do have general meanings that are known to everyone who knows the language. *Educational* means "something you learn from." It can describe anything from burning your finger to reading Aristotle; with a little imagination, you can apply it to any human experience. *Creative* describes someone who makes things that are innovative in some way. Even though this meaning is vague, not just any example of making something would support a claim with *creative* in it. Making hamburgers is not creative, but inventing a new pâté may be. Similarly, *neurotic* may or may not have a precise clinical meaning; ask any two psychologists to define neurotic behavior and you may witness a first-class argument. But for a general audience, *neurotic* describes any kind of habitually odd behavior not quite serious enough to institutionalize a person. In informal writing, terms like *neurotic* are used casually and only their general meanings are intended. But in certain fields such terms may have quite precise meanings.

Insiders' Words

It is always the audience that determines the arguer's need to define. To illustrate this point we can look at some slang terms like *geek, airhead, preppy,* and *nerd.* These words have very clear meanings to some people. If one high-school student said to another, "Jason is a nerd," no explanation would be necessary. But if that student characterized Jason in the same way to his great-aunt Tillie, she would probably ask, "A what?" Aunt Tillie needs a definition because she does not know high-school slang. Slang, by its very nature, is the private language of a group; when that language is carried outside its group, it must be defined.

Scientists, scholars, lawyers, and bureaucrats all use the "slang," or jargon, of their professions, terms that have very precise meanings for them though not for outsiders. When they argue with one another, they can use these terms freely without defining them (as long as the definition itself is not at stake). Literary critics can debate happily about *Bildungsroman,* rhetoricians about tagmemic theory, art historians about mannerism, and biochemists about allostery. But as soon as they address the uninitiated, they must translate their terms.

Without Definition, You Risk Circular Argument

What happens when your readers will not understand or not readily share the meaning of the words you use in the predicate of your claim? They read through a set of examples that supposedly link up subject with predicate. By the time they finish, they can define the predicate, but only in terms of the examples they have just read. Suppose you read through the following paragraph, not knowing the meaning of the slang term *preppy.*

> My roommate is preppy. Brenda is a nice girl, and we get along well, but she certainly is preppy. She usually wears Docksiders or L.L. Bean ducks. Mono-grams and brand names appear conspicuously on her clothes; her pink Lacoste shirts have alligators above the pockets, her green Shetland sweaters have her three initials embroidered in the center, and her leather purses have Aigner horseshoes. When she wears all these things together, she looks like a very preppy girl.

By the time you finish reading this, you have a pretty good idea what some of the characteristics of a preppy person are. But are you convinced that Brenda is preppy, which is the point of the whole little argument? The only way you could be—if you didn't know the definition of *preppy* before-hand—would be if you accepted the circular argument, which goes as follows:

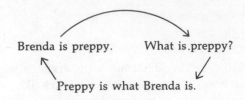

Brenda is preppy.   What is preppy?

Preppy is what Brenda is.

But without some external point of reference for the predicate term, how can you know you are not being fooled? How can you know the examples adequately define the term?

We are tempted to tell you always to define your predicates as a matter of intellectual honesty. But if we did that, we would be misrepresenting the way things are usually, casually done, even in written argument. It would be absurd to dash off a little article on "Art festivals are fun" (not very arguable to most audiences) and preface it with an eight-part diction-ary definition of *fun*. But remember, you can dispense with definition *only* when not much is at stake in an argument and your terms are thoroughly acceptable to your audience.

FOR YOU TO WRITE

Write a paragraph supporting a claim about the nature of things with a predicate that does not need definition for an audience of students. What changes would you have to make for an audience of parents?

Example: Many students "veg out" on weekends.

WHEN THE DEFINITION MUST APPEAR IN SOME FORM

In the following situations definition *must* be a part of your argument.

1. When you use a specialized, technical, or slang term with an audience that might not understand it.

2. When you put a signal in your predicate, such as "real" or "basically," announcing that part of your argument will be a challenging redefinition of the predicate.
3. When you have invented a new term or used a term metaphorically or created a new class to put your subject in.
4. When you redefine a broad term or apply only part of its meaning to fit your evidence.

In addition to these specific cases, remember that your particular audience always influences your argument. Whenever you sense that your proposition will meet with resistance from the audience you are addressing and that you have an uphill battle ahead, you may need to define your predicate in order to forestall your audience's objections.

Using a Specialized, Technical, or Slang Term for Outsiders

Someone arguing for any of the following claims would need to define the predicate terms for an audience of outsiders, though not necessarily for an audience who shared the terminology.

1. Aldous Huxley's *Antic Hay* is a *roman à clef.*
2. Marcel Duchamp was a Dadaist.
3. This book provides a heuristic of argument.
4. Russian biology in the twentieth century is Lamarckian.
5. Voltaire was a theist, not a deist.

Here is an example of a specialist briefly defining a term in an argument addressed to a student audience:

> Whitman was an advocate of "organic form," believing that poetry should grow naturally out of itself, like a plant in nature.
>
> —R. Secor, *Outline of American Literature*

Redefining a Term

Notice the italicized words that wave a flag in front of the predicate.

1. Joe DiMaggio is a *true* gentleman.
2. Audie Murphy was a *real* American hero.

3. Sir Lancelot was *essentially* a male chauvinist pig.

4. The U.S. system of government is *basically* socialist.

5. The movement for bilingual education is a *form* of civil war.

Other words that can similarly call for redefinition of the predicate are *actually, intrinsically, the quintessence of, by its very nature.* You can probably think of more.

Most audiences would find that the words italicized above add a challenge to the claims they appear in. What difference is there between saying (1) "Audie Murphy was an American hero," and (2) "Audie Murphy was a *real* American hero"? The first requires a rather bland demonstration; it is all but a fact. Audie Murphy was the most decorated soldier of World War II, and after the war he had an acting career in the movies.

The second, however, seems to both assert Murphy's claim to heroism and deny that of others; it has an argumentative edge. You can imagine several ways of carrying on an argument for this proposition. It could, for example, turn into a comparison between Murphy and other not-so-real American heroes. But no matter how you support it, you must work in a definition of "real American hero." You may demand, for example, that *a real hero have real rather than celluloid experience;* that would be the difference between Audie Murphy and John Wayne or Sylvester Stallone. Or you may require that *a real American hero have done more than survive the routine of war at the front; he must, in other words, have done something not only extraordinary and unprecedented, but something that endangered his life.* On January 26, 1945, Murphy saved his beleaguered unit by jumping on a burning tank destroyer and annihilating fifty enemy soldiers with its machine guns.

The italicized passages above *are* the definition; in an argument for a proposition containing a qualifier like *real,* giving facts about Murphy's life without tying them to a definition would not be enough. And notice too that our definition says as much what the real American hero is not as what he is.

Examples 1 through 5 above are in order of increasing abstraction and arguability. By the time you get to "socialist" and "civil war" your arguments will consist predominantly of definition. To define the U.S. system of government as a form of socialism is to challenge long and widely held beliefs. To call bilingual education a form of civil war is to refute other definitions of it as a constitutional right, a matter of ethnic pride, or a sop to minorities inspired by middle-class guilt. In short, when we put *basically, real,* or a similar word into our claim, we announce that the battleground is definition.

Inventing a New Term

The following claims differ only in degree from those we have looked at before.

1. Advertising "Opium" perfume is psychosocial pollution.
2. Gladys Frank's living room is a suburban salon.
3. State universities are intellectual brothels.
4. Children are an endangered species.
5. Most nineteenth-century poets were novelists.

These claims all take a word not usually applied to the subject at all and link it up to make a startling statement in order to stimulate an audience to see things in a new way. What results is often an overstatement, but one with some force in it if the arguer can find ways of supporting it.

The first three claims have newly created terms in the predicate. "Psychosocial pollution," "suburban salon," and "intellectual brothels" are terms invented for the occasion by combining things not normally combined. The predicates of sentences 4 and 5 are recognizable terms, but the whole propositions are startling juxtapositions.

All such invented claims demand definition of the predicate. What, for example, could possibly be meant by the term *intellectual brothel?* Because proposition 3 is an implied universal, something about the very nature of state universities must have inspired the writer to create a category to epitomize them. That category was formed by taking a word not usually applied to a university—*brothel*—and combining it with a word that usually is—*intellectual.*

> An "intellectual brothel" is a place where ideas are prostituted for the sake of a transient clientele. Knowledge in a state university is a commodity at the service of the students, rather than an ideal to be pursued. Occasionally, a good student falls in love with learning and redeems the commodity.

Proposition 4 is a bit different because the term *endangered species* is easily recognized by the average reader, though not with the meaning intended in this claim. All the effort in this argument will go into showing how the term *endangered species,* usually reserved for bald eagles or buffalo, could possibly apply to children. Obviously, this claim is not meant literally. This apparent universal can unfold into an argument about the declining birth rate and diminishing value of children in affluent Western countries. The arguer means that since children are decreasing in number and importance, they resemble an endangered species.

Redefining a Broad Term

What do these claims have in common?

1. American society is stratified into classes.
2. New Yorkers are provincial.
3. The Hudson River School of painting is literary.
4. Doing nothing is creative.
5. Whitman's *Leaves of Grass* is a great comic poem.

Each asserts something unusual about its subject. Each is, therefore, quite arguable. We usually think of the United States as the opposite of a society layered in classes and the inhabitants of its largest city as anything but provincial. And how can doing nothing be a form of doing something?

To support any of these claims requires defining the predicate to fit evidence about the subject. In effect, you must select part of a large, possible definition, and either ignore or refute the parts that do not fit. For example, suppose you wanted to argue for sentence 2. *Provincial* usually describes life away from a center of population, a life, presumably, of limited experience, narrow outlook, and unsophisticated manners. In fact, one of the dictionary meanings of *provincial* is "narrow" or "limited." Thus, applying this term to life in a big city is unexpected. How could it be done convincingly?

You could do it by emphasizing that part of the definition of *provincial* that suits your details. You might seize on the notions of "narrowness" and "limitation" and argue that New Yorkers can be narrow and limited, and in that sense provincial. Of course, eventually your argument must get down to hard evidence. Here is what part of your argument might look like. (Notice that we have emphasized the definition of *provincial*.)

> Life in the boroughs of New York is indeed provincial, and New Yorkers are *narrow and limited in their experiences* of places other than the square blocks around their homes. It is rare for a native of Brooklyn to leave Flatbush Avenue and venture on the Grand Concourse in the Bronx. I once met a Brooklynite who never set foot in the Bronx until she was twenty-one, let alone west of the Hudson. And even a Manhattan tower dweller, who partakes of "Culture" several times a week at the opera and museums, still experiences only a narrow band in the spectrum of possible life styles.

The word *provincial* is not bent totally out of shape here. Instead, one of its possible meanings has been selected and the evidence tied to that meaning. But the readers are, as they must be, explicitly informed of what parcel of the definition you were working with. They might disagree of course, insisting, for example, that "rusticity" is an essential of provincialism and that, according to their definition, it is impossible to live a provincial life in a major city. But that possibility for disagreement is what makes the proposition arguable in the first place.

Selective defining is a skill that requires sensitivity to audience and shades of meaning. On the one hand, you have to avoid defining your word so narrowly or oddly that your definition will be rejected; on the other hand, you cannot let your key term mean *all* the things it could mean because you would dilute your examples.

Let's look at the defining process in action once more. If you were to argue for sentence 1, you would obviously not mean that American society was divided into nobles, yeomen, and peasants with internal gradations in each class and no movement between. Instead, you might argue as follows:

> The class structure in America is not readily visible. Rather, we have classes in the sense of separate levels of existence that rarely mix with one another, the essence rather than the trappings of class. We don't have separate labels for our classes, we don't pray for their preservation in churches, we don't even identify ourselves as members of one class or another. Nevertheless, class distinctions are there in the discomfort we feel in the presence of members of another level.

The above paragraph presents a distilled definition of the broad term *class* that is easily understandable and acceptable to most audiences; this redefinition makes it possible to go on and talk about America as a stratified society. The next step in the argument would be to fit examples under this definition. Notice that *class* is not defined narrowly as "bloodline," or so broadly that it covers all distinctions of birth, education, dress, place of living, speech habits, income level, and occupation. Instead, we have taken just as much of the complete definition of class as our American examples might need.

The "selective defining" we have practiced on *provincial* and *class* is not all that difficult. After all, you must have some selective definition of your predicate in mind when you create a proposition in the first place. You have to articulate that definition.

FOR YOU TO WRITE

Try your hand at making up claims in the following categories:

1. Using in the predicate a specialized term from a course you have taken.
2. Using in the predicate a broad term that you will redefine, such as *political, sophisticated, street-wise,* or *conventional.*

3. Using in the predicate an intensifier like *real, basically,* or *true.*
4. Using in the predicate a new term or a startling juxtaposition.

WHERE TO PUT THE DEFINITION

Examples alone are not sufficient support for more arguable claims. You need definition as well, and that gives you an added organizational problem—where to put that definition. In a textbook, definitions are often underlined, boxed, or starred, making them as obtrusive as possible. And on an exam, you may want to be as forward as a textbook in your demonstration that you know the definition of a critical term. Similarly, in a technical or scientific article, definition is blunt. For such occasions, beginning with an explicit, isolated definition is usually the best tactic.

But in other writing situations—the essay about literature, the paper for a history course, the article for a general audience, the play review—two demands are made of the writer. The writing in such arguments must be both precise and easily read, even graceful in style. Precision requires that definition be present, but style often demands that some elements of an argument be unobtrusive. When the definition must be there yet not impede the flow of the writing, a dispersed, or emerging, definition can be used.

Isolated Definition

Sometimes an argument cannot get off the ground unless the predicate is defined all at once. When an audience is inexpert and the subject at all technical, definition must come at the beginning. You could not, for example, argue to the readers of a newspaper that "Lyndon Johnson had hubris," without defining *hubris* immediately, or that "Stockbrokers are Manichean," unless the very next sentence, or even clause, translated *Manichean* into everyday words for an everyday audience.

The *isolated definition,* the definition given all at once, can be as brief as a phrase. (We have just given you an example of that in our definition of *isolated definition.*) Or it can be a sentence, several sentences, even a paragraph or more. But no matter the length, it is delivered whole, in one installment, as in the following examples.

> Third in importance among the sources of medieval monastic culture is classical culture, the word "classical" having in this instance a meaning which requires definition but which, in general acceptance, can be taken to mean the cultural values of pagan antiquity.
>
> —Jean Leclercq, *The Love of Learning and the Desire for God*

For war, consisteth not in battle only, or the act of fighting; but in a tract of time, wherein the will to contend by battle is sufficiently known; and therefore the notion of *time*, is to be considered in the nature of war: as it is in the nature of weather. For as the nature of foul weather lieth not in a shower or two of rain; but in an inclination thereto of many days together: so the nature of war, consisteth not in actual fighting; but in the known disposition thereto, during all the time there is no assurance to the contrary. All other time is peace.

—Thomas Hobbes, *Leviathan*

Dispersed Definition

A second way to solve the definition problems of an argument about the nature of things is to use or create a definition with many parts. This definition is then dispersed throughout the argument, satisfying the logical demand for definition and, at the same time, organizing the essay.

Here's how dispersed definition works. Suppose you are arguing for a characterization like "Wilkie Collins's *Armadale* is a sensation novel." This proposition places a particular Victorian novel in the class "sensation novel," which has a precise meaning to the literary historian though not to the general reader. "Sensation novel" is best defined by a list of attributes.

1. The plot of a sensation novel concerns a mystery or secret.
2. The characters, if not always the reader, are kept in suspense.
3. The setting—houses, weather, landscape, or cityscape—is threatening.
4. The characterizations are often exaggerated.
5. The subject matter may include the occult, dreams, curses, omens, and ghosts.

Here are both a definition and an outline. Each of these attributes could sit at the head of a paragraph followed by supporting examples from Collins's *Armadale*. You could, of course, begin your essay by giving the full definition of "sensation novel" before dispersing it. That would serve the double function of explaining the predicate term immediately and foreshadowing the structure of the argument. Or you could end your essay by pulling the parts of the definition together, providing a summary. Everything depends on your audience and thus on how long, elaborate, and qualified your argument is. If it is short, you risk boring your reader with needless repetition.

Dispersing the definition works well with words whose meanings can be given as a list of attributes. But you would not bother to disperse the definition unless you had examples for each part of the meaning. However, defining your predicate term and finding examples are reciprocal processes; each feeds the other. That is, you won't know what examples to look for unless you know what they might be examples of. And a bag full of examples won't mean a thing without the organizing principle of a definition.

To illustrate, here is a proposition whose predicate requires us to invent a plausible list of attributes which we can then disperse throughout the argument. Our example is "Uncle Armand is an intellectual." Now *intellectual* needs a definition. We could think of synonyms—*smart, brainy, intelligent*—but these words are just as abstract as *intellectual* and they bring us no closer to supporting examples. Common sense tells us that if we want to get down to Uncle Armand and the things he has, says, and does, we must break *intellectual* up into smaller, more manageable terms, like a series of paths from the abstract to the particular. We can define *intellectual* as a list of activities and attributes. These help us bridge the gap between subject and predicate, between "Uncle Armand" and "intellectual."

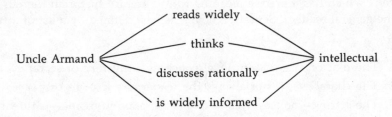

According to one part of our definition, an intellectual is someone who is well read. If Uncle Armand is to fit this part of the definition, we must demonstrate that he is well read. Now we bring in the evidence to convince our reader; we mention the 3,000 books in Uncle Armand's library and his many magazine subscriptions. He tells us that he never watches television, and we report that we have often seen him reading intently. We could do a similar piling up of examples and evidence for each of the four parts of our definition.

Our "Uncle Armand" proposition is an easy one to support. Let's look at a more challenging one: "Heavy metal rock is ritual music." What is our definition of *ritual music?* We have to construct one that covers examples from our subject and yet is plausible in itself. That double-duty defining is, as we have mentioned before, the essential skill in arguing for a claim about the nature of things. Our definition of *ritual music* might be the following list of attributes:

1. unvaried, incessant, heavy beat
2. undifferentiated vocal sounds
3. melody line relatively unimportant
4. dance use

Once again, as in the case of Uncle Armand, these attributes, with the exception of the last, have to be tied to particulars. The first defines the very nature of heavy metal rock; it makes the universality of this proposition possible.

FOR YOU TO ANALYZE

What claims are being supported in the following arguments? Pick out the elements of the dispersed definition.

Evolution, then, was "in the air" in the years immediately preceding the publication of *Vestiges* [Robert Chambers, *Vestiges of the Natural History of Creation,* 1844], in a number of specific senses. First, a fair number of scientists, from Buffon and Maupertius to Lamarck and Saint-Hilaire and Meckel, had given it the cachet of their approval; and while most of these were obscure enough, a few were of some importance in their fields or had taken pains to be noticed. Second, the idea had also attracted several nonscientific writers, ranging in influence and quality from Kant to Erasmus Darwin, and Monboddo. Third, there had been of late a considerable accumulation of technical findings leading in the same direction, most strikingly in geology, embryology, and comparative anatomy. Fourth, a good many of the neutral and half-convinced were recording the hypothesis honestly enough, sometimes even in popular treatises, as at least a possibility. Fifth, these influences had rendered the idea sufficiently conspicuous that even hostile writers, when addressing an informed audience, were forced to deal seriously with it, thereby giving it a sort of disagreeable publicity of their own. (Herbert Spencer was first seriously interested in evolution by Lyell's refutation of it in the *Principles.*)

—Milton Millhauser, *Just Before Darwin*

When the 14th century opened, France was supreme. Her superiority in chivalry, learning, and Christian devotion was taken for granted, and as traditional champion of the Church, her monarch was accorded the formula of "Most Christian King." The people of his realm considered themselves the chosen objects of divine favor through whom God expressed his will on earth. The classic French account of the First Crusade was entitled Gesta Die per Francos (God's Deeds Done by the French). Divine favor was confirmed in 1297 when, a bare quarter-century after his death, France's twice-crusading King, Louis IX, was canonized as a saint.

"The fame of French knights," acknowledged Giraldus Cambrensis in the 12th century, "dominates the world." France was the land of "well-conducted chivalry" where uncouth German nobles came to learn good manners and taste at the courts of French princes, and knights and sovereigns from all over Europe assembled at the royal court to enjoy jousts and festivals and amorous gallantries. Residence there, according to blind King John of Bohemia, who preferred the French court to his own, offered "the most chivalrous sojourn in the world." The French, as described by the renowned Spanish knight Don Pero Niño, "are generous and great givers of presents." They know how to treat strangers honorably, they praise fair deeds, they are courteous and gracious in speech and "very gay, giving themselves up to pleasure and seeking it. They are very amorous, women as well as men, and proud of it."

As a result of Norman conquests and the crusades, French was spoken as a second mother tongue by the noble estate in England, Flanders, and the Kingdom of Naples and Sicily. It was used as the language of business by Flemish magnates, by law courts in the remnants of the Kingdom of Jerusalem, by scholars and poets of other lands. Marco Polo dictated his *Travels* in French, St. Francis sang French songs, foreign troubadours modeled their tales of adventure on the French *chansons de geste*. When a Venetian scholar translated a Latin chronicle of his city into French rather than Italian, he explained his choice on the ground that "the French language is current throughout the world and more delightful to hear and read than any other."

The architecture of Gothic cathedrals was called the "French style"; a French architect was invited to design London Bridge; Venice imported dolls from France dressed in the latest mode in order to keep up with French fashions; exquisitely carved French ivories, easily transportable, penetrated to the limits of the Christian world. Above all, the University of Paris elevated the name of the French capital, surpassing all others in the fame of its masters and the prestige of its studies in theology and philosophy, though these were already petrifying in the rigid doctrines of Scholasticism. Its faculty at the opening of the 14th century numbered over 500, its students, attracted from all countries, were too numerous to count. It was a magnet for the greatest minds: Thomas Aquinas of Italy taught there in the 13th century, as did his own teacher Albertus Magnus of Germany, his philosophical opponent Duns Scotus of Scotland, and in the next century, the two great political thinkers, Marsilius of Padua and the English Franciscan William of Ockham. By virtue of the university, Paris was the "Athens of Europe"; the Goddess of Wisdom, it was said, after leaving Greece and then Rome, had made it her home.

The University's charter of privileges, dating from 1200, was its greatest pride. Exempted from civil control, the University was equally haughty in regard to ecclesiastical authority, and always in conflict with Bishop and Pope. "You Paris masters at your desks seem to think the world should be ruled by your reasonings," stormed the papal legate Benedict Caetani, soon to be Pope Boniface VIII. "It is to us," he reminded them, "that the world is entrusted, not to you." Unconvinced, the University considered itself as authoritative in theology as the Pope, although conceding to Christ's vicar equal status with itself as "the two lights of the world."

—Barbara L. Tuchman, *A Distant Mirror*

FOR YOU TO WRITE

Here are some claims with broad terms in the predicate. Outline arguments for them by creating a series of smaller claims, which make up a dispersable definition of the predicate term.

Example:

Shyness is a handicap.

Shy people have trouble in social situations.

Shy people are at a disadvantage in school.

Shy people go unrecognized in their jobs.

1. Much popular fiction is unreadable.
2. Musical comedy is a uniquely American entertainment.
3. Many elementary-school children have learning disabilities.
4. My friend _____ is gifted.
5. American public education discriminates in many ways.
6. Thomas Jefferson was a protean man.
7. The civil rights movement was not a regional phenomenon.
8. Hospital care in the United States does not treat the whole patient.
9. Computers are now used in businesses of all sizes.
10. The eastern coal industry is floundering.

6 | How to Define

By now you realize that definition is essential in argument. If you use any term that your audience will not recognize, either because it is unfamiliar or because you are using it in an unfamiliar way, you must define it. And most important is the definition of the predicate in a claim that names, describes, or characterizes. There, definition can determine the very structure of the argument; it is not just a passing clarification.

Many techniques of definition are available. The more possibilities you know, the more choices you have, and the more choices, the better your chance of finding one that works for your audience. You can even use several techniques of definition on the same word and attack it from different sides. This chapter gives you many models for constructing definitions for your arguments.

THE SYNONYM

Using a synonym is the fastest way to define. You simply follow the word to be defined with another word that means roughly the same thing but is more familiar to your audience.

74

litotes, understatement

febrile, feverish

dour, gloomy or sullen or severe

W.C., the toilet

masjid, mosque

dolce far niente, it is sweet to do nothing

The terms in the above list are probably unfamiliar enough to most audiences to need definition. But sometimes you do this kind of doubling for words whose meanings are more obvious. You might, for instance, say that something is "unique, one of a kind." Using a synonym does not make *unique* any clearer here; it's clear enough. The synonym adds emphasis.

Foreign borrowings—like *masjid, W.C.,* or *litotes*—are often easily translated by a synonym. In all these cases, the relationship between true synonyms can be expressed with an equals sign. But the synonym definition does not work for words that do not have precise equivalents, and for many words in English, no other single word means the same. Can you think of synonyms for words like *sociobiology, crenelated,* or *mauve*? For these words synonymous phrases are required.

The challenge of definition in argument is not always limited to a single word. Sometimes a phrase, a combination of words that no one would ever look up in the dictionary, needs the same kind of clarification that a synonym gives to a single word. Since precise meaning is so important in argument, you may find yourself using synonymous phrases to define groups of words in just the way you mean them. You might, for instance, describe an upcoming primary as "a crucial test for the president" and follow that phrase with the explanation "one that will determine whether he runs for reelection."

EXERCISE

Define the following words and phrases by using synonyms:

1. symmetry
2. sporadic
3. binary
4. solecism
5. naïve
6. pig in a poke
7. sabbatical
8. avatar
9. eidolon
10. caveat emptor

THE GENUS/DIFFERENCE DEFINITION

If you have been taught how to define, you have probably learned to use the genus/difference definition. This definition has two parts. The word to be defined is first placed in a genus, a larger class, category, or group it can belong in, and second, the qualities that distinguish it from other members of that class are named; those other qualities are called the *difference.* A harp, for example, could be placed in the genus *stringed instrument,* and distinguished from other members of that genus by a description of its appearance: It has strings stretched across a large open, triangular frame and is played by being plucked with the fingers rather than struck or bowed.

The difference section in a definition can be very short:

> An asteroid is a minor planet.

Planet is the genus and *minor* is the difference. Or sometimes the difference section can be very elaborate:

> A tabloid is a newspaper whose pages, usually about five columns wide, are about one-half the size of the standard newspaper page left flat after printing rather than being folded in the middle as is a standard-size newspaper.

Newspaper is the genus and everything that follows is the difference.

One of the skills in making a genus/difference definition is finding just the right words to convey shades of difference, especially in a crowded genus. You can see the importance of carefully distinguished differences in the following series of definitions:

pasta	any of various flour and egg food preparations of Italian origin, made of thin unleavened dough and produced in a variety of forms, usually served with a sauce and sometimes stuffed
tagliatelle	a kind of pasta made with egg in long, flat pieces
linguine	a type of pasta in long, slender, flat pieces
vermicelli	a kind of pasta in the form of long, slender, solid threads, resembling spaghetti but thinner
macaroni	a pasta prepared from wheat flour in the form of dried hollow tubes

rigatoni   a tubular pasta in short, ribbed pieces
fettuccine   pasta in the form of flat narrow strips

In each of these delicious definitions, the genus is *pasta.* The added words attempt to distinguish one kind of pasta from another on the basis of shape and size. Notice that the difference between *fettuccine* and *linguine* is almost too fine for words. (You might want to do further research to refine these definitions in an Italian restaurant.)

Another skill in putting together a genus/difference definition is finding a genus that is not too broad. If your genus term is too broad, you need too many distinguishing qualities. For example, if you had used the broader class *food* as the genus for *rigatoni,* the rest of your definition would have to read something like the following:

> Rigatoni is a kind of food made from a paste of wheat and egg forming an unleavened dough which is then rolled thin and shaped into short, ridged tubes.

You had to incorporate the definition of *pasta* as well as that of *rigatoni* because your original genus was too large. Of course, if your audience might not recognize the word *pasta,* the definition would have to be done that way.

After you put something in a larger category, you have to find ways of distinguishing it from other things in that category. There are several ways of doing this. You can distinguish one member of a large class from others by:

1. What it looks like.
2. How to make or do it.
3. What it does or is supposed to do.
4. What it is made of.

What It Looks Like

The definitions of the different kinds of pasta, given above, distinguish one from the other on the basis of appearance: macaroni is tubular; linguini, flat; rigatoni, tubular and ridged. This method of differentiating works only for objects, things that can be seen. You can distinguish kinds of pasta by what they look like, but you cannot, for example, distinguish the Department of Commerce from other departments in the government on the basis of what it looks like.

EXERCISE

Here are pairs of objects from the same genus. Distinguish them from one another on the basis of what they look like or on the basis of any other difference perceivable by the senses.

1. jeans: Levis and designer
2. small cars: Pinto and Chevette
3. flowers: daisy and rose
4. dogs: collie and German shepherd

5. fabrics: velvet and burlap
6. books: folio and quarto
7. guns: rifle and shotgun
8. herbs: basil and oregano

How to Make or Do It

Some objects are conveniently defined by how they are made. What is a quilt? It is a blanket or covering made by sewing several pieces of material together. A fresco is a wall painting made by applying pigment to wet plaster. Clay pots can be distinguished by how they are made: Some are coiled, some hand-molded, some thrown on a wheel. The ingredients are often mentioned in these how-to-make-it definitions, but the main emphasis is on the process.

Words labeling time-bound processes can best be defined by how to do them. Dances, like the waltz or the funky chicken, are most precisely defined by how they are done, though the task is often abandoned in favor of demonstration. Engraving processes like lithography and etching, laboratory procedures like titration and chromatography, physical actions like push-ups and throwing a discus can all be defined by how they are done. It can be very challenging to define a process for someone who has no mental picture of it or who might actually need to follow your description.

EXERCISES

Define the following by how they are made or done.

1. carving techniques: scrimshaw and intaglio
2. painting techniques: pointillism and impasto
3. forms of lace making: netting and tatting
4. exercises: split and sit-up

5. plant propagation: air-layering and cutting
6. decathlon events: pole vaulting and javelin throwing

Now define these more abstract processes by how they are done.

1. appealing a traffic ticket
2. serving on a jury
3. making a plane reservation
4. programming a computer
5. registering as a transfer student at a particular college or university

What It Does or Is Supposed to Do

Some things, and thus the words that stand for them, cannot be defined by how they look or what they are made of or how they are made. Instead, you may have to talk about what the thing does or is supposed to do in order to construct the difference for a genus/difference definition. Machines especially are known by what they do: a food processor chops, slices, grinds, mixes, blends, and purées; a centrifuge separates materials of different density. Workers too are defined by what they do: Drones do not work; electrologists remove unwanted hair with an electrified needle; napropaths massage connective tissues. Diseases, although frequently characterized by their causes, are also known by what they do to the body: Gout brings about pain and swelling in the joints; tuberculosis produces a cough and lung hemorrhage; shingles creates skin blisters; narcolepsy makes a person sleep compulsively.

Of course there can be quite a difference between what a thing is supposed to do and what it actually does, between what we might call an ideal definition and the thud of reality. If we define a babysitter by what he or she is supposed to do, a babysitter is someone who cleans, feeds, comforts, protects, and entertains a child. In reality, a babysitter may be one who plops the kid in front of the television set and keeps him quiet with a bag of candy. Ideally, a university may be an institution that produces an educated and competent citizenry; in reality, it may do no more than keep some people between the ages of eighteen and twenty-one out of the labor market. This difference between the ideal and the real can be serious. The painful gap between what a thing does and what we want it to do is a strong impulse to proposal making. Showing that the gap exists is evaluation (see Parts III and IV).

Some larger abstractions can also be defined by what they do or are supposed to do. The Little League is supposed to give children a chance to learn baseball and sportsmanship. Your freshman composition course is supposed to teach you to write clearly and effectively. Public-television stations are supposed to offer programming for limited audiences. Even broader abstractions can be defined by what they do: Try making your own definitions based on what they do for *sacrilege, hospitality,* and *literary criticism.*

EXERCISE

Define the following terms by what they do or are supposed to do. (Other methods might also be possible, but stick to constructing a difference by describing what these things do.)

1. aspirin
2. fraud
3. infatuation
4. hair dryer
5. welder
6. fixed term insur-ance
7. teacher
8. worship
9. prudence

What It's Made Of/What Its Parts Are

You can distinguish one member of a class from others by naming some or all of its ingredients. Quiches and flans, for instance, are both kinds of pies that can be distinguished from each other by their ingredients. A quiche is made with eggs, milk, and often cheese, while a flan usually has fruit. Obviously, this basis of distinction works well for things put together from ingredients, but prepared dishes are not the only things that can be defined by what they are made of. An electric fan, for instance, is made of a small electric motor, blades, a frame, and a protective grill. A kitchen stove can be defined as a combination of burner units, an oven, and a grill.

Nor are objects the only things that can be broken into parts. A larger, more complex entity like a university can be dissected in a number of ways in order to define it. It is an administration, a faculty, a student body, and a support staff, if you are thinking of people. It is a collection of colleges (science, liberal arts, engineering) and an administration, if you are thinking of it as a corporation. And it is a central quadrangle surrounded by dorms, classroom buildings, labs, offices, and sports facilities, if you are thinking of it as a physical place.

Whenever you define something by dividing it into parts, you create a potentially dispersable definition, a structure that can organize a paragraph or even a whole essay for you (see Chapter 5). If, for example, you wanted to argue that "this university is changing its notion of general education," you might define both *university* and *general education* by breaking them into parts. The university is students, faculty, and administration; changes in the notion of general education consist of an increase in the required number of general education credits, changed readings in a humanities course, the addition of courses in Eastern culture, and a new required course in computer literacy. These smaller claims, which define general education, can be dispersed throughout the argument, each tied to its own parcel of evidence.

EXERCISE

Define the following by breaking them into parts and describing what they are made of. Some can be approached in more than one way.

1. a playground
2. the Romantic movement
3. the Coast Guard
4. the state legislature
5. a graduation ceremony

6. a museum
7. the French Revolution
8. the football season
9. traffic court
10. a sonnet

DEFINITION BY EXAMPLE

Since many words stand for collections of things, they can be defined by singling out one or more examples from the collection. What, for instance, is an entrepreneur? When you give an example of an *entrepreneur*, you must name a particular person. If your audience is familiar with that person, the name alone will suffice: "An entrepreneur is Colonel Sanders." But rarely is this simple naming sufficient in writing; usually more information is added: "An entrepreneur is Colonel Sanders, who turned a chicken store into a red and white striped empire."

If your audience is completely unfamiliar with your example, you will have to add much more information: "An entrepreneur is someone like my friend Jack Kolln, who bought a run-down farm, planted four acres of grapes, taught himself wine-making, and built the first winery in central Pennsylvania." From an example like this, your audience can abstract a genus/difference definition; in this case, an entrepreneur is someone in business whose ambition makes a success out of a small, risky beginning.

When you use a single example for a definition, you run two risks. First, your audience might confuse unimportant details with essentials. If, for example, a reader of your Jack Kolln example abstracted a definition of *entrepreneur* as someone who makes wine, then that example failed to define *entrepreneur.* Second, if the example is overparticular, no general meaning will emerge. A long detailed biography of Jack Kolln would confuse the reader about what part of his life illustrates *entrepreneur.* The reader would then have no choice but to assume the *whole* life defined *entrepreneur,* and thus the example would fail again.

Nevertheless, for a writer, definition by example is an indispensable technique. It lessens the gap between words and representations by producing images for the reader. For instance, *epic hero* could well be defined by examples—by Roland, Beowulf, Aeneas, and Ulysses, by an account of their exploits and heroic journeys. Since definition by example can produce vivid writing, it can and should be used in conjunction with any other method of definition. Readers seldom tire of examples.

EXERCISE

Define the following terms by one or more appropriate examples.

1. superstar
2. virtuoso
3. cult movie
4. menial job
5. folk hero
6. underdeveloped nation
7. classic car
8. ghetto
9. congressional pork-barrel project
10. executive privilege

ETYMOLOGICAL DEFINITION

An etymological definition defines a word by identifying its origins or roots. It can help you seize on that part of a word's meaning which you may need in your argument. *Philogyny,* for example, comes from two Greek roots, *philo-* meaning "love" and *gyne* meaning "woman"; so *philogyny* means "love of women." This word is nothing more than the sum of its parts. Similarly, *republic* comes from two Latin roots, *res* meaning "thing" or "matter" and *publica* meaning—we have no other word for it—"public." However, the relationship between the modern meaning of *republic* and its roots is not direct. The roots add up to "public matter," a hint that the origin of *republic* as a form of government is the idea that government concerns public matters.

Sometimes an etymological definition is the most direct way to define an unfamiliar term. If you have to define a word that is a pure combination of its roots and nothing more, then an etymological definition is an efficient translation. Technical words are especially true to their roots and can easily be defined etymologically. To check this for yourself, look up the derivations of the following words: *zwitterion, cathode, poltergeist, plenipotentiary,* and *piedmont.*

In argument, an etymological definition can help you seize on the part of a word's meaning that will be most useful to you. Suppose, for example, you want to argue for the following characterization:

The liberal arts are educational rather than instructive.

You must, of course, clarify for your reader what you mean by the "liberal arts." But the essence of your argument depends on your definitions of those two predicate terms, *educational* and *instructive.* They look like synonyms. How can you distinguish one from the other when the common meaning of both is "teaching"? You can find the difference between them—and the point of your argument—in their roots. "To educate" comes from the Latin verb *educere* meaning "to lead forth"; "to instruct" comes from another Latin verb, *instruare,* meaning "to build in or insert." The difference, then, between *educate* and *instruct* is essentially the difference between *out* and *in.* That which educates leads outward, expands, opens up in many directions. That which instructs puts into the mind, stocks it with information the way a storeroom is filled with supplies. These etymologies help you to argue that the liberal arts broaden and direct the mind into many fields, rather than instruct the mind in one skill. With the help of etymological definitions, you are able to ignore the more common meanings of *educate* and *instruct* and focus on those that serve your argument.

EXERCISE

Define the following words etymologically.

1. technology
2. male chauvinist
3. controversy
4. diplomacy
5. argument
6. isometric

7. urbane   9. amnesty
8. sophisticated   10. eccentric

GENETIC OR HISTORICAL DEFINITION

The genetic definition gives the origin of the thing rather than the origin of the word that stands for it. It is a way of defining something by describing its history, how it came about, how it developed. The genetic definition is most useful for words that stand for ideas and objects with discoverable origins. Here, for example, is a historical definition of an object, the Conestoga wagon.

> During the early 1700's English and German traditional craftsmen—wheelwrights, blacksmiths, joiners, and turners—in the Conestoga valley of Lancaster County began to combine features of earlier European wagons—the road wagons of England and the large farm wagons of western Germany—to produce familiar but new styles of freight-bearing vehicles. By mid-century these wagons were generally known as Conestoga wagons.
> —*Pennsylvania 1776*

Note that the etymology of the word *Conestoga* itself, an Indian place name, is irrelevant to the definition of Conestoga wagon.

The term defined by a historical definition need not stand for a tangible thing like a wagon. It can stand for an idea or movement such as "The Great Awakening."

> A series of revivals, usually dated from the preaching of Domine Theodorus Frelinghuysen (1691–1748), a Dutch reformed minister in New Jersey, the establishment of Tennent's log college (1736), and the first visit of George Whitfield to Georgia (1738) and his later itinerant preaching from Maine to Georgia (1739–40).
> —*Encyclopedia of American History*

In what circumstances is a genetic definition most helpful? It can be useful when the term itself is not likely to mean anything to a reader; then giving the history of the thing or concept behind it is the best way to construct a working definition for your argument. You could not define words like *Schwenkfelder* or *phlogiston, orrery* or *spill*—dead ideas and dead things—without describing the historical origins of what they stand for.

Historical or genetic definition can also help you use part of the meaning of a word for the sake of an argument. Suppose you want to argue that "Henry David Thoreau was really epicurean." You certainly don't mean *epicurean* in its current sense as "someone fond of luxury and sensuous pleasures, especially eating and drinking." After all, Thoreau lived in a one-room hand-built cabin and dined off beans and coarse bread. For the sense of *epicurean* you want, you must go back to the historical origin of the idea. In ancient Greece and Rome, an Epicurean was a follower of Epicurus, a Greek philosopher who prescribed not sensual indulgence, but its opposite, a life of temperance and suppression of desire for anything beyond that which fulfills natural need. The followers of Epicurus sometimes lived in walled gardens, away from the temptations of urban life. The word *epicurean* has turned itself around in 2,000 years and now means quite the opposite of what it once did. To go against the current meaning in your argument about Thoreau, you need the authority of *epicureanism*'s origin.

The genetic definition is often the "difference" part of a genus/difference definition. The genus term for our definition of *epicurean* is "follower," a very unimportant part of the definition compared with the historical "difference." You will naturally find that for some words, especially those describing past ideas and things, history is the best definition.

EXERCISE

Write genetic/historical definitions of the following:

1. Yankee
2. sanscullotism
3. technocracy
4. ether
5. Skinner box

6. Arminianism
7. *primum mobile*
8. phrenology
9. aeolian harp
10. gnosticism

NEGATIVE DEFINITION

Sometimes the best way to say what something is, is to say what it is not. This technique is often preliminary to another form of definition; we use it to eliminate rival meanings, and that helps us isolate the meaning we want. Or sometimes a negative definition is as close as we can come to a meaning; we can only say what something is not, as in the following example:

Erica Jong's *Fear of Flying* is not fiction, because some of it is not made up; nor can we call it an autobiography, because it is not a literal rendering of the events in her life. Instead, it is something in between for which there is no word.

But when the term you want does exist, negative definition can be a prelude to positive identification:

An antique is not something of a certain age, that is, made before 1830, as some scholars claim, not necessarily something intrinsically precious, like gold or diamonds, not something of high style or artistic merit. An antique, rather, is anything that people consider worth collecting, so long as it is not still being made. Some people collect the baseball cards of ten years ago, and since they are not still being made, they are antiques.

In this example, elimination is a kind of ground clearing. If you remove all things your subject is not, your reader can see more clearly what it is.

You can think of *elimination* as a technique that removes several possible rivals to the definition you want. A *contrast* definition, on the other hand, carefully discriminates between close alternatives, as though you anticipated the possibility of your reader (1) confusing your word with one close to it in meaning or (2) confusing two possible senses of the same word. Here is an example of the first problem. Suppose you want to characterize someone as "frugal" rather than "stingy." On your way to defining *frugal* (so that your examples will fit), you can distinguish it from a word close in meaning, *stingy*. *Frugal* and *stingy* both describe a scrupulous caring for resources, but *stingy* suggests meanness as well, an unwillingness to spend even what is necessary. *Frugal* does not have the same negative connotation. And one of the best ways to point that out is to say, in effect, "When I mean frugal, I do not mean stingy."

The second problem is the necessity to make distinctions between two possible meanings of the same word. Consider a loaded term like "energy shortage," one that has picked up meanings and associations the way a ship picks up barnacles. Whether the "energy shortage" is "real" has been the subject of much public debate, often carried on without defining what an "energy shortage" is. It has been used to mean "distribution problems," and "high prices" as well as "running out of a natural resource." If you are going to use this term in an argument, you should limit its meaning. One way to do that is to bring up and dismiss other possible meanings by making fine distinctions: "An energy shortage is not really lines at the gas pumps or odd-even rationing systems. They are only examples of the energy shortage in the sense that the product is not getting to the consumer quickly enough. The energy shortage I am talking about is our dependence on a commodity whose supply and price we cannot control."

EXERCISES

Distinguish between the following pairs of words that are close in meaning.

1. disinterested/uninterested
2. sympathy/empathy
3. neurosis/psychosis
4. pathos/bathos
5. racquetball/squash

Define one possible meaning of the following words by eliminating others.

1. natural
2. tragic
3. revolution
4. physical fitness
5. handsome

FIGURATIVE DEFINITION

When Karl Marx defined religion as "the opium of the masses," he created a figurative definition, a definition that makes a creative comparison between the term under scrutiny and some other thing or quality that it literally has nothing to do with. Religion is not a drug derived from poppies, but, as Marx saw it, religion acts as a narcotic and dulls the indulger's sense of reality. Can you find the points of comparison in the following figurative definitions?

1. Congress is a beehive that buzzes but makes no honey.
2. A man's home is his castle.
3. Home is a girl's prison, a woman's workhouse.
   —George Bernard Shaw
4. Grief is itself a medicine.
5. Marriage is a war of attrition.
6. Repression is the gravity of civilization.

Figurative definition is perhaps the most graceful, memorable way of singling out a meaning of a word. In fact, such definitions are often so pithy that they survive in the language as aphorisms like the definitions of *home* above. They are also effective in argument because they convey attitude as well as meaning. Calling marriage a war of attrition, for example, defines it as essentially a kind of conflict, and conveys bitterness and skepticism about the institution.

Although they are fun to make, figurative definitions are useless if you need to give the literal meaning of a term. It would do no good, for example, to define *suttee* as a squandering of natural resources if your reader is unlikely to know what it is literally.

EXERCISE

Create figurative definitions for the following:

1. Studying physics is ———.
2. My bank account is ———.
3. A door-to-door salesman is ———.
4. Interstate highways are ———.
5. Fast food is ———.
6. Shyness is ———.
7. Our foreign policy is ———.
8. The state lottery is ———.
9. Compulsory education is ———.
10. Americans are ———.

OPERATIONAL DEFINITION

Operational definition presumably attempts to apply the scientific method to areas untouched before. Modern social scientists and psychologists, for example, cannot make scholarly arguments about grand abstractions like "poverty," "adjustment," "culture," "neurosis," or "success" until they give them measurable meanings. Yet when they construct operational definitions of such terms, they actually use a tactic of definition common in everyday life. Suppose, for example, your mother asks you to weed the garden and you have never done it before. You don't even know what a weed looks like. If your mother wants to protect her chrysanthemums from your indiscriminate hand, she had better tell you precisely that anything in the garden that does not have a dark green, multilobed leaf is a weed. That is an operational definition, one that defines *weed* for one particular time and place. This operational definition is nothing like the definition of *weed* in the dictionary. It is, rather, a definition you can operate or act on; it creates a test for discriminating in one particular circumstance.

An operational definition is particularly useful for setting boundaries. The definition of a "child" as "anyone who can walk under a turnstile and get into the circus free" sets a boundary, an upper limit for which there is an easy, immediate test. An amusement park can define a potential "dodge-em car driver" as "anyone who is at least as tall as a predetermined mark on a wall," setting, in this case, a lower limit. And an employer can define "eligibility for a three-week vacation" as "more than five but fewer than fifteen years of service," setting both an upper and a lower limit. Each of these operational definitions provides a simple test for belonging or not belonging under the term defined. Once an operational definition is in place, whether anyone or anything belongs to the category defined can be a fact. You either are or are not tall enough to drive a dodge-em car.

We can move from the amusement park to more problematic arenas for definition with equal practical success. For example, we can quibble endlessly about whether a particular president is successful or not, with no hope of resolution unless "successful president" is given a satisfactory operational definition, one or more tests of success that send us to facts. A satisfactory definition would be one that an audience or participants in a debate find plausible. If a successful president is defined as "one who brings the unemployment rate down under six percent during his term of office," we have a test that any individual president will pass or fail.

It looks as if an operational definition could settle any argument. All we have to do is define a critical term operationally and apply the tests to reality to generate facts ("President X kept unemployment below six percent during his term in office"), and we have said before that facts are not matters of argument. But arguments are not so easily settled. All we have really done is shift the ground of argument to the definition itself. The issue shifts from "Is X a successful president?" to whether it makes sense to define a successful president as one who keeps unemployment under six percent. Someone else may argue that a better definition of "successful president" is one who keeps *inflation* under six percent.

Many public debates revolve around operational definitions. For example, the current operational definition of a "high-school graduate" in many places is "someone who has a diploma testifying that he or she has survived four years of secondary school or its equivalent." There is a movement to change to another operational definition of a "high-school graduate" as "someone who can read and calculate at the eighth-grade level." That definition would snatch the diplomas out of many hands. So here you can see how operational definition can be the beginning rather than the end of the argument.

If your operational definition is accepted by your audience, it is possible to settle an issue. Since the stakes for acceptable definition are high, no wonder operational definitions are desirable. But they can go wrong in many ways. First, you can be fooled by the paraphernalia of quantification that goes into proving whether the tests set up by an operational definition have been fulfilled; the whole thing looks so scientific that you forget to ask whether the original definition is valid. For example, a sociologist might be investigating who is and who is not "successful" in a given society. She defines *success* operationally as average yearly income: the higher the income the greater the success. When she writes up her argument, she may have to spend considerable time explaining the difficulty of calculating average income, especially on the higher levels, where income is often sequestered. Or suppose she comes to the surprising conclusion that doctors are not as successful as judges because as a group their "average yearly income" is lower. She will have to explain that the lower average income of doctors comes from including low-paid interns and residents in the group. All this mumbo-jumbo of quantification and qualification distracts attention from the debatable operational definition of success as average yearly income. Can success really be quantitatively defined? Perhaps our sociologist should be talking just about average income, not success.

In some situations we allow certain people to apply for us the tests set up by an operational definition. The operational definition of strike, for example, a pitch above the knees, below the letters, and over the plate, is engraved in the rules of baseball. But the application of the test is left solely to the eye of the umpire. And your college handbook probably defines "A" as the grade for superior work. That is a somewhat vague general definition. Your instructor then both creates and applies the operational definition of an "A."

Some words resist operational definition. Suppose the Department of Labor wants to know whether assembly-line workers are satisfied with their jobs. A social scientist might come in and create an operational definition by defining "job satisfaction" as coming to work. Coming to work can be measured by absenteeism and worker turnover. That sounds like a workable definition, yet a large part of the meaning of "job satisfaction" has been lost. "Satisfaction" is a feeling that often is not even precisely assessed by the person who feels it. And after all, a worker may attend faithfully a job he loathes.

Go ahead and make operational definitions. They work well for anything that can be measured and then labeled, and they are satisfactory when partial definition is sufficient. But remember they do not work as well for abstractions because they cannot define the entire concept. If you try to make claims about "job satisfaction," defining it as "coming to work" and measuring it by "absenteeism," all you may really be talking about is absenteeism.

EXERCISES

Construct or find an existing operational definition of one of the following terms. Make sure your operational definition is a test by which the term can be measured.

1. intelligence
2. physical fitness
3. literacy
4. adolescence
5. love

6. readability
7. alcoholism
8. drug abuse
9. mental retardation
10. happiness

It is easier to write an operational definition in specific circumstances. Try the following:

1. Successful job performance at a local fast-food chain.
2. A teenager with a drinking problem.
3. An academically disadvantaged freshman in your college.
4. Musical talent in a very young child.
5. Intelligence in an animal.

SUPPORTING THE DEFINITION ITSELF

You now have many tactics of definition at your disposal—from the synonym to operational definition. You will find that the more carefully and explicitly you define your terms, the more credence and respect your arguments will earn from most audiences. The very act of saying "I mean precisely this, and not that" can go a long way toward convincing an audience. However, sometimes your own solitary definition will not be accepted by a certain audience. You may, for instance, want to make an argument for a challenging claim like this one: "The smallpox virus is utilitarian." The common meaning of *utilitarian* is "useful," but you mean it in the more precise philosophical sense of "producing the greatest good for the greatest number" and you intend to argue that the smallpox virus is utilitarian in this sense, because although it can kill people, its continued existence, at least in the laboratory, ensures that certain antibodies against related pox infections could be stimulated. Since most audiences will resist this argument, especially the initial definition, you can help the whole argument along by backing up and supporting your stipulated definition of utilitarian.

The best way to support a definition is to bring in an authority that has explicitly defined the word or has used it as you do. In the case of "utilitarian," that authority might be as accessible as the nearest good dictionary, which defines *utilitarianism* as

> the ethical doctrine that virtue is based on utility, and that conduct should be directed toward promoting the greatest happiness of the greatest number of persons.
>
> —*The Random House Dictionary of the English Language*

Another kind of authority is the inventor of a term or a scholar notable for his or her discussion of it. In the case of *utilitarian,* the authority is John Stuart Mill, who wrote the classic essay on utilitarianism. Here is Mill's definition:

> The creed which accepts as the foundation of morals, Utility, or the Greatest Happiness Principle, holds that actions are right in proportion as they tend to promote happiness, wrong as they tend to produce the reverse of happiness.
> —John Stuart Mill, *Utilitarianism*

What are the relative merits of dictionary definitions and definitions from individual authority? The dictionary gives a range of meaning; it describes the ways a word is actually used, and therefore it can lend the authority of common usage to your choice of meaning. But a dictionary will rarely support the very precise, qualified definition necessary in some arguments. Look at the following passage where the philosopher Sissela Bok uses an authority to back up her definition of *moral justification*:

> Moral justification, therefore, cannot be exclusive or hidden; it has to be capable of being made public. In going beyond the purely private, it attempts to transcend also what is merely subjective. Wittgenstein pointed to the elements of justification in observing that "justification consists in appealing to something independent."
> —Sissela Bok, *Lying*

She could not have found such a precisely limited definition in a dictionary.

HOW ARGUMENTS ABOUT THE NATURE OF THINGS CAN GO WRONG

An argument about a characterization or state of affairs goes wrong whenever the evidence and the thesis, particularly the definition of key terms, fail to mesh in a way acceptable to its audience. We can look at that potential discrepancy from the point of view of the evidence or from that of the definitions.

When the evidence does not support the exact degree of the claim, the arguer has committed the fallacy of hasty generalization. Suppose, for example, someone argues that "Most Mid State students are concerned about their future in the job market," and cites interviews with four students, one selected from each class. But Mid State has 35,000 students; in no way can those four, no matter how representative, be used to generalize about "most" of 35,000. Certainly this argument can and should feature the four interviews, but those examples should be backed up with a survey of a much larger number of students and/or what it is about the very nature of current Mid State students and the job market that adds up to worry.

The evidence brought in to support a claim can also be inadequate in kind as well as number. This double error is common in arguments characterizing things. A proposition like "Many athletes are overconditioned" should not be supported with only three examples from one high-school football team. How are readers to know that it is not only football players who can be overconditioned? How are they to know that the high school from which the examples were taken was not unusual? Those three high-school football players simply cannot represent "many athletes" in number or kind.

You can also focus on definition and criticize a claim as basically incorrect or inaccurately worded because it asks an audience to share an idiosyncratic and/or unsupported definition. In that case, no greater number or improved spread of examples will make it more acceptable. To say "*Hamlet* is a comedy" is to put the play in the wrong class, no matter how many funny scenes are mentioned or funny lines quoted. No acceptable definition of comedy could ever fit *Hamlet.* "Granted," you say in refutation, "*Hamlet* contains many jokes, puns, and funny exchanges of dialogue, yet those examples of humor have no significance in characterizing a play as tragedy or comedy. Whether a play is a comedy has nothing to do with a joke count." Or suppose your friend has characterized his sister as a genius and supported that claim by citing her straight-A grade average, her local ranking as "Outstanding Junior Amateur Tennis Player," and her election as Fire Company Carnival Queen. You could refute him by saying

"Yes, all of these may be facts, and they may show that she is bright and talented, but they don't add up to genius." The refutation of a claim about the nature of things, then, seizes on an implausible definition or on irrelevant, insignificant, insufficient, or unrepresentative evidence.

FOR YOU TO ANALYZE

I. Identify the technique or techniques of definition used in the following examples.

Stoicism is that Hellenistic philosophy which sought to make the personal and political lives of men as orderly as the cosmos.
—*Encyclopedia of Philosophy*

Good manners consist not only in our willingness to say what we are expected to say, but just as much in our self-control in keeping ourselves from saying what we really feel and really want to say, but which might hurt others. When someone says, "How are you today?" we say, "Fine, thanks, and how are you?"
—Daniel J. Boorstin, *Democracy and Its Discontents*

An eddy, or whorl, is a vortex such as you see in the water when a bathtub drains. Basically, turbulence is a chaotic assembly of eddies within eddies, all interacting intricately with one another to drive each bit of fluid along a different erratic path.
—Edward A. Spiegel, "Currents in Chaos," in *Science Year 1979*

Prehistory . . . applies in the Americas to everything before Columbus, before Cortez, before Pizarro, before Raleigh, the Pilgrim Fathers, and Penn.
—Nikolaus Pevsner, *An Outline of European Architecture*

A true staple [food] provides the people of a peasant countryside with considerably more than half of their calories, up to 80 or 90 percent.
—Philip Morrison, *Scientific American* September 1985

What is symmetry? If you look at me I am symmetrical, right and left— apparently externally, at least. A vase can be symmetrical in the same way or in other ways. How can you define it? The fact that I am left and right symmetric means that if you put everything that is on one side on the other side, and vice versa—if you just exchange the two sides—I shall look exactly the same. A square has a symmetry of a special kind, because if I turn it around through 90 degrees it still looks exactly the same. Professor [Hermann] Weyl, the mathematician, gave an excellent definition of symmetry, which is that a thing is symmetrical if there is something that you can do to it so that after you have finished doing it it looks the same as it did before.

—Richard Feynman, *The Character of Physical Law*

Man is but a reed, the most feeble thing in nature, but he is a thinking reed.

—Blaise Pascal, *Thoughts*

To alienate is to give or sell.

—Jean Jacques Rousseau, *The Social Contract*

When I say "modern physics," I can be very precise: physics after 1896 when the first breakthrough was made and, a most unexpected thing, made experimentally and not theoretically, in Röntgen's discovery of X-rays.

—J. D. Bernal, *The Extension of Man*

A majority taken collectively may be regarded as a being whose opinions, and most frequently whose interests, are opposed to those of another being, which is styled a minority.

—Alexis de Tocqueville, *Democracy in America*

Fractals, geometric forms whose irregular details recur at different scales, are often fantastically complex. And yet one can create a fractal merely by plotting points on a sheet of paper according to two simple rules, randomly applied. One begins at any point. The rules then might stipulate that the next point plotted always be either halfway toward the upper right-hand corner of the page or one-third of the way toward the center and rotated clockwise 40 degrees; a coin flip decides which rule is applied. The points seem randomly distributed at first, but after hundreds of coin flips a distinct form—a fractal—emerges.

—"Fractal Shorthand," *Scientific American*

II. Here are some arguments characterizing the nature of things. Identify the controlling claim in each argument. Is the predicate term defined, and, if so, how and where?

The pieces of the kiwi story can be put together in more than one way. I prefer to look on this curious bird as a classic example of convergent evolution. In this view an avian organism has acquired a remarkable set of characteristics that we generally associate not with birds but with mammals. That the temperate, forested New Zealand archipelago provides good habitats for mammals is indicated by the success of the exotic mammals introduced there. When there were no mammals present to lay claim to the niches in this hospitable environment, birds were free to do so.

The kiwi must still lay eggs; after all, it is a bird. It is nonetheless mammal-like in a number of ways. For example, Kinsky has reported that kiwis are unique among birds in retaining both ovaries fully functional, so that the female alternates between ovaries during successive ovulations, as mammals do. Also as with mammals the prolonged development of the kiwi embryo proceeds at a temperature below the avian norm. The 70-to-74-day incubation period of the kiwi is much closer to the 80-day pregnancy of a mammal of the same weight than it is to the 44-day period that should be enough to hatch a kiwi-sized egg.

When one adds to this list the kiwi's burrow habitat, its furlike body feathers and its nocturnal foraging, highly dependent on its sense of smell, the evidence for convergence seems overpowering. Only half jokingly I would add to the list the kiwi's aggressive behavior. In the course of my research at the Otorohanga Zoological Society I often had to enter a large pen that was the territory of a breeding male kiwi. When I intruded on his domain at night, he would run up to me snarling like a fighting cat, seize my sock in his bill and drive his claws repeatedly into my ankles until I went away. For this behavior and for the many other reasons I have cited I award this remarkable bird the status of an honorary mammal.

—William A. Calder, III, "The Kiwi,"
Scientific American

SAMPLE ANALYSIS

The thesis of this brief argument characterizing kiwis is not revealed until its last sentence: "For this behavior and for the many other reasons I have cited I award this remarkable bird the status of an honorary mammal." The proposition can be put even more simply in the form of a sentence with a linking verb: "The kiwi is an honorary mammal." The predicate term "honorary mammal" classifies kiwis metaphorically rather than literally, since obviously a bird cannot really be a mammal; it can only have mammal-like characteristics.

The writer's first task is to define "honorary mammal" so we can understand how an animal that is not a mammal can be like one. He does so in the first paragraph, where he talks about the kiwi as "a classic example of convergent evolution," a bird that has acquired mammal-like characteristics. After giving that general definition, Calder goes on to mention a number of the kiwi's attributes, or examples of typical kiwi behavior, that are mammal-like: two functional ovaries, long incubation period, burrow habitat, furlike feathers, nocturnal foraging, and even aggressive behavior. These attributes, which he has observed in kiwis, constitute a dispersed definition of "honorary mammal."

IS THE DISMAL SCIENCE REALLY A SCIENCE?

Herbert Stein

By calling economics the dismal science, Thomas Carlyle was saying something about how dismal it was. He wasn't answering the question of whether economics is a science. The answer to that is, "On the one hand . . . and on the other hand. . . . It depends on what you mean by science." That may sound like a typical academic economist's reply, but it's also a scientific answer. No scientist would consider the validity of a proposition before making sure the terms were precisely defined.

If by science you mean a subject in which everything that's known is known with a high degree of certainty, supported by conclusive empirical evidence, and attested to by the unanimous opinion of experts who approach the subject with objectivity, then economics isn't a science. But by that definition neither is physics nor geology nor anything else that's commonly called a science. Geologists can't tell us with much confidence when to expect an earthquake along the San Andreas fault. People who are unquestionably scientists seem sharply divided about whether a defense against intercontinental ballistic missile attack is possible in principle, much less in practice, and an outsider can't escape the impression that the positions of the parties in this debate are influenced by their political beliefs.

But if science is a subject about which some things are known with a considerable degree of confidence and other things are known with lesser degrees of confidence and are true only under certain conditions, and in which much is said that has little analytical or empirical foundation, then economics is a science. Put another way, there's some science in economics but much else that isn't science, just as there are scientific and unscientific portions of other sciences. Though I can't demonstrate this scientifically, I suppose that the ratio of science to nonscience is lower in economics than in many other fields, especially the physical sciences. . . .

The laws of economics, like most of the laws of other sciences, are statements of relationships between two or more variables, all other variables being held constant. In most physical-science laboratories, conditions can be created in which the other variables are actually held constant and the relationships between the variables under study can be repeatedly observed. Not in economics. Economists would like to examine the relationship between the price of wheat and the quantity of wheat demanded under the conditions in which the prices of all other products, incomes, and tastes are constant. But they can't conduct a laboratory experiment in which all those variables are constant. The best they can do is observe the history of all those relationships and hope it contains enough cases to permit the isolation of the relationship between the price and the demand from the effect of the other variables. But that's never completely satisfactory. To some degree this problem exists in other sciences, but it's much more pronounced in economics, despite the use of increasingly sophisticated statistical techniques.

Even if one could nail down what these relationships have been in the past, that wouldn't be enough to predict the future. Economists deal with the behavior of human beings and social institutions that aren't constant but constantly changing. The boiling point of water at sea level is the same today as it was in 1708, when Gabriel Daniel Fahrenheit devised his celebrated scale. But the way people react to a change in prices or wages or unemployment or the money supply is probably not the same today as it was in 1929, or even 1959, because people have been influenced by history.

Moreover, the body of data available to economists is severely limited in coverage and reliability. Many statistics that economists commonly work with don't go back more than 50 years in the United States and go back even less than that in other countries. What data exist are often flawed by difficulties of estimation and ambiguities in concept, and although the economic actions of individuals are in principle the building blocks of economics, most of the data relate to the behavior of large aggregates.

The difficulty of scientific analysis in economics is illustrated by one of the relationships most debated these days. Do budget deficits cause interest rates to rise? The real question here is whether, if everything else is constant, interest rates will be higher if the deficit is higher. But we can't create a condition in which everything else is constant. We can only observe deficits and interest rates under historical conditions in which business investment, private saving, state and local deficits, foreign budget deficits, cyclical conditions, inflation rates, and a number of other factors are all changing. Some of those other factors are expectations, which we can't measure at all but can only infer. It's hard to determine what part of the variation in interest rates is the result of variations in the deficit and what part results from variations in other factors. A similar problem exists in medicine, for example, where researchers can't determine whether a decline in the incidence of heart disease is the result of a decline in smoking, a change in the nation's eating habits, or other factors that have been occurring simultaneously.

Even if we knew the precise relationship between deficits and interest rates for the past, the same relationship might not hold today and in the future. The past experience may have changed the way people perceive the consequences of deficits and, therefore, the way they respond to them. Also, a number of conditions have changed. So, while we have hunches or make judgments, economists can't say with great confidence whether, if the deficit is reduced, interest rates will be lower in 1988 than they would otherwise have been.

Still, there are useful things that economists do know on the basis of considerable evidence. To cite a few examples: Critics used to say that if a parrot were taught to say "supply and demand," it would be an economist. But the laws of supply and demand are both valid and useful. Generally, all other things being equal, people will want to buy more of a product the lower its price is, and they will want to supply more the higher its price is. If people are free to trade with one another, the price will settle at a point at which the market clears—that is, where everyone who wants to buy or sell at that price can do so. This seems an obvious proposition, but it's still not known to everyone who ought to know it. People are still surprised when a ceiling on rents leads to a shortage of apartments, or when a floor on the price of cheese leaves the government holding a mountain of cheese.

Other things being equal, inflation is more likely to result when the money supply expands rapidly over a long period of time than when the money supply grows more slowly. The consequences of neglecting this proposition can be seen in Israel, Argentina, and a number of other unfortunate places.

An economy organized by voluntary exchange will be more satisfactory to most of its participants than one organized by the government. This is one of the oldest lessons in economics, one that isn't intuitively obvious, and one that has been disregarded at great cost in large parts of the world.

There are differences among economists about even these propositions, but at least in the Western world these differences relate more to the significance of exceptions than to the validity of the general principles. . . .

REREADING ROBINSON CRUSOE: *THE ORIGINAL "NONFICTION NOVEL"*

Diana Loercher Pazicky

We tend to think the fuzzy line between fact and fiction is a recent phenomenon. Remember, for example, the stir created in the 1960s by Truman Capote's *In Cold Blood,* which was hailed as the harbinger of a new literary genre, the "nonfiction novel," and spawned a host of imitations. How easily we forget that Daniel Defoe was there before him, in 1719 to be exact, with the publication of *Robinson Crusoe.*

Defoe, a compulsively prolific but frequently impecunious journalist, had little patience with works of the imagination and probably would have found the distinction posthumously conferred upon him—"father of the English novel"—a dubious one at best. Always on the lookout for a way to translate words into currency, Defoe knew a good story when he heard one and pounced on the tale of Alexander Selkirk with all the avidity of a contemporary gossip columnist getting wind of a celebrity scandal. Selkirk was a *real* English seaman marooned alone on a *real* desert island who learned to survive by his wits, and Defoe based his book on the various interviews conducted with Selkirk after his rescue. He may even have met Selkirk.

Rather than calling it a novel, Defoe would have been far more comfortable with the cumbersome but comparatively accurate labels, fictionalized narrative or fictionalized autobiography. In his preface he assumes the point of view of an editor and presents the narrative as Crusoe's own.

Nevertheless, Defoe takes great liberties with Selkirk's account, such as extending his sojourn from four to 28 years. That Crusoe retains his sanity, remembers his language, and never once thinks about women only heightens this implausibility.

It is clear that Crusoe is as much a product of Defoe's imagination as of Selkirk's experience and an early example of how the boundaries between fact and fiction blur, whether the genre be the nonfiction novel, "new journalism," or even conventional biography.

If its ambiguous genre makes "Robinson Crusoe" surprisingly contemporary, its ambiguous interpretation continues to tantalize the 20th-century reader. Although this novel is far too often consigned to the purgatory of children's classics, the scrupulous adult reader will appreciate that this is not a mere adventure tale but one that rebounds with social, political, religious, and even anthropological overtones.

"Robinson" has been variously interpreted as a survival myth in which "Everyman" overcomes the hostile forces of nature; an allegory about the rise of capitalism in which Crusoe turns a desert island into a mock bourgeois paradise; and a puritan fable in which the prodigal son who rebelled against his father by going to sea finds both punishment and redemption on his "island of despair."

To read the novel on one of these levels alone is to ignore the intricate network of ironies that gives the seemingly shapeless narrative an interlocking form and even humor. For example, Crusoe, who wants nothing more than to go to sea and see the world, spends 28 years in the most extreme isolation and confinement. Furthermore, having rejected the "middle station" of life that his father recommended and the circumstances of his birth assigned him, he devotes those 28 years to trying to duplicate not only the necessities of life but also the comforts of home.

These ironies are not lost on Crusoe, who is given to breast-beating and self-recrimination about his folly in succumbing to the irrational, e.g., "I that was born to be my own destroyer . . . ," and they reinforce the notion that "fate" or "divine providence" is conspiring to bring about his deliverance, not only from his situation, but also from himself.

Thrown back on his own resources, he busies himself with the fine art of survival, for which he develops a creative and innovative flair. He is proud of his ingenuity and his labor: "I had never handled a tool in my life; and yet, in time, by labor, application, and contrivance, I found, at last, that I wanted nothing but I could have made it, especially if I had had tools. . . ." This formerly feckless, lazy fellow develops qualities of patience and perseverance and can expatiate on his achievements with a reverential regard for detail.

The struggle to survive, Crusoe discovers, has a certain salutary influence on the soul. Like Thoreau he learns to rely on himself and live in harmony with nature. He also transcends commonplace social values with such insights as, "All the good things of this world are no further good to us than they are for our use . . . we enjoy just as much as we can use, and no more."

Defoe's novel is in many respects a paean to the indomitability of the human spirit. The ultimate irony is that it is only when Crusoe is stripped of civilization that he becomes most profoundly human. His fears, his needs, his wants, are no longer individual but universal. In getting back to basics, he becomes a mirror of man's best instincts, and we feel his continual efforts to make his life more comfortable are less a manifestation of materialism than of a fundamental need for stimulation and security. . . .

"AL JOLSON" IN THE PHILIPPINES

Stanley Karnow

"We must slay the father image," Raul Manglapus, the Philippines Foreign Secretary, remarked the other day. The metaphor, he explained, means that the time has come for Filipinos to shake off the influence of the United States and assert their own national identity.

He has a point. Former Western possessions all retain remnants of their colonial past, but I doubt that the old imperial legacy is more alive anywhere than in the Philippines, where America's presence seems to be almost as dynamic now as it was during the days when the United States controlled the islands. To exorcise it, as Mr. Manglapus and other nationalists propose, would require a monumental cultural revolution.

An American visiting Manila can feel as if he had never left home. The Greek-colonnaded public buildings were modeled on those of Washington by Daniel Burnham, a famous American city planner of the turn of the century, who also conceived the mountain resort of Baguio to imitate an Adirondacks vacation spot. The Manila Hotel, designed in 1912 by one of his American protégés, is the site of Rotary luncheons, Shriner conventions and June weddings.

Affluent residential neighborhoods resemble Beverly Hills, and the suburbs are a blight of used car lots and fast-food franchises, like the outskirts of Los Angeles. Taft Avenue honors the first American civilian governor, and Jones Bridge commemorates an obscure Virginia Congressman who in 1916 drafted the enlightened legislation that promised eventual independence to the Philippines.

The writer Carmen Nakpil Guerrero has observed that chic Filipino families, to emulate Americans, incongruously furnish their living rooms with fur pillows and leather sofas—protected against the fierce humidity by plastic covers

In a land lush with tropical fruit, snobbish matrons serve their guests canned American fruit cocktail. Kraft cheese and Hellmann's mayonnaise are manufactured under license, but Filipinos drive hours to Angeles, a town adjacent to Clark Field, to buy the same American-made items purloined from the PX. Doreen Fernandez, a cultural anthropologist, explains, "The prestige is the label 'Made in the U.S.A.' "

Filipinos, satirizing their foibles, joke about an injured man whose doctor prescribed a local anesthetic. "Please, doc," the patient pleads, "can't I have an imported one?"

Men with names like cigar labels—Benedicto, Bernardo and Benito—are known as Benny, Bernie and Butch, and women call themselves Penny, Popsy and Peachy. Gen. Douglas MacArthur's beautiful mistress, whom he secretly installed in a Washington love nest, was Dimples. The deposed President, Ferdinand E. Marcos, is Andy to cronies.

A statehood movement, founded early in the century, claims five million members. Nearly everyone has a relative in California, Illinois or New York, and lines form at dawn at the United States consulate, which handles close to 300,000 requests for visas a year. When I asked an applicant why he wanted to go, he replied, "America is my other country."

A captured Communist insurgent escapes from jail and flees abroad—not to Moscow, Beijing or Hanoi but to San Francisco. Her "three happiest years," President Corazon C. Aquino said in her address to the United States Congress in September 1986, were spent with her husband and children in exile in Boston.

The dream of every young Filipino is a college degree, and diploma mills grind out more lawyers than the society can absorb. But Ivy League credentials are supreme. In 1980, after Mr. Marcos released him from prison to have a heart operation in Texas, Benigno Aquino pondered ways to remain in America without violating his pledge to return home. "Marcos can't resist if I go to Harvard," Mr. Aquino said—correctly.

Nor is American influence confined to the urban upper classes. Led by nubile drum majorettes in miniskirts, bands at barrio fiestas invariably play Sousa marches with gusto.

Nothing illustrates America's impact as vividly as the widespread use of American English. Candidates campaign in English, delivering florid orations in the rhetoric of vintage American politicians.

The Government has been trying for years to promote Tagalog, renamed "Pilipino," as the national language. But Tagalog is spoken by only about 30 percent of the population, mainly in central Luzon, and in any case it is "Taglish." (The word for "toothpaste" is "colgate.")

Though Spain ruled for more than three centuries, its only durable heritage has been Christianity, implanted throughout the provinces by friars whose principal aim was to save souls. The United States, by contrast, hoped to turn the Filipinos into facsimile Americans.

The conquest, which began in 1898, was as ugly as any imperialist episode. But America soon started to atone for its brutality. On a sultry August day in 1901, a converted cattle ship, the Thomas, steamed into Manila Bay with 500 young schoolteachers aboard. Precursors of the Peace Corps volunteers, they fanned out across the archipelago, becoming known as "Thomasites," as if they belonged to a religious order. Their vocation, though secular, was evangelical— to Americanize the Filipinos and cement their loyalty to the United States. "We are social assets and emissaries of good will," wrote Philinda Rand, a Radcliffe graduate, to her parents in Massachusetts.

The early teachers remain legendary. Older Filipinos evoke misty memories of "Mr. Parker" or "Miss Johnson," who introduced them to reading or algebra. The diplomat Carlos Romulo accepted a Pulitzer Prize in 1942 with the words: "The real winner is . . . Hattie Grove, who taught a small Filipino pupil to value the beauty of the English language."

Pioneer Americans promoted baseball as an antidote to the addiction to cockfighting. Baseball, wrote the *Manila Times,* was "more than a game, a regenerating influence and power for good." The effort partly succeeded. Filipinos are avid fans and players, and their media detail American major league action. But cockfighting remains the national pastime.

American education transmuted pop culture. By the 1920's, the vernacular press was carrying komiks, with Filipino characters lifted intact from American strips; the intrepid Trece was none other than Dick Tracy in Tagalog. Ersatz American soap operas, at first broadcast on the radio in the afternoon to housewives, are now a staple of daytime television—complete with detergent commercials.

Essayists, novelists and poets began to write in English. Under the guidance of American editors, reporters replaced the elegance of Castilian with the razzle-dazzle of Chicago, so that the Manila press to this day identifies senators as "solons" and the president as "the prexy."

Superb performers, Filipinos adjusted to the Americans' arrival early in the century by discarding the zarzuela, the Spanish variety show, in favor of vaudeville, called bodabil—its performers billed as the "Filipino Al Jolson," the "Filipino Sophie Tucker," the "Filipino Bing Crosby." Subsequent years spawned "Filipino" Glenn Millers, Elvis Presleys and Barbra Streisands. Rock groups with names like Hot Dog and the Boyfriends emerged as clones of the Rolling Stones and Led Zeppelin, though they slowed their beat to the tempo of the tropics.

Nationalist militants, deploring all this as American cultural neo-colonialism, are searching for ways to combat it. Hernando Abaya, who once held down the city desk of the *New Haven Register,* wants to stage a wholesale purge of American names, like Taft and Jones, from Manila streets and bridges.

Some people insist that Tagalog replace English in courts and Government offices. It is bound to be a tough struggle. An activist named Cookie Diokno, whose English is as fluent as mine, has vowed to speak only Tagalog to her friends and family. But one morning I overheard her scolding her small son—in English. As she conceded somewhat sheepishly, she was doing what came naturally.

I spent an amusing afternoon at a rehearsal of an amateur jazz band composed of six or seven businessmen, lawyers and officials. Called the Executive Combo, they play occasionally at night clubs and parties. Their hero is Duke Ellington, their theme song is "Take the A Train" and their leader, a demon on both piano and drums, is Raul Manglapus, the Foreign Secretary.

FOR YOU TO WRITE

A claim about the nature of things can be the thesis of a longer argument when it presents new evidence to an uninformed audience and/or contains a challenging definition. The topics suggested below can stimulate your invention of such arguments that might be addressed to students or an instructor in an appropriate class.

1. Characterize the state of research on a particular problem in one of the sciences or social sciences. Remember that the exact wording of your claim may change in the course of your investigation. Be sure that your final thesis (which may be the title of your paper) is an accurate reflection of your evidence. Examples:

biochemistry   Research with hybridomas is a new and promising field.

psychology   ESP research has yielded no verifiable conclusions.

education   We still know very little about how people learn.

physics	Recent research on quarks has excited physicists.
physiology	Scientists are coming closer to an understanding of how the brain works.
biology	Currently two groups are hotly debating the mechanism of natural selection.
criminology	Forensic science has reached new heights of sophistication.
psychology	The University of Minnesota study of identical twins separated from birth tips the balance in the nature/nurture controversy.
anthropology	Archaeologists who study early humans in North America disagree over when the first migrations from Siberia occurred.

You can formulate theses like these in any area of study that interests you.

2. Much historical argument is a matter of defining and characterizing past events, eras, and important figures. History is therefore fertile ground for arguments about the way things happened or what labels best describe them. The following examples might jog your invention.

1. The cowboys of America's old west were riffraff rather than heroes.
2. The 1950s were a decade of political complacency.
3. Thomas Edison was a tinkerer, not a scientist.
4. Ancient Rome had periods of inflation and price control.
5. Intellectual life in France in 1830 was stagnant.
6. Mary Queen of Scots was a pawn, not a power.
7. Metternich was the architect of nineteenth-century Europe.
8. Chinese civilization is anti-individualistic.
9. Prince Albert was the real Queen of England from 1840 to 1861.
10. History is glorified gossip.

3. The arts and humanities—painting, architecture, music, literature, philosophy, rhetoric, language, and classics—are another rich source of claims.

1. Madame Bovary is an escapist.
2. The secret of Charles Dickens's art is his style.
3. The Pre-Raphaelite painters were obsessed by hair.
4. Postmodern architecture is eclectic.
5. Grand opera is a sublime irrationality.
6. Virgil was basically a farmer.

7. Baroque churches were built for God, not men.

8. Machiavelli's *The Prince* is not cynical.

9. Shakespeare really understood women.

10. Poetry is emotion recollected in tranquility.

4. Some of the most challenging and interesting arguments have to do with whether a state of affairs even exists. In such arguments, the emphasis is on marshaling evidence. We all hold many unsupported assumptions about what is happening and what isn't. Take one of these assumptions and see if you can actually gather evidence for it. Write your argument for the audience of a mass media publication (e.g., *U.S. News and World Report* or *The New York Times.*).

1. Organized religion is declining in Europe.

2. Every beach is in danger from sharks.

3. The people of India love American movies.

4. Most Americans are fat.

5. SAT scores have *not* declined in the last few years.

6. Many young people today think that the United States is facing a dismal future.

7. Pornography is on the rise.

8. Drugs are used extensively in professional sports.

9. The so-called sexually permissive society does not really exist.

10. Cheating is widespread on most campuses.

5. Many arguments about the nature of things set out to correct a prevailing view. No doubt you have often heard characterizations that you suspect are inaccurate. Imagine yourself correcting such a prevailing misconception with an argument supporting the more correct view. The thesis of your argument will follow this paradigm: "Most people think x is y, but x is really z."

1. Many people think that football is the most popular sport in America, but that honor really goes to baseball.

2. Many people think all emotional problems are mental, but many are really physical.

3. Potatoes are not as fattening as many people think.

4. Children can learn to read at a much younger age than most parents believe.

5. Most people do not really enjoy their vacations.

6. Contrary to popular belief, most bosses do not sexually harass their employees.

7. Most people think that learning to —— is difficult, but it really isn't.

8. Most people think the influence of organized religion is increasing in the U.S., but it is actually declining.

9. Most people think that left-handedness is random, but actually it is correlated with intelligence.

10. Many people think that lotteries equalize the tax burden, but they actually place it on the poor.

7 | More Arguments About the Nature of Things: Comparisons and Disjunctions

WHAT THINGS ARE LIKE: COMPARISONS

Some arguments support straightforward claims about the existence or nature of things. Still another way of getting at the nature of something is to say what it is like. Such a statement is called a comparison. Some philosophers argue that the act of comparing is a more fundamental operation of the mind than that of defining. Whether or not this is so, you will find that making comparisons comes naturally. But even though perceiving a likeness or difference may be a simple intuitive act, arguing for a likeness or difference is a process with many parts. We are going to analyze various kinds of comparative statements to discover how to support them. But first let's talk about why we might bother to argue for a comparison.

Levels of Arguability in Comparison

The least arguable comparisons point out likenesses between things that everyone believes are similar to start with: "Ohio State University resembles the University of Illinois." What else would you expect from two large Midwestern land-grant universities? You could certainly write 500 words about this subject; you could probably write 5,000. Such a comparison could entertain a reader, but the result, except in special circumstances, would be a rather obvious argument, one whose thesis most readers would grant immediately.

A comparison becomes more and more arguable as the two things compared initially seem less and less alike to the audience addressed. The following comparisons are arranged in order of increasing arguability with a contemporary American audience in mind:

1. My dorm room is just like my neighbor's.
2. Kansas City is like St. Louis.
3. *Star Wars* is like *The Wizard of Oz.*
4. French cuisine is like Chinese.
5. A modern shopping mall is like a medieval cathedral.

When a reader's initial reaction is "Those two things have nothing in common," then we recognize an arguable comparison in which the unexpected similarities must be pointed out. We expect dorm rooms to look alike, and it is not surprising that two Midwestern cities are similar. The comparison between *Star Wars* and *The Wizard of Oz* is not as immediately obvious, but it arouses curiosity rather than disbelief. But the initial reaction of a general audience to claim 4 would be puzzlement. Except for the fact that they are both foreign to an American, French and Chinese cooking appear to have little in common: Their basic ingredients are quite different, as are their techniques of preparation. So there is more resistance to overcome in that comparison, and a great deal to overcome in claim 5. Malls and cathedrals, in our superficial wisdom, are dedicated to wholly different functions, the worship of money and the worship of God. Showing how they are similar would intrigue most audiences.

Just as a comparison is more arguable the more unlike the two terms seem to an audience, so also is a contrast, a pointing out of differences, more arguable the more alike the two terms seem to an audience at first. There is no point contrasting things extremely unlike. Of course Roman Britain is different from modern Britain, and we need not point out that raising tropical fish is a different hobby from operating a ham radio. An interesting contrast argument finds differences between things that are apparently similar. We might take a boring comparison and make a lively contrast from it: Ohio State and the University of Illinois differ enormously.

Like comparisons, then, contrasts differ in degree of arguability. Here is a list of contrasts arranged, with a general American audience in mind, in order of increasing arguability:

1. The United States is unlike Bulgaria.
2. High-school football is unlike professional football.
3. Squash is not like racquetball.
4. Patriotism and love of country are not alike.
5. Congress this week and Congress last week are quite different.

The United States is so unlike Bulgaria that we won't get much of an argument out of a demonstration of the differences. And to most Americans, the differences between high-school and professional football are obvious, even though they are nominally the same game. When we get to claim 3, we have a topic an uninitiated audience may be less familiar with, although players of both games would be aware of every difference between squash and racquetball. In sentence 4, patriotism and love of country look like synonyms; to distinguish between them would require precise, explicit definition. And we usually talk about Congress as if it were an unchanging entity. Whenever we use a static word to describe a dynamic thing, our labels are bound to be imprecise. At one time, some language reformers recommended that whenever we talk about an institution or country, we should specify the time period. In other words, whenever we talk about the United States we should say the United States$_{1945}$ or Congress$_{1936-1938}$ or the Space Program$_{1969}$. We do not recommend such an artificial device, but it makes the point that institutions change, and because they do, a careful contrast, a now and then argument, can be drawn between various stages.

EXERCISES

How do you think an audience of your fellow classmates would rank the following comparisons from least to most arguable?

1. Studying science is like studying history.
2. *Time* is like *Newsweek*.
3. Watching television is like going to the movies.
4. Rollerskating is like skiing.
5. Squash is like racquetball.

How do you think your classmates would rank the following contrasts?

1. Black singers are quite different from white singers.
2. Students today are not like the students of twenty years ago.
3. The rich are very different from the rest of us.
4. Field hockey and ice hockey are quite unlike.
5. The Democratic party of today is not at all like the Democratic party of twenty-five years ago.

An entire class may do this exercise individually and then compare results to see how perceptions of audience differ.

How Do We Make Comparisons?

Arguing for a comparison is a bit more complicated than arguing for a direct claim about the nature of things. We have more things to think about at first. But eventually, we do get down to simple claims. Different kinds of comparisons make different demands, so in order to give any practical advice, we have to carefully distinguish types of comparisons.

Simple Comparisons

The simplest form a comparison can take is "x is like y."

1. The BMW is like a Mercedes.
2. JFK was like FDR.
3. Twentieth-century science is like thirteenth-century religion.

Notice that these are not all equally arguable to most audiences, though they are all comparisons. No matter what the level of arguability, this kind of comparison has certain requirements.

When we compare two things we are not saying "this whole thing is the same as that whole thing." Instead, we are saying they are alike *in some way or ways.* Thus our argument must name the way or ways in which the two things resemble each other, the points of similarity. The initial comparison statement must generate at least one more statement that names a point of similarity. Here's how it works:

Initial comparison: Twentieth-century science is like thirteenth-
century religion.

↓

Twentieth-century science and thirteenth-century
religion are both international institutions.

Now you already know how to argue for a claim like the second:

Twentieth-century science and thirteenth-century religion are both
international institutions.

| Twentieth-century science is an international institution. | Thirteenth-century religion was an international institution. |

Define or identify your terms, and link subject and predicate with verifiable evidence.

We have made this sample comparison generate only one proposition. It certainly could generate many more, and the more points of similarity, the stronger the comparison argument:

1. Twentieth-century scientists and thirteenth-century churchmen have private languages.
2. Both twentieth-century science and thirteenth-century religion are mysterious to the population as a whole.
3. Both are worshipped by the population as a whole.
4. Both offer prestigious careers.
5. Both are regarded as systems of salvation.

Each of these propositions can be supported as described in Chapters 3 through 6.

Arranging the Comparison

When you generate more than one point of similarity from a comparison, you have to decide how you want to arrange your whole argument. You have two basic choices. First, you could take up all the points that relate to one subject and then all of these same points as they relate to the other subject. In the science–religion example you might divide your paper into a section on twentieth-century science and another section on thirteenth-century religion. And in each section you would take up the points of comparison in the same order.

Second, you could take up each point of comparison in turn and say all that has to be said about it in relation to both subjects. Using our same science–religion example, you could have sections on language, careers, systems of salvation, and so on. And you could even mix the two methods.

Under what circumstances is one scheme of arrangement preferable to the other? The point-by-point method is best used when the things you are comparing come apart easily, as do many physical objects. When you compare stereos or cars or skis (perhaps to evaluate brands), you are most likely to do a point-by-point comparison.

1. Car X has front-wheel drive; car Y doesn't.
2. Car X has fuel injection; car Y doesn't.
3. Car X is an import and therefore expensive to repair; car Y is domestic.
4. Car X gets 30 miles per gallon of gas; car Y, 28.

The point-by-point scheme is useful not just for the comparative evaluation of things. Even events and abstractions—wars, for example—have identifiable parts like causes, purposes, turning points, treaties, leaders, and weapons, all of which can be separately assessed. So it is even possible to compare point by point wars separated by thousands of years.

You might also find the point-by-point scheme best when you have a more arguable, far-fetched comparison or contrast, one where you can expect your audience's reaction to be "those two things have nothing in common." An anticipation of audience resistance forces you to identify and line up the points of comparison for all to see, and when the comparison itself is surprising, that is not going to be easy. Our comparison of twentieth-century science and thirteenth-century religion, for example, is somewhat surprising and might best be handled in a point-by-point scheme.

When is the whole-subject method of arrangement most useful? A comparison always talks about the parts of its subjects, but in the whole-subject method that concentration on separate parts is less important. Instead, your purpose is to compare the things as wholes. In other words, a discussion of one entire subject yields a characterization or evaluation that can then be set against the discussion of the other. A tally of points is not important, but a sense of the whole thing is. When you are comparing two happenings, stories, biographies, or events in the form of narratives, the whole-subject method may be best for two reasons: It does not break up the narrative, and the subjects treated in narratives usually do not have parts that can be lined up with perfect symmetry. Suppose, for instance, you want to compare the lives of the Romantic poets Percy Bysshe Shelley and John Keats. Although these poets had enough in common to make comparison worthwhile, you cannot line up their lives precisely. Shelley was never apprenticed as a surgeon, and Keats never married and deserted a wife. Yet you do not want to leave out significant details, and you do want to convey a sense of what their lives were like. Thus, whenever you want to include nonparallel details or whenever your comparison involves narrative, you will devote separate sections to each part, in paragraphs, pages, or chapters, at whatever length best suits your overall purpose.

EXERCISE

Here are some subjects to compare or contrast. Specify a possible audience and decide which method, the point-by-point or whole-subject, would probably provide the better structure for your argument.

1. The summer I spent working. / The summer I spent going to school.
2. My sister before and after she got married.
3. Country music / Western music.
4. Football / ballet.
5. Ten-pin bowling / duck-pin bowling.
6. My hometown when I lived in it. / My hometown when I came back from college for a visit.
7. School in another country. / School in the United States.

Real comparison arguments, directed at real audiences, are often unsymmetrical. They can be lopsided, with more space devoted to the side of the comparison that needs more argument, either because it is less familiar or more difficult to argue with a particular audience. Take, for example, an argument comparing American baseball and English cricket for an American audience. No detailed explanation of the rules and customs of baseball would be necessary. Whichever scheme of arrangement you might use, your discussion of baseball will be brief because you can comfortably assume that your audience knows all about it. In a point-by-point comparison, only one sentence in a paragraph might touch on baseball, while the others will explain cricket in great detail. Or in a whole-subject comparison, the more familiar topic might be handled in a paragraph, while the rest of the essay is devoted to the less well known. A British audience, however, might know all about cricket but need to have every nuance of baseball explained.

And of course the same lopsidedness can hold for the individual points of comparison. Certainly you would not belabor an easy point or gloss over a hard one just to make the paragraphs come out equal. To return to our baseball example, if one rather obscure rule of baseball figured in your comparison with cricket, that one baseball point would receive more attention.

Metaphoric Comparisons

So far we have been talking about literal comparisons that line up things belonging to the same class. There is, however, another kind of comparison that can work even between things not in the same class. Such a comparison is metaphoric, one that makes a *single* startling link between two otherwise dissimilar things:

1. Poetry is a drop of water.
2. Knowledge unlearned is like a tennis court covered with snow.

These sudden illuminations of the nature of one thing in terms of another wholly different thing depend on only *one* point of similarity. No extended comparison is logically possible between poetry and water because these things do not belong to the same class. You can get them together only for a moment to make one point.

EXERCISE

Since simple comparisons often occur in extended arguments, you should be able to support a comparison convincingly even in the confines of a paragraph. Choose one of the following topics for a succinct comparison or invent one of your own.

1. My brother/sister and I are basically alike.
2. College and high school are surprisingly similar.
3. Compare
   two books by the same author.
   two movies by the same director.
   two movies with the same star.
   two record albums by the same performer.
4. Women's clothing is really just like men's clothing.
5. There is no significant difference between the Republican and Democratic candidates for _____ office.

Simple Contrast: A Statement of Dissimilarity

The simplest form a contrast can take is "x is not like y."

1. Levis are not like Wranglers.
2. Orville Wright was not like Wilbur Wright.
3. Deism is not like Unitarianism.

These statements divide their subjects from their predicates, but a contrast need not claim that two things are wholly unlike, only that there are significant differences between them. Finding these points of difference is the first step in constructing a contrast argument. Thus, the contrast statement must generate at least one other statement that names a point of difference:

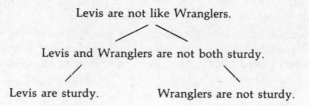

Levis are not like Wranglers.

Levis and Wranglers are not both sturdy.

Levis are sturdy.   Wranglers are not sturdy.

Once again, you come down to two simple claims and you are on familiar ground. Generally, everything we have said about comparisons holds for contrasts. The only difference is that one points out similarities, the other differences.

Comparing and Contrasting the Same Two Things

Remember that comparisons and contrasts are especially arguable when your audience assumes the opposite, when they resist the comparison of things apparently unlike and the contrast of things apparently alike. A wise tactic is to acknowledge your audience's initial assumptions by using both comparison and contrast; open your contrast with a comparison section, or your comparison with a contrast. For example, if you want to argue that country music and western music are really different, you must realize that many people think they are so alike that they are identical. So you begin your contrast by pointing out the well-known similarities that have created your audience's assumptions. Or if you are arguing for a challenging comparison like "Attending a football game is like attending a cocktail party," you would be wise to begin by acknowledging all the ways these two social events are obviously different.

EXERCISE

Since many arguments begin with a perception of dissimilarity, all writers need the ability to sketch in contrasts succinctly. Try writing brief contrast arguments on the following topics or, once again, invent one of your own.

1. Contrast two relatives (grandmothers, aunts, uncles, cousins) who are really quite different.
2. Contrast the spirit of two sports teams in your home town.
3. Contrast a person, place, or thing you are familiar with at two different times: a park you played in as a child then and now; the street you live on, now and five years ago; a friend as a child and the same friend grown up; the same job, two different summers.
4. Contrast your reaction to the same person, place, or thing at two different times. Here the emphasis is on your reaction, not on the thing itself: a friend; a teacher; a movie seen twice; a once favorite activity.
5. Contrast two things most people think of as indistinguishable: two pizza or hamburger franchises; two brands of the same piece of sports equipment; two closely related varieties of a plant or species of an animal; two professors of the same subject.

Comparisons and Contrasts with Degree

Unlike simple comparisons and contrasts, which have only two terms to begin with ("Dwight Gooden is like Roger Clemens"), comparisons with degree have a third term explicitly stated.

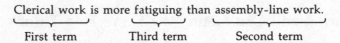

Clerical work is more fatiguing than assembly-line work.

First term   Third term   Second term

Claims of this type begin one level down from the simple comparison or contrast; they name a point of resemblance between the two subjects. Comparisons with degree assert that two subjects share a quality and specify how much sharing is going on. The sharing may be equal ("Dwight Gooden is as fast as Roger Clemens") or unequal ("Dwight Gooden has more control than Roger Clemens." "Roger Clemens has less of a curve ball than Dwight Gooden").

Some Have More and Some Have Less

The following comparisons assert inequality:

1. Women are less aggressive than men.
2. British imperialism was more successful than French colonialism.

3. Raskin-Bobbins ice cream is creamier than Greyers.
4. Chess players are more *macho* than football players.
5. The Roman Emperor Augustus was more power hungry than George Washington.

What are the problems if a statement like one of the above is the thesis of your argument? First, you must realize that behind a statement that two things share a quality, although unequally, lies the assumption that the two things can be compared. Behind the statement that Augustus Caesar was more power hungry than George Washington lies the assumption that Augustus and Washington are fundamentally comparable, in other words, that x is like y, a simple comparison. Is that initial comparison plausible? They were both leaders, and, furthermore, both were poised at the beginning of new orders of government. These superficial similarities make comparison possible in the first place; that is, you can put Augustus and George Washington into the same very general category. But might not someone respond that the differences of time, ideology, and circumstances are overwhelming? Someone bent on refutation would certainly reject the initial comparison, saying in effect that it is ridiculous to claim that Augustus was more power hungry than George Washington, because the two cannot be compared at all.

Because comparisons with degree depend on an unstated simple comparison, they are open to the kind of refutation that says "You cannot compare oranges and apples." The initial assumption of comparability is hidden in the statement, and you may forget it is there and so forget to defend a potential weak spot. If it needs defense, you can back up and support it just as you would support a simple assertion of similarity ("Augustus was like George Washington").

A second assumption lies behind a comparison with degree. Not only are the two things basically comparable, but they both possess the third term to some degree. Unless they both have it, how could you claim that one has more and the other less? So here is another assumption you may have to defend if your audience is not likely to acknowledge it. If you say, for example, "Women are less aggressive than men," you assume that both men and women are aggressive (to some degree). If aggression is not something they both have to begin with, then any comparison of degree of aggression is foolish. Now most people would agree that aggression is a universal human attribute; both sexes have it. So you would not have to stop and support this second assumption for most audiences.

But what if your degree comparison is sentence 4, "Chess players are more *macho* than football players"? Your first assumption is "Chess players are like football players." You might get over that, because after all they are both players of competitive sports. But the second assumption,

"Both chess players and football players are *macho* to some degree," is likely to give you some trouble. You should recognize by now that the trouble comes from the commonly held definition of the word *macho*. It usually suggests the external trappings of maleness, the posturing and exaggeration of physique so obvious in football. To get around that notion, you will have to redefine *macho* in such a way that it can apply to chess players, who do not obviously strut, swagger, and pull at their jerseys and who may be women anyway. Perhaps you will extend *macho* to cover the posing of intellectual aggressiveness, the snorting, staring, and defiant arm crossing that many professional chess players, who are flamboyant poseurs, engage in. Once again, careful definition is essential for convincing your readers that both chess players and football players are *macho* (to some degree).

Now you are ready for the problem posed by the original degree comparison, claiming more or less of the third term. This quantification problem is easily solved when the initial degree comparison simply requires verifying a potential fact. If you claim "I have more marbles than my friend," a count will settle the matter. But if you claim "I have more common sense than my friend," what do you count? How can you quantify common sense—or aggression, *machismo,* or hunger for power, for that matter—so that you can count it? If such attributes were quantifiable in the first place, no argument would be necessary. Since they are not, you must choose tactics that enable you to convey a convincing impression of "moreness" or "lessness."

Operational Definition

Suppose you are arguing that women are less aggressive than men, which is the same as saying that men are more aggressive than women. You have assumed the basic comparability of men and women, getting past step one, and you have assumed that aggressiveness is a basic human trait, getting past step two. Now you are ready to tackle the question of degree. You can begin by giving an operational definition of aggression, translating it into one or more observable acts that can be counted. How many men and women are arrested for *assault*? How many men and women engage in *contact sports*? How many men and women are charged with *reckless driving*? The italicized words might be part of an operational definition of *aggression*; research may yield answers to all these questions. Of course, you have not completely settled the argument, because your operational definition of *aggression* has limited its meaning to observable physical acts, leaving out verbal aggression, aggression in the pursuit of a career, in short, all the multiple meanings that *aggression* has accumulated. (For a fuller discussion of this problem, see the section Operational Definition in Chapter 6.)

Lining Up Evidence, More on One Side, Less on the Other

Remember that your second assumption was "Both men and women are aggressive to some degree." That compound breaks down into two simple claims: "Men are aggressive" and "Women are aggressive." By simply bringing more support to one side than the other, you can produce the impression of inequality you are striving for.

This impression can be produced by supporting the "more" side in the same way any claim about the nature of things is supported, combining definition with iterative and specific examples. Your support for the sample "more" proposition might include statements like these: "Men turn their frustrations into physical restlessness, which is a sign of aggression" (lower-level generalization). "Observe men waiting in line: they fidget, shift their weight, and turn around" (iterative example). "I once saw two men argue over a seat in a ballpark and then break into a fist-fight" (specific example). All of these statements can be used to support the assertion "Men are aggressive." Piling up statements like these on one side produces an impression of moreness; saying more about the aggressiveness of men suggests that more exists. And conversely, finding little evidence of the aggressiveness of women implies that little of it exists.

Of course, saying little is not necessarily the same as the existence of little to be said; you must never assume that your own ignorance means that no evidence exists or that your audience will not notice the imbalance. Nevertheless, in an argument, the statements you make explicitly imply much more than they say. All your statements about men, for example, say nothing about women, but they imply that women behave in just the opposite way. All by itself, a statement like "men fidget in line" says only that. But under the umbrella of the degree comparison, it implies that women do not fidget in line. So in a sense, an assertion on one side does double duty.

Some Are Just the Same

The following comparisons assert equality:

1. This auditorium is *as long as* a football field. (fact)
2. Alcohol is *as efficient a fuel as* gasoline. (near fact)
3. Law is *as overcrowded a profession as* accounting.
4. Unemployment is *as serious a problem as* inflation.
5. Piet Mondrian is *as fine a draftsman as* Rembrandt.
6. Altman movies are *as confusing as* Bergman movies.
7. Collectors who buy undocumented art objects are *as morally guilty as* art thieves.

If you find that you are supporting a thesis like one of the above, you must analyze what your audience is likely to understand by it. A statement like "Unemployment is as serious a problem as inflation" can have two possible meanings. If it means, simply, "Both unemployment and inflation are serious," it is just an idiomatic way of stating a compound. When you support a sameness statement intended in this loose way, you really support this compound, emphasizing the less obvious element. And you already know how to do that.

However, these statements of sameness disguise another possible meaning. They may be transformed into simple comparisons. If we say, for instance, that "Altman's and Bergman's movies are confusing," we may really mean something slightly different: "The confusion of Altman's movies is like the confusion of Bergman's movies." In other words, our statement of sameness is really a simple comparison. That is, the confusion produced in the average viewer by the movies of both directors is perhaps not *exactly* the same, but there are many points of similarity. If we were supporting the compound "Altman's and Bergman's movies are confusing," they could be confusing in entirely different ways. But if we say the confusion of one resembles that of the other, they must be confusing in similar ways.

Occasionally, a sameness statement may mean exactly what it says. It certainly does when it presents a fact like "This auditorium is as long as a football field." But even in a more arguable comparison, you may try to support that precise assertion of sameness. You do not mean simply that both have a third term, or that the third term of one is like that of the other; you really mean they are as alike as argument can make them. Look at sentence 7: "Collectors who buy undocumented art objects are as morally guilty as art thieves." You may mean that the guilt of both is just the same. How could you convince an audience of that? Here is certainly a place for lopsided argument. You assume that one side has the third term and work at making it stick to the other, usually by careful definition. Art thieves are obviously guilty of appropriating for profit what is not theirs; but so are unscrupulous art collectors who invest in *objets d'art* and never ask where the priceless treasure came from. In their intentional blindness they are as guilty (as you define *guilty*) as the deliberate thief. Both art thief and unscrupulous collector are greedy and willful deceivers; in that sense, their guilt is the same.

EXERCISE

Here are some comparisons with degree that could be theses of arguments. In each case decide first whether the two things being compared are comparable, second whether they both share in the third term, and finally how the moreness, lessness, or sameness could be argued for. Then choose one, stipulate an audience, and support it in a brief argument.

1. Pigs are smarter than dogs.
2. Women are stronger than men.
3. Physics is less difficult than chemistry (or vice versa).
4. People who live in small towns are just as cultured as people who live in cities.
5. Americans are less well educated than Europeans.
6. Conservatives are just as humanitarian as liberals (or vice versa, for a different emphasis).
7. Parents are more important to a child's education than teachers.
8. Children are more adaptable than adults.
9. Age discrimination is as much a problem as racial discrimination.
10. People who get all their news from TV are less informed than those who read newspapers.

DISJUNCTIONS

A disjunction is like a Y in the road: You have to go one way or the other. You cannot take both roads, and an error might have serious consequences. Disjunctions, in other words, divide a set of possibilities into two unreconcilable alternatives: "The United States can pursue a policy of peace or one of war." "You can either fish or cut bait." Logic books have much to say about propositions in this form, but they rarely occur as the main thesis in ordinary argument.

Perfect Disjunctions: Not Arguable

1. Either Louise is in California or she is not in California.
2. He either squeezed the trigger or he did not squeeze the trigger.
3. The dodo is either extinct or not extinct.

These propositions simply illustrate one of the laws of thought: A thing cannot both be and not be at the same time. Louise cannot be both in California and out of California at the same time. (O.K., she could straddle the state line.) Dodos cannot both exist and not exist at the same time. There is usually no need to argue for the perfect disjunction itself; it is self-evidently true. But you may want to go on and verify one half of it.

For example: "He pulled the trigger. I saw him do it." Or, "Louise is in California. I just phoned her there."

Imperfect Disjunctions: Arguable

1. She will either run or not run for the Senate.
2. She is either guilty or innocent.
3. Lawrence of Arabia was either a hero or a madman.
4. Either we develop alternative energy sources immediately, or we remain at the mercy of OPEC.
5. There are two kinds of houses: those that have had termites and those that will get them. (Terminex brochure)

A disjunction is arguable when the two alternatives it mentions are not necessarily the only ones. Logicians throw imperfect disjunctions out the window immediately as illogical because the framework of the statement is too rigorous for the content: "How," they ask, "can you say 'either/or' when common sense tells you that so long as other possibilities exist, 'either/or' cannot be true?" But a disjunction that is not self-evidently true can still be argued for; indeed, it is the only kind that can be argued for, because a perfect disjunction, self-evident to its audience, can be treated as a fact.

An imperfect disjunction is best seen as a rhetorical device, a way of expressing something that helps emphasize it and shape the pattern of a reader's thinking. Setting up a disjunction forces a reader to think in terms of a limited set of alternatives. You go on to support one of the alternatives and refute the other, as though the whole argument came down to a contest between the finalist you favor and the semifinalist who loses. The also-rans do not even get into the disjunction.

When you begin to argue for them, disjunctions break down into one positive and one negative claim.

Lawrence of Arabia was either a hero or a madman.

Lawrence was a hero.   Lawrence was not a madman.

Or the other way around, depending on what you want to argue for:

Lawrence was not a hero.   Lawrence was a madman.

You will go on to support one of these propositions, the positive or the negative one, if you can assume that your readers will accept the initial disjunction. In effect, you must ask yourself, "Can I assume that my readers will accept this disjunction, or must I defend it before I can go on?"

If you think you have to defend it, how do you do so? First, you must establish that the two possibilities you have named are the only likely ones, that they fill the field of realistic possibilities. For example, why couldn't Lawrence of Arabia be called a "charlatan" or "a product of circumstances" instead of a "hero" or a "madman"? Of course, you do not have to anticipate every crackpot possibility (such as "Lawrence of Arabia was really a woman"), only those that plausibly challenge your disjunction. These other possibilities must be refuted: "He wasn't a charlatan because ————." "He wasn't just a product of circumstances because ————." After you have eliminated rival possibilities, you are left with a defended disjunction, still not perfect, but quite respectable.

Now there is only one more objection the wily reader might raise: He or she might ask, "Why can't Lawrence of Arabia have been *both* a hero and a madman? Why can't both alternatives be true at once? Why should I believe they are mutually exclusive?" This challenge is hard to refute. It will inevitably take you into intricacies of definition. You will, for example, have to define the nature of heroism in such a way that it excludes madness. In other words, by skillful definition you try to make your disjunction as close to perfect as possible.

After you have completed any necessary defense of your disjunction, you go on to support the positive or negative proposition that you have broken it into. Remember that you do not always have to give equal time to both sides. In fact, logically you have to defend only one half. If your disjunction claims that "Lawrence was either a hero or a madman," and you support "He was a hero," the other possibility automatically disappears. Similarly, if you support "Lawrence of Arabia was not a madman," you have, under the umbrella of your disjunction, supported "He was a hero." However, if you do not want to rely on your readers' elimination logic, you might spend some time refuting the other possibility anyway.

FOR YOU TO ANALYZE

Read the following disjunction arguments. How convincing are they?

History shows that wars are divided into two kinds, just and unjust. All wars that are progressive are just, and all wars that impede progress are unjust. We Communists oppose all unjust wars that impede progress, but we do not oppose progressive, just wars. Not only do we Communists not oppose just wars, we actively participate in them. As for unjust wars, World War I is an instance in which both sides fought for imperialist interests; therefore the Communists of the whole world firmly opposed that war. The way to oppose a war of this kind is to do everything possible to prevent it before it breaks out and, once it breaks out, to oppose war with war, to oppose unjust war with just war, whenever possible.

—Mao Tse-tung

How praiseworthy it is for a prince to keep his word and live with integrity rather than by craftiness, everyone understands; yet we see from recent experience that those princes have accomplished most who paid little heed to keeping their promises, but who knew how craftily to manipulate the minds of men. In the end, they won out over those who tried to act honestly.

You should consider then, that there are two ways of fighting, one with laws and the other with force. The first is properly a human method, the second belongs to beasts. But as the first method does not always suffice, you sometimes have to turn to the second. Thus a prince must know how to make good use of both the beast and the man. Ancient writers made subtle notes of this fact when they wrote that Achilles and many other princes of antiquity were sent to be reared by Chiron the centaur, who trained them in his discipline. Having a teacher who is half man and half beast can only mean that a prince must know how to use both these two natures, and that one without the other has no lasting effect.

—Niccolo Machiavelli, *The Prince*

In the following examples, discuss how arguable the comparison or contrast is to begin with. Can the two things be brought into juxtaposition at all? What is the purpose of each comparison? Notice each author's choice of arrangement. How apt is it?

Indeed, scientists are in the position of a primitive tribe which has undertaken to duplicate the Empire State Building, room for room, without ever seeing the original building or even a photograph. Their own working plans, of necessity, are only a crude approximation of the real thing, conceived on the basis of miscellaneous reports volunteered by interested travelers and often in apparent conflict on points of detail. In order to start the building at all, some information must be ignored as erroneous or impossible, and the first constructions are little more than large grass shacks. Increasing sophistication, combined with methodical accumulation of data, make it necessary to tear down the earlier replicas (each time after violent arguments), replacing them successively with more up-to-date versions. We may easily doubt that the version current after only 300 years of effort is a very adequate restoration of the Empire State Building; yet, in the absence of clear knowledge to the contrary, the tribe must regard it as such (and ignore odd travelers' tales that cannot be made to fit).

—E. J. DuPraw, *Cell and Molecular Biology*

SAMPLE ANALYSIS

The above paragraph is an extended comparison between two things apparently unlike: Most of us think of scientists as highly sophisticated, civilized people, not at all like a primitive tribe. The initial comparison is therefore highly arguable, even shocking to most readers.

After making that initial juxtaposition, the writer goes on to talk about the tribe's attempt to duplicate the Empire State Building without a plan; he never again mentions scientists specifically. The reader is left to supply the missing term of the comparison and to connect the story of the primitive tribe to the enterprise of science. The Empire State Building resembles the intricate order of nature, whose entire plan none of us has seen. "Interested travelers" are like observers of nature who send back their reports, some of which are contradictory; "large grass shacks" are primitive scientific models or theories, which must be replaced by more solid structures; and the current version of science is just as unlikely to be an adequate representation of nature as a tribe's reconstruction of the Empire State Building.

The effect of this comparison is to make us regard our scientific achievements as tentative and incomplete but in the process of continual improvement; the more detailed the comparison, the more convincing the characterization of scientists.

The difference between certain practices at Dachau (organized in 1933) and Buchenwald (in 1937), reflects the growing depersonalization of all procedures during that period. At Dachau, for example, official punishment, as distinct from random abuse, was always directed at a particular individual. Beforehand he had a so-called hearing in the presence of a commissioned SS officer. According to Western legal standards these hearings were a farce, but compared to what later became standard procedure it showed great consideration for the individual because he was at least told what he was accused of and given a chance to refute the charges. If he knew what was good for him, he made no effort to defend himself. But he could add one or another detail and sometimes get off without punishment.

Before flogging, he was examined by the camp physician, another fairly empty procedure since the doctor rarely canceled the whipping, though he sometimes reduced the number of lashes. Even as late as 1939, prisoners at Dachau enjoyed some limited protection against too flagrant acts of injustice. When a guard shot or otherwise caused a prisoner's death he had to make a written report. That was all he had to do, but it was still something of a deterrent.

Such consideration of prisoners as individuals, though small enough, was out of the question at Buchenwald, which reflected a later phase of National Socialism. For example, prisoners who went insane—and there were quite a few of them—were no longer isolated, protected, or sent to mental institutions, but were ridiculed and chased about until they died.

But the greatest difference was that at Buchenwald it was nearly always the group that suffered, not the individual. At Dachau, a prisoner who tried to carry a small stone instead of a heavy one would have suffered for it; at Buchenwald the whole group including the foreman would have been punished.

—Bruno Bettelheim, *The Informed Heart: Autonomy in a Mass Age*

Physics is aware of phenomena which occur only at *threshold* magnitudes, which do not exist at all until a certain *threshold* encoded by and known to nature has been crossed. No matter how intense a yellow light you shine on a lithium sample, it will not emit electrons. But as soon as a weak bluish light begins to glow, it does emit them. (The threshold of the photoelectric effect has been crossed.) You can cool oxygen to 100 degrees below zero Centigrade and exert as much pressure as you want; it does not yield, but remains a gas. But as soon as minus 183 degrees is reached, it liquefies and begins to flow.

Evidently evildoing also has a threshold magnitude. Yes, a human being hesitates and bobs back and forth between good and evil all his life. He slips, falls back, clambers up, repents, things begin to darken again. But just so long as the threshold of evildoing is not crossed, the possibility of returning remains, and he himself is still within reach of our hope. But when, through the density of evil actions, the result either of their own extreme degree or of the absoluteness of his power, he suddenly crosses that threshold, he has left humanity behind, and without, perhaps, the possibility of return. . . .

—Aleksandr Solzhenitsyn, *The Gulag Archipelago*

WASHINGTON VS. NEW YORK

Mickey Kaus, Peter McKillop, Nonny Abbott, Howard Fineman, Timothy Noah, and Eleanor Clift

There's no use denying it anymore. On some nontrivial economic and emotional level, Washington's enemy is not Moscow, or Beijing, or Panama. It is the alien culture 250 miles to the north. America's seat of government and its largest metropolis are locked in a long twilight struggle over which will be seen as *the* city of the nation.

The battle has been going on, quietly, for some time. "In the [past] half century, the power of New York has declined almost in proportion to the imperious, if not altogether imperial, ascent of Washington," writes New York Sen. Daniel Patrick Moynihan, who has feet in both camps. But lately things have been heating up, as Washington again senses victory. Didn't giant Mobil Corp. flee the Big Apple and seek refuge in Washington's Virginia suburbs? Wasn't Washington now the richest of the nation's 10 largest metropolitan areas? Wasn't Bloomingdale's there? Wasn't the blockbuster Gauguin exhibit opening at the National Gallery? (Yes.) Would it go to New York? (No.) Riggs Bank, a Washington institution, has a sign at National Airport that reads "Welcome to the Most Important City on Earth!" Even New York's senior senator seems to agree: "New York is still a great city; but slowly, inexorably, Washington becomes the greater one."

In April, the Washington-based *New Republic* magazine published a cover story entitled "NYC, RIP," in which reporter Howard Kurtz outlined in gleeful detail New York's problems. Paired with Kurtz's article was a piece by Irving Kristol, the neoconservative writer, explaining why he'd moved from New York to D.C. New York was no longer "the nation's intellectual center." It "ceased being that about 20 years ago." In Manhattan's literary living rooms, this broadside brought a swift response. Kurtz? He was just whining because he had to live in Queens! Kristol? He'd always been a sucker for power. . . .

Let's settle this dispute once and for all. Herewith a scrupulously prejudiced evaluation of our two municipal contestants:

1. Cosmological Significance: "New York has all the money and money decides who goes to Washington," says New York developer Donald Trump. "Washington is just a place people happen to be. It's New York that gets them there." This is a profoundly myopic statement (see Provincialism, below). First, Trump is equating power in Washington only with elected officials, neglecting the Permanent Washington of regulators, lawyers and lobbyists, who are hardly beholden to New York. Even when it comes to elected officials, Trump's vision is almost Marxist in its exaggeration of financial power. If New York money picked the next president, for example, that will be news to Michael Dukakis, whose campaign was fueled mainly by Massachusetts businessmen and Greek-Americans from all over.

You could as plausibly argue that New York is a place where rich people happen to be. Manhattan has become a playland for the world's wealthy, with undeniable attractions (see Consumption, below). Increasingly, it is not where major economic decisions are made. The headquarters of 51 Fortune 500 companies are in New York. A decade ago there were 82. Addressing a breakfast crowd of New York City corporate leaders, Gov. Mario Cuomo referred to the problems of recruiting workers from the city's isolated, unskilled, despairing minorities. "You can't move away from them," Cuomo told the businessmen. Of course you can.

Washington is no threat to New York as a business center. (Only two Fortune 500 corporations are headquartered in the area.) Its claim to significance is based on power. Reagan was supposed to cut Washington down to size by reducing "big government." Washington survived. New York may have the three networks (though NBC had to be bribed into staying). But the major locus of the news they report is Washington. Which is more important to the U.S. car industry, a decision made in Washington to pressure Japan on import quotas, or a decision made in New York on the price at which to underwrite some auto stock? (Hint: don't buy the stock if they raise the quotas.)

Winner: Washington.

2. Livability: The Germans have a word—*Schadenfreude*—that means "joy at the suffering of others." For Washingtonians, the "Metropolitan News" section of the *New York Times*—page B-1—might be called the Schadenfreude Express. On a single day, recently, page B-1 brought news of the following: delays in the reconstruction of New York's West Side Highway, which collapsed 15 years ago. Runaway teenagers dying of AIDS. Pollution on the Jersey shore. A 43-year-old Queens woman shot to death while cradling her six-month-old son. A Long Island doctor found stabbed to death near her Mercedes. Two men charged in the killing of a "rap" disc jockey. New York dairies planning a cartel to fix city milk prices. And new layoffs on Wall Street.

No wonder Washingtonians claim New York is physically and socially falling apart, becoming unlivable. In part, this may be an illusion: New York is far bigger (18 million in the metropolitan area, compared with D.C.'s 3.6 million); of course it has more murders. Many whites, secure in their sprawling Northwest D.C. ghetto, never see the bleaker side of the capital.

But three factors decisively coarsen middle-class life in New York, compared with Washington. First is the sheer size and proximity of the underclass of addicts, drug dealers, robbers and punks that terrorize poor and rich neighborhoods alike. One goal of cities is to provide common space in which citizens can mingle. But, thanks in part to the ominous underclass, many of New York's famed public spaces are no longer places for civic interaction. Municipal libraries are crowded with fetid vagabonds looking for a place to nap. Smaller parks belong to drug dealers.

The second factor is an acute housing shortage, and its companion, rent control. Even without rent control, housing in New York would be costly. Construction codes and union rules drive up the cost of building to about 50 percent more than in neighboring New Jersey. The Wall Street whiz kids bid up prices on choice Manhattan properties. But rent control has undoubtedly made the situation worse by discouraging both new construction and maintenance.

The beneficiaries are the residents of about 60 percent of New York's apartments, who are protected from rising prices as long as they stay put. Which means few ever move. Even New York's mayor, Ed Koch, clings to his rent-controlled apartment in Greenwich Village. With fewer apartments opening up, and few being built, the market price for what's available is driven sky high. In Manhattan, the "market" rent for an apartment hovers around $600 to $700 a room. Newcomers sometimes spend years sleeping on friends' couches. Many wind up paying thousands of dollars in "key money" to obtain illegal sublets. A recent *Times* story on dating contained the complaint of a bachelor that women often moved in with him on the third date: "They say they like me, but they also need a place to live. That's not a sound basis for a relationship . . ."

Washington has rent control, too, but it's less severe than New York's, and it hasn't been in place as long. Washington apartments are cheaper and, more important, newcomers can actually find a place without going through the real-estate equivalent of hazing.

Finally, there's a general civility factor. A few years ago the *New York Times* matter-of-factly chastised its readers for their habit of defecating in building foyers or in the middle of the street. Is there another city in America where "squeegee men" routinely extort quarters by "washing" the windows of cars immobilized at busy midtown stoplights? (The *Times* once described these menacing characters as a "part of New York's great street theater.")

Washington, by contrast, is the Big Campus. There are gorgeous public parks, maintained through the generosity of the nation's taxpayers. There's a new subway, paid for by those same taxpayers, that's so clean it looks as if it might be an extension of the Whitney Museum. There are museums, too, paid for by you-know-who. In the white ghetto, old policy chums greet each other on the street and dish gossip.

Winner: Washington.

3. Equality: . . . Washington's median income is far higher than New York's. That's not because Washington has a lot of really rich people. It's because Washington has a tremendous number of pretty-well-off people. It's a town of Volvos, not Rolls-Royces.

One of Washington's dearest pretensions is that it doesn't care about money, in contrast to Mammon-worshiping Gotham. This is true, in a way Donald

Trump might not understand. "People who do have money try not to flaunt their money," says Sally Quinn, a Washington writer, who has it (and flaunts it). Quinn's husband, Ben Bradlee, is worshiped in Washington not for his wealth but for his role as executive editor of the *Washington Post*. When he retires, his cachet will vanish and be transferred to the next editor. Sondra Gotlieb, wife of the Canadian ambassador, destroyed her career by slapping her social secretary when she learned that Richard Darman, then a high Treasury official, wouldn't be attending her party. Darman is now a mere investment banker. "Nobody's going to slap anybody in Washington ever again if he's not at their party," notes Diana McLellan, a D.C. society writer. Washington's increasing wealth simply "means that those power people get taken to fancier lunches," says Charles Peters, editor of the *Washington Monthly*.

In fact, you don't need much money at all to be a social star in Washington, if you have the right role. Journalists and "public interest" activists are peculiar beneficiaries of this arrangement; in Washington they are kings as in no place else. A former Washington Post writer, Walter Shapiro, has written about driving his beat-up 1972 station wagon to embassy parties without a hint of status insecurity.

That doesn't mean Washington society is egalitarian, of course. It is, rather, a one-track status game. At the top, policy pundits compete desperately for slots on political talk shows that few people elsewhere even bother to watch. In the middle-management suburban trenches of Maryland, families plaster the back windows of their Volvos with decals of the prestigious colleges their children attend. In large families, whole expanses of glass are dangerously obscured.

New York, in theory, has the advantage of what columnist George Will calls "competing elites." If you're big in the art world, the theory goes, you're still humble because the bigs of finance don't even know who you are. On the other hand, the multiplicity of status ladders may only put a higher premium on the one yardstick on which they can be compared, namely money. "Competing elites" haven't stopped New York from being the most class-addled city in America, where the difference between taking a subway and taking a taxi, having a fawning doorman or a dangerous walkup, going to private school instead of public school, can be all the difference in the world.

Winner: Washington, barely.

4. Consumption: Not much contest here. New York's vastness and its ethnic variety give it a level of specialization Washington simply can't achieve. Walking around New York one can easily find a store devoted exclusively to saxophone and flute repair, a store that sells only light bulbs, a store that specializes in automotive books.

Meanwhile, Washington's Yuppie uniformity and anti-money pretension make it a grim killing ground for trendy purveyors of food and fashion. Glorious Food, a fancy New York caterer, tried expanding to D.C. and discovered that Washington wants "middle-end food," according to Sean Driscoll, the firm's cofounder. "It isn't our style, pigs-in-the-blanket on picks."

D.C. dress is almost aggressively antifashionable. For men, a typical Full Washington includes an off-the-rack suit, a too-short tan trench coat and wing-tip shoes. Yellow "power" ties are just catching on. (They're so passé in New York they sell them on the street.) Women's clothes are equally unhip. "You have to wear a very long skirt, clumpy jewelry, comfortable shoes and not be too fashionable," says Patrick McCarthy of W magazine. A D.C. department store, Garfinkels, recently converted almost totally to designer lines of women's clothes. Now it is rumored to be in financial trouble. "The Washington woman does not have the adventurous spirit of the New York woman to experiment with varied fashion statements," admits Aniko Gaal, Garfinkels's spokesperson.

Winner: New York.

5. High Culture: Another blowout. Washington has artsy pretensions, as does any healthy, growing American city. "We used to be a sleepy Southern town, but now we're a cosmopolitan center," is the ritual incantation. One Washington Post writer even called D.C. "a second Paris."

Get serious. The capital's artistic salvos tend to be of the hollow, "Ain't we got culture" variety. The National Gallery's Gauguin exhibit, the current hit, is so huge that, at one showing, bored Washingtonians practically ran through the last few rooms to get to the buffet. Some did stop to notice a carving called "Maison de Jouir," translated by a museum guide as "House of Pleasure." Actually, it means "House of Humping." Explained museum director J. Carter Brown: "Washington is a family town."

Washington does have the Kennedy Center, a hideous Culture Box squatting on the Potomac (built with . . . never mind). In it, Washingtonians flock to see (or be seen at) productions that seem to become more middlebrow by the week. The flamboyant Peter Sellars flopped as the center's theater director, either because he's a fraud or because Washington wasn't sophisticated enough to appreciate him, depending on whom you talk to. Under schmaltzy Mstislav Rostropovich, the National Symphony has climbed in esteem from third to second rate. That's enough for the Post to have recently devoted an embarrassing number of inches to a boosterish story on a single section of the NSO, the cellos. The only cultural institution that is really in tune with the official culture of Washington is the American Film Institute. It seems mainly to bring Hollywood celebrities to town for ceremonies and photo opportunities.

Winner: New York.

6. Provincialism: Washington can't claim to be a real intellectual center, because it has no great universities. A few years ago, when faculty members were asked to rate graduate schools in 32 fields, New York schools got 28 top-10 ratings. Washington got zero.

New York does claim to be an intellectual center, but that is now a matter of dispute. "The debates we have in New York are not about what is happening at the moment," says Podhoretz, "but really debates over the future." Hmmm. To the rest of the country, New York's heated intellectual tussles might appear a trifle insular and retrospective. How many more times are we going to read about the Rosenbergs, or the old *Partisan Review* crowd?

The *New Yorker* magazine's Statement of Purpose, in its first issue in 1925, reads in part: "It has announced that it is not edited for the old lady in Dubuque." Here is the New York parochialism that America hates. Life in New York is so unpleasant, apparently, that New Yorkers must constantly tell themselves it's all worth it, that New York is better than every place else—precisely *because* it's so unpleasant. Music sounds better in New York, argues John Rockwell of the *Times,* because of the city's "extremes of wealth and poverty." The "vitality of Wall Street," writes David Byrne of the Talking Heads, somewhat obscurely, "depends on its accessibility to the Bowery bums." Recently New

York's current hot magazine, *Spy,* published a special section "In Search of America." The title, "Big, Dumb White Guys With Guns," was only half ironic. "The Smithsonian is supposed to have American stuff," New York punkette novelist Tama Janowitz told *Newsweek:* "I don't know how they take all the stuff we have in America and make it palatable."

One of the attractions of Washington is that Tama Janowitz doesn't live there. Because the power of Washington is theoretically grounded in the ballot, the capital must at least keep up the appearance of friendly relations with the provinces. But the capital is insulated in its own way. Thanks to the permanent cadre of staffers and consultants, its economy is virtually recession-proof, protected from the ups and downs that afflict everybody else. Fact-finding missions into the Heartland are often called "field trips." And Washington is still segregated. Live in the white ghetto, and you would hardly know the city is 70 percent black.

Winner: None. Neither place is really part of America.

7. Morality: New York is not quite the capital of capitalism it's reputed to be. Comfort in New York too often depends upon some exemption from the market, some special little angle: a rent-stabilized pad. A tax break (Trump's favorite). A cushy union deal (New York firefighters have been excused from making inspections in "inclement weather"). Honesty is not the hallmark of New York's elite. Cartier recently pleaded guilty to cheating on state sales taxes. The Metropolitan Museum of Art was caught inflating attendance figures in order to get more in grants. Yuppies buy children's books from shady sidewalk vendors. Only New York could make Dr. Seuss seamy.

Washington is less visibly dishonest. Its immorality is more profound. Start with the city's original sin, which is that it has profited from the nation's tragedies. Washington grew as a result of the Civil War and World War I. The Depression and World War II made it a boomtown. Add its isolation, the inability to judge its product by any clear "bottom line," the way it has grown fat spending other people's money—the taxpayers', the money of corporations convinced they must hire a lobbyist with an expense account (either to protect themselves from Washington, or to glom a favor from Washington).

Indeed, the executive, civil-service branch of government hasn't grown much over the past two decades. What has grown—the source of Washington's new wealth—is the economy of hangers-on, of lawyers and consultants and think tanks and interest groups and trade associations. A "parasite culture," Washington writer Fred Barnes labels it. At some point, these Washingtonians achieved critical mass, and from here on out they can put their kids through college by taking in each other's policy, as it were. At the top, there's now an established "three step" procedure, Barnes notes: "You get a job in Congress or on a presidential campaign, step up to the administration, and finally go on to easy money," lobbying. Permanent Washington doesn't really care which party is in power. It's in business either way.

If Washington is now ascendant, and New York descendant—as seems to be the case—we'd be well advised to remember that our capital was built on this questionable economic base. Washington is in many ways already a nicer and "greater" place than New York. It would be even nicer if it would forget its absurd attempts to achieve parity in the cultural arms race. But it will be hard to reform the corruption at its soul. Maybe we should do without a capital for a while.

FOR YOU TO WRITE

Any of the topics suggested in exercises throughout this chapter could be expanded into full-length essays. The theses we suggest here are of more academic interest. We overstate them; you will undoubtedly qualify any you investigate. For example, we exaggerate the disjunction "For energy self-sufficiency, the United States must go either coal or solar"; it might be modified to "If our relations with the Arab nations do not improve, the United States must go either coal or solar for its energy self-sufficiency."

Careful discrimination between rival theories or hypotheses is a staple of scientific thinking. Here we suggest a few rather obvious comparisons, contrasts, and disjunctions drawn from various sciences. They may stimulate you to think of others.

1. Darwin's views on evolution were more courageous than Wallace's.
2. Chimpanzee and human language learning are quite dissimilar (or similar).
3. The human mind works like a computer.
4. The atomic theory of Democritus is not at all like the atomic theory of Rutherford.
5. All modern economies are in a state of either inflation or recession.
6. Many plants are more complicated than animals.
7. Older people are just as capable of learning as any age group.
8. The abilities of the right side of the brain are quite different from those of the left.
9. For energy self-sufficiency, the United States must go either coal or solar.
10. Exploring under the sea is more difficult than exploring outer space.

Historical figures, events, and epochs are often better understood when their similarities and dissimilarities are pointed out.

1. Roman law and Napoleonic law are more alike than different.
2. The Egyptian and Mayan civilizations have many striking similarities.
3. Warren G. Harding was either a scoundrel or a fool.
4. The space program since the Challenger disaster bears no resemblance to the space program in the 1960s.
5. The 1960s were more optimistic than the 1970s.

6. All emerging nations are either dictatorships or politically unstable.
7. The political terrorists of our times are like the anarchists of the nineteenth century.
8. Nineteenth-century England was very much like sixteenth-century England.
9. Benjamin Franklin was the American Voltaire.
10. Political history is less revealing of an age than social history.

Our understanding of ideas, movements, and artistic productions is enhanced by comparison and contrast.

1. Tennyson was as much a self-conscious poseur as Walt Whitman.
2. Descartes was a less systematic thinker than Hobbes.
3. Monet and Manet have more than a letter difference between them.
4. Mozart and Haydn are almost indistinguishable.
5. John Stuart Mill was the Aristotle of the nineteenth century.
6. Most modern poets are more like self-advertising politicians than artists.
7. All twentieth-century philosophers are either idealists in the camp of Bradley or logical positivists in the camp of Wittgenstein.
8. The development of Woody Allen's career parallels Charlie Chaplin's.
9. *Gone with the Wind* tells us more about the Civil War than any history book.
10. All science fiction can be described as either hard or soft.

Formulating straightforward claims and making comparisons or contrasts are both ways of defining the nature of things. A simple claim and a comparative thesis can be added together to make an extended argument, which gets at its subject from two different angles. Here are some pairs of theses that approach the same subject in different ways.

1. People today have very inaccurate notions about the 1960s. Actually the 1970s were as polarized as the 1960s.
2. Science education is de-emphasized in the schools today. We are back to where we were before Sputnik.
3. Few great musical performers are teachers. Those who do teach treat their students with either contempt or maniacal obsession.
4. Indian food is gaining in popularity in the United States. It is not at all like Chinese or mid-Eastern cuisine.
5. Many students prefer pass–fail grading for electives. But they work less hard at such courses than they do in courses with regular grading.

You should try to support each thesis in a pair separately. However, for some audiences you might be able to assert one of the elements without going into detailed support.

8 ‖ Verification in Argument

Would you believe an argument proposing a certain kind of nuclear-waste disposal if its writer showed no knowledge about radiation, or a defense of the electoral college from someone who knew no American history, or a claim that Cal Ripkin, Jr., is baseball's greatest shortstop from someone who never heard of Ozzie Smith, Luis Aparicio, Ernie Banks, Honus Wagner, or Pee Wee Reese? Certainly not. You must have solid, verifiable evidence to support a claim about the nature of things or to back the causal, evaluation, or proposal arguments you will learn about in later chapters.

You would not even bother to read an argument written by someone who betrayed fundamental ignorance on the subject. Now think of yourself as a writer rather than a reader. Being well informed on your subject is your first obligation. You should read what is available, talk to those who can help you, even collect evidence first hand. Nothing can replace a solid background. But to get the greatest benefit from it, your reader should know it is there as well. We are not concerned in this chapter with how to create knowledge in the first place (the search depends on the discipline you are working in), but with how such knowledge should appear in written argument.

How do you let your reader know you have solid evidence to support your argument? You can, of course, explicitly tell your reader what personal experiences you had, present the research you conducted, refer to books and articles you read. Or, in less obvious ways you can reveal the thorough background knowledge that your reader has a right to expect and that in turn reflects credit on you. (See also Building Author Credibility in Chapter 15.) Before we can look at those ways, we have to focus on a critical question every writer must ask about an intended audience. What is that audience's state of knowledge compared with yours? Do they know more than you do, less, or about the same? (Your audience's assumptions and beliefs are as important as their knowledge, but we discuss such matters under each type of argument.)

If they probably know more, then your major task is to show that you know at least enough to argue on the subject. It is difficult to address an audience that has superior knowledge, but if you are a student you are familiar with this difficulty. Your papers and exams are written for your superiors in knowledge, your professors. In such cases you show your knowledge by (1) defining the important terms in the field, (2) mentioning the work of experts, and (3) referring to pertinent books and authors.

You can show your competence in the same three ways if your audience is approximately your equal in knowledge. But writing to those who know less than you do creates different problems. You cannot cite books and experts your readers have never heard of without straining their comprehension and inviting accusations of pedantry and pomposity. Instead, you must identify every unfamiliar term, every new concept, every name or book or technique. You have to give enough background information so that your readers can place new ideas in a familiar context. For example, if you are going to quote an expert unknown to your audience, you will have to present that expert's credentials. You write not just "Linus Pauling," but "Linus Pauling, the Nobel Prize-winning chemist." Or if you refer to a book your readers probably have not read, you would name its author and identify its contents. You write not *"A Tale of Two Cities,"* but *"A Tale of Two Cities,* Charles Dickens's novel about the excesses of the French Revolution." Or if you name an unfamiliar place, then it is not just "the fens," but "the fens, that flat, marshy expanse of land in the east of England." Whenever your argument depends on specific information, information you cannot assume your readers have, you must stop and inform them, at whatever length necessary.

THE BRAIN SCAN

A critical problem for you as an arguer is presenting information to your readers in a credible way. Think about how you respond to statements presented to you as facts. Your response depends on what is already in your mind. There are, to begin with, some facts that everybody in our culture seems to know. If your high-school science teacher mentions that the solar system has nine planets, your brain will register approval because you have that same fact stored away from elementary school. So of course you accept as fact any statement you have previously accepted as fact. That observation sounds crushingly obvious, but you must remember that you began stocking your brain before you were old enough to know what you were doing. Some of these "facts," like "Santa Claus brings toys at Christmas," do not survive the test of time and experience; and as you grow more critical in your thinking, more of them will be discarded. Or new information may come along to replace or alter the old.

Now suppose someone tells you a "new fact," something you have never heard before. How do you respond? Your brain does something like a quick scan of its stores of information, without your even realizing it, to find out if this new fact fits in with what you already know. Suppose, for example, you read that Abraham Lincoln is buried in Springfield, Illinois; although you have never heard that before, it does not bother you, because your brain scan, in effect, lines up this new fact with your existing knowledge of Lincoln's associations with Illinois. The new fact fits, so you accept it readily. But if someone told you Lincoln was buried in Hawaii, your reaction would be quite different.

Some new facts will not fit at the first scan. You hear or read the tidy little fact that "the opossum is a marsupial." "I didn't know that," you respond, surprised. On the first scan, the word *marsupial* may call to mind Australia, kangaroos, and koala bears, while the word *opossum*, on the contrary, disconcertingly suggests an animal that can be found in your own back yard. These tidbits of information seem to contradict each other and doubt is cast on the new fact. How can an anomaly of Australian evolution wind up on your side of the world? If the statement had been worded more precisely in the first place—"The opossum is the only North American marsupial"—this new fact would have passed the scan more easily. Those careful qualifications "only" and "North American" show that the framer of the statement was aware that your predictable previous knowledge would make the simple assertion "The opossum is a marsupial" a shade difficult to accept.

Since the wording can be so important, try to anticipate your readers' brain scan of any statement you present as a fact. Are they likely to know it already? If they are, then a simple assertion of the fact is enough. The easily accepted fact will not need the clarification a startling new fact needs. The earth revolves around the sun, hot air rises, and rubber is a poor conductor of electricity. The barest prose suffices for these simple, well-known facts.

If the fact is not so obvious—if it probably will not pass the first brain scan—you need to clarify or qualify. How much clarification is necessary depends on your understanding of your audience. For example, in Japan you could not say that "Hank Aaron is the home-run king of baseball."

Your audience would demand the qualification "of American baseball." And any audience, with the possible exception of one of professional geographers, would balk at the statement "Mauna Kea is the tallest mountain in the world." Everyone knows it's Everest. You would have to add the necessary qualification "if we measure from the bottom of the ocean." Then the fact will probably pass the first scan.

HOW TO VERIFY A CLAIM IN AN ARGUMENT

Sometimes you need more than careful wording to help a statement pass a reader's brain scan. You need to demonstrate that a convincing connection links the *statement* with what you want it to represent. In short, you must *verify*. We have already defined a fact as a statement that can be verified. Sometimes that verification must be an explicit part of your argument. How do you do it?

The means of verification are exactly the same as the ways in which you take in information in the first place. You simply reproduce in writing whatever verification convinced you. Basically you are convinced of facts in three ways: (1) you have seen and experienced them; (2) people you trust have told you about what they have seen and experienced; and (3) experts have communicated the facts in books or articles on a particular subject or in reference books like encyclopedias or dictionaries.

Verification from Personal Experience

Many of the arguments you write will arise from situations in your own life: your dorm needs better security; the library should be open for longer hours; your community needs a new parking lot or swimming pool and does not need a new courthouse or another shopping mall. You select these subjects for argument because you have been frightened by a stranger in the dorm, unable to study in the library on a Saturday night, frustrated looking for a parking place downtown, or sweltering on a hot summer afternoon with no place to swim. All of these experiences are facts. They have actually happened; they have happened to you. When the topic of your argument grows out of personal experience, you can regard your experiences as fact and use them in your argument.

What is the best way to present your personal experience in an argument so that your readers will find it believable? Tell them what actually happened to you; give the details of time, place, and circumstance but downplay your feelings about them. For example, suppose you are writing a letter to your town newspaper, arguing the need for another municipal parking lot and basing your argument in part on personal evidence. Here are two possible sample paragraphs from this letter. Both use "I" to convey a personal experience, but which is more credible and therefore convincing?

> Last week, when I drove downtown, I couldn't find a parking place for the longest time. Boy, was I mad. I got angrier and angrier as I drove around town. The sweat was pouring down my face, and I was red as a beet. I was so frustrated I felt like swearing. What an experience!

> Last Wednesday morning I had a dermatologist's appointment. I was downtown twenty minutes early, yet I was fifteen minutes late. I drove up and down several blocks around the Glennland Office building, looking for a meter, but every space was taken. I checked the two municipal lots on Garner and Fraser Streets—both full. I drove around and around all five levels of the parking garage—also full. I waited a hopeful five minutes double-parked by a yellow Mercedes that two old ladies were chatting next to. Instead of getting in they walked away. I finally parked illegally in the "customers only" lot behind Centre Hardware store and got a ticket.

Everything is ineffective in the first paragraph. The writing is vague, imprecise, and cliché-ridden. But more important, it is particularly ineffective support in an argument whose first purpose is to convince your readers that something has happened (in short, to verify your experience as fact). Only after your readers are convinced of the reality of your experience, can you—should you—get them to share your reactions to that experience.

The second paragraph records personal experience in specific detail. Of course, personal experience alone would not be enough to support the demonstration section of an argument that a city needs a new parking garage. You would also need far more detailed statistics on traffic flow, the number of parking spots available, and the typical demand as measured, perhaps, in parking revenues. But your personal experience is valuable evidence as well. First, it shows that parking problems are not just statistics, but inconveniences that affect individuals. The more typical your experiences are, the more likely to happen to your readers, the better. Second, your personal experience makes your argument lively, more interesting to read, and therefore more likely to be read. So, once again, if you have a legitimate personal experience at the core of your argument, *use it.*

Verification from Hearsay

Hearsay is a word with negative connotations, associated with gossip, rumor, and unfounded accusations—just the opposite of what you want when you try to verify facts. In its loosest meaning, *hearsay* is anything heard from another person, about anything from the price of eggs to the fate of the universe. Someone can make a factual claim to you directly, or say that somebody else told it, and so on. Although you take in a great deal of information by hearsay every day, you cannot hand that information back in argument as verified fact. No statement is a fact *just* because someone told it to you. For example, your roommate may tell you that the bursar at your college occasionally falsifies tuition records. Your roommate's testimony, however, is not sufficient verification that such a crime happens. He or she may have heard a rumor, have misinterpreted a remark in passing, have a lively imagination, or even hold a grudge against the bursar. You would not base any official complaint against the bursar solely on your roommate's hearsay accusation. Your school newspaper, however, might run an article citing many student complaints about the bursar.

Although often inadmissible in formal situations such as the courtroom, hearsay is used extensively in argument as a source of verification. Let us define *hearsay* as someone else's testimony of firsthand experience—what happened to another, what another saw and did. This kind of hearsay verification is then no different from verification by personal experience, only this time the personal experience is the other person's, not yours. That means that your personal experience is actually hearsay to your readers, and the hearsay information you pass along in writing is in a sense twice hearsay to them. Your readers believe your "hearsay" only out of trust in you; they will believe the hearsay you report only if you likewise convince them your source is trustworthy. You say, "Dana fell down a hole." Someone says, "Verify that please." You say, "Dana told me so." You tend to trust people when they are talking about their own experience and when they can pass tests of credibility.

Obviously, we do not accept hearsay verification without making the crucial assumption that our informant, our verifier, has no reason to deceive us or is not in turn deceived. A reader who has no reason to doubt the objectivity of a writer, who does not question the writer's memory, prejudice, or ability to comprehend, will probably never doubt the accuracy of personal or hearsay testimony. Most of the time we extend such credibility to our informants. Why should Dana lie about falling down a hole?

Under what circumstances should we withhold belief in hearsay verification? Although no codified rules exist for when to doubt and when not, common sense suggests circumstances for suspicion. We tend to distrust stories that are too good to be true: "I always win at the race track." "All my stocks go up." "I climbed Mt. Everest without oxygen." Heroic feats of memory also make us skeptical; we wisely doubt the ability of ordinary minds to remember large verbatim chunks of conversations (she said, then

I said, then she said, then I said) or the exact wording of pages of written material.

Once a person is caught in a serious lie, all his or her subsequent testimony is subject to doubt. Harsh but true. Embellishing the truth, however, is more common than outright lying. In some cases, embellishment is no more than an imprecise use of language to dramatize the truth: "I was up half the night." "My children are driving me crazy." People say they waited longer, worked harder, ate more, drank less, were angrier or more in love than they actually were. Embellishments like these make life a bit more interesting and we normally don't challenge them. But if the accuracy of a fact verified by hearsay is in any way crucial ("Where were you at 9:35 when the murder was committed?" "I was waiting for my date, who was hours late"), we will demand more precision than embellishment gives us.

The value of hearsay verification comes down to the objectivity and competence of the witness. To report a fact, you must first take it in, and many factors distort perception. The most basic source of distortion is personal bias. If you have watched your favorite football team lose, are you likely to be objective about the conduct of the referees? If you saw someone you love in a fight, could you fairly report what the other person said or did? And if you had just been fired, could you give an accurate account of what your boss said to you? The same bias you will admit to in your cooler moments exists in every other human being.

If you are going to use the personal testimony of a witness to an event, you will of course make sure that the witness was actually at the scene and able to see and comprehend the event. But think of the kinds of competence required simply to take in what happens. Could you give an accurate report of the proceedings of the Japanese Diet (parliament), not knowing the language? You don't even have to go to the other side of the world to have difficulty taking in an event. You might have a medical examination and not be able later to give a clear report of what was done to you, or you could be in the control room of a nuclear-power plant when an accident occurred and not even realize it. A great deal of prior knowledge may be necessary simply to take some things in.

Hearsay in print is more believable when the source is identified and justified, and we have certain conventions about what constitutes adequate identification. Journalists, for instance, will credit hearsay to "a White House source" or "a Pentagon informant," thereby creating a sometimes spurious sense of authority; but in a courtroom, evidence from an unnamed source is inadmissable. Hearsay is often defended by adding further claims about the veracity of an informer: "The President's aide told me, and he knew because he sat in on the meeting."

Whenever you have reason to doubt your informant, hearsay testimony is no longer good enough. You must seek further verification. The testimony of a suspected embellisher evokes skeptical follow-up questions like "How big did you say that fish was?" Or, when the story sounds hard to believe, and the teller's self-interest is obvious, you ask for more verification. For example, when Peter Habeler and Reinhold Messner claimed to have climbed Mt. Everest without oxygen, they were asked to produce evidence other than their mutual corroboration.

Again, all of this checking has to be done if you question the competence or objectivity of your hearsay source. If the evidence you have gained from someone else is important enough to appear in your written argument, it is better to be suspicious than naïve about its accuracy. The most accurate and therefore valuable hearsay evidence comes from a source so competent and trustworthy you can call it authority.

Verification by Authority

An authority is a person or a source that is widely trusted to give accurate information and careful judgments. *The Statistical Abstract, The Handbook of Chemistry and Physics, The Oxford English Dictionary, Encyclopaedia Britannica*—these are famous, authoritative reference books, and there are thousands of others, compendiums of information on everything from abacus to zygote. They are not 100 percent accurate—that is an impossible state of perfection—but those that have been continually updated have been acknowledged as trustworthy over the years. If you find yourself writing on a recognized topic, something in history or politics or science, you will do well to pull these heavy books from their shelves to look for and check on basic information.

When you need information that is too current to have found its way into the thin pages of a reference book, you must turn to more frequently published newspapers and journals, which differ in their credibility. Although you wouldn't consult the supermarket copy of the *National Enquirer* for a complete text of the president's speech the night before, that's exactly what you will get in the *New York Times.* There are other relatively credible widely distributed newspapers published in major cities. Your local paper may not be as reliable or detailed on big events, but it may be your only source of information on events in your community. To compensate for any inaccuracies in local coverage, you might be able to do some verifying yourself in your own community.

You may also learn about current events from magazines like *Time* or *Newsweek* or *Sports Illustrated,* which offer enjoyable and often informative reading. But keep in mind that mass-circulation magazines often bend and color facts, or leave out tedious but important details, in order to entertain. Such magazines should not be used alone as sources of verification.

Television falls in this slightly unreliable category too. An enormous amount of information is presented on television, but it is very difficult to trust it implicitly or to use any of it authoritatively. You don't usually take notes while you watch television newscasts, and the time restrictions of television programming create more distortions than are found in print. Just when interviews and discussions turn interesting, the moderator faces the camera and says, "That's all we have time for now." Unless you can obtain the transcript or tape of an interview, a talk, or a documentary, you cannot cite a television program as a source of verification.

So far we have considered certain publications as possible authorities on current matters. But another very obvious meaning of the word *authority* is a person who is an expert on a subject. Experts present their information, and much more, in books and articles, so when you want to know anything about a field, find out who the experts are. But don't go at it the other way and assume that anyone who has written a book about a subject is an expert. At first glance, books look equally authoritative, but not all are written by conscientious and thoughtful scholars. How do you tell the difference? To begin with, you can check the credentials of an author by seeing what else he or she has published. If the previous book was an exposé of the secret life of Elvis Presley and the most recent a harangue on the dangers of cloning, you might doubt your author's authority. But if the author has published other reputable books, you can feel more confident. You can also check the credibility of a book by looking up reviews of it in journals and newspapers that send books to other experts for assessment. The book itself will also give some clues as to its credibility, and the more you know the subject, the more the quality of the book will be evident to you. For example: Is the book published by a reputable publisher? Does the author show sources, just as you do when you write a paper?

When you want to verify a claim for readers, bring in the authority that verified it for you in footnotes, in-text citations, or the very wording of your argument. Accurate documentation is not only a matter of intellectual honesty; it is also a mark of respect for your audience as alert, intelligent readers. Consult a handbook for the method of documentation appropriate to your discipline and format.

FOR YOU TO ANALYZE

Read the following paragraphs and identify the statements of fact. Which are verified and which are not? Taking into account the author and where these passages appeared, does the absence of verification weaken credibility at any point?

Nearly two years ago a former Navy employee who had left the Government to work for a military contractor received a call offering for sale some inside information from the Pentagon, according to Federal investigators.

The caller was a consultant, one of many people in the Washington area who use their knowledge and expertise to help military contractors in their dealings with the Pentagon.

The former Navy employee alerted the Naval Investigative Service and agreed to record subsequent conversations with the consultant in which the details of the deal were fleshed out. . . .

That operation proved successful, and shortly afterwards investigators had the evidence they needed to secure the consultant's cooperation in an investigation. He allowed the Federal authorities to make a recording as he dealt with a Pentagon official who was providing him with material useful to military contractors.

That single operation led investigators to an interlocking network of consultants and a far-reaching fraud case that is shaking the multibillion-dollar military-industrial complex to its foundations. Investigators have not disclosed the names of the former Navy employee or the consultant who began cooperating in the investigation.

—Stephen Engelberg, "Inquiry into Pentagon Bribery Began With a Telephone Call," *The New York Times*

The number of cattle on New York farms has dropped to the lowest level since the state began keeping records in 1867, the New York Agricultural Statistics Service reported this week.

The agency put the number of beef and dairy animals at 1.7 million as of Jan. 1, 8 percent less than the year before. The record is 2.6 million head, in 1888.

The major cause for the drop was a reduction in the number of dairy cows as part of a Federal program to cut national dairy surpluses, according to Don Keating, an agricultural statistician here.

Under the $1.8 billion Federal program, partly paid for by the farmers themselves, about 14,000 farmers slaughtered 1.5 million dairy cows and calves in 1986 and 1987 throughout the United States.

In New York, the dairy termination program resulted in a milk-cow population of 844,000 as of Jan. 1, down 6 percent from 900,000 the year before. That total, the Statistics Service said, was a record low number of milk cows in New York.

—Harold Faber, "Count of New York Cattle Lowest on Record," *The New York Times*

The study of the time and circumstances of the human colonization of the New World has preoccupied archeologists for more than a century. The earliest universally acknowledged North American sites are those that were occupied by people who made distinctive fluted stone projectile points approximately

11,500 years ago and who are usually given the name Clovis, after a locality in New Mexico. Although many sites and study areas have been presented as providing evidence for pre-Clovis human occupation in both North and South America *(1)*, the validity of this evidence is not accepted by all investigators *(2)* Reexamination of one such body of evidence shows that four artifacts from the Old Crow locality in the northern Yukon Territory, Canada, which were previously thought to be of late Pleistocene age, were in fact from the late Holocene.

1. A. L. Bryan, Ed., *Early Man in America from a Circum-Pacific Perspective* (Occasional Papers 1, Department of Anthropology, University of Alberta, Edmonton, 1978); R. L. Humphrey and D. Stanford, Eds., *Pre-Llano Cultures of the Americas: Paradoxes and Possibilities* (Anthropological Society of Washington, Washington, DC, 1979); R. Shutler, Jr., Ed., *Early Man in the New World* (Sage, Beverly Hills, CA, 1983).
2. F. H. West, *The Archaeology of Beringia* (Columbia Univ. Press, New York, 1981); D. E. Dumond, *Am. Antiq.* **47**, 885 (1982); D. F. Dincauze, in *Advances in World Archaeology,* F. Wendorf and A. E. Close, Eds. (Academic Press, New York, 1984), vol. 3, pp. 275–323; R. C. Owen, in *The Origins of Modern Humans,* F. H. Smith and F. Spencer, Eds. (Liss, New York, 1984), pp. 517–563; E. J. Dixon, *North Am. Archeol.* **6**, 83 (1984–85).

—D. E. Nelson et. al., "New Dates on Northern Yukon Artifacts: Holocene Not Upper Pleistocene," *Science*

FOR YOU TO WRITE

Write a paragraph supporting a claim about a state of affairs, using as many factual details as possible to support your thesis. After you finish your paragraph, ask yourself whether it contains any facts a very skeptical reader might doubt. Might anything be the product of biased perception? Might a reader doubt your memory, competence, or objectivity? Might a reader doubt the authority of your sources? If so, go back and substantiate your facts with corroboration.

Part Two
HOW DID IT GET THAT WAY?

9 | The Kinds of Causes

Perhaps the most basic question we ask ourselves is one about identity. Does a certain state of affairs exist? What is this thing I am confronting? What is its nature? What qualities does it reveal? Answers to these questions, as we have shown in Chapters 3 through 7, can range from simple claims to complicated comparisons.

In its next basic operation, the mind enters time. It sees things not simply as "being"—having existence, attributes, and definition—but as "becoming." We see things come into existence and pass out of existence in time. We see a before and an after and ask, "Why? How did it get that way?" The answer to this question is a *cause.* We see a flower blooming in the evening, and the next morning we find it shriveled and faded. When we ask the *why* of before and after, we can find an answer in various ways, depending on the system of thought available to us: the flower's soul grew weary and fled; a frost last night froze the water in the plant tissues and broke them; an evil sprite punished the flower because someone left food in a bowl overnight. Of course, only one of these answers satisfies the system of thought we currently work in, but all of them could be called causes because they account for the change from before to after. We can even distinguish one culture from another by the kinds of causal explanations that satisfy it.

When we look for causes we look back in time; we start with the completed event or thing and look back to see what might have caused it. But causal thinking can work in forward as well as reverse. We can confront an event or thing and ask what *effect* it will cause. *Effect* is the after and *cause* the before. When we see the fingers of frost on the window at midnight, we can reason forward to the death of the flower in the morning.

The first answer to the question "Why?" is often not enough. If you try to explain to a four-year-old that a flower died because the frost came, the child will want to know why the frost came. If you answer that the frost came because it is the season for frost, the child will still ask, "Why?" Most attempts to answer a four-year-old's "Why?" turn into cosmological explorations until the child learns the futility of going back too far in the search for causes. Nevertheless, we often have to go partway back, and that is the first complication in finding a cause. What causes the cause? We can get into an infinite regression looking for the cause behind the cause behind the cause. Practical purposes determine when we stop.

Sometimes even without going back, we cannot give only one answer to the question "Why?" Suppose you want a new flower to replace the one blighted by frost. If you think you can do anything about causing a new flower, you have already done some causal reasoning: "A flower grows from a seed. If I put a seed in the ground, a flower will grow." So you take a seed from the dried flower, place it in the ground next to the dead one and wait. All through November and December nothing happens. It does not take a brilliant mind to realize that planting the seed was not enough, that something else must be necessary to produce a flower. A flower is an event with more than one cause. Here then is the second complication: Sometimes several causes have to come together to produce a single effect.

How we answer a causal question also depends in part on what we want to do. If we want to repeat an event, like growing a flower, we have to know all the causes that are required to bring it about. But what if we want to stop or prevent something? Suppose you want no more flowers to grow by your doorstep because the death of the last ones distressed you so. You know that the seeds are in the ground, and next spring the sun and rain will make them grow. You cannot turn off the sun and rain, but you can prevent them from germinating the seed. You can dig up the seed and feed it to your canary, put a rock over the spot that no shoot could move, or saturate the soil with poison so that nothing grows there for a century or more. Here, then, is a new wrinkle in answering the question of cause. You have zeroed in on those causes that you can remove or block. When you interfere in causal processes, you look for the causes that are within your grasp, the ones you can do something about.

Our thinking about causes, then, is shaped by what we want to do with them. We may simply want to explain them to our own and others' satisfaction. Such explanations are still arguments because competing versions can be constructed. Or we may want to repeat them to bring about an effect again; or we may want to block them to stop the result or even to change them to improve the effect. To do any of these things, to any degree, we need to understand causes as fully as possible.

To help our understanding of causes, we can learn to label them in a number of ways; each way gives us a slightly different notion of how a cause works. In order to make these labels usable as aids in thinking about causes, we have organized them into sets. Here is the procedure for using these sets. First have a clear idea of what you are investigating. Are you looking for the causes of a physical object or state, an isolated event, or a trend? Are you sure the effect whose causes you are investigating really exists? There is no sense investigating an increase in the average size of women's feet if there has been no such increase.

Next you can try a set of causes the way you try out a frame for a picture. This frame can work in two ways: It can send you looking for something that will fit in it, or it can impose order on the information you have already found. Some of the causal terms in the following list will fit the information you find and thus give you a useful vocabulary for talking about the case at hand. Use this list, in the first place, as an aid for your own thinking. Some of these terms overlap and not all of them will be equally useful. The same cause can sometimes be called by several names; call it by whichever name is most useful, and don't assume that you have to find a cause to match every label. Think of this list primarily as an impetus for causal brainstorming, for building a model of the relationships among the possible causes you identify.

SET 1: CONDITIONS, INFLUENCES, AND PRECIPITATING CAUSES

Conditions

Usually, many conditions lie behind an event—the physical setting, the social climate, the historical time, all the attendant circumstances natural and artificial. Conditions make up the background for an effect, but they are not necessarily separate events themselves; they can be situations that persist in time, like force fields that shape an event within their domain.

Some conditions may be crucial, others not worth mentioning, given your audience and purpose. If you are explaining the causes of a forest fire, you would mention the crucial conditions of a prolonged dry spell and a prevailing wind. But if you are talking about a freak accident, someone killed by a cornice falling off a tall building, for example, you would not mention gravity as an important condition behind the event. Everyone knows gravity is a condition behind every event that occurs on the earth.

We usually think of a condition as passive, the setting for the action initiated by the more important causes. Nevertheless, we cannot put on a play without a stage. There could have been no great age of European exploration without certain conditions—ships that could cross the sea and unexplored lands on the other side. Conditions are usually part of causal arguments when our main purpose is explanation. They figure in historical arguments and arguments about the success or failure of a person, or business, or other social enterprise.

Influences

In common usage, *influence* is really just another word for condition. But we are reserving *influence* for those conditions affecting the rate at which an effect takes place or the degree to which it happens. That is, an influence cannot bring about or prevent an effect, but it can make the effect happen more quickly or more slowly, intensify or diminish it. Think of influences as cheerleaders at a football game. They do not really cause the cheering; spectators always do some cheering. But cheerleaders do intensify the cheering and speed it up, getting cheers from the crowd even before the game begins. The sharp stock market decline of October 1987 had multiple and complex causes, but many experts investigating the event cited the use of computerized trading as an influence, a cause intensifying the effect.

Precipitating Causes

Conditions and influences prepare for an effect, but a *precipitating cause* comes along and actually forces it to happen. A precipitating cause is like that one extra salt crystal that precipitates a solid out of a supersaturated solution. The precipitating cause usually happens right before the effect, like the last straw that breaks the camel's back.

Remember the conditions for a forest fire—a dry spell and a prevailing wind. A bolt of lightning could act on these conditions as a precipitating cause, igniting the forest. Or an earthquake that shakes a loosened cornice, which falls and kills a pedestrian, would be a precipitating cause. It is the last thing that needs to happen before the event itself.

We usually think of wars as having precipitating causes that act on ripe conditions. The assassination of the Archduke Ferdinand at Sarajevo is considered the precipitating cause of World War I; the abduction of Helen of Troy was the precipitating cause of the Trojan War. And even trends can have a precipitating cause: The Beatles' long hair precipitated a decade of change in the appearance of young people. But it is easier to see precipitating causes when they themselves are dramatic events and when they precede events with clear beginnings.

Precipitating causes are not by nature different from any other kind of cause. You cannot say with certainty that any particular kind of event is a precipitating cause. A border raid by Arabs or Israelis, for instance, may or may not precipitate a wider conflict. In the case of war, we can identify a precipitating cause only by hindsight. But in other cases, particularly where nature's laws take over, we can be more certain. Touching a match to a firecracker will inevitably precipitate a reaction.

EXERCISE

Here is a list of events. Think up some of the plausible conditions or influences behind them and the precipitating causes that could have acted to bring them about.

Example	The seizing of the American embassy in Teheran by Iranian militants.
Condition	Deteriorating diplomatic relationship between the United States and Iran.
Influence	The coming to power of the Ayatollah Khomeini.
Precipitating cause	The shah's entry into the United States for medical treatment.

1. The Three Mile Island nuclear reactor accident.
2. President Nixon's resignation.
3. The Soviet withdrawal from Afghanistan.
4. The beginning of World War II for the United States.
5. The popularity of Michael Jackson.

These specific examples may jog your imagination into recalling other events whose causes can be examined usefully this way: any political victory or defeat, any sports victory or defeat, business success or failure, any sudden fame or infamy. You can even look for conditions, influences, and precipitating causes of events in your own life.

SET 2: PROXIMATE AND REMOTE CAUSES

Unlike the model presented in set 1, which sees background conditions operated on by a precipitating cause, a framework of proximate and remote causes helps us separate causes according to time.

Proximate Causes

A proximate cause is one that comes close to an effect in time. A precipitating cause can also be a proximate cause, but an effect can have several proximate causes though only one precipitating cause.

. It is useful to distinguish passive persistent conditions from proximate causes that are unique events themselves. Suppose we are looking for the causes of the final selection of a presidential candidate. The choice is the result not only of conditions that have built up over the last four years and even longer—the economy, foreign relations, the energy situation. It is also the result of events that happen during the months and even days before the party's final choice is announced at a convention—the various primary victories, media disasters, deals, and withdrawals that sway delegates' votes. These happenings can be labeled proximate causes because they occur relatively close in time to the final effect, the choice of a particular candidate.

Remote Causes

A proximate cause operates immediately to bring about an effect; a remote cause is best seen as the cause of a cause. Some causal explanations will not satisfy an audience unless the causes behind causes or before them in time are examined. Obviously, all events are connected with events before them, but we do not have to go back to the dawn of history to give satisfactory explanations. We would not explain the explosive growth of microcomputer technology by going back to Stone Age reliance on chipped flint arrowheads. We have to sense how far back we need to go given the topic and audience.

In general, a significant remote cause is one linked to its effect by an inevitable chain. It has been argued, for example, that the building of the Great Wall of China was a cause of the fall of Rome. That is about as remote as a cause can be, but these two events, widely separated in time and space, can be connected by identifying the links between them. The barbarians, stopped by the Great Wall to the east, bounced back to the west and did not rest, in fact, until they got to Rome.

When do we look for remote causes? We look for them especially when we analyze historical events; we could even say that history is the search for remote causes. History goes back in time to identify roots and comprehend what needs to be known to produce a sense of understanding or perhaps of control. The same search for remote causes is often necessary when we want to understand the causes of individual personal actions; we want to know the significant starting points of a neurosis, a marital breakdown, a successful career, an Olympic gold medal. We go back until we think we have found all the causes that contributed significantly to the effect; and in considering natural phenomena, where we deal more with fact than speculation, we go back until we have a full set of causes, enough to repeat the event if we could.

Of course, where proximate causes end and remote causes begin is a matter of debate, resolved in part by the purpose of your causal argument. If we are focusing on an event at the end of a week, what happens one day before can be proximate and six days before, remote. But in the case of a presidential nomination, what happens on the first day of the convention, or the week before, or during the primaries, or just after the previous election—any of these can be thought of as a remote cause, the cause of a cause. It all depends on your time frame. The distinguishing feature of a remote cause, then, is not any set quantity of time between it and the effect, but that it is the cause of a cause.

EXERCISE

Look for remote and proximate causes of events like the following.

1. The stock market crash of October 1987.
2. The disappearance of the dinosaurs.
3. The move of any sports team from one city to another.
4. Marilyn Monroe's suicide.
5. The victory of FDR in 1932.

SET 3: NECESSARY AND SUFFICIENT CAUSES

We use the framework of necessary and sufficient causes particularly when we want to know what is required to repeat, slow down, prevent, facilitate—in short, to interfere with a causal process. We want to know only what is required to bring about or prevent an effect. We do not necessarily want to trace causes any further than is sufficient to give us power over them.

Necessary Causes or Conditions

As its name tells us, a necessary cause or condition is one in whose absence an effect cannot occur. It is permanently and in some cases uniquely associated with its effect. For example, oxygen is a necessary condition for a fire; in fact, we would not even bother to mention it as the cause of a fire because we take its presence for granted. Similarly, a virus is the necessary cause of a cold. If you can distinguish your symptoms from hay fever or allergy well enough to know you have a cold, you can be certain that a virus has colonized your mucous membranes. In the case of many infectious diseases, once we have identified the disease correctly, we know exactly what kind of virus or bacteria caused it; there is a unique association between a virus and its disease, between some necessary causes and their effects.

The distinguishing characteristic of a necessary cause is that we can reason back to it with certainty. Given the effect, we know that certain causes or conditions *had* to be present to bring it about. If you know that someone has a valid college diploma, you can infer with certainty that he passed a required number of courses. You cannot infer anything with certainty about what he has learned. If you meet someone with a National Merit Scholarship, you can infer that she received a very high score on the SAT exam; Merit Scholarships are not awarded through a local politician or on the basis of need, or because of a promise to serve in the Navy for four years after college.

Even though you can reason back with certainty from an effect to a necessary cause, *you cannot turn the process around.* That is, the presence or occurrence of the necessary cause is *not* always enough to predict the effect. Not all high-scoring high-school seniors win National Merits, and you do not have a fire just because you have oxygen.

You can always invent a necessary cause: The necessary cause of poverty is not having enough money; the necessary cause of a dent in a fender is that something hit it; the necessary cause of famine is not enough food to go around. All of these statements are facts; they name necessary causes that you can reason back to with certainty. But they do not help your thinking about causality very much. You really want to know what caused these inevitable necessary causes.

Another kind of cause that is *always* necessary is the absence of anything to prevent the effect. We know that when anything happens, nothing stopped it from happening. If a house burns down, the fire was not detected and put out in time. Searching for a cause that would necessarily block an effect is useful if you want to reverse the causal process. In your next house, you will install smoke alarms and fire extinguishers.

Sufficient Causes

Once again, imagine yourself confronting an effect and trying to reason back to its causes. Let us say it is that same forest fire. You can be certain that the necessary causes and conditions were present: combustible material, oxygen, an igniting agent, and the absence of what would have stopped the fire. But even though you know an igniting agent would have to be present, several possibilities could fill that niche—a carelessly thrown match, a bolt of lightning, an imperfectly extinguished camper's fire, or carefully planned arson. These rival possibilities can be described as *sufficient causes.* Any one of them, given the necessary conditions, could have started the fire. *A sufficient cause is one in whose presence the effect must occur.* Sometimes several causes must combine to satisfy this requirement.

Suppose you stumble over a dead body. You know that the necessary causes of death are the cessation of heartbeat and breathing and the absence of anything to keep them going artificially. But no coroner's report ever recorded the cause of death as cessation of breathing. That is not an interesting answer.

The coroner called to the scene will test out a number of explanations. Death has many sufficient causes, causes in whose presence it must occur if nothing intervenes: heart failure, stroke, strangulation, hemorrhage, poison. Of course, examination of the body will narrow down the list of sufficient causes; if the body is unmarked, then death by violent external means is ruled out. Autopsy will eventually reveal the sufficient cause. We talk about sufficient cause, then, when an event has many possible causes, any one of which is enough to bring it about.

In human affairs, most sufficient causes are not necessary causes. Take divorce as an example. It can be brought about by a number of things—desertion, adultery, mental cruelty—no one of which is a necessary cause, one in whose absence divorce cannot occur. Any one of them may be sufficient, however.

EXERCISE

What are the necessary and/or sufficient causes behind the following effects?

1. Getting an A in a course.
2. A particular plane crash.
3. The popularity of a particular movie or kind of movie.
4. The expansion of deserts around the world.
5. A disease, such as cancer, or phenomena such as strokes or heart attacks.

OTHER KINDS OF CAUSES

Common usage has given the word *cause* many meanings that we must consider because they are important in causal argument.

Responsibility

Obviously, responsibility as a cause exists only in human affairs. It often comes up when we examine events that people have helped bring about, and what people have brought about includes all the domain of history and the social sciences, and most of what gets into the daily newspaper.

Responsibility can be assigned because of what someone either has done or has not done. For example, an ambassador who sets up a conference can be a cause of improved relations between two countries. On the other hand, an ambassador who initiates no overtures to the host country—sets up no conferences, throws no parties—can by such inaction cause deteriorating relations between two countries.

Right away, we can see that in considering a human being who either acts or doesn't act, we are also considering the idea of *intention.* What does a person mean to cause by either acting or not acting, and to what extent is a person responsible for what he or she does not intend? Consider the enormous difference it makes deciding punishment for someone's death if the act was done intentionally or not. We think of human intention as a cause; if someone wills a result and acts on that will, then that person is a cause. If, for instance, you want to celebrate your birthday, and you invite thirty people and buy the cake, then you are the cause of a birthday party. If you want to be physically fit, and you run, do push-ups, and play tennis, your will is then as much the cause of improvement in your body as any exercises you do.

These are examples of intentional acts (sending out invitations and doing exercises) that are causes. It is also possible to intend not to act, and doing nothing can also be a cause. Foreign policy, for example, which we assume is largely a matter of human intention, consists as much of actions deliberately *not* taken as of actions taken. Decision makers in the State Department resolve not to interfere, not to send letters of protest, not to invade, not to respond to provocations, and these intended omissions can have their effects as well as intended acts.

We are on sure ground in identifying responsibility when the acts whose causes we are investigating fall within someone's *domain of responsibility.* Doctors' domain of responsibility is the health of their patients; teachers', the instruction of their students; parents', the welfare of their children. If a patient dies because a disease was misdiagnosed, we do not ask any questions about intentions. The effect was clearly in the doctor's domain of responsibility. Whenever we can place an effect within someone's domain of responsibility, it does not matter whether the human cause of that effect was intentional or not.

Questions of responsibility lead us into deep ethical waters. Sometimes it is difficult to decide whose domain of responsibility an action falls under or how far a domain of responsibility extends. Were the citizens of the United States responsible for the internment of Japanese-Americans at the beginning of World War II? How do you judge the French who collaborated with the Nazis? Or the candidate whose aide misappropriated campaign funds supposedly without the candidate's knowledge?

EXERCISE

What human responsibility was involved in the coming about of the following events?

1. The execution of Julius and Ethel Rosenberg.
2. The Iran-Contra scandal.
3. The success of the first moon landing.
4. The chemical contamination of the Love Canal area.
5. The space shuttle Challenger disaster.

Absence of a Blocking Cause

When is the lack of a cause a cause? How can something that does not happen cause something that does? Picture a wedding. The clergyman looks around and asks, "Is there any reason why these two should not be joined together?" If no one steps forward and the ceremony is completed, we can say that one cause of the marriage was the absence of interference. Something that did not happen helped to bring about something that did. Thus, the absence of restraints, impediments, blocks, inhibitions can actually help bring about an effect.

We can also turn the example around. Suppose your friend Bernie never gets married. The cause of this event not happening is the absence of what it would take to make it happen: No one asked him, and he asked no one. Therefore, when something does not happen, the absence of what would make it happen is a cause of its not happening.

We can always claim, as we said before, that a necessary cause is the absence of anything that would have prevented the effect. However, we seldom bother to reckon up all the missing causes when we are trying to explain why an event came about. But we certainly would pay attention to possible blocking causes when we want to prevent an effect. For instance, we might say that the cause of a forest fire's spreading was the absence of a firebreak to stop it. If we want to prevent future forest fires from spreading, we will provide a blocking cause like a firebreak. Of course, looking for absent blocking causes can be endless. If the forest fire were started by careless campers, it would be senseless to speculate about what might have prevented them from going camping that weekend.

EXERCISES

To what extent did the following events occur because of the absence of causes that would have prevented them?

1. The Iran-Iraq war.
2. The disappearance of the Midwestern prairie.
3. The loss of a famous monument or building.
4. Dutch elm blight.
5. The spread of the gypsy moth or Japanese beetle.

Think of things that diminished or happened less frequently because something prevented them.

1. Fewer people have been voting in recent presidential elections.
2. The failure of the revival of the miniskirt.
3. The absence of progress in the space program.
4. The decline in the birth rate in the United States in the 1960s and 1970s.
5. The decline in foreign-language programs in American high schools and universities.

Reciprocal Causes

Informing all our discussion of causes so far is an image of causes and effects lined up along a one-way street. We begin at a cause and we move ahead to an effect farther down the road, and that effect can be the cause of something still farther down. But this model of a one-way street, clear and tidy to our minds, can oversimplify reality. Instead, we can have a situation of *reciprocal causality* where cause and effect feed each other. In other words, traffic on the "causeway" can go in two directions; an effect can turn around and influence the cause that caused it.

Here are some familiar examples of reciprocal causality: Higher prices cause increased wage demands, and increased wage demands cause higher prices; success causes self-confidence, and self-confidence causes success; consumer demand inspires the development of new products, and the development of new products creates more consumer demand. In all of these situations, a one-way model fails to represent the actual two-way traffic pattern. These examples of reciprocal causality are all generalizations; they stand for a number of similar instances and they abstract from them a persistent pattern of causality. In fact, reciprocal causality can exist only on the level of generalization. When we deal with unique, individual events, we are better off with the one-way model.

A repeating sequence of cause and effect is a sign of reciprocal causality. Suppose you hear a joke that makes you laugh. That laughter makes the next joke seem even funnier, and in a few minutes even jokes about chickens crossing roads convulse you. We can look at this sequence of events as a one-way chain of cause and effect.

funny joke ⟶ laugh ⟶ funnier joke ⟶

more laughing ⟶ a real knee slapper ⟶ hysteria

This is a correct diagram of the events in time, but when we see that the events are really repeating themselves, we can pull the chain around to make a circle that represents reciprocal causality.

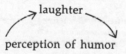

laughter

perception of humor

Even when a repeating series is not obvious, you can still try out a reciprocal model and see if there is any evidence to make it stick. You may know, for instance, that sunspots made Skylab fall. Is it likely that Skylab had any influence on the sun? Of course not. No two-way causality there. But suppose you are analyzing the factors that have influenced the size of cars Americans buy. You begin with a simple one-way model: Automobile manufacturers have created the taste for large cars. Historically, American car manufacturers have made the most desirable, top-of-the-line cars look like large, heavy boats. Now you can ask yourself, can the causality go the other way as well—has public demand been influencing the size of the cars Detroit produces? Is there any evidence that the public ever had a chance to choose smaller, economical cars over big gas guzzlers? Some might argue yes, because smaller American cars have regularly appeared on the market, from the Studebaker to the Vega to the Fiesta. The public has had a choice and therefore a chance to influence Detroit. In this case, reciprocal causality has been at work: Detroit certainly has influenced public demand for big cars, but the public in turn has influenced Detroit.

Causality in human affairs is especially likely to be reciprocal. When we try to impose a causal model on the mass of individual and group interactions that make up a society, we find things bouncing back and forth. When causes persist, effects can continue as trends rather than appear once as single events. What has caused the increase in the number of divorces? Why are more people entering business schools? The causes of social trends like these are complicated. Perhaps at some point we ought to abandon our model of reciprocal causality as a two-way street for some image of a Roman piazza crisscrossed by free-for-all rush-hour traffic.

EXERCISE

Think of causes for the following phenomena which can, in turn, be caused by their effects.

The commission of an unusual kind of crime, such as an airline hijacking, results in a news report, and extensive news coverage causes others to commit the same crime, leading to more news reports.

What can both cause and be caused by the following?

1. The rejuvenation of some inner cities.
2. Dressing well for work.
3. The run of similar television programs.
4. Mental depression.
5. The desire to learn.

Chance

Many people think that chance is the opposite of causality, that some things "just happen" and others are caused. Meeting your Aunt Tillie "by accident" on the street is a chance event, but meeting your friend at 3:00 at the lion statue in front of the Art Institute is caused by intention. Does that mean that all events that happen by accident are beyond causal explanation? Not so. In a sense, both kinds of events are caused even though we could label the one event chance. There was a cause (reason) for Aunt Tillie to be walking down the street where she was and a reason for you to be in the same place at the same time. We can reserve the word *chance* for the fact that these two things happened at the same time. *Chance is the unexpected coming together of things that have their own causes.*

One kind of chance is the occurrence of a random event. The physical world provides us with many examples of random events: the tunneling of electrons, the passage of cosmic radiation through our bodies, the spontaneous mutation of the DNA molecule, the emission of radiation from a decaying radioisotope. We cannot pinpoint exactly when such events will happen, but we can know when they are more likely to happen. No one can predict exactly where and when lightning will strike; but that does not make it sensible to stand on a treeless hill, wear metal-spiked shoes, and brandish a golf club during an electric storm.

We cannot predict the precise result of the toss of a coin, the throw of dice, or the turn of a card. But since we know all the possible results, we can calculate the *probability* of any one result occurring. The chance of a coin turning up heads is one in two, of a die showing two is one in six, of an ace appearing is one in thirteen. That kind of chance can be expressed as a mathematical probability. The other kind of chance, the "just happened" kind we discovered in our Aunt Tillie example, is beyond precise mathematical prediction, but the separate things that come together have their own causes.

EXERCISE

What causes had to come together in order to produce the following effects?

1. The invention of Teflon.
2. The way you met your best friend.
3. Last year's World Series or Superbowl victory.
4. Any major airplane crash.
5. The discovery of a political scandal.

THE CASE OF GEORGE

Let us take one event and think about all the possible causes behind it. We can stimulate our thinking by taking our sets of causes and seeing how many we can fill in with the facts of the situation. Here is the event whose causes we are examining: Our friend George has just flunked freshman chemistry, Chem 13, the first course for chemistry majors at the university.

Set 1

Conditions

The conditions of our friend's failure are all the persisting circumstances behind him and the course. The search for conditions can thus go very far back. In George's case, the existence of the university, of chemistry as a discipline, and the pressure on young people to go to college are all, in a sense, conditions behind his failure. But, obviously, these givens of reality are not worth mentioning, even in a thorough search for causes. Even George himself, wondering why he failed, would not think of these. The following conditions, however, might be worth mentioning:

1. Chem 13 is a fast-paced course.
2. The chemistry department uses Chem 13 to weed out potentially weak chemistry majors.
3. George's lab instructor spoke very poor English.
4. George's personality—he is lazy and tends to blame others.
5. George had a poor high-school background. His school offered only one term of chemistry, the instructor was old and taught outdated concepts, and the lab was underequipped.
6. Chem 13 met at 8:00 A.M. three days a week.

Influences

Influences are difficult to distinguish from conditions and perhaps separating them is sometimes arbitrary. But certainly the pressure of these external problems accelerated George on the road to failure:

1. George had trouble with a roommate who never studied.
2. This was his term for fraternity rushing.
3. George partied every Wednesday, Friday, and Saturday night.

Precipitating Cause

This is the event that comes closest in time to the effect and makes it happen. In fact, if the precipitating cause had not happened, the final effect, the failure itself, would not have happened.

1. George flunked the final, which counted for 60 percent of the grade.

Set 2

Remote Causes

Remember that we must set our own limits as to what we will call remote in time from the effect. In this case, it seems reasonable to call a remote cause anything relevant that happened before George took Chemistry 13.

1. George's high-school preparation in chemistry was poor.
2. His parents fostered negative qualities in his personality.
3. His desire to major in chemistry was probably unrealistic.
4. George's adviser placed him in a course beyond his preparation.

Proximate Causes

Since we have labeled "remote" significant things that happened before George took the course, then we must label "proximate" whatever happened during the course.

1. George's attendance was poor all term; he missed one and sometimes two or three of the weekly lectures.
2. He got a D on the midterm.
3. He did not complete two out of five lab experiments.
4. Two weeks before the final, George caught the flu.
5. He did not study for the final.
6. He did not know enough chemistry to pass the final.

Set 3

Necessary Cause

This is, quite simply, the cause without which the effect would not have occurred. It is the only cause to which we can reason back with certainty, even when we know nothing else about an effect except that it happened. Often, the necessary cause is a restatement of the effect.

1. The necessary cause of flunking Chemistry 13 is failure to meet the requirements to pass it.

Sufficient Cause

This is the cause in whose presence the effect must occur. As the semester unfolded, two sufficient causes developed to guarantee that George would fail the course:

1. Not completing all lab work satisfactorily.
2. A failing average on the two exams.

Set 4

Responsibility

George is a human being, and a human being wrote the F on his grade card, so we here must consider all the complications of intended and unintended acts that add up to human responsibility. This is the list of people implicated in George's failure:

1. *George's parents* were all too willing to sympathize uncritically with him, never suggesting he might be responsible for his own failures.
2. *His high-school chemistry teacher* was uninformed and uninspiring.
3. *His adviser:* In a sense George's adviser is responsible for letting him take a course he was unprepared for. George's schedule was his domain of responsibility. But could the adviser have known how unprepared George really was?
4. *George's fraternity brothers* made unreasonable demands on his time.
5. *The chemistry department professor* refused to give George the deferred grade he asked for after his bout of flu, two weeks before the final. Was the professor also responsible for allowing someone incompetent in English to teach a lab section? (But then, did the chemistry professor distribute the teaching assistantships?)
6. *George himself.* Of course.

Absence of Cause

These are the causes that could realistically have prevented George's failure and did not.

1. George could have taken command of himself (imposed a strict study schedule and hired a chemistry tutor) when he discovered early in the course that he was not comprehending the material.
2. A deferred grade would have prevented, or at least postponed, that final F.
3. George could have dropped the course while it was still possible.

Reciprocal Cause

This is a cause that intensifies or perpetuates the very thing that caused it.

1. Because he had not studied enough, given his deficiencies, George got a D on the midterm. Getting the D disheartened rather than stimulated him. As a result, he applied himself even less in the second half of the course, so that by the time he caught the flu, all was lost.

Chance

Two kinds of chance plagued George. A random natural event struck him down, and he was also the victim of an unfortunate combination of conditions.

1. He caught the flu two weeks before the final, although in crowded dorm conditions it is not surprising George picked up a virus.
2. Poor motivation, distractions, an inadequate background, and a hard course—all these conditions and more came together at one time for one person.

George's Case

A comprehensive listing of causes is only a preliminary step. In making a causal argument, the arguer, always with a particular audience and purpose in mind, chooses and arranges causes from that complete list. George has to account for failing chemistry to a number of audiences—his parents, his adviser, his professor, and even himself. He chooses, in effect, from the master list of causes and makes different arguments for different audiences and purposes.

First, George calls his parents to warn them about the F in chemistry coming in the mail. He tells them how he was wiped out by flu the last two weeks of the term. He tried to study, but his temperature was 102 degrees. The course is designed to flunk out as many students as possible anyway, he tells his parents, and the exams are ridiculously hard. Furthermore, he complains, when he went to talk to his professor, the guy was never around. In response to this tale of woe, George's parents murmur sympathetically, "How unlucky our George has always been."

Later that day, George goes to his adviser to justify his failure. He tells him about the flu, complains that he never understood the lab assistant and that the professor refused to give him a deferred grade a week before the final. He also informs his adviser that he talked to other students taking the course and discovered how poor his own high-school chemistry program was in comparison to theirs. He wonders out loud to his adviser whether he should have been allowed to take Chem 13. Perhaps he should have taken an easier chemistry course first.

At the beginning of the next term, George goes to his Chemistry 13 professor to see if he can do anything to get the grade changed. He pulls out the flu, the insufficient high-school background, the poor advice he received, the lab assistant's broken English—all the causes beyond his control. He even remarks that the professor was not around when he came to look for him after the midterm. The professor asks if George came during office hours. George says no, he had a class then. The professor replies that George should have asked for an appointment, either before or after a lecture, or with the department secretary.

Then the unimpressed professor gives his version of the causes behind George's F. George's attendance was poor throughout the course, he did not complete his lab reports, his midterm grade was D, and he failed the final. Therefore he failed the course. In short, the professor pays no attention to all the remote causes and conditions that worked on George. He acknowledges only the presence or absence of sufficient cause to pass the course. The question of who was at fault or whether there were extenuating circumstances is of no concern to him.

George goes away upset and admits to himself for the first time that, in spite of all the excuses, he was responsible for his own failure. He simply had not studied enough. Between his fraternity rushing and partying with his roommate, who seemed to be majoring in leisure, he had filled all his weekends and many of his week nights. True, he was ill-prepared and the course was hard, but he had been too lazy to get up for many of the 8:00 A.M. lectures. He had planned on cramming for the final when the flu intervened. But he had to admit that by the last two weeks of the term, all was hopeless.

Like most human events, George's failure had many causes. Though he may not have formulated a list of all possible causes, as we did above, George argued instinctively by selecting causes to fit his purpose and audience. He told his parents only what would arouse their sympathy. He omitted mentioning how much time he had spent on partying and rushing activities. For his adviser he also brought out only the things that would arouse sympathy, and he emphasized his poor high-school background and placement in a difficult course, stressing the one cause within the adviser's domain of responsibility. George tried a similar approach on the professor. This time he stressed his bad background and causes within the professor's domain of responsibility—the lab assistant, the difficulty of the course and of finding the professor, and the refusal of a deferred grade.

What George did, in effect, was shape each argument so that one cause dominated, and in human affairs the dominant cause is often seen as a person responsible. In making his case to his adviser and his professor, George identified the dominant cause as the one that moved responsibility into their domain; talking to his parents, George was concerned only with removing responsibility from himself. In other words, these different audiences shaped George's argument. But when the audience was George him-self, then he was most willing to take on personal responsibility. He looked at what *he* might have done to prevent failure, rather than at what others did or what circumstances influenced.

When George singled out a dominant cause, he said really that that one cause was enough to bring the effect about and that without it the effect would not have occurred. You should recognize this combination as the definition of a necessary and sufficient cause. In blaming his professor, George assumed that his professor had an active responsibility to help each of his students pass the course. He also assumed that if his professor had been more helpful, all the other causes would have gone for nothing. In effect, he elevated his professor's positive responsibility into a necessary and sufficient cause. George's professor would not share this assumption; most people do not believe that they are responsible for guaranteeing the success of others.

When George admitted to himself that he was the cause of his own failure, he operated on the assumption that we are all responsible for most of what happens to us. He realized that he should have been able to overcome his poor background and all the other conditions against him. In the end George agrees with his professor on the dominant cause in this case. A fatalist, looking down on the whole situation, unconcerned with assigning responsibility or finding alterable causes, might call it all un-changeable bad luck.

CONCLUSIONS FROM GEORGE'S CASE: THE TWO THINGS CAUSAL ARGUMENT CAN DO

We have presented both an elaborate accounting of the causes behind George's failure and George's own attempts to single out dominant causes for different audiences. These once again illustrate two major purposes of causal argument.

First, you may simply be interested in explaining as many as possible of the causes behind an effect. You want to identify the proximate and remote causes, the conditions, every responsible agent, the role of chance, and any plausible blocking causes that were not there. Anyone interested in completeness might make a case study of George's failure and produce a list similar to the one we did above.

You may think that a full accounting of causes behind an event is a piece of informative rather than argumentative writing. Not so. Although argu-ing that many causes produce an effect is less challenging than arguing that only one or two did, you may still have to convince your reader that the causes you name are plausible and that a different version of the events is not plausible. And to have to convince is to argue. Let's return to George to explain this point. Suppose you have come to condition number 5, his poor high-school background. You may be able to assume the connection between a poor high-school background and trouble with a college chemistry course, but you must give some concrete evidence that his background was indeed poor—for example, the fact that his high-school course used a fourteen-year-old textbook. Furthermore, a causal explanation is still an argument because you exclude some causes too remote or too obvious to mention, like George's childhood or the pressures that overload the chemistry department with majors who must be weeded out. So a full causal explanation is still an argument, although an easy one with most audiences.

The second purpose of causal argument is to emphasize one cause from among many. This emphasizing can be done either to assign responsibility or to intervene in the causal process. If the first, your purpose is similar to that of a judge in a courtroom who simply wants to know if any party is responsible under the law. If the second, the cause you single out depends on how you want to intervene in the causal process. If you want to prevent, then you look for a missing blocking cause to replace, or a necessary cause to remove. If you want to foster, then you look for causes or influences that can be created or initiated or charged up to increase the effect.

FOR YOU TO ANALYZE

The following passages show their writers' attempts at causal model building, that is, at explaining the proper relationship among causes. Identify the various kinds of causes, using the labels introduced in this chapter.

All specific advice concerning how to read, how to take notes, how to tackle problems, how to form good study habits, is secondary. There is one fundamental and indispensable requirement for effective study more basic than any rules or technique. Without it real study is impossible though everything else be favorable; with it results can be achieved even in ignorance of all the fine points of how to study. This key requirement is a *driving motive*, an intense desire to learn and to achieve, an interest in things intellectual, a "will to do" in your scholastic work. If you would learn to study, first develop a feeling that you *want* to master your studies and that you *will* master them. All else is subordinate to that.

—Arthur W. Kornhauser,
How to Study

Schizophrenia probably has its roots in a biochemical abnormality within the body. While there are those who dispute this view, the evidence at this point appears highly persuasive and comes primarily from two sources. First, a large body of research data indicates that schizophrenia has a genetic component. That is to say, the tendency to manifest schizophrenic symptoms under stress is, in large part, genetically based. While it has been known for many years that schizophrenia tends to run in families (and, indeed, this knowledge has been causal in the suspicion that faulty family rearing practices cause schizophrenia), it is only recently that adoption studies and twin studies have helped to tease apart the genetic and environmental contributions to the illness. While the genetic contribution is clear, nongenetic factors have also been implicated by these same studies. Nonetheless, insofar as genes provide us with our basic physical equipment, a genetic predisposition toward schizophrenia means that some part of the body is malfunctioning or likely to malfunction under a certain set of circumstances. Analogies with other medical diseases are common. Both diabetes and hypertension run in families. They are not *solely* genetically determined. Rather, what is inherited is a *predisposition* to become ill in this way, given the right set of factors.

The other major source of evidence for a biological predisposition to schizophrenia comes from a recent treatment innovation. In 1955, clinicians in the United States began using chlorpromazine (Thorazine) to treat schizophrenia. The results were overwhelmingly positive. Many patients who had been withdrawn became communicative; many patients who had been assaultive became calm; many patients who had lost touch with reality regained it. Both recent clinical experience and controlled scientific studies have confirmed the initial impression that the symptoms of schizophrenia are markedly and lastingly reduced in many patients through the use of chlorpromazine and other related drugs. . . .

> —Richard R. D. Lewine and
> Kayla F. Bernheim,
> *Schizophrenia*

JETLINER CREW BLAMED FOR SAN DIEGO CRASH

Mark Stevens

The National Transportation Safety Board (NTSB) pinned responsibility April 20 for the nation's worst air disaster on the crew of the Pacific Southwest Airlines (PSA) jetliner that crashed last Sept. 25, but exhibits within the testimony gathered by the NTSB—and made available to the Monitor—strongly suggest that Federal Aviation Administration (FAA) directives regarding "visual separation" procedures at San Diego's Lindbergh Field would also lead the NTSB to attach blame to the air-traffic controllers.

At the heart of the matter are FAA regulations which require pilots to "see and avoid" other aircraft when landing under Visual Flight Rules (VFR) as the PSA 727 was doing when it collided with a small Cessna, killing 137 persons on both planes and 7 persons on the ground.

But one of the nation's leading air traffic safety experts, Dr. Maurice A.

Garbell, believes that the current system of air traffic control is unworkable because it mandates that a pilot *see* other aircraft when the best a pilot can do is *look*.

By a 3 to 1 vote, the NTSB said it was the responsibility of the flight crew to keep the planes separated by visual means from other aircraft and that the crew failed to "inform the controller when they no longer had other aircraft in sight."

The board also cited the lack of any FAA rules which require controllers to notify aircraft every time they appear on a radar screen to be on a potential collision course with another plane.

On its approach to Lindbergh Field, the PSA jet was under visual flight rules. Cockpit tapes show that the crew had been advised that a small plane was in the vicinity but that the crew lost sight of the smaller plane—if they ever saw it—and was still looking when the two craft crashed.

The safety board said that the air traffic controllers also were misled by their previous experiences with similar problems in the past that had required no action on their part.

The FAA directives—exhibits 3M and 3H in the NTSB evidence—clarify the procedures which air traffic controllers are supposed to follow in avoiding midair collisions in San Diego. They show that air traffic controllers at Lindbergh Field and at nearby Miramar Station are required to ensure visual separation for aircraft making practice approaches at the field. The Cessna carried a student pilot and his instructor who were in the process of a training flight.

The Cessna was in radio contact with Miramar Station. The PSA jet, while in contact with Miramar during the approach to San Diego, had switched its ground communication to Lindbergh tower just prior to the collision.

A letter of agreement between Miramar and Lindbergh says that "the tower shall insure visual separation between all aircraft executing VFR practice approaches." In clarifying that letter, the FAA said May 13, 1976, that "it is the intention of this statement that this visual separation will only be provided by the tower controller, i.e., he sees the aircraft involved and assures that the separation will remain constant or increase."

In at least two other memos issued after that, including one just eight days before the crash, the FAA reiterated the same procedures to controllers at Miramar and Lindbergh.

While the exact circumstances of the crash were not explicitly addressed in the FAA orders, Dr. Garbell says that "I feel the concept of visual tower control is necessary—even for VFR aircraft in these conditions—and it is so clearly spelled out that it should be binding on the tower."

Lengthy debate over the cause of the crash preceded the final vote, but in the end only board member Francis H. McAdams said he felt the accident should be blamed equally on the PSA flight crew and the air traffic control system.

The FAA investigation into the crash led the agency last December to begin upgrading the radar capability at 124 airports around the country, including Lindbergh Field.

SAMPLE ANALYSIS

In the case of major airplane accidents, our government requires that an appropriate federal agency investigate, sort out the relation of the various causes, and finally determine the predominant cause. Since human beings both acting and not acting—as well as machines, weather, and chance—are usually involved in such accidents, the issue of responsibility, and of blame given the disastrous outcome, often comes in.

The newspaper article reprinted here reports on the causal decision of the National Transportation Safety Board in the case of a crash between a jetliner and a small private plane at the San Diego airport. The plane was landing, at the crew's request, under visual control. According to the regulations for such a landing, the crew was required to avoid any aircraft that it saw. Unfortunately it could not see the small plane rising beneath it; the two collided. Since the accident occurred while the crew was fully in control of landing the plane, and no mechanical failures occurred, they are held responsible for the crash as the first sentence says. This was the legal decision of the NTSB. Much is at stake in such decisions by investigative agencies. Their nominations for chief cause and responsibility may make or break later court cases.

One member of the NTSB, however, would have named the entire air traffic control system at fault as well as the crew in one ill-fated plane flying under its procedures. As safety expert Dr. Garbell points out as well, the crew can only look for other planes; they cannot avoid one they cannot see. Any landing procedures that do not take this possibility into account are faulty, and, therefore, perhaps this background condition should be seen as the major cause of the accident.

The article also strongly suggests that the air traffic controllers at Lindbergh Field were also to "blame," or that, in other words, their deeds and omissions might be seen as the most important cause. By chance the planes were in radio contact with different ground controllers at the time of the crash. But an FAA directive had clearly established the tower at Lindbergh Field over the station at Miramar as the responsible agent for maintaining visual separation between planes in the area. Although the exact circumstances of this crash were not outlined in the directive, the tower controllers were under an obligation to ensure separation between the planes. But how far did they have to go to fulfill this obligation? They did inform the crew of the jetliner that a small plane was in their vicinity. Therefore, technically they had fulfilled their responsibility. The crew, in turn, failed to report when they no longer had this aircraft in sight, if they ever did have it in sight, and so the responsibility, and status as prime cause of the crash, falls once again on the dead.

The reader may possibly have heard of a peculiar theory of the emotions, commonly referred to in psychological literature as the Lange-James theory.

According to this theory, our emotions are mainly due to those organic stirrings that are aroused in us in a reflex way by the stimulus of the exciting object or situation. An emotion of fear, for example, or surprise, is not a direct effect of the object's presence on the mind, but an effect of that still earlier effect, the bodily commotion which the object suddenly excites; so that, were this bodily commotion suppressed, we should not so much *feel* fear as call the situation fearful; we should not feel surprise, but coldly recognize that the object was indeed astonishing. One enthusiast has even gone so far as to say that when we feel sorry it is because we weep, when we feel afraid it is because we run away, and not conversely. Some of you may perhaps be acquainted with the paradoxical formula. Now, whatever exaggeration may possibly lurk in this account of our emotions (and I doubt myself whether the exaggeration be very great), it is certain that the main core of it is true, and that the mere giving way to tears, for example, or to the outward expression of an anger-fit, will result for the moment in making the inner grief or anger more acutely felt. There is, accordingly, no better known or more generally useful precept in the moral training of youth, or in one's personal self-discipline, than that which bids us pay primary attention to what we do and express, and not to care too much for what we feel. If we only check a cowardly impulse in time, for example, or if we only *don't* strike the blow or rip out with the complaining or insulting word that we shall regret as long as we live, our feelings themselves will presently be the calmer and better, with no particular guidance from us on their own account. Action seems to follow feeling, but really action and feeling go together; and by regulating the action, which is under the more direct control of the will, we can indirectly regulate the feeling, which is not.

Thus the sovereign voluntary path to cheerfulness, if our spontaneous cheerfulness be lost, is to sit up cheerfully, to look round cheerfully, and to act and speak as if cheerfulness were already there. If such conduct does not make you soon feel cheerful, nothing else on that occasion can. So to feel brave, act as if we *were* brave, use all our will to that end, and a courage-fit will very likely replace the fit of fear. Again, in order to feel kindly toward a person to whom we have been inimical, the only way is more or less deliberately to smile, to make sympathetic inquiries, and to force ourselves to say genial things. One hearty laugh together will bring enemies into a closer communion of heart than hours spent on both sides in inward wrestling with the mental demon of uncharitable feeling. To wrestle with a bad feeling only pins our attention on it, and keeps it still fastened in the mind: whereas, if we act as if from some better feeling, the old bad feeling soon folds its tent like an Arab and silently steals away.

—William James, "The Gospel of
Relaxation," *Talks to Teachers on Psychology:
and to Students on Some of Life's Ideals*

FOR YOU TO WRITE

A. Consider each of the following situations or trends and, using the sets of causes outlined in this chapter, think of as many plausible causes for them as you can.

1. College freshmen tend to gain weight.
2. Attendance at major-league baseball games has increased.
3. Symphony conductors tend to live a long time.
4. Enrollments in colleges of engineering have increased.
5. The unemployment rate has decreased.
6. Coffee consumption has declined in the United States.
7. The average temperature has increased worldwide.
8. Soccer has become a much less popular sport.
9. Fewer women wear pants in public.
10. Interest in the liberal arts is increasing.

B. You have just performed the first step in brainstorming a causal argument. Now you can investigate to find out which of the causes you have hypothesized really operated significantly.

C. Write up a causal argument that emphasizes either a full accounting or one dominant cause. You might find that one paper can combine these two assignments.

D. Which cause you choose to emphasize out of a complete set of causes depends on your audience and purpose. Here are some events and several different audiences who would require different causal arguments. How would your arguments differ for each audience? Choose the harder-to-convince audience and write up your argument.

1. The decision to attend your current college.
   a. To a friend who chose a different college.
   b. To your parents.
2. The decision to turn down a date.
   a. To the person you refused.
   b. To a close friend.
3. Your A in a course.
   a. To yourself.
   b. To a friend who didn't do as well.
4. The causes of the women's movement.
   a. To a man.
   b. To a woman.
5. One candidate's victory in any presidential election.
   a. To a Republican.
   b. To a Democrat.

10 | The Tactics of Causal Argument

Now that you know the kinds of causes and the general purposes of causal argument, you are ready for the next question. How can you actually convince an audience in writing that a cause and effect are linked? It is one thing to name a possible cause, quite another to convince an audience that it operates. Fortunately, convincing an audience is easier than you might think because both arguer and audience will share a storehouse of assumptions about what causes what. You draw on that storehouse in causal argument, just as you appeal to shared definitions in arguments about the nature of things. If, for example, you argue for the characterization that "Benedict Arnold was really a patriot," you must try to evoke a sharable definition of *patriot.* Similarly, if you argue for the causal claim that "Benedict Arnold's treason caused others to abandon the American side in the Revolution," you are appealing to a sharable assumption, namely, that one person's action can influence others.

AGENCY: OUR BASIC ASSUMPTION ABOUT WHAT CAUSES WHAT

What convinces us that one thing causes another? Suppose we see a two-year-old child fly forward on a swing, the mother pushing from behind.

This is a capsule case of cause and effect, for we know that the mother's push causes the child's motion on the swing. When we can see the actual push and the forward motion that follows it, we have the most satisfying kind of evidence of a causal connection between two actions, in this case the push and the swing.

We need a word to stand for this most basic connection between a cause and an effect. Let us use the word *agency* for this "touching" of cause and effect, this link between them. In a sense, agency is the smallest unit of cause. The simplest kind of agency is literal physical contact: the mother's hand *touches* the child's back; lightning *strikes* a dry tree to ignite it; a car *bumps* into a store window and shatters it.

We intuitively understand such physical agencies of force, motion, resistance, and reaction. (And, of course, there are many other chemical and physical agencies in nature, such as light, heat, motion, and chemical reagents.) Even if we are not scientists, we have a common-sense understanding of how things work in the natural world. We know that plants need water and sunlight to grow, although they can get too much of either. We know that we cannot fry an egg without heat, that if we eat too much we get fat, that cars need fuel.

But what agencies operate in individual lives, in social and historical events? In any society, at any time, there are quite a number of accepted agencies whose operation we believe in as readily as we believe in the operation of physical law. Philosophers, psychologists, anthropologists, and social scientists debate about what to call these agencies—motives, instincts, or learned patterns of behavior. But we all recognize a believable appeal to the way human nature works, in the same way we recognize how physical nature works. We no more accept happiness as a motive for murder than we would accept the power of rocks to fly.

What are some of these accepted agencies of human behavior? We believe that people do things to *imitate* one another, and that they also do things *to be different from one another.* We believe that people usually act *to maximize their own good* (as they see the good) *with the least amount of effort.* We also believe that people act *to avoid pain.* But since this text is not the place for an analysis of human motivation, let us just say that certain fundamental motives, causes, or agencies of human action are widely accepted. And these same agencies that move individuals also move groups, communities, and even nations. They too imitate, rebel, seek their benefit, and minimize pain and expense.

We will be able to understand the concept of agency better if we look at some human cause-and-effect relationships and identify the assumed agency in each. If we say that watching violent programs on television causes violent behavior in children, the assumed agency is imitation. If we say that living in a tract development caused Bertha to paint her house pink, the assumed agency is the desire to be different. If we say that the citizens of a community voted to increase taxes because they want to build a new school, the assumed agency is the desire to maximize their own good. If a nation builds a system of dams to prevent floods, the assumed agency is the desire to avoid disaster. Of course, less obvious agencies may also be operating; whether we argue about them depends on how much we want to elaborate on the springs of human action.

Often when we connect a cause and an effect in argument, as in the cases above, we do not even mention the agency between them. We *assume* it. Fortunately, people in the same culture share more or less the same assumptions about causal agency, about what causes what. So we are usually able to claim that one thing causes another without going into elaborate explanations. We develop our argument to the point where we and our audience share assumptions about agency. We want the readers to nod and say to themselves, "Yes, I believe that could cause that."

With agency in mind, we can distinguish between causal arguments that assume agency and those that do not, those that get the reader's nod easily and those that do not. Let us first look at a causal argument where agency is obvious enough to be assumed.

Suppose you want to argue that juvenile pot smoking in a particular community is in part caused by parents' drug and alcohol dependence. Depending on your audience, you could spend much of your time in this argument presenting evidence of the large number of children who smoke pot and of the large number of their parents who smoke pot, take Valium, and drink excessively. In short, your effort would go only into proving the simultaneous existence of the two events you call the cause and the effect. In this case, you bring the cause and the effect into juxtaposition and stop because your audience will most likely assume the agency between them. The agency between the parents and the children is imitation; you could mention it to be emphatic, but you probably would not need to.

Now let us look at an example where agency cannot so easily be assumed. Two types of arguments fall into this category. First, there are implausible agencies. Any argument that depends on an implausible agency is likely to arouse the resistance and incredulity of its audience. If a woman claims, for example, that her presence in a room causes spoons to bend, books to levitate, and lamps to shatter, she is assuming an unbelievable agency. Most of us do not accept telekinesis as an agency connecting the human mind and physical movement. There are many other such agencies currently unacceptable to educated audiences: copper bracelets that cure arthritis; the Bermuda Triangle, which makes ships and planes disappear; vision into the future by dreams, astrology, or biorhythms. With an audience of unbelievers to assume that any of these is a causal agent would be the death of argument. With such an audience an arguer who seriously wants to claim that one of these mysterious forces caused something must move the argument to a different level. He must argue for agency itself, and establishing a new agency requires a major intellectual effort.

The other kind of argument where agency cannot simply be assumed involves a distant cause. That is, the cause and the effect are so far apart that we cannot see immediately the agency between them. If we claim that a childhood disease is the cause of a heart attack at age sixty-five, that an army's need for spurs gave rise to feudalism, that greased cartridges led to the Indian Mutiny of 1857, we are likely to lose our audience because assumable agency, the link between cause and effect, is missing. In these cases we can supply agency by establishing a *chain of causes*. (See below for a fuller discussion.)

You can now see the crucial importance of *agency* in causal argument. In fact, the essence of causal argument is getting down to assumable agency that your audience will accept. If you have assumable or acceptable agency, you spend all your time in causal argument showing that cause and effect exist and lining them up by any of the methods that follow. If you do not have agency, you have to establish it. If you cannot establish it, you have no causal argument.

EXERCISE

Describe the agencies that would plausibly operate between the following pairs of causes and their effects. Are any of the linkages implausible because no assumption of agency is possible?

1. Parental strictness causes teenage rebelliousness.
2. One seventh-grade girl gets her ears pierced; two weeks later, fifteen other seventh grade girls get their ears pierced.
3. An old woman looks at a cow; the cow stops giving milk.
4. The salesman was physically out of shape, so he failed in his career.
5. France refused to boycott the Olympics, so the Russians held a special summit meeting with the French.

TACTICS FOR SUPPORTING A CAUSAL RELATIONSHIP

Mill's Four Methods

The English philosopher John Stuart Mill gave us a detailed explanation of how to carry on a causal investigation. He was concerned with identifying potential causes and making the connection between cause and effect as certain as possible. In the laboratory, once a potential cause-and-effect relationship is identified, it can usually be tested and established with certainty. That one thing causes another becomes a fact. However, in most ordinary causal investigations, outside the controlled conditions of a laboratory, certainty is an unreachable goal. We settle for probability. That one thing causes another becomes a matter of argument, not proof, because most human actions cannot be repeated in a laboratory.

Nevertheless, in supporting a causal argument, we use versions of Mill's basic tactics in two ways. First, they help us find or single out a dominant cause; they are especially useful when we have a number of sufficient causes to choose from and need something to convince us that a particular one was working. Second, the same tactic that helped us select a dominant cause can also be used to convince a reader. In other words, if one of Mill's tactics convinced us, it will also convince our audience.

The Common-Factor Method (Mill's Method of Agreement)

The common-factor method works only when the effect we are interested in occurs more than once. People catch the same disease, nations invade one another, and some people have difficulty waking up every Monday morning. Investigators looking into the causes of any events like these first assume that the cause(s) came before the effect in time. They look at the events that came before the effects to see if they have anything in common. Assuming agency, the simplest unit of cause, they reason that the common factor is likely to be the cause.

Here is a fuller example of how the common-factor method works. A literary historian interested in how some prolific novelists accomplished so much looks for anything alike in their very different lives. She may find that many of them (Charles Dickens, Anthony Trollope, George Eliot, Edith Wharton, Henry James) set aside a time in the morning, even if only a few hours, for uninterrupted writing. She can then reasonably infer that this common factor, regular morning work habits, was the cause of their productivity, rather than some other possible cause such as intermittent inspiration. When she writes up her argument, she can assume that readers will accept the agency linking regular work habits and great productivity.

A search for the cause of food poisoning is a frequently cited example of the common-factor method. If six people come down with the symptoms of botulism, health officials will obtain a list of what the victims ate in the past twenty-four hours and check for things in common. They will eliminate the salad or coffee that all six had because they know that *Clostridium botulinum* grows only in an anaerobic (airless) environment. But when they find that all six ate the canned vichyssoise at the local diner, they can be certain that they have found the cause. Health officials looking for the source of botulism have an easy time because they know exactly what they are looking for; botulism has only one necessary and sufficient cause.

But in the famous case of the so-called legionnaire's disease that struck 182 conventioners at a Philadelphia hotel in 1976, some time went by before a possible cause was located. Investigators did not know at first what they were looking for; they had not identified the agency. They tried every possible common factor—food, water, air, location of rooms, even whether all the victims passed through the same lobby.

Notice the difference between the food poisoning example and the one about the novelists. The health officials' knowledge of the cause of botulism simplified the investigation and led to a certain conclusion, but in the example about the novelists, the conclusion is only probable. Though we know the necessary cause of botulism, no one has yet identified a necessary and sufficient cause of productivity (one in whose presence productivity must follow).

Remember that frequently your purpose in causal argument is to persuade your audience that a dominant cause indeed produced the effect. If you discovered this cause by the common-factor method, you can simply relate that process. Write it out in your argument; it may read like a detective story. The health officials will explain in the local press how they tracked down botulism to the vichyssoise. The literary historian will describe the working habits of each individual novelist and point out the common pattern and the common result: how Trollope had a servant wake him each morning with a cup of coffee at 5:00 A.M.; how Dickens went every morning to a little house built for him to write in, complete with a mirror to make faces in; how Edith Wharton wrote on a lapboard in bed. Since such an argument is not scientific, the literary historian may have to refute or concede other possible sufficient causes of prolific writing such as vital energy or a need for money. The need for money could be refuted by pointing out that it is not really a common factor, since at least one of the novelists (Edith Wharton) had plenty of money, or the literary historian may concede that all the novelists had extraordinary vital energy, and that is exactly what caused them to get up early and write every morning. Thus, vital energy is a cause of regular work habits and a remote cause of prolific output. All the novelists may have had brown hair too, but it is not easy to imagine any agency between hair color and creativity.

EXERCISE

This exercise will show you how the common-factor method is both a tool of causal investigation and a convincing technique in causal argument.

Here are some situations that lend themselves to the common-factor method of analysis; after you have identified a dominant cause, write up your argument by explaining how you did it.

Begin by identifying a group of at least five incidents or five people who have some effect or condition in common: people who scored the highest on a recent test; people who have chosen the same major, especially an unusual one; people with unusual diets, hobbies, exercise routines; the accidents that have occurred in one location; the best-selling hardbacks or paperbacks or record albums for a single year.

Now look for a common factor shared by all the members of the group. You might even come up with several factors, but some will have to be rejected as implausible or insignificant. Don't be dismayed if all the members of your set do not share one common factor. You may simply be dealing with an effect that has several sufficient causes. But at least you will have identified one of them.

The Single-Difference Method (Mill's Method of Difference)

The single-difference method works only when there are *at least two* similar situations, one leading to an effect and the other not. One seed grows, another doesn't; one president's term is peaceful, another's is full of conflict; one sponge cake rises, another flops. You look for the possible cause that was missing in one case and present in the other—the single difference. You assume that if everything else is substantially alike in both cases, the single difference must be the cause—the sandy soil that one seed was planted in, the international inflation that faced one president, the thundering herd that passed through the kitchen of the flopped cake.

Here is how the single-difference method works in an extended example. Two students in a course have a B+ average on the exams, but one gets an A and the other a B as a final grade. Both students attended class regularly, both sat in the second row, both were attentive in class; but the one who got the A participated in class discussion, while the other did not. If you know that this participation was the single difference between their performances, you can reasonably conclude that it caused the difference between their grades.

If you argue for a cause discovered by the single-difference method, you must first persuade your audience that the two cases being considered are substantially alike. Convincing an audience of such a comparison is sometimes difficult, for rarely in human events are two situations *exactly* alike. You can, however, establish likeness in two ways: List all the important things the two cases have in common, or show how any differences other than the one you are interested in are insignificant or trivial. For instance, if the student who got the B missed one more class than the one who got the A, you may have to argue that such a difference was insignificant in determining their grades.

If you are arguing a case like the one above, you must be especially careful not to overlook any other possibly significant difference. If someone else were to point one out, your argument would be weakened. So you have to anticipate any plausible rival difference and refute it. For example, someone may point out that the student who got the A was a man and the one who got the B a woman. That may be a significant difference. How would you argue that it wasn't?

EXERCISE

This time you will have to find pairs of similar situations, one in which an effect occurs and the other in which it doesn't: two tests in the same subject, one that you do well on, the other less well; two dates with the same person, one a success, the other a failure; two attempts to do something (pole-vault, get elected), one successful, one a failure; two very similar international crises, one resolved peacefully, the other not; two lab experiments, one that yields a result, the other not.

Try to find the single difference between these two situations. That single difference may be the cause of the effect occurring in one case and not in the other. Remember that when you nominate a single difference as a cause, other factors must be alike in both cases. You have to convince your reader of similarities or argue that apparent dissimilarities are unimportant.

The Method of Varying Causes and Effects (Mill's Method of Concomitant Variation)

The concomitant-variation method can be used only when an effect persists and varies. Sunspots come and go, SAT scores rise and decline, the cost of living rises, the stock market lurches. Faced with fluctuations and trends, you look among the possible causes to find at least one that persists and varies in a similar way. In doing so, you assume that the correlation between the cause you are supporting and the effect is evidence of their connection. But you can make this assumption only when the agency is plausible.

Both cause and effect may increase together, decrease together, or one may increase while the other decreases. They may even jolt up and down together in absolute harmony. Sunspots may increase when electromagnetic activity on the sun increases; SAT scores may decline while the number of students enrolled in advanced high-school English and math courses declines; and the standard of living may rise when family size decreases. In each of these cases, an assumption about agency is as necessary to your argument as the rising and falling patterns of cause and effect. That is, your audience must see the plausible connection between the two. It is easy, for example, to see the agency between declining SAT scores and declining enrollments in advanced math and English. If students are not learning skills, they will not do well on tests of verbal and mathematical ability.

Let us look at a more complicated case where concomitant variation is the key to causal argument. The library in Centreville keeps careful records of the number of books taken out per year. The librarians noticed that over a period of ten years, from 1950 to 1960, the number of books taken out decreased from 30,000 in 1950 to 15,000 in 1960, despite a population increase of 10 percent in the town. Casting around for an explanation, the librarians discovered that the number of TV sets in the community increased dramatically during this ten-year span. The agency between TV sets in the home and library books still in the library is obvious. And in this case, the relationship between cause and effect is inverse: As one went up, the other went down.

Between 1974 and 1976 the librarians were pleased to notice a sudden upsurge in the number of books taken out. This time there was no single obvious explanation, so they noted a number of trends that might have contributed to the increase: the sudden increase in the price of oil, a big rise in community enrollment in night-school courses, a steep rise in the rate of inflation, an increase in the number of fast-food chains, and an increase in the number of senior citizens living in the area. None of these is an obvious cause of increased book circulation without further explanation.

Let us compare how difficult it would be to convince an audience of causes for the decline or the increase in library use in these two instances. Persuading an audience that it was an increase in the number of TV sets that led to a decrease in the number of library books taken out would not be very difficult. You could simply present statistics of increase and decrease; as we said, the agency between them is obvious: Most people cannot read and watch TV at the same time. You could, of course, make your argument more interesting by giving a detailed, specific example of one family whose evening reading had been replaced by TV watching.

But making a causal argument out of the relationship between book circulation and any of the other simultaneous trends between 1974 and 1976 might be more difficult. There is no obvious connection between an increase in the price of oil and an increase in book circulation. If you suspect they are causally related and want to convince yourself and others, you must construct a chain of causes to connect them. Your argument might go something like this: An increase in the price of oil leads to an increase in the price of gasoline. An increase in the price of gasoline leads to fewer nonessential car trips, so people find themselves at home with more time on their hands. To fill that time, they may turn to their local library instead of simply turning on the television set.

Arguing a causal connection on the basis of concomitant variation can depend in part on forestalling some obvious objections. First, even though trends vary in the same way, they may be unrelated. For example, the increase in the number of fast-food chains and the increased book circulation probably have nothing to do with one another.

Second, both the supposed cause-and-effect trends may really be the effects of yet another cause. For example, increased book circulation and an increased number of senior citizens may both be the result of an overall increase in the population. Third, the trends may be the cause and effect of each other—remember reciprocal causality. For example, a rise in continuing-education enrollment could lead to more books being taken out, which in turn could lead to more continuing-education enrollment. It takes skillful arguing to maneuver around all these pitfalls and place causes in their proper relation to one another.

EXERCISE

Think of some trend that has been either increasing or decreasing over a period of time: vandalism in your town; drug use in your former high school; enrollments in certain kinds of courses (for example, business, classical languages, forestry); summer unemployment among young people in your area; increase in the number of special-interest magazines; female crime in the United States.

Among plausible causes of these trends, try to find one that has increased or decreased in a similar way. Remember that in your argument you will probably have to support the existence of both trends with the techniques learned in Part I. And be careful that the two trends you line up are not better seen as effects of yet another trend or cause.

The Elimination Method (Mill's Method of Residues)

Like Mill's three other methods, the process of elimination is both a method of arguing about causes and a method of writing about causes. As a method of investigation, scientists use elimination in controlled experiments, doctors use it in diagnosis, Sherlock Holmes used it to find criminals, and common sense makes it available to everyone. If your car stalls in traffic, you systematically eliminate all possible causes, beginning with the most likely, until you find the cause—gas, water, battery, oil. Obviously, the elimination method works only when an effect can be produced by several possible sufficient causes. We assume that since only one cause was needed to bring the effect about, only one cause operated. (This assumption is a potential weak spot in this method.) In the process-of-elimination method, then, we argue for one dominant cause, not by proving it happened, but by proving that the other possibilities did not.

The success of convincing an audience by this method in argument depends on how complete the initial set of possible causes is and how validly the other members of this set are eliminated. For example, in the story "The Adventure of the Speckled Band," Sherlock Holmes considered all the possible means of entering and leaving a bedroom. The room was sparsely furnished, so no one could hide in it. The door was locked from the inside, so no one could either enter it from the outside or, once inside, leave it without a sign. The window was shuttered from within, and no one could open it from without. After Holmes eliminated these obvious possibilities, he concluded that the only remaining way of getting into the room was through the very small ventilator above the bed, "So small that a rat could hardly pass through." Thus, by the process of elimination, Holmes concluded that he was not dealing with a human intruder. (If you want to know whodunit, read the story.)

Such Holmesian thoroughness is possible only when the set of causes is limited, as it is by the physical facts of a room. More often, we use the process-of-elimination method loosely. That is, we argue by simply eliminating the most *obvious* possible causes—other than the one we are interested in, of course. Setting up and then eliminating the *entire* set of possible causes is not always necessary. Since we are not often involved in matters as crucial as identifying murderers, it is usually enough to dispose of only the most likely of other possibilities, especially those that the audience of the argument might anticipate.

For example, you may want to persuade your audience that media favoritism was the cause of one candidate's victory in a Senate race. One tactic you could use to support this case would be to eliminate obvious rival causes. One such rival cause might be the candidate's support for a tax cut, a position that certainly attracts votes. But if the other candidate supported the same tax cut, you could certainly eliminate this cause of your candidate's victory. You could go on to eliminate other possible causes such as the candidate's attractive spouse, family's wealth, and dedicated staff. You may decide not to bother with some of them, but *only* if you think them insignificant and *only* if your audience is likely to ignore them too. You must always remember that you risk easy refutation if you leave out anything likely to occur to your audience.

EXERCISE

List at least four possible causes of the following effects. Try to show that three of them could not have operated.

1. The increase of foreign tourism in the United States and the Soviet Union in the 1980s.
2. Deterioration of the coral reefs off the Florida keys.
3. One student's dropping out of high school.
4. The decline of polygamy among Mormons.
5. The decline of travel abroad from 1985 to 1986.

Mill's Methods and Agency

Mill's methods will convince an audience whenever agency can be assumed. But what do you do when agency cannot be assumed? Say you have some evidence that two things are causally connected. Your evidence comes from one of Mill's methods in the first place—you have identified a single difference, a common factor, a concomitant variation, or have eliminated everything else. But there is no obvious connection, no agency between the cause you have identified and the effect.

If you are left with a gap between cause and effect, you have to do some imaginative model building to close it. Two rules govern this imaginative model building: (1) The agency you invent must be in line with accepted causal laws; that means no magic. (2) You should apply the centuries-old wisdom of Occam's razor, or the Principle of Parsimony. Occam's razor advises looking for the simplest agency that explains the effect, rather than an elaborate Rube Goldberg contraption with fourteen interlocking steps between cause and effect.

OTHER RHETORICALLY EFFECTIVE METHODS

Mill's methods are rhetorically effective but complex. In newspaper editorials, magazine articles, speeches at meetings, and so on, we often use simpler, almost shorthand methods to support causality. Instead of telling a long story, we may combine several of the techniques listed below to indicate a likely causal connection. These methods may not be as rigorous as Mill's, but they can be convincing when agency is assumable. They are better as methods of *presenting* causes than of finding them in the first place.

Chain of Causes

Often you may want to link two events whose connection as cause and effect will not be obvious to your audience. The cause might be incongruous or remote. For example, it has been argued that the deforestation of England in the sixteenth century led to the industrial revolution, that not learning to crawl leads to reading problems, and that the rising divorce rate leads to a boom in the kitchen appliance industry. We are likely to respond to any of these statements with "Huh?" When an audience is likely to find a causal connection implausible, a chain argument is often called for.

A chain-of-causes argument is a persuasive way to support an improbable or remote causal link. Such a chain divides the big leap between cause and effect into a series of little steps, making it easier for you and your audience to share assumptions about agency.

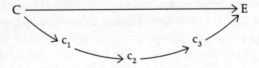

Here is an example of a chain-of-causes argument. NASA announced that sunspots caused Skylab to fall in its orbit. That sounds magical, but NASA persuaded the public by establishing a chain of cause-and-effect relationships between sunspots and Skylab's fall. Its argument went like this: Sunspots are a sign of magnetic storms on the sun. These storms hurl a stream of charged particles, called the solar wind, into space. The solar wind heats the thin gases in the earth's outer atmosphere, which then expand into Skylab's orbit. The expanded gases increase the drag on the craft, which then slows down and falls, as Skylab did.

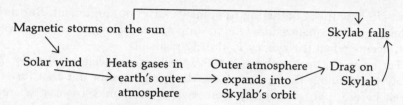

This chain of causes looks very persuasive. But, like any chain, it is only as strong as its weakest link. It works by appealing to an audience's assumptions about what are believable causal links.

EXERCISE

To get some practice in describing a chain of causes, try linking these remote causes with their effects by describing the intermediate steps between them. Notice that there may be several ways to get from one to the other.

1. A childhood interest → a career choice.
2. A misunderstanding → a broken friendship.
3. A political crisis → a war.
4. Shutdown of a major industry → the decline of a town.
5. Clear cutting of a forest → increase of deer population.

Time Precedence

We are often warned not to assume that one thing causes another just because it came before the other in time; to do so, we are told, is to commit what is called the *post hoc fallacy* (*post hoc ergo propter hoc,* after this, therefore because of this). The man who plugged in his electric broiler a split second before the East Coast blackout in 1965 may have felt a surge of fear and thought, "What did I do?" But although his act immediately preceded the effect, he was not responsible. Nevertheless, although there are many such examples of exact time sequence without causal connection, causes *do* precede or accompany their effects in time. Can you think of an exception?

This notion of cause first and then effect is our most primitive causal assumption. (Here is our one-way-street model again.) Lightning strikes the transformer and then the electricity goes out; the voyages of discovery took place in the fifteenth and sixteenth centuries and then the colonization of the New World began; the spoon falls in the garbage disposal unit and then the unit breaks. We usually assume this order of cause first and then effect without bothering to point it out in our argument. But mentioning a time sequence does tend to support a causal relationship between two events when the agency is already plausible.

For example, on October 19, 1987, stock prices declined sharply. An analyst explaining the causes of the drop might point out that just the week before, two economists from two major banks forecast a credit crunch. Making a causal connection between the experts' pronouncements and the decline in stock prices simply required presenting the two events in sequence. The writer could assume that an educated audience would understand the impact of experts' predictions on the world of finance. Thus, time precedence by itself is enough support only when we can assume agency very comfortably.

EXERCISE

Which of the following sets of events paired in time order seem plausible because agency can be assumed?

1. The secretary of the treasury predicts recession.
   The stock market declines.
2. The president announces he will seek reelection.
   The stock market declines.
3. A student takes a study skills course.
   The student's grades improve.
4. A student changes roommates.
   The student's grades improve.
5. A roller-skating rink opens.
   The orthopedist gets more patients.
6. A roller-skating rink opens.
   A bowling alley closes.
7. The prime interest rate goes up.
   The sale of houses declines.
8. The prime interest rate goes up.
   The export of steel declines.

Singling Out Examples

Causal propositions can be either generalizations—"TV violence causes violent behavior," or specific cases—"Because the defendant watched *Miami Vice,* he committed this crime." As you learned in the section on arguments about the nature of things, generalizations can be supported by examples. Thus, any causal statement that stands for a number of instances can be supported by describing one or more of those instances.

Here is an example of using examples. A social scientist may want to persuade us about the effectiveness of halfway houses for parolees as a cause of their successful reintegration into society. The argument will be persuasive if it describes some detailed case histories of former prisoners successfully rehabilitated in halfway houses. Of course, the case histories presented, no matter how inspiring and persuasive, may have little to do with the overall statistics of success versus failure. After all, we may be given as examples the only three successes the system produced and the eighty-seven failures may be ignored. Thus, this technique can falsify the facts of the case.

However, when this method is used legitimately, the examples are backed up either with overall statistics or, in the absence of exact evidence, with an assessment (as accurate as possible) of the relationship of the examples to the whole. The social scientist, arguing for a very specific thesis such as "The Barrabas Halfway House rehabilitates its residents" would have access to the kind of exact evidence we mean; he or she should have at least counted all the Barrabas alumni who stayed out of jail and all those who went back.

But what if exact evidence is impossible to attain? Suppose, for example, you are arguing for the proposition "Running frequently produces a sense of well-being." Your causal argument is ultimately based on the common factor method and time precedence: Running frequently is accompanied by a sensation of euphoria. Since you could never know how every runner feels, you have not worded your proposition to suggest all. But even though you cannot know all, you can know some. You might create a sample and compile statistics about it ("Of the ten runners I talked to, nine claimed to be suffused with well-being after running"). Or, you can simply give your few examples (yourself, your friend, and your brother) and leave it at that, letting the reader assume they are typical. Your reader could skeptically respond, "So that's ten. What about the other 25 million?" Examples of causal relationship also require the assumption of agency. What is it about running that actually produces euphoria?

EXERCISE

Here are a few common causal generalizations. Find two or more examples to support them.

1. Absence makes the heart grow fonder.
2. Lying hurts the liar.
3. High expectations create success.
4. Friendly parents increase the popularity of their children.
5. Idleness produces mischief.

Analogy

You use analogy when you establish one cause-and-effect relationship by comparing it with another. This other relationship, which is held up as a model, should be familiar and acceptable to your audience. If it is not, you must back up and clarify it.

Like the use of examples, analogy is a common technique in supporting a causal argument. FDA scientists, for example, used mice to test the cancer-causing effects of saccharin. When they found that large doses of saccharin produced cancer in mice, they announced that saccharin is dangerous to humans. The persuasive power of their argument depended on the acceptability of the analogy between human and rodent physiology, diet, and metabolism. Most people find such animal-human analogies convincing; many theories about human disease, learning, and behavior are based on animal experiments.

Analogies can be used to argue for the causes of events in the past and to predict events in the future. When we argue for the causes of a completed event, we can compare that event with another whose causes are better known. For example, the causes of the Athenians' difficulties in the Peloponnesian War can be compared with the causes of America's problems with guerrilla warfare in Vietnam. (We take up predictions in Chapter 11.)

EXERCISE

Below are some possible causal analogies. Choose one and make an extended argument for it, or argue for a similar analogy of your own.

1. Ecologists know that even a small disturbance in a delicately balanced ecosystem can lead to its destruction. Think of a neighborhood as a kind of ecosystem, and construct a causal argument based on that analogy.
2. Historians have argued that many wars (World War I and the Vietnam War especially) are the result of diplomatic blunders and an overriding will to go to war. Could you argue that similar causes could produce a marriage?

3. The well-known Peter Principle says that a worker will be promoted until he or she reaches his or her level of incompetence, and there he or she will stick. Can you use this principle in any other domain, such as the growth of institutions or students' choices of careers?

4. The second law of thermodynamics, the law of entropy, states that all systems tend to disorder unless energy is invested to maintain their stability. Use this law analogically to argue for a tendency you have observed in your own life or in the life of any group from community to nation.

5. A classic law of physics states that for every action there is an equal and opposite reaction. Could this law be used analogically to explain phases in history, the 1950s and the 1960s, the 1960s and the 1970s, the 1970s and the 1980s?

HOW CAUSAL ARGUMENTS CAN GO WRONG: COMMON DIFFICULTIES IN CAUSAL ARGUMENT

The most important characteristic of causal argument is plausible connection between cause and effect, that is, believable agency. Without it, no causal model building or application of Mill's or any other tactics will make a convincing causal argument. An argument that claimed, for example, that closing the university library at 10:00 P.M. caused depression among students could not get by without explaining agency, what comes between such an implausibly paired cause and effect. To refute such an argument you would ask, in effect, "What on earth is the link between closing libraries and student depression?"

Even when agency is plausible, a causal argument may require further support to show that a particular cause operated. It is one thing to be convinced that a cause *could* have operated, another to be convinced that it *did*. A critical audience needs to have cause and effect linked by the tactics described in this chapter. One of the most common faults in a causal argument is to underestimate the audience's need for this additional support. Though everyone knows cyanide can kill, that known agency is not enough to convince a jury that it did kill the body in question.

We have already pointed out the pitfalls of the various tactics used to establish or emphasize a particular causal connection. The common-factor method works only when there are no unrefutable rival factors; the single-difference method requires convincing an audience that any but the singled-out dissimilarity is insignificant; the problem with concomitant variation is that the supposed cause and effect may both be the effects of still another cause; and elimination arguments depend on the plausible completeness of the original set of possible causes. The other tactics, which are less rigorous to begin with, have their dangers as well: Time order may be coincidence, not cause; analogies may be more apparent than real; examples may be atypical; and chains may break at the weakest link.

We have said that causal arguments aim to depict the interaction of causes or to emphasize the power of a particular cause. The causal model of an argument may be inadequate for either of these purposes. A causal explanation can be too full, going farther and farther back, finding influences on causes and multiplying conditions, until the coherence of the whole is lost in a dissolving view. Or the single cause featured in an argument may be unable to bear the importance placed on it. Another way of oversimplifying is to ignore reciprocity, to miss a mental U-turn and fail to see the effects operating on their causes.

EXERCISES

Identify the techniques of causal investigation or argument used in the following examples.

Pistachio I Scream!

"My car won't start when I buy pistachio."

The manager of a Texas automobile dealership thought the woman who confronted him with this bizarre statement must be crazy. It seems that on hot summer days she would drive to a certain shop for ice cream to take home. It never failed, she said: the car would always start when she bought chocolate, vanilla or strawberry—but when she bought pistachio, she got stranded.

The manager had to see this to believe it. He tried a chocolate trip, and the car worked fine. Vanilla or strawberry—no problem. Then came the trip for pistachio and, sure enough, the engine refused to start.

It was an engineering troubleshooter whose insight solved the problem. He observed that chocolate, vanilla and strawberry were pre-packaged flavors, sold right out of the freezer. But take-home orders of pistachio were hand-packed at the shop. The time needed to have the pistachio packed was just enough for the car to develop vapor lock in the summertime Texas heat. The woman wasn't crazy after all—her car *wouldn't* start when she bought pistachio.

—Bulletin of the Greater New York
Automobile Dealers Assn., quoted in
News and Views

SAT SCORES—HOW TO STOP THE DROP

Jane Whitbread

Scholastic Aptitude Test (SAT) scores—a critical factor for college admissions—have slipped in the past 15 years. The decline, seen as a sign that American education is on the down-grade too, has been blamed on everything from marijuana use to divorce. Now the National Association of Secondary School Principals may have a simpler answer: *too many elective courses* and *too few required courses in English and math*—the skills SAT's are designed to test.

While SAT scores in most of the country's 20,000 high schools have dropped by more than 50 points in English and about 30 in math since 1963, in about 100 schools, scores have remained level or even gone up. Concluding that these schools might have something to teach the rest, the Principals' Association looked at 34 of them and compared them with similar schools whose scores had dropped the most. What stood out was the total dedication of the successful schools to giving the kids the best possible preparation for college:

- College-preparatory students *must* take at least two years of math and four years of English—literature, language (grammar, spelling, punctuation, vocabulary) and writing.
- Teachers stress good writing (clear, precise expression) in *all* courses.
- Qualified college counselors help students choose appropriate colleges and follow through so they take *the courses required for admission* before they take nonqualifying electives.
- Students, particularly in math and English, are grouped by ability. Thus, the faster may go farther, and the others can learn more effectively, free from pressure to rush.
- Teachers in success schools had an average of five more years' experience than those in low-scoring schools.
- Faculty efforts have the support of the entire school administration. Excellence in scholarship is valued as highly as skill in sports. "Our student body is as proud of the winning math team as they are of our champion athletic groups," says A. R. Cramer, principal of Newtown High School in Connecticut.

SAMPLE ANALYSIS

The effect that is the subject of causal investigation in this short article is not an event but a trend, the infamous fifteen-year decline in SAT scores. The opening paragraph makes passing reference to the large social conditions (such as marijuana use and the increasing divorce rate) that have been cited as causes of the drop. But among all the factors influencing such a complex phenomenon, this article focuses on a more immediate cause: the education that high-school students receive prior to taking the test. Such a cause can be changed, while the larger social conditions of the past fifteen years cannot. Not surprisingly, the people responsible for high-school education, the National Association of Secondary School Principals, sponsored the investigation.

Behind the investigation is the assumption that learning is a cause of test performance; this assumption is so obvious it need not be mentioned. Since education should make a difference, the principals want to know what kind of education does. The investigative technique employed is first of all the single-difference method. Among the nation's 20,000 high schools is a small set of 100 high schools in which scores have not declined. Thirty-four of these are compared with "similar schools" in which scores have declined. That simple word *similar* represents a crucial step in the method. The schools compared must be similar (even paired) in location, size, affluence of the school district, and so on. In other words, any other differences that might be causes of test performance must be cancelled out so that differences in education alone can emerge. The investigation is designed to yield the kind of cause the investigators are interested in, but this does not mean that the cause is any less real.

Once the single-difference method has produced the comparable schools, the common-factor method takes over. What do the successful schools have in common that could produce the kind of education that yields better test scores? Six common attributes were discovered: four years of required English and two of math, emphasis on clear writing in all courses, qualified college counselors, ability grouping, greater experience of the staffs, and administrative support.

Whether these common attributes can be seen as causes depends on whether we can construct plausible agencies between them and the effects. It is fairly easy to see how four years of solid instruction in English vocabulary, grammar, and writing would have a strong effect on results in the verbal component of the SAT, but what about the greater experience of the teaching staffs? Could their greater experience mean something about different teaching techniques? We might need a chain to connect this particular discovery of the common-factor method to its effect. And the last common factor, the administrative support and equal emphasis on academic as well as sports excellence, looks as though it may reflect a difference in the local community's values, values that in themselves may be a quite important cause of good SAT performance.

In New England, Canada and western Europe the summer of 1816 was extraordinarily cold. A meteorological record for New Haven that had been kept by the presidents of Yale College since 1779 records June, 1816, as the coldest June in that city, with a mean temperature that would ordinarily be expected for a point some 200 miles north of the city of Quebec. . . . In New England the loss of most of the staple crop of Indian corn and the great reduction of the hay crop caused so much hardship on isolated subsistence farms that the year became enshrined in folklore as "Eighteen Hundred and Froze to Death." The calamity of 1816 is an interesting case history of the far-reaching and subtle effects a catastrophe can have on human affairs.

The chain of events began in 1815 with an immense volcanic eruption in the Dutch East Indies (now Indonesia), when Mount Tambora on the island of Sumbawa threw an immense amount of fine dust into the atmosphere. . . .

This eruption, which was considerably larger than the better-known one of Krakatoa in 1883, reduced the height of Mount Tambora by some 4,200 feet and ejected some 25 cubic miles of debris. Ash was encountered by ships at sea as large islands of floating pumice as much as four years after the event. Climatologists rank the eruption as the greatest producer of atmospheric dust between 1600 and the present. The dust circled the earth in the high stratosphere for several years, reflecting sunlight back into space and thereby reducing the amount of it reaching the ground.

The idea that dust in the upper air can result in lower temperatures at ground level is quite old. Benjamin Franklin invoked it to explain the cold winter of 1783–84. Today the idea can be confirmed more conclusively through long records of temperature from many parts of the world, which can be compared with the fairly complete record of the volcanic eruptions that have been observed during the past two centuries.

As the dust in the upper atmosphere circled the earth after the eruption of Tambora, it gradually shadowed the higher latitudes. The first two months of 1816 were not exceptionally cold in New England, but by May observers had begun to comment on the lateness of the spring. June began auspiciously, and crops that had survived the unwonted frosts of mid-May started to progress. The first of three unseasonable cold waves moved eastward into New England early on June 6. The cold and wind lasted until June 11, leaving from three to six inches of snow on the ground in northern New England. A second killing frost struck the same areas on July 9 and a third and fourth on August 21 and 30, just as the harvest of twice-ravaged crops was about to begin. The repeated summer frosts destroyed all but the hardiest grains and vegetables.

> —Henry and Elizabeth Stommel, "The Year Without a Summer," *Scientific American*

During a period of severe depression several years ago I began to study jujitsu. My purpose was to feel safer on the streets of New York City; everyone I knew seemed to be getting mugged. The immediate results, however, were totally unexpected. Within two weeks I found that the training had begun to have a dramatic effect on my life.

My posture and my mood changed markedly as passivity and depression gave way to energy and euphoria. In the next several months I was able to seize the initiative in several important areas of my life. I applied for a grant to write a book, entered and won a competition for a writing award, and began the steps out of a difficult relationship. Although I was also in psychotherapy at the time, I believe that the jujitsu and the physical fitness that came with it had a significant effect.

Many other women have had similar experiences. One friend of mine took up running and discovered a new sense of calm and ease. "I feel freer, as though I've recovered a lost part of me," she says. "I have a sense of wholeness—body and mind come together in a way they don't otherwise. Although the running, changing and showering take up an hour a day, I feel as if I have more time, not less. Whereas I used to push things out of my life to save energy, I now feel able to investigate some of the things I always wanted to do but thought I didn't have time for."

Margo Lawrence, a TV producer, took up ballet three years ago and now goes to class four or five times a week. Although she has changed physically, it's the psychological change that's dramatic. Her image of herself is so improved that she recently auditioned to appear on camera. "I was tubby as a teenager and as a result I've always had bad feelings about my body," she says. "I can't tell you how exhilarating it is to stand up and let myself show."

—Susan Edmiston, "The Surprising
Rewards of Strenuous Exercise,"
Woman's Day

THE BUBONIC PLAGUE

Colin McEnedy

Finally, after innumerable cycles of onslaught and retreat, the [bubonic] plague disappeared from Europe. London's last experience with the disease, the Great Plague, began in 1665 and ended in spectacular fashion with the Great Fire of 1666. At that time it was natural for Londoners to believe they owed their deliverance to the purifying conflagration. Later it was suggested Londoners owed their resistance to the plague to the reconstruction that followed the fire and the fact that the rebuilt city boasted brick houses and wide, rubbish-free streets in place of the higgledy-piggledy structures and malodorous alleys of medieval times.

This explanation is attractive but does not hold up under scrutiny. One reason is that the fire destroyed only the central part of London, the area least affected by any of the outbreaks of plague earlier in the century, leaving untouched the overcrowded suburbs that had provided the disease with its main lodging in previous times. A second reason is that other cities in Europe, such as Paris and Amsterdam, became plague-free during the same period—a phenomenon that could not be linked to the Great Fire of London.

A somewhat more convincing (but still flawed) theory suggests that the disappearance of the plague coincided with a slow rise in prevailing standards of health and hygiene. Although hygiene cannot be eliminated as a factor, it does not explain why subsequent outbreaks followed the standard course, complete with high rates of mortality, but were farther and farther away from the center of Europe each time they appeared. It was almost as if Europe were developing some form of resistance to the plague that kept the infection from propagating in the usual way. In the north the path of retreat was to the east; in the Mediterranean it was to the south. The later the epidemic, the less it seemed to be capable of spreading. This, moreover, was at a time when, according to every available index, traffic by land and by sea was increasing.

When the role of rats was finally established late in the 19th century, it was suggested that the subsidence of the plague could be explained by changes in the population dynamics of the black rat, *Rattus rattus*. During the 18th century it had been observed that the black rat, the historic carrier, had been largely displaced by a new species, the brown rat *(Rattus norvegicus)*, which would have been a much poorer vector of the plague: the brown rat is as susceptible to the plague bacillus as the black rat but does not normally live in close proximity to humans. Brown rats typically live in dark cellars or sewers, whereas black rats overrun the upper rooms and rafters of a house. Because the oriental rat flea has a maximum jump of 90 millimeters (a little more than 3.5 inches), the difference in preferred habitats may have been enough to isolate humans from plague-infested fleas.

The brown-rat theory seems plausible but does not fit the geography: the brown rat spread across Europe in the 18th century from east to west, whereas the plague retreated from west to east. The brown rat was in Moscow long before the city experienced a particularly severe epidemic of the plague in the 1770's; it did not reach England until 1727, more than 60 years after that country's last bout of the plague.

The late Andrew B. Appleby of San Diego State University suggested an alternative theory, namely that a certain percentage of black rats became resistant to the plague over the course of the 17th century and that the resistant animals would have increased in number, spreading across Europe during the next 100 years. Although these rats might still be infected by the plague bacillus, they would not die from it and therefore could support a large population of fleas, rendering it unnecessary for the fleas to seek other hosts. This theory, however, does not conform to what is known about resistance to plague in animal populations. As Paul Slack of the University of Oxford has pointed out, rat populations often develop resistance when exposed to a pathogenic bacterium or virus, but such resistance is short-lived and is therefore unlikely to have been responsible for broad-based immunity to the plague.

A more plausible theory suggests that a new species of plague bacillus, *Yersinia pestis*, may have evolved that was less virulent than the previous strain. Being less virulent, it might have acted as a vaccine, conferring on infected animals and humans a relative immunity to more virulent strains of the bacterium.

The bacteriological theory is acceptable on several grounds. First, it conforms to the dictum, proposed by the American pathologist Theobold Smith, that "pathological manifestations are only incidents in a developing parasitism," so that in the long run milder forms of disease tend to displace more virulent ones. Second, it explains why the decline of the plague is associated with a failure to spread beyond local outbreaks: a disease cannot travel far when the number of people susceptible to it is low. Third, it is supported by the existence of a close relative of the plague bacillus, *Yersinia pseudotuberculosis*, which does not induce visible illness in rats but does confer on them a high degree of immunity to the plague.

Did *Y. pseudotuberculosis*, or a relative with similar properties, gradually spread through the rodent population of early modern Europe, making it impossible for *Y. pestis* to gain a foothold there? Although no direct evidence exists to support that hypothesis, it seems more reasonable than any other. . . .

FOR YOU TO WRITE

We cannot ask you to discover new cause-and-effect relationships in chemistry, astronomy, or physics. Instead of research, then, do some reading in the extensive and accessible literature of science, so that you can synthesize already existing information and interpretation in any of the following areas or on similar topics. You should frame all your arguments for an educated but inexpert audience.

1. Trace the causes and/or the immediate and long-term effects of a natural disaster, such as the eruption of Mt. St. Helens, the drought in the United States in the summer of 1988, or any of the scourges of flood, earthquake, or pestilence.

2. Write an argument singling out the predominant cause for the extinction of a species, such as the passenger pigeon, the dodo, the great auk, or the Irish elk. You may even wish to take on the great question of paleontology: Why did dinosaurs disappear from the earth with such apparent suddenness in the late Cretaceous period?

3. What is the latest causal explanation of a disease or phenomenon that has stumped medical investigators? Examples: sudden infant death, senility, multiple sclerosis, Legionnaire's disease, lupus, or Kawasaki's disease.

4. Trace the causes and/or effects of a form of pollution or a particular incident of pollution. Examples: acid rain, ozone depletion, automobile exhaust, sewage in lakes and rivers, any particular oil spill, Love Canal, a train derailment leading to the release of toxic chemicals.

5. Try your hand at cosmological causality. Why should there be volcanic activity on one of Jupiter's moons and not the others? What are the causes and effects of sunspots? What is the origin of the moon/earth system?

6. What technological advances have made today's computer revolution possible, and/or how are its effects taking shape? Or what have been the effects of computerization on any particular business or industry?

7. Why have we not been able to progress in some area of science or technology: exploring and using the resources of the ocean, interfering with the weather, harnessing a particular form of energy?

8. Argue for the importance of a particular animal or plant in an ecological nexus: bears, squirrels, ragweed, aphids, purple martins, dung beetles, bats, or the bacterium *E. coli*.

9. Identify the most important effect of an advance in agricultural technology: the McCormick reaper, a particular pesticide, drip irrigation, a breeding technique.

10. What was required to create a new development in transportation? Examples: high-speed trains, the monorail, trailer trucks, automatic transmissions on automobiles.

Searching for causes in the social sciences rarely means finding a cause that is both necessary and sufficient. Instead, social scientists usually discover influences, contributing factors, and responsible agents. What can current research offer as answers to the following causal questions?

1. Identify a large-scale social trend, like the increase in divorce rate, decline in birth rate, increase in cocaine abuse, or the increase in teenage pregnancy. Such trends are the products of many causes, but try singling out one you find significant and relating others to it. Remember that you may have to document the existence of the trend.

2. What, would you argue, is the dominant cause of job satisfaction in any particular field?

3. What psychological factors influence success in a sport? Do different sports attract different personalities, and if so, why?

4. Using the common-factor method, can you argue for a dominant influence in alcoholism, drug addiction, agoraphobia, or stuttering?

5. Can you make a causal connection between any method of instruction and success at learning? Examples: drill in math instruction, grammar in composition instruction, learning a foreign language at the elementary level with later language learning.

6. What does current research say are the causes of sleep disturbances or dreams?

7. Why do people fall in love, or do they?

History

1. The cataclysms of history—wars, revolutions, plagues, and other upheavals—prompt the question "Why?" Against the background of conditions and factors, argue for one overriding cause behind an event such as the Spanish–American War, the bombing of Pearl Harbor, the battle of Gettysburg, the 1967 Arab–Israeli War, the overthrow of the Shah of Iran in 1979, the Iran–Iraq War.

2. The perception of unexplained difference also leads historians into causal investigation. Why, for instance, did the South have slaves and not the North? Why has Japan been influenced by the West more than China? Why did France have a revolution in the eighteenth century and not England? Why are there more labor unions in the North than in the South?

3. Economic historians analyze changes, fluctuations, and cycles, often finding evidence of reciprocal causality. What brought about the rise and fall of strip development in the suburbs of U.S. cities? Can you argue for any predominating cause behind any identifiable recession or boom? What has caused any particular change in banking or credit policy?

4. The biggest questions in history concern the growth and decay, the rise and fall of nations, peoples, religions, even whole civilizations. Any full answer to such questions would require a book, but a shorter argument can place

deserved emphasis on one major cause. Consider, for example, the decline of the Minoan civilization of Crete, the Etruscans of Italy, the Mayans of Mexico, the Shakers or other such utopian communities in the United States, or the flourishing of the Shiite Moslems, the Hasidic Jews, or the economically powerful Japanese.

5. Ideologies and isms of all kinds are moving forces in history. Their effects tend to scatter, but in a chain argument you can follow an idea into action. Argue for at least one important effect caused by Malthusian ideas on population, Russian nihilism in the nineteenth century, Saint Simonian or Fabian socialism, populism, or civil rights in the United States.

6. History is made not only by people and ideas, but also by technological innovation. Again looking to effects, what is or has been the impact of the astrolabe, the Jacquard loom, the cotton gin, nylon, cable television or the VCR, the photo-duplicating machine? In military history what have been the results of inventions like radar, the tank, the machine gun, the missile?

In the study of languages, literature, art, and philosophy we engage in a kind of open-ended causal inquiry that relies heavily on time sequence, analogy, and assumptions about intention. You can fill in the following causal propositions with specific content drawn from works and artists you are familiar with.

1. Trace the origins of a movement in any of the arts. Examples: English Romanticism, punk rock, art deco, abstract expressionism, Pre-Raphaelite painting, the Victorian Gothic revival, the blues.

2. Argue for the influence of one artist on another. Is pointing out similarities enough evidence of influence, or do you need to establish agency? Examples: English novelist Anthony Trollope on Russian novelist Leo Tolstoy, Paul McCartney on Billy Joel, Frank Sinatra on Barry Manilow, Fred Astaire on Michael Jackson, Jack Benny on Johnny Carson, Beethoven on Brahms, Ravi Shankar on the Beatles, Japanese watercolorists on James McNeill Whistler.

3. Why did a particular popular art form or style flourish and decline? Examples: the mini-skirt, the blond furniture of the 1950s, disco, movie musicals, pop art, front porches.

4. Explore the motivation of a major character in a novel or short story or drama you are familiar with. Can you argue for one predominant cause behind that character's behavior?

5. Choose a book you think important and argue that it has affected the way some people think and act. Such a book can be a precipitating or remote cause of other events. Examples: *Unsafe at Any Speed* by Ralph Nader, *The Feminine Mystique* by Betty Friedan, *Walden II* by B. F. Skinner, *Silent Spring* by Rachel Carson, *The Jungle* by Upton Sinclair, *Looking Backward* by Edward Bellamy, *The Interpretation of Dreams* by Sigmund Freud, *Origin of Species* by Charles Darwin, *Free to Choose* by Milton and Rose Friedman, *In Search of Excellence* by Tom Peters, and *Cultural Literacy* by E. D. Hirsch.

11 | Precision and Prediction

We spent a great deal of time looking at the exact wording of claims to see what that could tell us about supporting them. Now that we have surveyed causes—what kinds there are, what tactics of support we can use, and how important agency is in causal argument—we are ready to examine the wording of causal propositions. They come in five possible forms. The way the proposition is worded suggests how to support it. Reviewing these forms will help you make a proper adjustment between the wording of your thesis and its supporting arguments.

CLAIMS WITH CAUSAL VERBS

Some claims have verbs that clearly indicate causality and often reveal something about the degree and kind of the causality. Some verbs indicate immediate or precipitating cause, others remote; still others show that the cause under consideration may be only one of many, and a weak one at that. The verb may also suggest the nature of the causal connection—that is, whether one thing creates, destroys, or alters another.

Here are some of the more common verbs that turn their subjects into causes.

1. These verbs suggest weak causality such as that produced by a condition, a remote cause, or one cause among many.

add to	lead to	increase
affect	make a difference	influence
contribute	modify	reduce
decrease	go along with	stimulate
elicit/enhance	have a hand in	take away from
evoke	have an effect on	
be associated with	improve	

2. These verbs suggest stronger causality such as a precipitating, sufficient, or necessary cause.

bring about	effect	necessitate
cause	eliminate	produce
compel	exhaust	result in
create	force	set off
decide	impel	trigger
destroy	initiate	
determine	make	

Notice in the following examples how a difference in a causal verb calls for quite a different argument.

1. Deciding not to go to college *affects* your future.
2. Deciding not to go to college *determines* your future.

Arguing for the first statement is not very difficult. Your argument would simply point out that one thing influences another; you need to show only a modest change to make your case, since the decision not to go to college may be one of several factors affecting one's future. But arguing for the second statement requires strong evidence as well as the refutation of other possibilities; you would have to show how a college education is the necessary and sufficient cause of the pattern of one's future.

EXERCISE

How would the choice of causal verb in the following examples affect an argument?

1. The noise level in a classroom (influences, determines) how much a child learns.
2. Participation in organized athletics (enhances, creates) ambition and competitiveness.
3. Taking cram courses (guarantees, leads to, can help students achieve) higher SAT scores.
4. The amount of sleep you have been getting (affects, decides) your ability to fight off viral infections.
5. Moving to a new area (stimulates, produces) anxiety.

THE CAUSAL ASSERTION AS A CLAIM ABOUT THE NATURE OF THINGS

Many statements that would have to be supported by causal arguments *look* like generalizations about the nature of things. In fact, we can get into a muddle about why we bother to distinguish them. After all, "the reasons" for putting any subject into a class are in a loose sense "the causes" behind making the claim in the first place. For instance, if we say that "Albert Einstein was a genius," his being a genius "causes" us to make the assertion. But we would do nothing with Mill's methods to support that claim; we would use definition and example. How are we defining genius? What attributes did Einstein exhibit that fit that definition? We could go off into these separate questions. But we will ignore the quibble and distinguish between the two kinds of claims on the basis of how they are supported.

Only a few claims about the nature of things truly require causal argument, and here are two signs by which we know them.

An Adjective in the Predicate That Describes an Effect

This effect can be general:

1. Current auto emission standards are *ineffective*.
2. Living together is *disadvantageous*.
3. A college education is *beneficial*.

Or specific:

1. Drinking gin is *unhealthy*.
2. Eating pinto beans in moderation is *healthy*.
3. Reading Russian novels is *depressing*.
4. Keeping bees is *uplifting*.

Let us work through an example in detail to show how it requires causal argument and what the complications are.

If you assert that something is "beneficial," you claim that it causes good. One of our examples claims that good things follow from a college education. (See Part III on evaluation.) To support that statement you have to name those good things *and* show convincingly how a college education caused them. One good effect or benefit might be more money, and a large part of your argument might be a demonstration that college graduates do indeed earn more money. The tactic of supporting the causal connection between college education and income could be concomitant variation: The more years of education the higher the income. The agency connecting those two—that jobs requiring intellectual preparation pay well—is acceptable enough to most audiences without further support. Another good effect or benefit of a college education might be job satisfaction. First, you could define job satisfaction in some measurable way and then identify two groups, one that has it and one that does not. Then you might identify the single difference between the two groups as a college education, thereby convincing your readers of a causal connection.

The Predicate Names a Class Defined by Its Effects

1. Prostitution is a *victimless crime.*
2. Perfume is a *pollutant.*
3. Sunshine is a *carcinogen.*
4. The MIRV is a *deterrent.*

These are ordinary-looking claims, but when you start defining their predicates you will find yourself talking about causes and effects. A "victimless crime" is one that causes no harm, a pollutant causes pollution, a carcinogen causes cancer, and a deterrent prevents an effect. Therefore, to place a subject in one of these classes is to claim that it has certain effects. Perfume a pollutant? Well, a pollutant can smell good even while it contaminates the air.

Do not worry about how to classify claims like these. You do have to define the predicate, but then the predicate is defined by its effects, so you are back with causal argument.

SIGN ARGUMENTS

We have just shown how some causal claims look like claims about the nature of things. But sometimes a straightforward claim about the existence of something can lead the arguer to claims about causality, arguing backward from a cause or effect to existence. The ancient rhetoricians called this kind of reasoning "sign arguments." A sign argument offers as evidence things that the audience either already believes or is persuaded into believing are natural accompaniments of the real subject of an argument. If these exist, then the things they are signs of must exist also. We are probably most familiar with sign arguments in the natural world: the increased red shift in the spectrum of distant stars is taken as a sign that the universe is expanding; the presence of certain antibodies in the blood is taken as a sign that a person has been exposed to a particular infection; the discovery of a crafted tool in a certain stratigraphic layer is taken as a sign of human presence at a certain point in the past. Indeed sign arguments may be so convincing to certain audiences that they are accepted as establishing facts rather than probabilities. Succeeding generations, however, have a way of undoing the sign arguments that seemed "scientifically" factual to audiences in the past. We no longer believe, for example, that the size of one's cranium is an invariable sign of the degree of the cranium owner's intelligence.

In the grayer area of the social sciences and humanities, sign arguments support probabilities. The prosecution in a murder trial, for example, may wish to characterize the accused as in a state of anger toward the victim in order to support a further claim that the murder was premeditated. The prosecution will undoubtedly resort to a sign argument, detailing acts and words on the part of the defendant that most audiences, and especially the jury, would take as signs of anger: The defendant swore at the victim in the presence of witnesses, defaced the victim's car, tore up the victim's picture.

The relation between a sign and the thing it indicates determines how the claim will be supported. It makes all the difference in the world if a sign is merely associated with whatever is the real goal of an argument, or if it is causally related to it. In order to understand this difference, let's look at a deliberately extreme example. Ancient astrologers consulted the heavens for "signs" of events on earth. If they saw something unexpected in the night sky, they were persuaded that something unusual had happened on earth—perhaps the birth of a new leader. The sign in the heavens was not the *cause* of the event on earth; if anything, the astrologers may have believed that both were caused by some anterior intention on the part of a divine being.

These days we believe less in associated signs and far more in connected causes. The migration of birds is no longer a sign of the changing seasons but a result, a consequence of shorter days and the effects of less light on the biochemically mediated behavioral "clocks" in birds. Indeed much modern research is aimed at replacing mere associations between signs and phenomena with thoroughly explicated causal pathways. The term *sign* is still very much with us; semioticians/semanticists use it in the old sense to indicate the largely arbitrary connection between words and meanings. Perhaps only our modern soothsayers, the economists, still resort to sign arguments based on association when they talk of "leading indicators" for this and that phenomenon. Given the complexity and high variability of economic events, economists may not be able to trace the precise causal connections between stock market cycles and deficit spending, or consumer confidence and the money supply, but they may nevertheless have evidence of a past association between the two and so reason from the existence of one to the existence of the other.

Because of the preference of most modern audiences for causal relationships, arguments that attempt to substantiate the existence of something from its signs may have to turn to causal relationships for support. If the causal relationship is one an audience will readily believe, an arguer need only convince an audience that the sign exists to convince them that the cause exists. If you want to argue that deer you have never seen live in the woods behind your house, the presence of undisputed deer tracks should be convincing. Deer tracks are caused by deer. (Why doesn't this tactic work for Bigfoot?) If, however, your audience does not accept the causal relationship between the sign and the phenomenon whose existence you are arguing for, you will have to shift to causal argument. Why should an audience believe that a reduced white cell count is a sign of marijuana abuse if they have never heard of a causal connection between the two? Chapters 9 and 10 explain the special requirements of causal argument.

Are sign arguments a wholly different kind of support for claims about the nature of things? From one point of view they are not. Let's return to the example of the prosecuting attorney who wants to convince a jury that a defendant was angry by bringing up evidence of the defendant's swearing and violence. From one point of view we can say that the defendant's anger *caused* the demonstrable acts that we have direct evidence of. From another point of view we can look at this situation as one that calls for argument from definition. Anger is *defined* as uncontrolled acts of swearing and aggression. It does not cause those phenomena, it *is* those phenomena. Which tactic is stronger?

EXERCISE

What combination of causal and definition arguments would you use to support the following claims?

1. Eating fatty foods is (or is not) unhealthy.
2. Travel is not always broadening.
3. The free agent draft has been harmful to baseball.

4. Bats are beneficial.
5. Many science-fiction stories and movies have stimulated real invention.
6. Rewards are an incentive to achievement.

IF–THEN CAUSAL STATEMENTS

So far, we have seen causal statements lurking in generalizations about the nature of things or declaring themselves openly in propositions with causal verbs. They can also split themselves in two, and instead of taking the form "X causes Y," they take the form "If X then Y."

1. If you want to go to medical school, you must have high grades.
2. If the Japanese had not bombed Pearl Harbor, the United States would have remained neutral in World War II.
3. If John Wilkes Booth shot Lincoln, he must have been insane.
4. If you touch those wires, you will electrocute yourself.
5. If you study with a virtuoso, your chances of becoming a great musician yourself are improved.
6. If the president fired the Secretary of Commerce, he must have deserved firing.

All these statements can be reworded into direct causal propositions. Sentence 2, for example, becomes "The Japanese bombing of Pearl Harbor caused the United States to enter World War II."

One more qualification is necessary. Some if–then statements are not cause followed by effect but *antecedent* followed by *consequent.* An antecedent is not exactly a cause; it is simply something that comes before something else. Consider this example: "If it is day now, then it will be night soon." Day is an antecedent of night, as night is of day, but not a cause. So an if–then statement does not tell you for sure that you have a claim about causality. For an antecedent to be a cause, an agency must connect it to the consequent or effect. Because there is certainly no agency between day and night, we definitely have a case of antecedent/consequent—not cause/effect. You must examine if–then statements carefully to see which kind you have.

EXERCISE

Which of the following if–then statements are causal, and which are only antecedent/consequent?

1. If you pass this course, you can take an elective in English.
2. If you do not study tonight, you will not pass the test.
3. If winter comes, can spring be far behind?
4. If you learn another language, you learn another way of thinking.
5. If you turn right at the fork in the road, you will come to a sign that says "Marengo 5 miles."
6. If the onion snow has fallen, then it is time to plant peas.

FACT-PLUS-CAUSE STATEMENTS

We have said that we do not argue about easily verified statements; we call them facts. But if we can take a fact and add a reason or explanation for it, then we may have an arguable statement. The entire statement is a causal claim naming an event or effect and its cause. For example, it is a fact that dinosaurs are extinct, but scientists do not really know why, so they argue with each other about the causes. For example, consider the following:

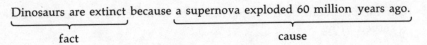

Dinosaurs are extinct because a supernova exploded 60 million years ago.

        fact   cause

Here is an arguable statement that a scientist must do two things to support: First, show the likelihood of a supernova explosion 60 million years ago, and second, show how a supernova explosion would cause dinosaurs to die. The same steps that are needed to support any causal claim may be needed to support a fact-plus-cause statement:

1. You may need to convince your audience that the cause really exists or existed.
2. You may need to convince your audience that the cause could have brought about the effect. In other words, if you cannot assume agency, you must work at establishing it.

EXERCISE

How would you argue for the following fact-plus-cause statements for an audience of fellow students? Would you need to establish the existence of the cause or could you assume it? Would you need to establish agency?

1. Registration for the draft was reinstituted in 1980 because the all-volunteer army was judged inept.
2. Tornados are frequent in the Midwest because there are no mountains.
3. SAT scores have fallen because a larger proportion of high-school students are taking the tests.
4. The Hall of Fame pitcher Sandy Koufax retired at the height of his career because his arm was about to be permanently damaged.
5. Picasso did not leave a will because he didn't care about his family.

PREDICTIONS

What do fortune cookies, Jeane Dixon, and prestigious think tanks like the Rand Corporation have in common? They are all in the business of predicting the future, an occupation that has inspired the highest wisdom and basest hokum. We all want to know what will happen tomorrow. Some fortunetellers try to appease our curiosity by sharing their divinations and hunches with us. Soothsayers read death in chicken entrails, gypsies see "tall dark strangers" in palms and tea leaves, and psychics just "know" where next year's hurricane will hit and what movie star will get divorced.

Unlike these leaps in the dark, rational predictions can be supported only by careful argument. To convince a reader of our vision of the future requires all the skills of causal argument. Causal analogy is particularly important in prediction arguments, for we believe that if A produced B in the past, and we find ourselves with A now, we can predict that B will follow. Or, if we think we have the first link of a well-established causal chain in hand, we can construct a chain into the future, a series of inevitable small steps leading to a coming result. Or we can try to construct a causal law governing the event we are predicting, a law that has worked in the past and we are convinced will hold in the future.

What Do Predictions Look Like?

Our most common verbs for the future are *will* and *is going to*.

1. Great Britain will be economically healthy in the 1990s.
2. The divorce rate will decline for the rest of the century.
3. Rudyard Kipling's reputation as a novelist will revive.
4. College enrollments will decline in the mid-nineties.
5. The United States will have an energy crisis by the end of the century.

You must be careful, however, because the simple verb *will* has many meanings, not all of which concern predictions. We can distinguish three main uses of the future tense (and especially of the word *will*) that you should be aware of.

Intentions

If you make a statement about what you intend to do in the future, you are really talking about the present. Even though you use the verb *will* and what you intend may take place in the future, the intention to do it exists in the present.

1. I will (plan to/intend to) begin my vacation Friday.
2. I will (plan to/intend to) marry George next year after we both graduate.

Such statements of personal intention are not subjects for argument. You cannot and need not support a personal intention with any kind of evidence. If you intend it, you intend it. But a claim about another person's intentions may be arguable. Since such a claim concerns a state of affairs (a quality in another person), it is supported like any claim about the nature of things. For example, you would argue for a statement like "The State Department intends to improve relations with Cuba" by saying what it means to intend to improve relations with Cuba, and then finding examples or signs of this "intent" in recent activities.

Generalizations Using the Future Tense

We often use the future tense to talk about things that happen all the time. If we feel confident enough to phrase a generalization in the future tense as a kind of causal law, we must believe that the causes bringing the event about always hold. We may not bother to mention the causes; we may not know them. We simply assert that the effect always occurs:

1. Radioactive isotopes will decay.
2. Iron will melt at 3,000° F.
3. Flowers will bloom in the spring.
4. Broken bones will knit.

Using the future tense here is not necessary; it is simply a convenient way of expressing our certainty that these things always happen—past, present, and future. They are facts.

But any time collective or individual humanity is involved, we are less certain that things will always turn out the same way. There are always exceptions to the laws describing human behavior. According to the Peter Principle, for instance, "Any executive or administrator will be promoted to his level of incompetence." That is not just a prediction; it describes the way things usually work. But they do not always work that way. Certainly a few executives have shown competence at every rung of the corporate ladder.

Folk wisdom gives us many such generalizations about how people behave:

1. Social climbers will forget old friends.
2. Politicians will do anything to get elected.
3. Absolute power will corrupt absolutely.
4. Boys will be boys.

Since these statements are supposed to hold for all time, the future tense is not essential, though it is used for emphasis. If you find yourself in the position of having to argue for one of these, you can treat it either as a definition or as a causal argument. You can argue that forgetting old friends is part of the very nature of social climbing or talk about how social climbing causes people to forget old friends.

True Predictions

A true prediction talks about an event or process that is completely in the future:

1. It will probably rain tomorrow.
2. In the next decade, colleges will alter their recruiting policies.
3. The Soviet Union will eventually go to war with China.
4. The Mets could win the pennant this year.

Or about one that exists now and extends into the future:

1. Baseball will continue to be the most popular sport in America.
2. College enrollments are likely to decline even more in the next few years.
3. Funding for the space program will increase in the twenty-first century.

A true prediction is neither a statement of personal intention nor a statement about a causal law phrased in the future tense. The causes that bring about the prediction may exist in the past or the present, but some or all of the process or the event itself is yet to be.

How to Argue for a Prediction

The only way to argue for something in the future is with a causal argument. You cannot convince anyone but the credulous to follow your leap into the dark because you have a hunch or an inspiration. If you want to predict the future, you have to use the facts and assumptions of the present. Your laser into the future is made with the materials of now. If you predict rain tomorrow, it is because a front is approaching *now.* If you are convinced that college enrollments will continue to decline, it is because the birth rate has already declined over a number of years. If you think funding for the space program will increase in the next century, it is because of causes, even causes of causes, that exist now.

When you argue for a prediction, you try to convince your reader that all the causes needed to bring about the event are in place or will fall into place. You build a causal model, using any of the sets of causes we described in Chapter 9. You might bring together necessary and sufficient causes, show how a remote cause constitutes the first link in an inevitable chain, show how the conditions are ripe for a precipitating cause that is likely to occur, or show how the removal of a blocking cause will bring about some inevitable effect.

Here is how you might argue for the modest prediction "The Mets could win the pennant this year." You identify the set of causes sufficient to produce a pennant: good pitching, steady fielding, improved batting averages, and so on. You show that the Mets have these attributes; this can engage you in some difficult evaluation arguments. But once you have polished them off, if nothing else intervenes, like injury to the star pitcher, you have made a good case for the future success of the Mets.

Predictions can also be supported by analogies. The predicted event can be compared with a completed event in the past. Once again, the causes of the completed event, the model, should be familiar and acceptable. Once the model has been described (or simply referred to), you point out the existence of similar causes in the present. You claim that these similar causes will lead to similar effects in the future.

For example, a historian who predicts that the Soviet Union will go to war with China may reason from analogy. He may compare the present situation between the Soviet Union and China with the past situation between Russia and Japan that led to war at the beginning of the twentieth century. For an audience of historians, this will be a familiar example. But again, the argument is only as good as the analogy, which sometimes must itself be supported.

FOR YOU TO ANALYZE

What combinations of tactics are used in the following prediction arguments—analogies, causal laws, chains into the future? How convincing are these predictions?

FOR HEALTH AND FOR WEALTH

Kenneth R. Sheets with Robert F. Black

Alchemists they aren't. But a $5-billion-a-year investment in research and development by drug companies in America is generating a wave of breakthroughs—from tension relievers and cancer therapies to baldness cures and heart-attack medications—and positioning pharmaceuticals to become the glamour industry of the 1990s.

The wonder medicines working their way through the research pipeline and emerging from the labs will allow the pharmaceutical industry to keep its golden touch well into the next century if companies can circumvent several obstacles along the way—the exploding cost of developing new compounds, a hostile regulatory environment and growing government pressure to hold down health costs by squeezing profit margins on drugs.

Despite those hurdles, the drug industry is pushing ahead with a financial record that few businesses can match: A 10 percent annual rate of growth in sales and a 186 percent gain in after-tax profits—from $14 billion to $36 billion—since 1977. During that time, the after-tax profits of all American industry rose 65 percent. "More new products are coming out than at any time in the past 15 years," says Robert Hodgson, an analyst at Oppenheimer & Company. "Most are superior to anything on the market."

Permanent customers. Demographics also point to a bright pharmaceutical future. The 65-and over population is swelling, and persons in that age group use three times as many prescription drugs as those under 40. Many of the diseases under attack by new drugs—such as high blood pressure and diabetes—are chronic, and patients will take the medications for the rest of their lives. For young and old alike, drugs rather than surgery are considered the more promising medical treatment for a growing assortment of ailments.

Not since the 1950s, a decade that brought forth vaccines against polio as well as powerful new antibiotics, have so many exciting new drugs begun appearing at neighborhood drugstores. Merck's Mevacor, which lowers cholesterol, is now available by prescription, and some analysts believe its sales may eventually top $1 billion a year. Genentech recently began marketing Activase (t-PA), a biotech drug that reduces coronary risk by dissolving blood clots that damage heart muscle. Eli Lilly got a go-ahead from the Food and Drug Administration (FDA) in January to sell Prozac for the treatment of depression. This year's projected sales: $50 million. That sum will multiply if tests show that the drug can also be prescribed against obesity.

Even more promising remedies should emerge in the next decade. Cancer researchers are focusing on proteins that stimulate the body's immune system. A case in point: Interleukin-2, which did well in short-term tests on patients with renal-cell cancer or malignant melanoma but still has serious side effects that must be overcome. Hundreds of scientists are also involved in a quest for medicines to curb AIDS. Nearly a score of antiviral drugs for treating the killer disease are under development.

Improved blood-pressure drugs may result from research on renin, a protein suspected of contributing to hypertension in 58 million Americans. Scientists at several companies believe they've found a drug that suppresses the body's production of renin. By the year 2000, some researchers believe, the need for many coronary-bypass operations will be eliminated in favor of treatments with drugs that dissolve clots and plaque in the bloodstream.

Strokes and baldness. With the graying of America well under way, nearly every pharmaceutical company is pressing hard for products that will help the aged. Several companies are developing treatments for prostate trouble, common among older men. Upjohn has Rogaine, a hair-growing minoxidil preparation that is being sold in Canada and is nearing FDA approval. This summer, the company also begins human tests on lazaroid compounds designed to attack "free radical" molecules that damage cells in the wake of strokes and injuries to the head or spinal cord. Some lazaroid compounds may also help treat Parkinson's and Alzheimer's diseases and other central-nervous-system disorders.

Few of these developments would be possible without dramatic changes in the way research is done. For nearly a century, pharmaceutical researchers relied on the "screening" method, in which promising natural and chemical compounds were run through test after test to determine their benefits and drawbacks. Over the years, almost every known chemical, bacterium, fungus and countless combinations of them were tested. Now, that method is giving way to "rational drug design," a technique in which researchers first identify a target and then design a treatment. "Instead of searching for the key to unlock the disease, we first design the lock and then the key that will fit it," says Stanley Crooke, president of SmithKline's research center at Upper Merion, Pa.

Rational discovery methods have been greatly accelerated by the emergence of biotechnology, in which genetic material is manipulated to fit the needs of researchers. Once almost the exclusive tool of start-up firms such as Genentech, biotech expertise now is a necessity in nearly every major pharmaceutical house. Some companies build their own teams. Some buy out smaller companies. In the last two years, Bristol-Myers bought Genetic Systems for $300 million and Eli Lilly got Hybritech for $350 million.

Thanks to biotechnology, labs are creating compounds of remarkable complexity. Genentech started it all a decade ago by cloning the human insulin gene to create the first genetically engineered drug (now marketed by Eli Lilly as Humulin). Then came the discovery of interferons and lymphokines, proteins thought capable of boosting the body's immune system. Most biotech drugs proved disappointing in tests, but alpha interferon now is sold as a treatment for hairy-cell leukemia, a rare form of cancer.

Biotechnology also played a major role in Upjohn's research on renin. Because renin is found only in tiny quantities in human blood, researchers could not get enough for testing. So Upjohn cloned the human renin enzyme and then inserted the gene into hamster ovary cells growing in test tubes. Those cells now produce unlimited amounts of human renin for research.

Patent woes. The new generation of pharmaceutical compounds is arriving at a propitious time. Until recently, Wall Street analysts complained that drug companies were showing signs of hardening of the arteries. Almost all of the top 100 prescription drugs on the current market will lose their patent protection by the mid-1990s and become vulnerable to the swelling market for low-cost generic medicines. And many "me too" drugs with similar properties are competing head to head. For example, Merck and ICI Pharmaceuticals recently introduced hypertension drugs to rival Squibb's breakthrough medicine, Capoten. SmithKline's revolutionary ulcer-treating Tagamet was replaced as the No. 1 prescription medicine last year by Glaxo's Zantac. Two other companies have similar ulcer drugs.

Though drug sales look healthy in annual reports, the reality is that most of the gains stem from repeated price hikes. Drug charges have climbed an average of 9.4 percent a year in the past 10 years, a period in which yearly inflation has averaged only 6.5 percent. The industry is quick and vigorous in defense of its profits, which can exceed 60 percent on some formulas. On average, new patent-protected drugs cost more than $125 million to develop, compared with $50 million a decade ago. Only 1 in 4,000 compounds tested in the labs survives a rigorous series of regulatory hurdles that can eat up more than half of the 17 years it gets in patent protection. The cost and time of testing show signs of increasing as the new drugs and the diseases they treat become more complex.

Although the FDA has managed to reduce the time needed to approve new drugs used to treat AIDS and other life-threatening diseases, pharmaceutical executives still gripe that the process takes too long. "The agency is too busy with AIDS and politics to approve new drugs," asserts analyst Neil Sweig, who follows the industry for Prudential-Bache.

Even after winning FDA approval, there are no guarantees that a drug will thrive in the marketplace. Valium was one of the most widely prescribed drugs in the world until it proved addictive. The FDA has ordered Hoffmann-La Roche to place the picture of a deformed infant on the label of its new acne drug, Accutane, as a warning that it can cause birth defects if used by pregnant women. Congress is investigating the approval and sale of Versed, a Hoffmann-La Roche anesthetic associated with three dozen deaths in the past two years.

The industry's ability to pass costs on to consumers is running into heavy opposition. Many health-insurance plans are rejecting higher prescription charges, and some lawmakers even hint of price controls in the decade ahead—a move that would sharply curb profits.

Another possible headache is the catastrophic-health-care bill now about to emerge from Congress. While the bill will make drugs more affordable for millions of elderly Americans, it also is likely to generate closer federal scrutiny of prices. European nations already limit drug charges, and Japan has cut its prices 40 percent since 1982. If the bill becomes law, "the cloud of potential federal drug-price regulation will hang on the horizon, a prospect that is not eagerly anticipated by the brand-name pharmaceutical industry," says Ira Loss, an expert with Washington Analysis Corporation, an economic consulting company in the nation's capital.

Drug firms recently got a whiff of what may be ahead when federal health officials notified hospitals that the government for the time being would refuse to pay the $2,200-per-dose cost of Genentech's t-PA. The government argues that t-PA has not yet proved significantly better than older but cheaper anticlot therapies, such as streptokinase.

The generic challenge. Congress's bill also is expected to mandate the use of generic drugs whenever they're available. That would give a big boost to the small companies that live off the discoveries of major pharmaceutical houses. Generics now hold 35 percent of the prescription market, compared with 7 percent in 1980. By the early 1990s, William Haddad, chairman of the Generic Pharmaceutical Industry Association, expects generics to command 50 percent of the market. Many name-brand firms have cut prices to meet the generic threat. SmithKline now offers discounts to hospitals that buy large volumes of patent drugs. Several companies have promised not to raise prices to customers who sign contracts for big orders.

Although U.S. companies are world leaders in research and sales, they operate in a global arena where competition is formidable. Eleven of the top 20 companies in the world, led by Merck, are still American, but eight are European and one is Japanese. American companies last year sold $3.3 billion worth of drugs abroad, while foreign companies sold $2.8 billion worth in the U.S.

Pharmaceutical firms see their current push to develop revolutionary drugs as the only way to outmaneuver the competition in the coming decade. Their $5 billion yearly investment in research and development takes a variety of forms. Many companies have formed research alliances, some with smaller firms, some with companies abroad. Others have channeled millions of dollars to university labs around the world in exchange for the marketing rights to new discoveries.

The effort is paying off in the lab, but success is not guaranteed in the marketplace. Products must earn their way by demonstrating a clear therapeutic advantage over existing drugs or by reducing the need for other treatments, such as surgery or long hospital stays. "The companies that develop these products will be rewarded," says Bill Lalor, president of ICI Pharmaceuticals. "Those that don't may not survive."

The survivors' rewards will be rich: The gratitude not only of medical patients who may live longer and better but also of shareholders happy to be a part of a glamour business.

HYBRID AIRCRAFT

Thomas Kiely

A decade from now, air commuters may fly on a novel aircraft under development in both the United States and Europe. Called a tilt-rotor, it will have movable rotor units on each wing tip. When the rotors tilt vertically, the craft will fly sideways, hover, take off, or land like a helicopter. Tilting the rotors horizontally will transform the craft into an airplane.

Proponents argue that this hybrid offers an affordable solution to air-traffic congestion. LaGuardia, Kennedy, and Newark airports, serving New York City and New Jersey, "are near saturation point right now," says Al McDonough, Federal Aviation Administration (FAA) program manager for East Coast heliports. "Probably 50 percent of the traffic at those airports are for passengers going less than 350 miles."

One reason tilt-rotors may help alleviate the situation is that they can operate out of existing heliports or small regional airports, as well as specially designed metropolitan or suburban "vertiports." They would be ideal for short air trips and could even decrease the time passengers spend commuting to airports.

Since tilt-rotors are part airplane, airlines and passengers may accept them more readily than redesigned helicopters. Conventional helicopters are expensive to maintain, noisy, and too slow to satisfy the potential market for alternative air transportation. A 1987 study, conducted by NASA, the FAA, and the Defense Department, argues that tilt-rotors would be far quieter than helicopters, perhaps even during liftoffs and landings. The study suggests that a commercial tilt-rotor could carry 75 commuters from downtown New York to downtown Washington at a speed of 300 miles per hour. The entire trip would take 40 minutes. And tilt-rotors would be far cheaper to maintain than helicopters, though more expensive than airplanes.

To take advantage of tilt-rotors, cities would construct downtown landing sites, equipped with advanced landing systems. The study estimates that a vertiport could cost between $11 million and $80 million, excluding the price of the site. By comparison, new metropolitan airports cost between $4 billion and $6 billion.

The FAA will have to certify the craft, a much longer—and therefore more expensive—task than approving new versions of existing craft. The FAA must also fashion discreet routes for tilt-rotor air traffic.

Which Market?

A commercial tilt-rotor is at least a decade away, but a military version already exists. A V-22 Osprey, constructed by Boeing Helicopters and Bell Helicopters Textron under contract to the U.S. Navy, will have its maiden flight this fall. Following several years of tests, the first V-22s will go to the Marines, probably in the early 1990s. The two companies reportedly invested $90 million in V-22 development between 1982 and May 1986, when they received a $1.81 billion contract for six flyable and three non-flyable prototypes.

Eventually, the Marines hope to get 552 tilt-rotors to replace their amphibious-assault helicopters. The Air Force wants 55 for special operations; the Navy will use 50 for air/sea rescue and is considering another 300 for anti-submarine warfare. The Army originally wanted 231 Ospreys, but backed out at least until 1994 because of budget constraints.

The V-22's body is fabricated almost entirely of solid-laminate graphite epoxy composites, and the rotors are advanced fiberglass structures. The craft will come with sophisticated electronic flight controls, similar to those in the new F-16 fighter. Equipped with a special fuel bladder, the V-22 could carry three people 2,100 miles with one-fourth the noise of a helicopter.

Since Bell and Boeing would be obliged to swallow costly overruns on V-22 production, the firms will probably not work on a commercial tilt-rotor at least until the mid-1990s. However, a consortium of aerospace and helicopter firms from France, West Germany, Spain, Italy, and Britain is more committed to a civilian project. They launched a tilt-rotor program last January and hope to sell a craft by the late 1990s, the earliest a U.S. version could be available.

Jacques Andres, a spokesman for Aerospatiale, a French firm in the consortium, says European governments will commit 50 to 60 percent of the program's funds to design and manufacture the tilt-rotor. Eurofar, as the venture is called, has already spent $30 million on research. According to Andres, the European tilt-rotor will look similar to the Osprey and also be made of composite materials. In the Eurofar version, only the rotors and not the entire rotor cell will tilt.

The consortium plans to build a 30-passenger vehicle, which Andres says will serve a different market from the probably larger Bell and Boeing craft. "We see a potential market for 1,000 machines," Andres estimates.

Eurofar worries proponents of a U.S. civilian craft, including Rep. Tom Lewis (R-Fla.), a member of the House Committee on Science, Space, and Technology. Tilt-rotors could be a billion-dollar industry by the year 2000, and James Greene, an aide to Lewis, believes the first commercial product available will take the lion's share of the market.

Meanwhile, the Pentagon is bullish on the tilt-rotor. Advocates had worried that since most major military programs are under review, the $23.7 billion price tag for the craft would make it an obvious target for Pentagon belt tightening. But the Defense Department's review staff decided in July to accelerate the program, not to cut it. While the final decision rests with Congress and the president, the Navy and the Marines look forward to an early delivery of V-22s.

FOR YOU TO WRITE

1. Choose a new product or technology and convince an audience of nonspecialists that it will have important effects.

2. Write a letter to a parent or adviser predicting what you will be doing five years from now, based on what you are doing now and the causal laws of your own personality.

3. Choose a current domestic problem or crisis in foreign affairs about which you either are or can become fairly knowledgeable. Predict its outcome in a letter to the editor of a newspaper.

4. What will be the state of your favorite sport in five years? Do you think a new sport will catch on or an old one become more popular? Address your prediction to a fellow sports enthusiast.

5. Where do you think popular music is headed? What artists or types of music do you think will go out of style or be revived? Imagine your prediction as an article in *Rolling Stone*.

6. The further into the future, the more difficult the prediction argument. Try your hand at a long-range prediction about life in the twenty-first century for an audience of people your own age.

7. Bankers, brokers, and marketing analysts are in the business of predicting. If you have some knowledge of or interest in economics, you might try to (a) recommend a long-term investment or savings plan, (b) predict the next step in an economic cycle, or (c) foresee the possibilities for a new market for a product.

Part Three

IS IT GOOD
OR BAD?

12 | Evaluation

Once you understand arguments about the nature of things and about causes, you have grasped the fundamental methods of argument, tying evidence to definition and linking two occurrences by agency. As you know, each of these tactics is associated with its own kind of claim. Two other kinds of claims also appear as the theses of arguments, the evaluation and the proposal. Fortunately, these require no new methods of argument, only a judicious combination of the types of argument already discussed.

In this section we take up *evaluations,* arguments for value judgments. Whenever we attach a label like "good," "right," "beautiful," "bad," "wrong," or "ugly," we are evaluating. If challenged, we ought to be able to defend our evaluations, and to do so we have two tactics of support at our disposal. First, we can measure the subject of our evaluation against an ideal definition of what it ought to be, a standard of perfection for its type. This tactic brings us back to the first type of argument. If you say, for example, "I have a really great Honda," that claim translates flatly into "My Honda is good." Everything you know about arguing for a claim about the nature of things still works, even though you have placed a value-judgment term in the predicate. You have to identify the subject for your audience, if necessary, and your supporting evidence must be fairly representative. And if you cannot count on your audience's immediate understanding of the predicate term "good Honda" or "good motorcycle," you must define your standard of "goodness" in a car or motorcycle so the subject term fits comfortably under it.

The definition of the predicate of an evaluation is called the *criterion* or *standard.* The criteria behind an evaluation are as critical as the definition of the predicate in an ordinary argument about the nature of things. If these criteria are not acceptable to an audience, you may have to stop and argue for them just as you would have to stop and argue for a definition.

The second tactic for supporting an evaluation is causal argument. Although evaluations resemble definitions in form, they frequently require causal argument in support, for the criterion or ideal definition we measure our subject against often includes good or bad *consequences.* If we say, for instance, that "properly conducted drill is a good teaching method," our definition of "good teaching method" must certainly include "has good effects." How else can a teaching method be good unless students learn from it? To show that drill satisfies this part of the criteria of good teaching method we will have to link drill *causally* with certain results, perhaps by the single-difference method, showing that students who have been drilled in math facts fifteen minutes a day retain more information longer than a similar group of students who have been taught the same material in a less formalized manner. Our criteria for a good teaching method might also include the absence of certain bad consequences as well as qualities like "thoroughly tested," "traditional," or "approved by prominent educators."

EVALUATION IS NOT A MATTER OF TASTE

You may think that anyone who judges value and makes claims like "Mary Cassatt was a wonderful painter" or "Government funding of science is poor policy" expresses a purely personal opinion, a matter of taste that, according to our discussion in Chapter 2, is not arguable. However, when sharable criteria or standards can be found, evaluation becomes legitimate argument. Of course, we often express value judgments without defending them, venting pleasure, approval, irritation, or anger. But if we want to move an audience to judge as we do, we must argue from external grounds rather than our own emotions. We do this either by appealing to standards we believe our audience holds with us, or by working to establish such sharable standards.

SUPPORTING THE CRITERIA WITH A SPECIFIC AUDIENCE IN MIND

You will not have to defend any criteria your audience are likely to share; at most you may remind them of your shared criteria. If, for example, you claim your friend is a "good student," you would probably not have to defend the criteria for a "good student." But what do you do if your audience does not automatically accept your criteria of evaluation? To begin with, ask yourself whether you can support them on any but personal grounds. A number of tactics are available for such support.

The first tactic for supporting criteria is an appeal to your audience's values. If you can show that your standard of evaluation falls under one of your audience's basic assumptions about what has value, then you have supported your criteria, at least for that audience. For example, the novelist John Gardner evaluated much modern fiction as "trivial and corrupt." He claimed as his criterion for that evaluation that fiction should be a moral art. How could he back up that criterion, one with which many modern novelists and readers disagree? He could place that criterion under one of our basic assumptions by appealing to the self-evident goodness of what is moral. *Moral* is another word for choosing the good and repressing the bad, and if we argue that trying to live according to this policy is admirable in life, shouldn't it also be admirable in fiction?

Second, you can appeal to authority. What if your audience does not automatically acknowledge the higher value you have appealed to, a value you think self-evident? You can remind them that a famous thinker, a religious leader, a great philosopher, the law, or the Constitution has supported your view. John Gardner backed his criterion for fiction by an appeal to the theory and practice of the great Russian novelist Leo Tolstoy.

Third, you can make an appeal to consequence, an appeal to the good and bad effects of following your criterion. John Gardner, for example, could have argued that morality is a good standard to judge fiction by because art that follows a standard of morality makes people behave better. If readers see characters in fiction engaged in serious moral conflict, trying to make right choices, they will have good models to imitate in their own lives.

Fourth, sometimes you can create a comparison to support a criterion. A standard of morality in art might be defended by comparing it with a standard of morality in life. You might support this criterion by arguing that just as a parent should point out to a child the rightness or wrongness of an action, so also should a novelist point out to readers the rightness or wrongness of a character's action. Of course, such a comparison assumes that your readers accept the basic comparability of a novelist and a parent. But if they do, you have defended this criterion.

If you think about all these methods of supporting the criteria that support the evaluation, you can see yourself getting into an infinite regression, going back and back, supporting one appeal with another and that appeal with another, and so on. Suppose, for example, you make an appeal to good consequences. How can a consequence be called "good" except by some prior evaluation that has labeled it good? At some point, and that point will depend on your audience, you simply call a halt. If you have touched common ground with your readers' values, you should be all right.

You can see how criteria of evaluation work if you look at what you evaluate. The following sections will help you think of subjects for evaluation and will suggest how to go about evaluating with ideal definitions and causal arguments. The subjects of evaluation are divided into four categories—things, people, acts, and finally abstractions, a special category that in some ways combines the other three.

EVALUATING THINGS

Things have material existence, and anything you can trip over can certainly be evaluated. Although things have no upper and lower size limits, for convenience we have divided them into the natural and the constructed.

Natural Things

It may seem futile and arrogant to evaluate the givens of the universe, but we do evaluate natural things both for their consequences and their beauty. Our notion of the consequences of natural things depends on our point of view. A child's book says, "Ladybugs are good insects." They are the gardener's friends because they eat the plant-destroying aphids. Actually, ladybugs simply behave like ladybugs, but what they do happens to have good consequences for people. If aphids could write, ladybugs would be bad insects. Similarly, almost no one has a good word to say for termites, which have very bad consequences for wooden houses, although in a forest they may be tolerable. We make the same kind of consequence evaluation of all the orders of animals and plants, according to how they affect us, even though ecology has taught us a broader kind of consequence argument. We have learned that an animal or plant species may produce no immediate consequence for us and yet may be a vital link in a chain of consequences for all living creatures.

We also evaluate natural things on aesthetic grounds, labeling them beautiful and ugly from a human point of view. Most people find centipedes and roaches ugly, swans and flamingos beautiful, especially from a distance. Do we also attach the labels *beautiful* or *ugly* on the basis of consequence? That is, do we call whatever species is good or at least neutral for our welfare beautiful, and whatever harms us ugly? Yes, consequences influence aesthetic judgments, but do not control them.

The shiver of repulsion we feel at the sight of a snake can exist simultaneously with an admiration of the snake's beauty. Coral snakes, for in-

stance, are magnificent but deadly. If something that has hideous consequences can still be beautiful, then the two appeals (aesthetic and practical)
must be separable. (For a discussion of aesthetic evaluations, see the section below.)

One curious object is perhaps constructed rather than natural, and that
is landscape. We certainly evaluate natural scenes as dull or exciting,
picturesque or sublime. But are we evaluating something that nature has
produced or something that the perceiver has created even though not a
bush has been touched? In other words, can we have landscape without
human point of view? Probably not. In fact, no one evaluated landscape
until only a few hundred years ago. Landscapes can be considered constructed in another sense, when they contain the farms and tilled fields that
are signs of human habitation. Thus, landscapes can be evaluated on
practical or aesthetic grounds.

Constructed Things

We spend a great deal of time evaluating constructed things, perhaps
because we feel we have some control over them. We choose among them,
improve them, reject them. Some of these evaluations are practical, others
are aesthetic, and a few are both.

Practical Evaluations

We make practical evaluations of constructed things according to how
close they come to fulfilling their functions. We have, as it were, *ideal
definitions* in mind of what good things of their kind should do or be, and
we measure individual things against these ideal definitions. For instance,
the good refrigerator keeps fresh food cold and frozen food frozen with no
effort on the part of the owner. We might even add the criteria of silence,
energy efficiency, and reliability. Of course, manufacturers and advertisers
add other attributes to the ideal definition of refrigerator—unlimited supply of ice cubes, cold drinks through the door, special storage compart-
ments, and a surface that won't show fingerprints. We always have to
decide which criteria we think important and which trivial. Consumer
magazines provide us with models of the practical evaluation of everything
from spaghetti sauce to outboard motors.

Practical evaluations are little trouble to an arguer because the criteria
are usually easy to define and win audience agreement for. We can all agree
that a television set should give a sharp picture in natural color, have
excellent sound reproduction, require little maintenance, and not cost too
much. The practical evaluation of a particular set is only a matter of
comparing it against the easily defined criteria.

EXERCISE

Establish criteria for evaluating any of the following.

1. popcorn popper
2. sleeping bag
3. electronic keyboard
4. personal computer
5. airport
6. public washroom
7. skis
8. CD player
9. 35 mm camera

Aesthetic Evaluations

Some things we evaluate not for their usefulness, but for their beauty, and therefore the pleasure they give to the perceiver. We evaluate all kinds of artistic products like poems, plays, piano music, and the work of artists from Pindar and Picasso to Proust and Puccini. Everything we call Art with a capital A is the province of aesthetic evaluation, as well as much else that contains an element of aesthetic appeal.

You are probably thinking that preferring Rockwell to Renoir, Beethoven to the Beatles, or Melville to Michener is simply a matter of personal taste and that arguing the superiority of one artist or work over another is futile. It is true that some people do refuse to argue any aesthetic issue, choosing to halt with "I like what I like" or "That's not art to me." Since these cliché responses are not based on impersonal grounds, they spell the end of arguable evaluation.

But impersonal grounds do exist. For anyone willing to put aside personal preference, arguments supporting aesthetic evaluations are possible. They work just like any other evaluation argument: The object at hand is measured against defined or assumed criteria. But aesthetic criteria may not be as obvious as those for evaluating useful objects. In fact, the criteria are rarely stated in the aesthetic evaluations you are most likely to read— reviews of books, movies, records, and art. They are simply assumed. Nevertheless, we can identify and define some common elements in aesthetic criteria. These are all aids to your invention, to help you make aesthetic evaluations.

PROPORTION

It is impossible to conceive of beauty without proportion.
—Johannes Winckelmann

We can admire a thing for the fitness of its parts and how they combine to form a whole object. A Greek temple, for example, has columns of fixed proportion, tapered finely to produce an illusion of straightness; the relationship of the size of columns to the size of the whole temple is fixed. In classical music a sonata has three parts in proportional relation to each other, and in poetry a sonnet is frozen into fourteen lines, each of fixed length. In any of the arts, to fulfill an expectation of appropriate proportion or form is to satisfy an aesthetic criterion, while to violate such an expectation can be an aesthetic flaw. A popular song with too short a bridge may be judged imperfect, a novel without an ending disappointing, and a picture with everything crowded to one side out of balance. Such works may be considered lacking in proportion, the perfect relation of parts to whole. When we find that a work of art is satisfying in its proportion, we sometimes bring in another word and praise its unity. To say that a work of art has unity is to say that its parts fit together so well that they become one thing.

SLIGHT DISTORTION

> There exists no excellent beauty but in strangeness of proportion.
> —Francis Bacon

Perfect proportion and slight distortion are rival criteria of beauty. They have never been reconciled, probably never will be, and need not be. The first may be called "classical" and the second "gothic" or "romantic." Art critics have used both authoritatively as standards of evaluation.

We have already considered proportion. What can it mean to call something beautiful because its proportions are slightly exaggerated or distorted? To begin with, distortion cannot be extreme, because extreme distortion is ugliness. The features of a gargoyle, for example, may be compelling but never beautiful. To turn to another more familiar art form, in a movie we are surprised and delighted by the occasional odd camera angle, the face reflected in calm water which is then stirred up. But a whole movie with the camera first at knee level, then on a helicopter, then looking in a mirror or through a keyhole, would distort perception beyond beauty. When the form is extremely distorted—whether it is the form of picture, poem, or music—it can interfere with our appreciation of the object.

The complementary criteria of proportion and slight distortion can be used in the evaluation of any art form. For instance, just as we can talk about the perfection in form of a Mozart symphony, so also can we admire Mahler's controlled distortion of the length and content of his symphonies' movements. Just as proportion pleases by fulfilling expectation, so also does slight exaggeration or compression give us the thrill of a ripple in the form.

CONTRAST When we appeal to contrast as an aesthetic criterion, we are admiring a juxtaposition, a placing next to each other, of two differing elements of form, color, or content. We can admire the contrast between the craggy vertical mountains and placid horizontal lake in a landscape painting, the dramatic play of light and shade in a Rembrandt portrait, the sudden shifts from *piano* to *forte* in a piece of music, the comic and tragic plots that twine in a Shakespeare play. We find it pleasing when vivid differences are brought together, perhaps because each element is intensified by juxtaposition. Too much contrast, however, can be an aesthetic defect, if it jars instead of pleases.

HARMONY Just as proportion and slight exaggeration are in conflict with each other, so too are harmony and contrast in never-ending tension. The appeal to harmony as an aesthetic criterion claims that pleasure can be derived from gentle or subtle rather than extreme variations. When we are not distracted by gross contrast, we can admire fine gradations and small details. In the absence of mountain and lake, we can appreciate the undulation of prairie wheat in the wind, and in pastel paintings, all harmoniously light, we can enjoy the subtle variations of color. The painting we know as *Whistler's Mother* was called by the artist *Arrangement in Grey and Black* to call attention to its delicate harmonies of dark shades, its lack of contrasting bright color. In music, a lullaby is harmonious not just in melody, but also in dynamics (loudness and softness) and tempo. In architecture, harmony can mean staying with the same style throughout a building. Putting modern floor-to-ceiling windows in a Victorian house could be considered a violation of harmony.

Too much harmony, the defect we call monotony, is the excessive repetition of the same form, a lack of sufficient variety to keep the observer's attention. A song that repeats the same phrase or chord progression over and over again, a film that repeats the same action over and over again (like pornography or cartoons), a housing development that repeats the same model over and over again—all these are monotonous.

CRAFTSMANSHIP All the aesthetic criteria we have discussed so far are formal; that is, they deal with the disposition of the basic elements of art like shape, color, and sound, rather than content. Now let us turn to those criteria that depend on the human maker and perceiver of a work of art. We can also base an argument that something has aesthetic value on the skill, ingenuity, inventiveness, or persistence of its maker. All of these are elements of craftsmanship, a criterion of value that can be applied to any made object.

How can we judge the skill of the maker? Sometimes we can infer it from the object itself. If we examine the dense pile of a handmade rug, we realize how many knots per square inch it contains, and therefore how much time and effort it took its weaver. In music, we may admire both the skill of the composer and that of the performer. We can admire the composer Liszt for his skill in intricate modulation, and admire any pianist who is technically competent to play Liszt. We are in awe of poets like Dante who can sustain an intricate verse form over thousands of lines, and of painters like Sir Peter Lely who can paint satin so skillfully we can almost feel it.

How well we infer the skill of the maker from examination of the object depends on how much we understand of the craft to begin with. We can look at a Seurat painting and say "how pretty" because we admire the light and shade of the soft colors. But if we look more closely, we see that each bit of color has been applied as a tiny separate dot. When we realize that Seurat's most famous painting, *Sunday Afternoon on the Island of La Grand Jatte*, is approximately 9 feet by 10 feet, we may well be in awe of the skill and patience of the artist. And anyone who has ever struggled to play a two-octave scale on the piano smoothly will have a much better appreciation of the skill needed to play the floating arpeggios of Debussy's *L'Ile Joyeuse* than a non-musician would.

When we construct aesthetic evaluations, however, we usually do not judge objects solely on the basis of craftsmanship. The work of art may have been difficult to create, but at some point we may ask the question "Was it worth making?" Someone may take twenty years to build a minia-ture castle out of toothpicks, but is the result art? A piece of music may be fiendishly intricate, but the result musically banal. The works of many great technicians in all the arts are unremembered because they do not fulfill any criterion but craftsmanship.

ASSOCIATION Like craftsmanship, association is another nonformal crite-rion by which we evaluate art. We can turn to human perceivers and ask what "meaning" the work of art has for them. What ideas does it suggest to them, what emotions does it arouse, what does it tell them about life? Although some critics discount "meaning" as a criterion of evaluation, most people prefer art whose content has relevance for them. They want to take something away, in the form of a message, from a work of art. Of course, some works yield a meaning more readily than others and some messages are more complex than others. It is easier to get the message from Norman Rockwell's painting of a Thanksgiving feast than from Picasso's *Man with a Guitar*. But for some people the quality or complexity of the message is related to the ease with which it can be extracted.

What kinds of messages do we get from works of art? How can we argue for our evaluation by referring to content? Although we cannot answer these questions here in the detail they deserve, we can suggest some of the large categories of association. The first category is an appeal to one of the basic human emotions: the love between mother and child in a Raphael madonna, the ecstasy of Bernini's St. Theresa with the angel's spear poised above her heart, the fear of Janet Leigh in the shower in *Psycho*, the tenderness of Romeo and Juliet, the hatefulness of the bad guys in an Arnold Schwarzenegger movie, and the laughter inspired by Charlie Chaplin's struggle with an escalator.

Second, associations can be historical or social, political or religious—in short, have mental rather than emotional content. We can admire the New York skyline not only for its formal characteristics and for the craftsmanship of the buildings, but also for the associations that skyline evokes—the spectacle of a powerful, technologically adept civilization. Such admiration may have an emotional component, but it is primarily intellectual.

Some people see works of art primarily as vehicles for ideas. An idealogue, someone possessed with an idea, looks at a work of art for its political orthodoxy, as the social realists of Russia do, or for its religious content, or for its truth to Freudian or Jungian psychology, or even for its ethnic purity. Many critics have ridden these ideological hobby horses and asked, "Is this painting an example of Marxist realism?" "Is this novel truly Catholic?" "How Irish is this song?" A limited ideological appeal will not go over well in an evaluation unless your audience shares your ideology. If they do not, the ideology itself would have to be argued for, which is no easy matter and which would take you far from your original purpose of evaluation.

Any work of art will spin a web of associations in your mind, but some of them will be too personal to use as criteria for aesthetic evaluation. A painting may please you because it reminds you of a favorite cousin; a song may recall the happy time you first heard it. But you could not convince an audience that the painting was good or the song beautiful because of those personal associations.

To be useful criteria of evaluation, the associations a work of art raises must be sharable rather than private. Only then can you hope to arouse the same admiration in another. For example, if you look at a painting by the French artist David, you may see a historical message in its depiction of stoical Roman Republican virtue and argue, "This is a great painting of the French Revolution." You may defend the value of the painting on the ground of its historical associations. Your mild assumption is that a work of art that represents its period has value, and the historical associations you find could also be appreciated by someone else.

MORAL CONSEQUENCES OF ART One common form of art criticism bypasses formal criteria, completely assumes the associations that the work arouses, and then goes ahead to evaluate the work on the basis of consequences. This kind of criticism asks, "What moral effects will this work of art have on the beholder? Will reading this book, seeing this movie, looking at this painting, or watching this TV show tend to produce good or bad actions?" According to such a criterion of evaluation, anything that produces good effects is good and anything that produces bad effects is bad. For example, a movie called *The Warriors* showed teenage gang wars and depicted in dramatic detail all the trappings of this subculture. An increase in vandalism and street fights occurred in many towns where this movie was shown; in short, a strong case could be made that this movie caused violent behavior. According to the moral criterion of aesthetic evaluation, this movie was bad because of its bad effects.

In the case of *The Warriors* the link between the object and its effect was easy to trace. An aesthetic evaluation based on moral consequence, then, requires some form of causal argument to convince the audience that the object could lead to the consequence claimed. But often that link is tenuous. In Eastern Europe, for example, abstract art and rock music are frowned on as causes of social and political backsliding and therefore considered inferior art forms.

In these nations, moral evaluation leads very quickly to censorship. But we want to stress that any connection between judging a work of art and censoring it is not inevitable. Even if we believe that a book or a movie does or could have bad effects, and that therefore it is a bad work of art, it does not necessarily follow that we should burn the book or confiscate the movie. Whether or not a work of art is censored depends ultimately on where we think moral responsibility for action lies, with the individual or with society; if with the individual, we make our evaluation and stop.

Using Two Standards of Evaluation for the Same Constructed Object

A wooden chopping block made of carefully matched end-grain pieces of hardwood, a van with Day-Glo flames consuming its sides and red velour upholstery, hand-painted English bone china in a delicate floral pattern, a low-slung, aerodynamically designed racing car, a Louis Quinze writing table, a Paul Revere silver teapot—here are objects we can evaluate both for usefulness and beauty, both practically and aesthetically. Beauty and function can be connected in two ways. Sometimes the beauty is obviously added on to the functional thing, like the decorated side panels of a van. Or sometimes the beauty is in the perfection of the functional design, as in the falconlike elegance of the Concorde.

EXERCISE

The following is a list of constructed objects that can be evaluated aesthetically or practically or both. Decide what criteria of evaluation you would use for each of them.

1. the photography in a fashion magazine
2. the cover of this book
3. the last movie you saw
4. a leather jacket
5. an apple pie
6. a Christmas tree
7. any symphony by Mozart, any quartet by Beethoven, and any song by Schubert.
8. a small foreign car or a large domestic one
9. your local landscape or cityscape
10. a music video
11. an F-16 fighter jet
12. the words to a popular song

EVALUATING PEOPLE

Though wisdom warns us to judge not, we constantly evaluate people either in the roles they perform or in their whole lives. For example:

1. My neighbor is a good mother.
2. Dr. Bright is a fine scientist.
3. Wellington was a great general.
4. My grandmother is a good person.

Evaluations like these use the tactics of definition and causal argument. Once again, if you want to establish that your neighbor is a "good mother," you have to define what a "good mother" is and then give evidence from your neighbor's life to show that she fits the definition. Part of your definition will include certain qualities she possesses, such as warmth and concern for her child's education. Another part might concern the effects she has on her family's spirits and health and thus require causal arguing.

In essence, what you are doing is holding an individual up to an ideal definition of a role. Actually, the most arguable part of your evaluation could be that ideal definition. What, for example, is a "good mother"? That's a sensitive issue nowadays; you cannot rely on any miscellaneous audience sharing assumptions about motherhood, as they might have a hundred years ago. Defining a "good electrician" would be much easier. And what about the definition of "a good teacher," "a good doctor," or "a good president"? These become increasingly difficult.

What happens when we turn from roles and try to evaluate the whole person, calling him or her "good" or using some synonym that suggests general approval? Again, nothing new. A vague "good" used to evaluate a person desperately needs definition, like any abstraction. Some ready-made systems can suggest criteria for judging the "good" person; Christianity, Judaism, Buddhism, Islam—all the major religions, and even smaller isms like dialectical materialism, deism, and vegetarianism, offer criteria for evaluating the good person. Once again, depending on your audience, you may have more argument over the standards than over the person you are canonizing.

EXERCISE

Construct and defend if necessary for a specified audience ideal definitions of the following. You may go on to compare a particular individual against one of the ideal definitions in a full evaluation argument.

1. a good child
2. a good sister or brother
3. a good mechanic
4. a fine guitarist
5. a competent waitress
6. an adequate dentist
7. an excellent senator
8. an effective clergyman
9. an inspiring piano teacher
10. a good pastry chef

EVALUATING EVENTS AND ACTIONS

Natural Acts and Events

At the mercy of wind, fire, and water, we can do little but hurl our evaluations back into the face of nature. But just as we judge natural objects according to their usefulness, so also do we judge natural events and actions by their consequences. We even have the arrogance to evaluate the weather. In one university town, for example, the local weather service grades the weather every day from A to F: "Today will earn only a C in the morning, but will improve to B in the afternoon when the cloud cover breaks." Any evaluation of a natural event will depend entirely on consequence and point of view. A flood that deposits rich, alluvial soil in the Nile valley is good, but a flood in Johnstown, Pennsylvania, that washes away lives and property is disastrous. A volcanic eruption may be an exciting and magnificent spectacle, but when we put a price tag on the damage that results, it becomes a catastrophe.

Human Acts and Events

In the arena of human actions we have enormous territory for evaluation, taking in everything from cheating on an exam to invading Afghanistan. But as in the case of natural acts, our heaviest reliance will be on consequence. A good action is one that produces good consequences and a bad one produces bad. In effect, when we judge an action, we are making two evaluations, one of the situation that precedes it and one of the situation that follows it. A good action *improves,* changes a situation to a better one. Hiring a new secretary is a good action if messy files get organized and lost letters found. The intervention of the United Nations is good if it stops a war and brings about a cease-fire. An action can also have both good and bad consequences: A tax cut can be good if it encourages the private sector and bad if it feeds inflation. When an action has a double effect, an overall favorable evaluation would depend on minimizing bad effects and maximizing good ones.

Do we ever bring in ideal definition to judge an action or event? Yes. We often call an action "wrong" because it violates some ethic, some code or standard of right action, regardless of whether the act has good or bad consequences. For example, because it is a form of dishonesty, cheating on an exam is considered, by definition, a bad or wrong action, even though it can temporarily produce good results for a person of hardened conscience.

The Variety of Ethical Appeals

It may be a good idea to pause here and consider how many kinds of ethical appeals there actually are. The word *ethics* might make you think of the Ten Commandments, the golden rule, philosophy, or the kind of moralistic preaching about good behavior that comes down from authorities and has seemingly little to do with day-to-day activities. Actually, we all must have a sense of what actions are right or wrong—that is, a sense of ethics. Ethics affect not only our personal lives, but also our deeds in groups, professions, and even nations. We all like to see the right thing done, whether that right thing is as individual as going to visit a sick friend in the hospital or as national as taking in refugees adrift in the ocean on rafts.

Might not all of the following be ethical warrants for the evaluation of actions and events? We can appeal to these warrants as the "right thing" with certain audiences. *Self-actualization* is considered a good thing. It means becoming whatever we can become, even if we must put our own interests ahead of the demands of others. Self-actualization can be used as ethical justification for just about anything from jogging to studying Greek. The opposite value of *altruism,* indifference to one's own welfare for the sake of the good of others, is held by many as a higher ethic.

Family loyalty is another ethical motive for action. You would not cheat your mother by selling her a lemon of a used car. Even the law respects the loyalty between husband and wife and does not ask them to testify against each other. And we all belong to larger "families" which have their own standards of right and wrong. *Being a stool pigeon* is as ethically wrong to the member of a street gang as *failure to help a partner* is to the policeman.

Professions are groups with their own codes of behavior. These codes may be as formalized as the *Hippocratic oath* or *union bylaws*; a teamster considers crossing a picket line unthinkable, and a doctor is supposed to treat anyone in need. The ethical codes of some professions are not formalized at all, but that does not mean they are any the less there. Scholars, for example, swear to nothing and sign nothing, but they share a strict understanding that plagiarizing (using someone else's ideas or work without acknowledgment) or intruding on someone else's declared area of study is unethical.

Institutions such as hospitals, universities, and corporations also have ethical responsibilities or duties, more or less codified. A hospital should treat the indigent; a corporation has duties to the public that buys its product as well as to its own stockholders. Any institution, from country club to nursing home, tries to live up to an ideal definition of what it should do and is evaluated positively when it does, negatively when it does not.

Religions and nations are even larger groups that declare standards of right and wrong, usually in writing. The volumes containing the law of the land fill many shelves, and all religions have their texts and commentaries on morality. Since their standards are written down in such detail, we think of law and religion first when we think of morality or ethical correctness. *Criminal* and *civil law* define what is wrong in human interactions, but we also carry in our minds a sense of what is right for us to do as citizens. We respect an appeal to *patriotism* (short of the jingoism that equates love of country with the mindless desire for warfare), no matter what nation we come from. And as citizens of the United States, we find an *appeal to the Constitution* a strong ethical argument.

A few general ethics cut across national and religious boundaries. As we might expect, these are vaguer but no less powerful than written laws. One of the strongest is an appeal to *fairness* or *justice* itself. A desire to be fair is the ethical standard behind many an evaluation, from a good way to share Halloween candy to the proper way of taxing large corporations. Most people also respond to the rightness of *preserving tradition*. We can evaluate the wholesale leveling of inner-city neighborhoods as bad because the past is being indiscriminately destroyed, or country auctions as marvelous because they preserve folkways. And these days, a very common appeal to tradition, although we might not recognize it as such, is any claim that it is right to preserve the world, its land, its species, just as they are today.

Similarly, an appeal to *progress,* the opposite of tradition, can evoke an immediate response. That same leveling of an inner-city neighborhood could be evaluated as good because it means new buildings for the city and hence progress. Many people feel it was right to go to the moon, regardless of the cost, because in that act mankind "progressed." In the same way, it is "right" to climb mountains never climbed before, to explore Antarctica, and to cross the ocean in a balloon. It may be difficult for us to explain why such acts are right, but we have a sense that it is right for men and women to extend the capabilities of our species. Here, a vague claim of general "rightness" brings us full circle to that most personal of ethical motives, self-actualization. Anyone who takes a giant step for mankind may also be motivated by the desire to take a small step for himself.

EXERCISE

How would you evaluate the following actions or events? By their consequences, by measuring them against an ideal definition, or both?

1. a rock concert
2. a football game
3. a political campaign, at any level
4. a thunderstorm
5. a diplomatic action
6. buying prewritten term papers
7. the 55 mph speed limit
8. a marriage ceremony you have witnessed
9. a Saturday night party
10. a forest fire

EVALUATING ABSTRACTIONS

Abstractions like "life style," "marriage," "management," "a sports program," and "the Supreme Court" are made up of things, people, and actions. "Life style," for example, a concept of recent invention, is certainly made of things—cars, tennis rackets, condominiums, and grand pianos; of people—health conscious, self-aware, up-to-date; and of actions—taking vacations in Antigua, skiing, jogging, dedicated shopping. All of these elements coexist in a life style and will furnish the examples for the evaluation of that abstraction. That is, if you want to argue that a certain life style is good, your criteria and evidence will include things, actions, and people.

Once again, you will use ideal definition and consequence to support the evaluation of an abstraction. But with an abstraction, ideal definition will dominate and will itself, very often, be the focus of the argument. In fact, every society engages in an ongoing debate over the ideal definitions of important abstractions. What is the ideal Supreme Court—strict constructionist or activist or something else? What is the best kind of institution of higher learning—large university, small liberal arts college, technical institute? What is the best life style—raise-your-own-rutabaga, hard-headed pursuit of a career, or every-house-its-own-recreational-vehicle-and-swimming-pool? Of course, these labels are tongue-in-cheek but they should remind you of what a volcano of controversy can erupt over an ideal definition.

The second line of defense in evaluating an abstraction is likely to be consequence. If, for example, you argue that "Urban renewal is a bad idea because it has destroyed working-class neighborhoods," you are appealing to consequence. But that consequence is bad only if you and your audience have in mind an ideal definition of a city as a place where working-class neighborhoods thrive close to its center.

You can see that consequence predominates in evaluating actions and useful objects, while in evaluating abstractions, works of art, and people, ideal definition comes first. You can make your evaluation even stronger by calling on other standbys of support.

First, authority. Why should your audience accept your ideal definition of a good painting, person, or institution rather than someone else's? One way of heading off refutation is to bolster your definition with authority. For example, bring in the Constitution to support your definition of the Supreme Court, Benjamin Franklin to support your definition of a good library, or quote a Nobel prize winner on good science.

Second, comparison. If you can count on your audience's predictable evaluation of anything as good or bad, you can compare whatever is under scrutiny to whatever is unambiguously admired or execrated. For example, we have all heard what a magnificent city Paris is. Perhaps Washington, D.C., falls short of that ideal in some respects but approaches it in others. Thus, an evaluation of Washington may be carried on by comparing it to Paris. Similarly, almost no one admires fascism, so to compare any ideology with fascism is to give it a very negative evaluation.

EXERCISE

Evaluate the following abstractions. First you must define them as some combination of things, people, and actions. Make appeals to both ideal definition and consequence and bring in any other lines of support.

1. your state legislature or city council for an audience of local citizens
2. your local public library for people who don't use it
3. adolescence for parents of adolescents
4. the stock market for potential investors
5. the high school you went to for fellow students
6. the revival of interest in crafts to nonparticipants
7. standard of living to a foreigner
8. retirement to someone about to retire
9. affirmative action to a member of a minority
10. political advertising to a TV audience
11. television programming to a steady viewer
12. the police (campus, town, state) to the group served

WEIGHTING CRITERIA

Suppose you are evaluating personal computers. You will have little difficulty setting up a list of standards that a good personal computer must meet.

1. speed
2. expandability
3. memory capacity
4. user friendliness
5. compatibility with other brands
6. software availability
7. price
8. dependability

Two people might nod yes to this list of standards, and yet when faced with a choice among real computers, each may choose a different one.

Why? *Because even though they agreed to the same standards, they weighted them differently.* By weighting we mean nothing more complicated than ranking standards in order of importance. One evaluator may put compatibility with other brands at the top of the list; another, large memory. Since any real object is unlikely to have all the ideal attributes, we have to make a best choice among what is available, and that is why weighting can lead to different choices. If price is important and the one personal computer that does and has everything costs $10,000, out it goes.

In evaluating an object for personal consumption, weighting may be an individual matter. Whenever we are going to spend our own money, an evaluation must take into account our personal preference. That is, someone in a technical field might put memory capacity or speed at the top of the list, while someone with more money might put price at the bottom.

The ranking of criteria for anything you do not personally consume can be made on more impersonal grounds. Whenever you put together an evaluation argument, you not only can but must weight your criteria, and you may even have to defend your weighting. What, for example, is the most important quality of a good manager—flexibility, sensitivity to employees, an eye on the balance sheet, or the ability to handle detail? If you were the chief executive officer in a company evaluating the managers under you, you would have to decide which quality is most important and defend that emphasis. You would probably concede the importance of the other standards but emphasize one by claiming that without it the other standards will not work. Such an argument for weighting one criterion of a good manager over others might look like the following:

The ability to handle detail is the most important quality of a good manager. A manager can be imaginative in dreaming up new programs, sensitive in handling personnel problems, and know enough accounting to make the budget look balanced, but if the manager doesn't answer mail, return phone calls, and get memos out on time, business will slip into chaos and all the dreaming, sensitivity, and creative bookkeeping will go for nothing.

Any any other techniques you want to bring in to support your weighting of criteria are fair—authority, comparison, examples.

WEIGHTING VALUES: ETHICAL ARGUMENT

Suppose you were a judge faced with the following case requiring your ethical evaluation: Is it right for the Amish to refuse state-mandated secondary education on the grounds that any education beyond eighth grade conflicts with the practice of their religion? Here is a case not of right action versus wrong action, but of two positive values in conflict, education and religious freedom. How would you decide which is more important? The United States Supreme Court decided that although a state has the right to insist on compulsory education to the age of sixteen, that right or value was not as significant as freedom of religious practice. So long as the Amish could demonstrate that secondary education disrupted their religious beliefs (and the Amish of Wisconsin did), the Court's ethical decision was in their favor.

What the Supreme Court did was weight one value over another. Ethical argument involves making such very fine discriminations, ordering values in a hierarchy to make possible the judgment of an action. In an ethical argument, you and your audience might agree on certain values, but not necessarily order those values in the same way. Your job in argument is to weight one value, the one that will become the critical criterion of judgment, above another. Evaluating values in this way is a matter of appealing to higher values or to consequences. You might argue, for instance, that faced with a choice, being well educated is better than being wealthy. Though both are good, the first has primacy because education cannot be taken away, has greater benefits for the soul, and enriches all experience so that life is fuller.

No matter what you are evaluating, from an object to a value itself, most of the time weighting will be the crucial issue with your audience. People are likely to agree about the relevance of a set of criteria but disagree about which is most important in a given situation.

EXERCISE

Here are five lists of standards for the evaluation of (1) a thing, (2) a person, (3) an action, (4) an abstraction, and (5) an ethical problem. Rank the criteria in each list in two different ways and defend each version. You need not work with all the criteria given.

1. Thing: an apartment (one-room studio)
   a. amount of rent
   b. efficiency of kitchen
   c. quiet (or insulation)
   d. size
   e. convenience of trash disposal
   f. closeness to public transportation
   g. parking facilities
   h. cleanliness/general condition
   i. storage facilities
   j. maintenance

2. Person: a lecturer
   a. clear speaking voice
   b. sense of humor
   c. command of material
   d. interest in subject
   e. good organization
   f. writes clearly on board
   g. uses audiovisual aids
   h. pleasant-looking

3. Action: a football game
   a. home team wins
   b. close score
   c. full stadium
   d. lots of cheering
   e. good tailgate party
   f. quality of half-time show
   g. quality of cheerleaders
   h. number of injuries
   i. weather

4. Abstraction: a university
   a. variety of curricula offered
   b. quality of individual colleges
   c. number of nationally famous scholars
   d. adequacy of dorm space
   e. strength of fraternity (Greek) system
   f. male/female ratio
   g. reputation of sports teams
   h. closeness to an urban center
   i. beauty of campus

5. Ethical problem: affirmative action
   a. fairness to minorities
   b. good of the profession, institution, etc.
   c. fairness to the well-qualified applicant
   d. absence of discrimination on the basis of age, race, or gender
   e. welfare of those served by the profession, institution, etc.
   f. the right of a profession or institution to select its own members
   g. the individual's right to pursue the profession or calling of his or her choice

COMPARATIVE EVALUATIONS

All our evaluations so far have been in the simple form of X is good, bad, mediocre (or some other judgment word). But evaluations can take two other forms, which we will deal with briefly.

The Evaluation as Comparison with Degree

1. Woody Allen is better than Mel Brooks.
2. Swimming is better than jogging.
3. Paris is better than London.
4. Solitary confinement is worse than physical abuse.

The support for such statements cannot begin until you come up with one or more classes or categories to which the objects of comparison can belong. For example, if you say, "Woody Allen is better than Mel Brooks," you probably mean "Woody Allen is a better actor/writer/director/comedian than Mel Brooks." Or if you say, "Swimming is better than jogging," you might mean "Swimming is a better therapy/muscle builder/improver of circulation/aerobic exercise than jogging." How might Paris be better than London? "Paris is a better art center/tourist city/place to do business/representative of its country/place to eat than London." If you come up with one or more categories in which one thing can be better than the other, you can make and organize an evaluation-with-degree argument. Each category will need to be taken care of separately in its own mini-argument.

What is the technique in each of these separate mini-arguments? The category that both subjects belong in will provide the criteria for evaluation. Those criteria may amount to an ideal definition of the class "comedian," for example, that both Woody Allen and Mel Brooks belong to. Both the subjects, Brooks and Allen, are evaluated against that definition and whoever has more of the ideal qualities of a "comedian" is judged the better. Here weighting the criteria will be a critical part of your argument. If slapstick is high on your list of the criteria for a good comedian, you will favor Mel Brooks; if intellectual wit comes first, Woody Allen wins.

EXERCISE

Here are some comparative evaluations. What categories, generating criteria for evaluation, could both objects in each comparison belong to?

1. Jazz is better than rock.
2. Tennis is better than squash.
3. Science fiction is better than detective stories.
4. American cars are worse than foreign cars.
5. It is better to have loved and lost than never to have loved at all.

Superlative Evaluation

1. The Library of Congress is the best in the United States.
2. The Rolls-Royce is the best car made.
3. Warren G. Harding was the worst president the United States ever had.
4. Albania is one of the worst countries in the world.
5. Charity is the greatest virtue/Pride is the worst sin.

When you argue that something is the best or worst, you will always identify at least one category to which your subject belongs: The Library of Congress is a library, the Rolls-Royce a car. Once you have a category, you can construct criteria of evaluation.

For superlative evaluations you have two special tactics of support at your disposal; you can use one or both. In the first method, you come up with an ideal definition of "best library," "best car," "worst sin," "greatest virtue," etc. In effect you create a class that can have only one member, and you go on to show how the subject term fits into that exclusive class. If you want to argue "Pride is the worst sin," you begin by defining "worst sin." You might say pride is that sin from which all others flow, the sin of the fallen archangels. Only one sin can be the origin of all the others, so you have created a class with only one possible member.

In the second method, you define a somewhat larger class, the class of near peers. In other words, you would not define "worst sin" but simply "mortal sin"; not "best library" but "good library." A class like "good libraries" has several members that are competing for the title "best," so you can now proceed by refutation, showing that the other contenders do not fulfill the criteria as well as yours. To do this, you can make a series of "better than" or "worse than" arguments, each of which names a different attribute or a different near peer. For example, if you are supporting "The Library of Congress is the best library in the United States," you could come up with a series of comparative evaluations that assert the superiority of the Library of Congress over other good libraries.

1. The Library of Congress is a better manuscript repository than the New York Public Library.
2. The Library of Congress has more newspapers than the Widener Library at Harvard.
3. The Library of Congress is easier for scholars to use than any other library.

If you have a reasonable, easily accepted set of near peers, you can bypass any explicit criteria for a "good or bad————" and get right into evaluative comparison.

EXERCISE

Here are some superlative evaluations. Defend them by setting up an ideal definition of "best" or "worst" or a set of near peers.

1. ——— (you fill in the blank) is the worst movie ever made.
2. ——— (you fill in the blank) is the best Democratic/Republican presidential candidate.
3. ——— (you fill in the blank) is the worst team in baseball.
4. Chess is the best game ever invented.
5. Honesty is the best policy.
6. Down is the best filling for comforters.

HOW EVALUATIONS CAN GO WRONG

The potential weak spots in an evaluation argument are first the criteria, second the weighting, and third the evidence that the subject evaluated fits the criteria. If you want to strengthen your own evaluation argument or refute someone else's, the place to probe first is the criteria, once you find them. They are always there but often not explicitly stated. You might first ask, "Are the criteria sharable and plausible?" A judgment on the basis of personal taste should not masquerade as an evaluation argument. If a movie reviewer writes, "I did not like *A Fistful of Dollars* because I don't like westerns or Clint Eastwood," you should complain loudly that this is no argument, just a statement of personal taste. Or if the reviewer of a TV comedy writes, "Yes, it was side-splitting and rollicking, but it had no deep social significance. It does not help the working class face economic reality," you might well ask if deep social significance is a plausible or appropriate demand to make of a sitcom.

Even if the criteria in an evaluation are plausible and impersonal, you can still question their weighting. Is the evaluator making too severe a judgment based on too minor a standard, or perhaps too generous an assessment on the basis of an unimportant criterion? Would you, for instance, accept the following favorable evaluation of a deposed dictator: "True, he slaughtered thousands of his countrymen, but he was a wonderful leader because he was so colorful and did things with such panache!" Surely you could attack such an argument on the grounds that aesthetics are not as important as moral consequence in judging human actions.

Finally, an evaluation argument must convince its audience that the subject really has the qualities of the criteria. For instance, you might agree with an arguer that "versatility," the ability to portray a wide range of characters convincingly, is a quality of a good actor, but disagree whether Debra Winger, Meryl Streep, Tom Cruise, or Michael J. Fox has really demonstrated versatility.

FOR YOU TO ANALYZE

Read the following evaluation arguments and identify the criteria or standards of judgment, whether implicit or explicit. Are any completely personal, implausible, or incorrectly weighted? Do the authors present enough evidence to warrant the subject's evaluation?

POLLUTION IS GOOD FOR YOU

Philip W. West

In general the environment is self-purifying. The end result of this is good and is appreciated by all thinking people. What is overlooked, and thus not appreciated, is the fact that the purification process itself is of the utmost value. It is basic in the providing of foods and material things; it is basic to sustaining life itself. It must be concluded, therefore, that some or even most pollution is necessary.

There are many examples. Sewage and salts such as those of iron, zinc, manganese, and copper are essential contaminants or pollutants when discharged into rivers or the sea. After all, pure water, which even children know is simply H_2O, must be contaminated with oxygen to sustain zooplankton and fish life and with carbon dioxide to support aquatic vegetation such as phytoplankton.

It appears that every individual and all groups and governmental agencies abhor the thought of sewage or metal salts being discharged into waters. But without iron in the water how would fish produce their blood, or where would their essential trace metals come from if not from the water?

And what about food? Much of the world's population depends heavily on seafood, but what do the shellfish and fish eat? The food chain can be considered as starting with plankton along with other small organisms which thrive on organic matter such as sewage and so function in the biodegradation and thus ultimately in the bioenhancement of the pollutants. Thus, the small organisms thrive on the pollutants and contaminants and in turn are devoured by larger organisms, and these provide food for still larger creatures, the ultimate consumer being man.

The conversion of pollution to food supplies can be seen in Louisiana where the Mississippi River carries essential metal salts as well as sewage from hundreds of towns and cities and discharges the pollutants into the Gulf. The enriched waters support one of the most productive fish populations in the world. So much nutritional material is discharged by the river that not only the Gulf Coast is enriched, but the Gulf Stream itself is enriched and carries the nutrients past Florida and north, making commercial and sport fishing profitable for hundreds of miles within its currents.

It should be observed that even a few miles away from the Gulf Stream fish are so scarce that fishing is unprofitable. There is no pollutant enrichment in the middle of the Atlantic or Pacific Oceans; that's why Russian and Japanese trawlers must look elsewhere for their catches.

Can anything good be said about contaminants or pollutants in air? Again the answer is yes, although it is more difficult because, unlike pure water, air is a mixture of many molecular and atomic species. Dirt in the air provides the nuclei required for the precipitation of atmospheric moisture. Without dust there would be no rain or snow, and so there would be no grass, trees, crops, lakes, rivers—no you or me.

There are many other "goodie" pollutants in air such as oxides of nitrogen and sulphur, trace metals, salts of potassium, etc. In other words, there are many nutrients in air as emphasized by the growth of plants such as Spanish moss, bromeliads, and orchids, all of which get their food from the air in which they live. In addition to the air plants, plants in general must get much of their nutrients directly from the air through the stomata of leaves or indirectly through the roots which pick up nutrients washed out of the air by rain and snow.

The viewpoint just outlined may stir up emotional objections, but the facts presented can hardly be debated. Absolute purity in the environment would be not only impossible but disastrous.

It must be recognized that some kinds of pollutants present very serious problems and their introduction must be minimized. For most, however, the bad changes to good as natural processes transform and utilize them. Pollution is like food in that to have none is a tragedy, to have too much can cause problems. There is a sensible range between the extremes.

SAMPLE ANALYSIS

"Pollution Is Good for You" is an evaluation whose thesis is its title. The argument depends on two definitions: one of "pollution" and one of "good for you." Its main appeal is to consequences: That which is good for us enables us to thrive in our environment. To support that causal claim the author constructs a chain-of-causes argument. People eat fish, fish eat plankton and other small organisms, and these organisms thrive on pollutants and contaminants. Similarly, polluted air contains nutrients that are taken in by plants and dust particles that are necessary for rain, which is necessary for plants, which are necessary for us. Thus, according to this argument, pollution is necessary for our survival, and certainly most of us will grant the assumption that our survival is a "good."

Although it is difficult to attack any specific link in the chain of causes that the writer presents, the argument becomes more shaky when we pick up the beginning of the chain and examine the definition of the subject, *pollution.* Granted that small organisms thrive on organic matter like sewage and dirt in the air provides a nucleus for raindrops. But is a biodegradable amount of sewage and dirt what most audiences usually understand as pollution? The author's definition of pollution seems to include all decaying organic matter and particles in the environment; the absence of such pollution would be "absolute purity," which is impossible and undesirable. The author does not indicate when necessary and natural impurities become excessive and result in bad consequences, such as dying fish or acid rain.

AMERICAN MADE: THE 1958 CADILLAC

By Olivier Bernier

Brilliant colors, dashing form, and lots of chrome: that, as any American car manufacturer knew in the late 1950s, was what the public wanted, and in an age when more was better and most was best, it stood to reason that the grandest (and largest) of automobiles must also be the flashiest. The roads were open, the interstate network was growing, the suburbs were expanding, and in that lavish and somewhat naive world, a Cadillac was the reward of success.

The 1958 [Cadillac] convertible in fact, says it all. Sculpted by General Motors' tremendously influential designer Harley Earl, it embodied his fascination with the wartime twin-boom Lockheed P-38. The fins at the rear, the wraparound windshield, the instrument panel—all was supposed to make the driver feel like a pilot. Indeed, the fin itself was the special mark of the Cadillac, the design element that at first differentiated it from all other General Motors cars, but then it turned out to be so popular that slowly it made its way throughout GM and the whole automotive industry.

Looks meant a great deal, but the rest also mattered. The V-8 engine represented a new standard of automotive achievement. This compact, lightweight (seven hundred pounds dry), and silent six-liter engine developed 325 gross horsepower and could push the car effortlessly to speeds of one hundred miles per hour. That was combined with the exceptionally smooth and efficient automatic Hydra-Matic transmission, while air conditioning—still a thrilling novelty—was available on sedans and coupes, and the convertible boasted an automatically raised and lowered top.

All the chrome, the new dual headlights, and the technical innovations did not come cheap. The Cadillac Eldorado Brougham hardtop sedan listed at thirteen thousand dollars (about fifty-two thousand 1988 dollars, a huge sum for an American 1958 car), more than double the price of the standard model, but that was all right. Here was achievement, visible spending on a large scale, and the buyers wanted everyone to know it, so the fin prospered. From an odd-looking little bump over the fender in the mid-fifties, fins grew and grew until in 1958 they were as conspicuous as those to be seen on the new jet planes.

Outlined in chrome, sprouting from chrome-wrapped brake and backup lights, the fins adorning Cadillacs looked, by 1959, as if they had developed a life of their own. Immensely high, and made to look even larger by the sloping line of the trunk, they erupted in the middle with a pair of pointed taillights that emphasized their already spectacular thrust. At a time when technological progress was still thought to be progress itself, the Cadillac was less a car than an early-model rocket ship made for the American highway.

These immensely comfortable, powerful cars were not inexpensive to run, however. They consumed a great deal of gas and oil, but in an era when natural resources seemed inexhaustible and were, in fact, cheap, it hardly seemed to matter, especially since the automobile, and all that went with it, was deeply felt as a symbol of prosperity. Year by year more cars were produced, more miles of superhighway were built, more drive-in conveniences were invented. Diners remind us of the thirties, but the fifties were the time of the carhop, meals on trays, drive-in movies, drive-in banks. As thousands of housing developments sprouted across the country, all far away from shops and public transportation, cars became more necessary than ever. But they were also much more than that: they were instant and visible glamour—and no one could mistake or ignore a Cadillac's fins.

Then, too, their difference was especially prized in an age of uniformity. When all those hundreds of thousands of new ranch houses looked the same, when all businessmen wore their hair short and their suits gray, the mass-produced automobile was, paradoxically, an expression of individuality. Bright, shiny colors, lots and lots of chrome, endless options—all these inventions of the designers in Detroit became a way for customers to affirm themselves, and the manufacturers knew it. "You can design a car," Harley Earl said, "so that every time you get in it, it's a relief—you have a little vacation for a while."

What came to matter most was the eagerly awaited yearly styling change, because candy-colored bodywork and lots of chrome sold cars. In the years ahead, less and less attention would be paid to technological innovations and, finally, to the quality of manufacture itself. But none of this seemed to matter as long as this year's fin sold the car, as long as last year's fin looked shamefully out of fashion.

Automobiles—and the Cadillac—of course, are still status symbols, but in the late fifties these vast, gently swaying dreamboats were more than that: they were the visible sign that this was the American century. Like other such signs, their meaning has changed in retrospect. What was seen as a mark of dominion now reads as a poignant appeal to our vanity. But for all that, the 1958 Cadillac retains its place in a permanent corner of the American psyche.

THE DIGNITY OF NURSING

George F. Will

Lytton Strachey dipped his pen in the acid of his malice in order to etch word sketches of "Eminent Victorians." However, one of his subjects proved impervious to his considerable powers of disparagement. She was Florence Nightingale, the founder of nursing as a modern profession. Strachey, unable to suppress an emotion strange to him—admiration—wrote that in the filth and carnage of the Crimean War she was "a rock in the angry ocean." She profoundly influenced hospital construction and management and nurses' education. Amazing, said Strachey, for someone who was "merely a nurse."

Well. A nurse is a remarkable social artifact, and there are not nearly enough nurses, in part because of backward attitudes packed into phrases like "merely a nurse." Today's nursing shortage is not just another crisis *de jour.* By the end of this century—in just 12 years—the demand for nurses will be double the supply. Fourteen percent of hospitals in large urban areas and 9 percent in small urban areas are delaying admissions because of the shortage. The shortage has strange aspects. More nurses are needed because Americans are healthy longer. And although we have more nurses than ever—about 2 million—more are needed because people are sicker when admitted to hospitals.

The advance of medicine and public health accelerated in the late 19th century with improved control of infectious diseases. Then the 20th century's characterizing phenomenon—war—brought progress in surgery and trauma control. Next came rapid strides in diagnosis and pharmacology. Today, and partly as a result of these advances, the most pressing medical problem is care for the chronically ill. This usually requires intense application of nursing skills. And because demography is destiny, we know that the need will intensify. The number of Americans 85 or older is rising six times as fast as the rest of the population.

Important basic needs of the chronically ill are emotional and social. But the intense specialization and technological emphasis of modern medicine have diminished the ability and willingness of doctors—once upon a time they were esteemed for their "bedside manner"—to satisfy such needs. The American ideal of a doctor—kindly, caring, reassuring Dr. Welby—was, says Lucille Joel, essentially a nurse. She is one. She also is a Rutgers professor and a forceful advocate of the proposition that nursing should be accorded the dignity of a profession parallel to that of doctors.

The crux of today's deteriorating physician-nurse relations is that many physicians cannot understand, or will not accept, that nurses can, should and want to do more than carry out doctors' orders. Nurses should be regarded by physicians more as complementary and less as subordinate professionals. Physicians are an episodic presence in the life of a patient. Nurses control the environment of healing. Assisting the rehabilitation of a stroke victim or monitoring and coping with chronic disease is essentially a nurse's, not a physician's function. A nurse—a mere nurse—superintends complex technologies, dispenses information and health education and strives for a holistic understanding of patients' needs, which include empathy.

For various reasons, ranging from AIDS (in New York City AIDS patients occupy about 5 percent of all hospital beds) to the use of toxic substances in treatments, nursing is still a dangerous profession. It also is increasingly demanding, physically and emotionally. Most people in hospitals are hurting and frightened and their families are in distress. This is increasingly true because, for cost-containment reasons, hospitals are increasingly reluctant to admit people unless they are quite ill. More and more patients are older and sicker and require more nursing. There is an 86 percent higher ratio of nurses to patients than 12 years ago. Then there were 58 per 100 patients, now there are 91 (spread over three shifts).

Patients progress quickly when they can get ample assistance in walking, eating and other elemental matters when they need it. Because of the nursing shortage many patients either take longer to heal or are discharged feeling more unwell than they would if given needed nursing. Furthermore, cost-cutting hospitals are trimming the staff (ward clerks, secretaries, transport and laboratory aides) that supports nurses, who now do extra duties. Nurses are paying a price for their reputation for versatility and dependability.

Sensibilities required: The nursing profession has a supply-side tradition of generating a high flow of highly motivated nurses and not worrying about retention. However, the emancipation of women, opening careers to talents, has enlarged women's choices while making nursing, a female-dominated profession (only 3 percent are male), less attractive to young women. There are, Joel believes, severe limits to the ability to attract male nurses, partly because of the difference between the sensibilities required for nursing and those produced by the socialization of men.

Nurses' salaries are low, starting, on average, at $21,000, and the ceiling can be hit in less than seven years. Many 20-year nurses make less than $30,000. An attorney in private practice can reasonably hope to increase his or her salary more than 200 percent in a career. A nurse can expect an increase of less than 40 percent. Add to monetary deprivation the denial of the psychological income of status, respect and intellectual growth and you have a recipe for a shortage.

Nightingale set a tone of brisk practicality for the nursing profession when she noted dryly that whatever else can be said of hospitals, this must be said: they should not spread disease. They should not be dangerous places, but they are becoming more so because of society's neglectfulness regarding nurses. Such neglect can have consequences for you, mortal reader. "If we live long enough, something wears out. I don't care how much oatmeal you eat," says Joel, viewing the columnist's breakfast with as much distaste as he does. The nursing profession must be nurtured with financial and emotional support. Otherwise, someday when you are in a hospital and are in pain or other need you will ring for a nurse and she will not come as soon, or be as attentive, as you and she would wish. And the chances are, aging reader, that the day will come when you will ring.

WILL THE WEATHER CHANNEL SAVE AMERICA?

James Gorman

I don't want to say flat out that the Weather Channel is the best thing on television. That would leave out the fishing shows. Actually, the fishing shows are the best thing on television. I saw one in which two old southern boys sat in a boat for half an hour without catching anything. That's right, two guys in a boat talking about what it would be like if they did happen to catch something. Zen TV.

They weren't unhappy. They just sat there, chatting, flicking their lures out and reeling them in. That was it. That's all that happened. The effect was that slowly, inexorably, the compelling lack of action drew the viewer into the same state of enlightened nothingness that fishermen experience on a slow day on a hot lake. Largemouth bass Nirvana.

Compare this with *Miami Vice*, the television show that introduced to the world the genre of action-couture. In the archetypal *Miami Vice* episode two different scenes were crosscut, or interweaved, much the way tulle and taffeta might be combined in a ballet costume. In one scene thugs were murdering some poor woman. In the other Don Johnson was making love to another poor woman. (My memory is hazy, but I'm sure it wasn't the same woman.) The viewers were heaved back and forth from Don Johnson and his victim to the thugs and their victim until the death of one and the presumptive orgasm of the other occurred simultaneously.

Now I certainly wouldn't want to go around picking on every television show that made me want to throw up. I'd have no time left for fishing. And my complaint about this sex-death bit doesn't have to do with its stomach-turning quality alone. Either scene, on its own, would have made me sick. No, what was sad about this episode was that somebody felt it was necessary to have two nauseating scenes at once. And that's what's wrong with television today—too much stuff happening. On television these days there's no end to the stuff that happens—murders, sex, car chases, wardrobe changes. And now, I suppose, we're going to have to have them all at once.

It's not just the action-couture series either. Television science shows (at least those that deal with subjects other than meteorology) have succumbed to this same undeniable urge to make everything overexciting. Salmon are always spawning, stars are dying and being born, the universe is whirling apart, dinosaurs are going extinct, people are evolving. On the nature shows there is the constant drama of slaughter. (I wonder if the Public Broadcasting System understands how small a role—in terms of protein—the predator-prey relationship plays in the life of the average American.)

You could say this is all just sour grapes on my part because my life is so dull, but you'd be wrong. I change my wardrobe, I have sex—not as much as on *L.A. Law,* but then neither does anybody else—and I was even in a car chase once. It's true. Some lunatic driving a giant bus tried to run me off the Long Island Expressway, all because of a vulgar gesture I happened to have made when he cut in front of me. People are so sensitive.

No, sour grapes is not the ax I have to grind. I like my life. I prefer my clothes to Don Johnson's. And I didn't like being in the car chase at all. I just want TV to reflect my life-style, one which I think is shared by the majority of people in this country. It is a life that consists largely of getting the oil changed in the car and trying to figure out, at the supermarket, whether to buy 80- or 85-percent-lean ground beef. On a big day, I go fishing and don't catch anything.

That's what was so great about the No Fish Fish Show; it was a little bit of actual life that somehow leaked into the television world. It was just like reality. They had only one or two camera angles, which is what we've got in our house. And the show obviously wasn't planned to come out this way. Nobody had edited this film to provide the suspense of fishlessness before the fish finally started to bite. These guys just weren't catching anything. They had gone out in a boat to do their show, and another boat with cameras had followed them, and the people in both boats had spent all day on some stupid lake fishing and talking and filming, and they hadn't caught a damned thing. Then they put this on television.

It was a shock, like when Lex Luthor takes over the television networks in Superman movies. I felt like Winston Smith in *1984*. I had managed to remember who we were at war with. I had remembered that this was what life was actually like—sitting in a boat with no sound track not catching anything. I took the moment as a kind of epiphany vouchsafed to those television viewers with an interest in bass fishing. I had no hopes to see anything like it again. I was satisfied that one such experience was as much as anyone could hope for. But I was wrong. I didn't know, then, about the Weather Channel.

I don't think any of us really expected science to revolutionize television, let alone meteorology. I know I didn't. Like most people I had pinned my hopes on our regional playwrights. In hindsight, now that I've experienced the Weather Channel, I can see why meteorology was such a likely candidate. It has to do with something people understand, for one thing. Rain is a far easier concept to grasp than, say, quantum gravity, or superstrings. You can see rain. You can even see the clouds that make it, in the satellite pictures. Like most Americans I'm a sucker for satellite pictures. This is one reason why there are so few television series on mathematics. No satellite pictures.

Of course, it would be disingenuous of me to suggest that meteorology did it all. A technological breakthrough was also necessary—cable TV. With cable, and with the wide dissemination of remote control for television, people are able to lie on the couch and zip through 20 or 30 or 50 channels and then back again. This makes the surfeit of action on the tube even more obvious. If you do this for a while, you realize very quickly that there's no point in figuring out what show you're watching or what the plot is. All television is made up of inter-changeable action modules, and you can switch from car chase to sex to shooting to car chase, never knowing who is chasing or kissing whom, and never caring.

With cable, people watch not shows but the television itself, as if they were looking through a window to check what's going on in the street, or what the weather is. The realization of this fact no doubt inspired the creation of the Weather Channel. Somebody said: Let's forget the whole notion of shows— the viewers have. Let's just have one endless weather forecast that repeats itself over and over. And let's forget about lying to the audience and claiming our channel will be exciting. Let's just claim that if people tune in, we'll tell them about the weather.

The result is something very much like the fishing shows, except that you don't have to like fishing. You don't even have to like the weather that much, because you don't have to watch for very long to find out what's going on. The Weather Channel doesn't really have shows. It has the weather, 24 hours a day, seven days a week, 365 days a year, delivered in bits and pieces, some as short as a minute, some as long as three minutes. You can tune in and tune out anytime you want. There's no violence and no kissing.

During the few weeks that I did my heaviest Weather Channel watching, I admit that there were no hurricanes or deadly tornadoes to throw the channel into frenzy, so my view may be slightly skewed. But this is what I saw: two men, or a man and a woman, with pretty unremarkable haircuts and clothes and looks, not like Diane Sawyer making the rest of us feel dumb and ugly. And they wouldn't talk to you as if something big were happening and you'd better listen up, the way Dan Rather does, because something big wasn't happening.

Mostly they talked about the temperature in different places. They'd tell you the international temperatures—84 in Rome, 92 in Bucharest. And they'd tell you the temperatures in our country and talk about our clouds and our highs and lows and where and when it would rain and snow. One day I learned that it had been 18 in Great Falls the night before and 90 in Miami. It made me think. What a diverse country we live in, I thought, and yet we're all Americans. It was kind of amazing. And when I saw that blue jet stream, done as a kind of video Slinky snaking across the weather map, or looked at the satellite pictures that showed the swirling clouds uniting us all in the movements of the cold fronts and the warm fronts, I felt not only that this channel related to my life—in that the weather they were talking about was the same weather I walked around in—but that I was part of a nationwide weather community. That is the level of excitement I like on my television. And that's the charm of the Weather Channel. In a world of video tarts shaking their goodies all over the screen saying "Hey baby, want to party?" there is one plain, unadorned, mousy little channel that says, "Hi. Some rain, huh?" To me it's irresistible.

Not that it's perfect, yet. We don't really need the maps and the blue snaky jet stream and the suits and ties. And we don't need lots of different weather people. All we really need are two guys, preferably southern, to just sit and chat about the weather. And then, if we could just, well, I know this is asking a lot, but if we could just put them in a boat and let them fish while they talked. Do you see how good that would be? Once in a while they'd catch some fish. It would rain now and then. A little drizzle, nothing big. And they'd talk about the weather. Snow in Colorado, sun in Florida, thunderstorms in Kansas. You could turn to them any time you wanted. Any time of the day or night you could switch to the Fishing and Weather Channel and there they'd be, not Crockett and Tubbs shooting up Miami, but two regular guys, your friends and mine, fishing and talking about the weather.

FOUNDING FATHER

Hugh Lloyd-Jones
THE HISTORY OF HERODOTUS. *Translated by David Grene. University of Chicago Press.*

For all practical purposes, historical writing in the West starts with Herodotus; there is no denying his importance. Had he not written, we should be painfully ignorant of the history of the Mediterranean and the Middle East up to his time. Also, Herodotus is a marvelously entertaining writer who, thanks to the astonishing variety of his subject matter and to his wit, humor, and narrative skill, can be read continuously or dipped into with delight even by those whose ignorance of Greek prevents them from appreciating his writing to the fullest. He is the father not only of history but of ethnology, even of anthropology. There is no denying either his importance or his readability. But is the father of history truly a great historian?

Since his own century, a strong body of opinion has accused Herodotus of credulity, of indifference to truth, even of downright falsification. Thucydides, who was only a generation younger, must have had Herodotus in mind when he wrote that his own history's lack of a mythical element might displease some readers, but that it was not intended simply to win immediate success, and also when he remarked that most people take little trouble to find out the truth. That view of Herodotus has its upholders to this day, as I shall show presently. But there is an even graver charge against him. It has been alleged, and by no mean authorities, that his ethical and religious beliefs precluded him from making a correct assessment of historical motives and connections. Wilamowitz found that Herodotus "had neither political understanding, historical sense, nor a firm and clear world outlook, but wavered between rationalism and superstition." Felix Jacoby thought Herodotus to be "hopelessly handicapped by the religious outlook which he had inherited." David Grene, however, would, I think, agree with me that the religious outlook inherited by Herodotus was one singularly well qualified to help him to survey world history from a detached and enlightened point of view.

Herodotus was born during the eighties of the fifth century B.C. in Halicarnassus, a Greek city of Asia Minor then under Persian rule. After his extensive travels, he made his way to Athens. His historical subject was the invasion of Greece in 480 B.C. by the king of Persia, Xerxes, with a vast naval and military armament, and Xerxes' defeat by a temporary coalition of most of the Greek communities, with Athens and Sparta playing the chief parts. Few historical events have been more surprising or have had more momentous consequences. In order to give an adequate explanation, Herodotus thought it necessary not only to recount much Greek and other Mediterranean and Oriental history of the preceding time, but also to offer much ethnographic and geographic information, mostly about the countries of the Persian Empire, which at that time stretched from Egypt as far west as Bactria and from the latitude of the Black Sea as far south as that of the Persian Gulf. Egypt in particular was given extended treatment, dependent, Herodotus claims, on autopsy, and occupying the whole of the second of the nine books into which the history is divided. Similar treatment was given the remote region of Scythia (South Russia), to which most of the fourth book is devoted. This kind of material occupies most of the first six books, and the actual narrative of the war is contained in the remaining three.

The difficulty of acquiring the information necessary for such a work, and of seeing that it is reasonably accurate, can hardly be exaggerated. A few minor historical works that may or may not be earlier than Herodotus may have helped a little, but the only major work that can have been of much use was that of Hecataeus of Miletus, who was a geographer and a genealogist rather than a historian. The information had to be collected laboriously from diverse informants and in the course of extensive travels. Since Herodotus does not claim to speak any foreign language, he must have depended on the services of many interpreters. Undoubtedly he took great trouble to collect his material and where possible to verify his facts; but he operated with such remote and varied communities and at a time when the borderline between myth and history was so indeterminate that from the beginning his veracity could be doubted, all the more easily because his power as a storyteller is so compelling.

Herodotus warns his readers that he puts down what he has been told, often giving more than one version of a story and often telling us from what source it comes; that is not necessarily a less scientific procedure than that of Thucydides, who gives only one version of each story and does not name his source. Many of his stories are clearly myths, but that does not mean that he takes them literally or that they lack interest or significance.

For example, Herodotus tells a story of the early years of Cyrus, the founder of the Persian Empire, which has many of the standard features of the myth of the birth of the hero as it is described by Otto Rank. The story is certainly not true, but as the foundation myth of the great empire, it is of great interest. Again, Herodotus alleges that after the defeat of the mysterious successor of the Persian king Cambyses, the three Persian nobles who had played the chief parts in that defeat held a debate, in which one suggested that they should establish a democracy, another pleaded for an oligarchy, and the third, Darius, argued successfully for the continuance of monarchy. Such a debate cannot have taken place; but as a specimen of the Greek political theorizing of the time, the story is not uninteresting. The intelligent reader will know how to interpret mythical narrations of this kind. But anyone who takes Herodotus's apparent naïveté for real is being naive himself and has failed to reckon with the historian's wit, humor, and irony.

Certainly Herodotus tells his story in a framework provided by religion; but Greek religion is totally unlike dogmatic monotheism. Its gods do not arbitrarily change the course of nature, but work through natural processes and human passions. Thus Herodotus can remark that it makes sense to say that the passage through which the great river of Thessaly, the Peneus, flows between the mountains to the sea was made by the god Poseidon, because anyone who thinks Poseidon causes earthquakes will believe this, and it was clearly an earthquake that made the passage. In this religion the chief god, Zeus, punishes men's crimes against each other; but the punishment is often long delayed, falling not on the criminal but on his descendants, so that the working of divine justice is not easily perceived by short-lived mortals. Thus the usurpation of Gyges, the founder of the Mermnad dynasty of Lydian kings, is punished only in the fifth generation, when Croesus is conquered by the Persians under Cyrus. Herodotus often speaks of envy felt against mortals by the gods. From the human point of view, it is natural for a believer in Greek religion to think of the gods as envying or resenting excessive prosperity on the part of mortals; yet a god might retort, as gods do in Homer, that the so-called envy is merely the gods' wish to defend their own due honor and the prerogatives that it entails.

Human beings, Herodotus in accordance with his religion thought, cannot attain or keep prosperity without hard work. A family or a nation rises to power, but then grows weak and self-indulgent and must pay the penalty. This may be seen as the operation of divine justice or of divine envy, but in any case it is a process so natural as to be inevitable. The Ionian Greeks revolted against the Persians, but refused to endure the strict discipline that the naval commander Dionysius tried to impose on them, and so were defeated and reduced to servitude. The mainland Greeks, on the other hand, could defeat the Persians because the Spartans had long lived a hard life and practiced for war and because Themistocles had persuaded the Athenians to use their find of silver at Laurium not for a general handout but for the building of a battle fleet. The Persians, hardy mountaineers, overcame the Medes and then the Lydians, lords of the rich provinces of Asia Minor; later the Persians in turn grew weak from pride and luxury and were defeated, against all expectations, by the Greeks. At the very end of the history, Herodotus tells how after the conquest of Lydia certain Persians proposed to Cyrus that they should now abandon the mountains of Iran and live in the rich and comfortable countries they had conquered. Those scholars who have supposed that because the history ends with what seems to them a trivial story it must have remained unfinished understand little of Herodotus's methods.

Dogmatic monotheism assumes that there is only one right answer to every moral question. But for the Greek religion there can be more than one answer, and from the clash between conflicting imperatives, tragedy results. The predecessor who influenced Herodotus most was, beyond all comparison, Homer. Just as Homer takes a tragic view of the siege of Troy, Herodotus takes a tragic view of the history he records. He can observe the bad as well as the good qualities of great men and the bad as well as the good consequences of great events; he can treat men and nations, even those with whom he feels a special sympathy, with sovereign impartiality. He is able to describe the diverse customs and institutions of many different human communities without patronizing them from the standpoint of his own culture. The contempt that Greeks came to feel for "barbarians" after the defeat of Xerxes formed no part of Herodotus's way of thinking.

While the academic rationalism of the late nineteenth century was at its height, Herodotus was often severely handled by scholars, as my earlier quotations from Wilamowitz and Jacoby will serve to indicate. But from about 1930 a reaction set in. First, Orientalists found new evidence that confirmed many of Herodotus's statements, and later, certain historians—notably, Arnaldo Momigliano—vindicated Herodotus's historical methods. During the last few years, indeed, his veracity has again been challenged, by Detlev Fehling in Germany and O. K. Armayor in this country. These critics have indeed cast doubt on the truth of a number of Herodotus's allegations, but they are far from having established the general unreliability even of his account of Egypt, from which most of their examples have been taken. But even if some of his claims, such as his belief in the flying snakes of Arabia, cannot easily be accepted, his essential veracity as a historian must surely be acknowledged, as it has by the late eminent historian Hermann Strasburger.

Anyone who can understand his religion must recognize Herodotus as a great historian. The power of his tragic vision of history is enhanced by his possession of literary gifts of the very highest order. His prose is clear, rapid, euphonious, marvelously varied according to variations of his subject matter; he can write in a plain and simple manner, with short sentences loosely strung together, but he can also build up elaborate periodic structures, making effective use of many poetical words. As a stylist, no other writer of classical Greek prose except Plato and, in certain of his works, Demosthenes, can be compared with him. . . .

FOR YOU TO WRITE

This chapter's classification of subjects for evaluation (things natural and constructed, people, events, actions, and abstractions) has perhaps suggested many topics for argument. The following list of potential evaluation theses from several disciplines may also contain one that captures your interest or stimulates your invention of a similar one. In each case, before beginning to formulate your argument, specify what audience in what situation you might address.

Science and Technology

1. Evaluate any recent invention or technological advance. Does it satisfy any criterion of design, or perform its function more efficiently, or lead to good or bad effects? Examples: superconductors, lasers, fiber optics, automatic teller machines, VCRs, microwave ovens.

2. Evaluate the work of any particular scientist, living or dead. Investigate not only the good or bad effects of the scientist's discoveries, but also whether his or her work approaches an ideal of good science.

3. Evaluate an agricultural or environmental policy or practice: clear cutting forest land, the use of a particular pesticide or fertilizer (you may want to compare two products here), no-till farming, factory farming of chickens, bear hunting, the attempt to build up populations of wolves and cougars in North American forests.

4. Evaluate the United States space program at any point or any period in its history.

5. Evaluate an energy source or possibility or policy: wind energy, geothermal energy, wave energy, orbiting solar collectors, fusion, or any national energy policy.

6. Evaluate any medical breakthrough or therapy or practice: new imaging techniques such as NMR or the CAT scan, organ transplants, routine chest x-rays, the use of any particular drug for depression, electric-shock treatment, HMOs, the use of paramedics and midwives in place of physicians.

7. Evaluate a weapon or weapon system: the neutron bomb, the M-16 rifle in the Vietnam War, the MX missile system, the use of defoliants or biological warfare, electronic countermeasures.

8. Evaluate the work of an individual science writer, such as Stephen Jay Gould or Robert Cowan, or the quality of a science magazine intended for the general or educated public, such as *Scientific American, Science,* or *Natural History.*

9. Evaluate an engineering accomplishment for both its practical and aesthetic merit: the Concorde, the Brooklyn Bridge, the Hoover Dam, the Paris sewer system, the Los Angeles freeway system, Roman aqueducts or baths.

10. Evaluate by using ethical criteria as well as consequence some significant scientific breakthrough: recombinant DNA technology.

History and Social Studies

1. Evaluate a technological innovation that has been historically significant: the longbow, the tank, the telescope, the atomic bomb. You might even do a comparative evaluation: "British ships in the sixteenth century were better than Spanish ships."

2. Evaluate an educational method or policy: the mainstreaming of handicapped and retarded children, the Montessori method, special programs for the gifted, busing to achieve racial balance, equal funding for men's and women's sports, required musical or art education.

3. Evaluate a legal practice or a law enforcement policy: televising criminal trials, the legal-aid system, no-fault divorce, mandatory sentencing, job training programs in prison, restitution as a substitute for imprisonment, grade average requirements for juvenile offenders, and plea bargaining.

4. Evaluate media coverage of a particular event, such as a political convention or an international crisis. You can even do a comparative or superlative evaluation to decide which network or newspaper or magazine coverage was better or best.

5. Evaluate some historical or contemporary figure in a particular role: a president, a prime minister, a senator, a general, a Supreme Court justice, an industrial leader.

6. Evaluate a social or psychological theory: B. F. Skinner's behaviorism, E. O. Wilson's sociobiology, Sigmund Freud's theory of penis envy, R. D. Laing's theory of madness, Carl Jung's theory of the collective unconscious, Jean Piaget's theory of cognitive development.

7. Evaluate an economic theory or practice: Adam Smith's laissez-faire economics, credit unions versus banks, the gold standard, government control of industry, the social security system, computer trading on Wall Street, arbitrage; or do a comparative evaluation of several different kinds of investments, takeovers, or mergers.

8. Evaluate an American foreign-policy decision, either recent or historical: the Monroe Doctrine, the Kellog-Briand Pact, the Marshall Plan, United States involvement in Korea, the INF Treaty, or our relations with a particular country over a limited time period.

9. Evaluate the performance of an athlete or a team at one event or over a season or throughout a career: Greg Louganis at the 1984 and '88 Olympics, Dwight Gooden in any particular year, Carl Yazstremski over his whole career.

10. Evaluate a political theory or practice: Machiavellianism, the American primary system, the Taft-Hartley Act, any particular department or agency of the federal government, such as the Department of Energy or the FCC, or do a comparative evaluation of the parliamentary system of government versus the American.

The Arts and Literature

1. Evaluate a TV performance or series or network, or a TV personality such as Johnny Carson, Oprah Winfrey, Al Michaels, or John Madden. Do a

comparative evaluation of PBS or a cable channel versus the commercial networks.

2. Evaluate a movie. Rather than evaluating the entire movie, you might concentrate on the acting, script, direction, or special effects. Or you might do a comparative evaluation of two movies of the same type or by the same director. Or do a superlative evaluation, identifying the best movie by a certain director or the worst performance by a certain actor or actress.

3. Evaluate a painting or the work of one painter or a school of painting. Imagine that you are trying to move an uninitiated audience to admiration or distaste.

4. Choose a building you particularly admire (a house, a church, a campus building, a store) and analyze its appeal according to clearly articulated aesthetic and practical criteria.

5. If you have recently attended a concert or rock festival or live musical performance of some kind, evaluate its total effect. More than the performer's virtuosity may be involved. Or you may do a comparative evaluation of two recorded performances of the same piece: Ashkenazy and Vásáry playing Chopin's Second Piano Concerto, or the Beatles' and Jerry Lee Lewis's versions of "Roll Over Beethoven."

6. If you know something about musical composition, you can evaluate a piece of music itself, either as representative of its composer or of its type: the best work by a composer, the best cut on an album, the best or worst piece of its kind. If you know anything about the electronics of sound reproduction, you can evaluate the technology of an album.

7. Write a book review in which you try to interest or discourage another reader by your evaluation. The object of your review could be anything from a short story to an extended work of nonfiction. Be sure you define and defend, if necessary, your criteria. If you are studying literature, you are in the process of learning appropriate criteria of evaluation.

8. Given the variety of poetry that has been written, establishing criteria for evaluation of a poem is especially difficult. Try to convince a friend who does not read poetry to see the merit of a poem you admire.

9. Imagine that you are writing a travel brochure to convince tourists to visit a scenic spot you are familiar with. Your description of that place will contain an evaluation and should reveal your criteria of judgment.

10. Evaluate the interior design of a room and its contents. Of course you may judge its beauty, but you may instead or also apply criteria of comfort or utility. A dorm room, for instance, may not be beautiful, but it may be functional.

Ethical Issues

In the following controversial issues, two or more apparent rights conflict. To argue about any of them requires an ordering of values according to importance. Take a stand on any of these issues or a similar one you find compelling. Come up with a thesis that has "right" or "wrong" in its predicate. Carefully qualify your thesis to include any necessary contingencies. For example, "Is it right for women as well as men to serve in combat zones?" On the one side is the belief that if the sexes have the same rights, they should have the same responsibilities; on the other is the force of precedent and the physical disparity between men and women. Possible thesis: "With the exception of mothers, it is right for women to serve in combat zones."

1. Is it right for a physician to give a patient a placebo, that is, a drug without pharmacological effect, which the patient believes to be active medicine, even though some patients do improve after taking placebos?

2. Is it right for adoptees to have access to their birth records in order to discover their biological parents, even though the parents gave them up on the guarantee that the records would remain sealed?

3. Is it right to open the day in public schools with a time for silent meditation, even though agnostics and atheists claim that such meditation is an unconstitutional form of religious activity?

4. Is it right for a landlord to refuse a lease on the basis of race, religion, occupation, sexual preference, family size, or pets, even though the property to be rented is clearly the landlord's and the landlord is responsible for its maintenance?

5. Is it right to grant a woman alimony after a divorce, whether or not she initiated the divorce, whether or not she has children at home, whether or not she has ever worked outside the home during the marriage? Is the length of the marriage or the extent of the husband's financial resources relevant?

6. Is it right for non-English-speaking United States residents to be taught in their own language in the public schools, even though such instruction can produce financial inequity in a school district and may slow down the minority's assimilation and further education in the dominant culture?

7. Is it right for employers to require mandatory drug or AIDS testing, whether or not the job involves risk to the public, whether or not the tests are reliable, whether or not other dependencies or defects are tested for?

8. Is it right for the United States to extend political asylum to the children of diplomats who wish to remain in this country rather than return to their own, even though their parents want to return and even though the practice establishes a precedent for American diplomatic families living abroad?

9. Is it right for the economically ailing United States of the 1980s to refuse refugees from political, economic, religious, or racial oppression, even though the nation was built by such refugees?

10. Is it right for television news shows to broadcast nationally the projected outcome of elections on the basis of sample precincts, even though voters in parts of the country where the polls have yet to close may be influenced by such projections?

Part Four

WHAT SHOULD WE DO ABOUT IT?

13 | The Proposal: Arguing About What Should Be Done

When we learn that something is going wrong—our football team has lost its last five games, seventh graders are smoking pot, people are starving in Ethiopia—we ask the fourth and most practical of the great questions: "What should be done about it?" The argument that answers this question is a proposal. Such an argument "proposes" or urges some action; it says that something ought to be, should be, needs to be, or must be done.

A proposal is a very common kind of argument. We make proposals in every relationship and area of life: to ourselves and to each other, at home and at work, in our community and in government. The following proposals demonstrate this range:

1. I should practice piano two hours a day.
2. We should put a new septic tank in our back yard.
3. We need to expel the troublemakers from the sixth-grade classroom.
4. We must conserve paper in this office.
5. Our community should build a new indoor swimming pool.
6. Our state ought to have a scholarship program based on merit only.
7. The United States should intervene in Angola.
8. Mankind must preserve the earth for future generations.

Arguing for a proposal does not require any new techniques. You have already learned all the techniques you need when you learned how to argue about what things are and how they got that way. The proposal simply combines tactics you are already familiar with—definition, evaluation, comparison, and causal argument. Constructing a persuasive proposal is a matter of choosing the necessary arguments and arranging them in a convincing structure.

In the following sections we will show you the balanced structure of a full, formal proposal, take a look at several types of arguments that are not quite full proposals, and suggest when either the full or short forms are useful.

KINDS OF PROPOSALS

Before we talk about the contents of the full proposal, we should look at one important way to distinguish one kind of proposal from another. To put it simply, some proposals are more specific than others. We can have proposals as vague as the following:

1. We should do something about this problem.
2. This situation needs to be improved.
3. We must not tolerate this state of affairs any longer.

And we can have very specific proposals:

1. I should get up at 6:30 tomorrow morning and run three miles around the golf course before breakfast.
2. The Cessna 250 needs a green knob on the wiper control on the left side of its instrument panel.
3. The Secretary of State should meet with the Cultural Affairs Minister of Bulgaria in the lobby before the opera.

Actually, we can think of proposals as on a continuum from the vague to the specific:

1. Our high-school science program needs to be improved.
2. We should upgrade our lab equipment.
3. We need to buy seventeen new stereo-microscopes for the biology labs.

The situation and audience will determine how specific a proposal needs to be. If you are just sitting around griping with your friends about what is wrong with your science program, you might come up with the first proposal above. If you talk to the teachers or principal about the problem, you might come up with the second proposal in addition to the first. But if you go to the school board to get some action finally, you will also have to come up with the most specific proposal, the third one. How specific the proposal is determines the content of the argument supporting it. The more specific the proposal, the fuller the argument has to be, though not necessarily the longer. It may not be difficult to convince people that improvement is necessary, but if you want money to buy microscopes, you need to do some hard arguing.

THE PARTS OF THE FULL PROPOSAL

We are going to give you advice on how to argue for the most specific proposal because it requires the fullest treatment. But you can adapt the method, choosing the parts you need for audiences in situations where a full proposal is unnecessary or inappropriate. In its fullest form, the proposal argument breaks into two parts that flank the proposal statement itself. You can think of the full-proposal argument as an hourglass, with the proposal statement at the neck. Here is the typical arrangement of these three essential parts:

1. preliminary arguments—convince an audience that a problem exists
2. proposal statement—suggest general or specific response to the problem
3. supporting arguments—convince an audience that a specific action should and can be taken

Each of these sections can be further broken down.

PRELIMINARY ARGUMENTS

The Demonstration: "We Really Have a Problem"

What is the aim of the proposal argument? It asks for action from its audience, either to change the way something is being done now, to initiate something new, or even to stop something. In most cases, the arguer will begin by pointing out that things as they are now are not the way they should be. Therefore, a proposal argument often opens with a demonstration that the present state is in need of improvement. In effect, the arguer points a finger and says, "Look at that mess!"

Just how much of a demonstration section your proposal needs depends on the obviousness of the problem and the awareness of the audience. If you are standing in downtown Johnstown the day after a flood and proposing a rebuilding project to the former residents, you will not need much of a demonstration section. You can literally point around you. But if you are writing to the appropriate agencies in Washington to get funding for this same rebuilding program, you will have to demonstrate in words just how bad things are in Johnstown.

If the audience is not aware at all of the problem that needs to be solved, a demonstration section will be a necessary and important part of the argument, maybe even the bulk of it. Imagine, for example, you want to propose to an audience of consumers that factory farming be replaced by more humane methods of raising animals. Since most people are not aware of the techniques used in factory farming, any proposal to enlarge cages, provide straw, light, and fresh air for chickens or better diet for calves would first have to inform its general audience that these basic comforts are absent.

An audience can be anywhere between complete ignorance and full awareness of a problem. Sometimes the demonstration section may simply have to remind them of a problem they are already more or less familiar with. For example, the residents of a particular community may have heard about the problems of senior citizens, but they may have general rather than specific information. They may not be aware that in their town 3,000 men and women above sixty-five live alone in substandard housing, that 20 percent of them suffer from malnutrition, and that last winter three old people froze to death in their unheated apartments. You must provide this kind of specific information to make the unaware aware.

As the above example shows, the demonstration section can give an overall picture, provide trenchant statistics, and bring generalizations alive with specific examples. Thus, while the demonstration section informs, it has another function as well. It can begin to arouse the convictions and emotions that will bring your audience to support your proposal.

The demonstration section of the proposal argument has a claim about a state of affairs for its thesis, e.g., "Many old people live in poor conditions." Remember the steps for supporting such a claim. Do you need to define any terms? How much evidence might your audience need? These matters are covered in Part I.

You will get a better sense of the full-proposal argument if one sample proposal is carried through all the stages. Here is the demonstration section of an argument written for a university newspaper.

> Last Friday night, I had an English paper and a set of chem problems to work on, so I turned down my roommate's invitation to go party hopping at fraternities. While my roommate showered I sat down at my desk with self-righteous

satisfaction. I lined up my calculator with my open chemistry book; I had a clean page before me and a sharpened pencil. As I wrote down the first problem, my roommate slammed back into the room, unpacked her closet, and emptied her drawers looking for something to wear. That was the first of eight interruptions in thirty-five minutes. I can be exact about that number because I had pencil and paper to keep score, and they were useless for doing chemistry problems. Three people came in to borrow clothes, records, and money; one came in crying because she and her boyfriend had just had a fight. Two girls down the hall were having a water battle with their dates, someone across the quad was testing the range of his stereo equipment, and my mother called to ask how I was doing in my courses. So much for chemistry; I gave up and went to the party with my roommate.

The next day, football Saturday, I had band practice in the morning and spent the afternoon at the game. I had set aside Saturday night in my mind to tackle my chem problems again. This time I was wise enough to get out of my room. Since the main library was closed, I headed for the study lounge on my floor. That was a mistake; there were sixty people dancing in there, the nucleus of the floor keg party that spilled out into the hall in both directions. Maybe the student union lounge would be quiet on a Saturday night? Well, it was relatively quiet—but crowded as well. Every seat was taken. Since I didn't feel like sitting on the floor, I walked back to my dorm, past the closed library.

Am I so unusual? I wondered if other students, any other students, ever tried to study on a weekend night and found it impossible. So on Monday morning, I took a survey in my English and chem classes. Since most freshmen take these courses and there is nothing unusual about my sections, I had a representative sample of freshman opinion. I found that roughly one-fourth of the students studied—or tried to—on either Friday or Saturday night. Now one-quarter of the freshman class is roughly 1,000 students, wandering around campus with calculators and pads of paper, trying to find a quiet place to work.

Undesirable Consequences of the Situation

Your demonstration section may convince your audience that a situation exists, but not necessarily that this situation is a problem. To create in your audience a conviction that a situation is a problem is quite simply to evaluate that situation as bad. As you know from the preceding chapter on evaluations, you can do so by showing that the situation has undesirable consequences or is ethically wrong or both. Let's consider the first method, showing how the situation leads to undesirable consequences: how, for example, arson leads to inflated insurance rates, how wife abuse produces maladjusted lives, how aerosol sprays affect the ozone layer. These consequences are established by causal arguments.

Consequences may be either relatively obvious or not. If they are not obvious, you should certainly trace them for your audience, and if you can bring the bad effects home to your audience, you will arouse in them a very strong incentive for change. How, for example, can lawn-proud suburban-ites be persuaded not to use chemical fertilizers? Only by having a very undesirable consequence shown to be harming them: The fertilizer chemi-cals are seeping into their own drinking water.

Before you construct your "bad consequences" section, think over the following ways in which an audience can be unaware of the effects of a situation.

Ways an Audience Can Be Unaware

First, people may simply be *ignorant* that any effects exist at all; the public did not know, for instance, that some insecticides irreversibly build up in the fatty tissues of animals in a food chain until Rachel Carson pointed that out in *Silent Spring.*

Second, consequences may appear bad only from a certain *point of view.* Machine-dialed commercial phone calls, for example, may be of some benefit to the stores, mail-order houses, and magazine agencies that make them, but they can be an intrusive nuisance from the consumer's point of view. Often an arguer needs to show that a group the audience identifies with or has sympathy for is harmed by a situation.

Third, the audience may be unaware of the *extent* of the consequences, even though they may know that a consequence exists in any single instance. We all know that arson destroys lives and property, but we may be surprised to learn how many lives and how much property. The very extent of a problem can produce its own consequences: The prevalence of arson leads to increased insurance rates and cost of fire protection for all property.

Why Inform the Aware?

Often the undesirable consequences of the situation are well known to the audience, but even then pointing them out may be worthwhile. Probably everyone is familiar with the effects of cigarette smoking, but if you are trying to persuade your father to stop smoking, you should pull them all out again. Listing effects when they are *not* known serves the two purposes of informing and convincing; listing them when they *are* known may still be convincing. What everybody knows, nobody cares about. So the art of the arguer is to turn dull acknowledgment into vivid awareness. Any push toward action, such as the emotional appeal of bad consequences, is useful.

Evaluating the Consequences

There is one crucial thing to remember about consequence arguments. Behind every demonstration of bad consequences stands an ethical evaluation, a judgment that the consequence is bad. Demonstrating that a situation has consequences can be one thing; showing that these consequences are bad or undesirable may be another. We may, for instance, agree that the consequence of putting a bounty on wolf pelts is the extinction of the species. But some people may say, "So what?" They may not think that the extinction of wolves is such a bad idea. To substantiate the badness of a consequence that is not self-evidently undesirable to a particular audience may require *another* consequence argument or an ethical appeal. To continue the above argument, for example, we may have to argue further that the extinction of wolves would be bad because the forest would become overpopulated by deer.

Let's now find out how the situation of not being able to study in the dorm brings about bad consequences.

> After that frustrating Friday and Saturday, I spent all day Sunday trying to do chem problems while I felt guilty about not doing my English paper, or working on my English paper while unsolved chem problems nagged at my mind. I ended up doing neither assignment well despite the good intentions that made me attempt to start Friday night. I owe a C on an English paper and a backlog of chem problems to that frustration. I imagine that many other students are suffering from the same problem.
>
> Since that weekend, I have given up trying to study on Friday and Saturday nights. I now go partying with my roommate even though I probably need to study more than five nights a week to get good grades. But what's the use when there is no place to study anyway? I often wonder how many of the students I see wandering around downtown from pinball parlor to pizza palace wouldn't just as soon be in a quiet place, pulling their heads together and their grades up. It's no wonder that 20 percent of the freshman class flunks out the first year, and only 50 percent of each entering class graduates four years later.

An Ethical Assessment of the Situation

Here is another way to convince your audience that a situation is a problem. You can say that a situation should be remedied not only because of its undesirable consequences, but also because it is simply wrong, no matter what the consequences. Any appeal to an audience's sense of what is right or wrong is an *ethical appeal*. (See the sections on The Variety of Ethical Appeals and Weighting Values: Ethical Argument in Chapter 12.) If you can assume that your audience will immediately agree with your ethical appeal, all you have to do is claim that the situation you want to change is wrong.

The Assumable Response

For example, everyone will agree that child abuse is a moral horror. Of course, its consequences are damaging too, but even if it had no consequences it would still be wrong in itself. We all agree that slavery is wrong, even if it had some good consequences, at least for the owners of the slaves and the economy of the country, if not for the slaves themselves. Some audiences will automatically perceive birth control, divorce, welfare, gun control, or the Chicago police as absolutely wrong in any or all circumstances. You should know when you can expect from a particular audience such a unanimous response to an ethical appeal. When you can, you do not need to argue ethics; you simply appeal to them.

What to Do When the Response Is Not Assumable

On the other hand, many issues do not call forth an immediate ethical response and many audiences will not easily see the ethics of an issue. Whether it is the audience or the issue that will not come around easily, in such cases you have to work for an ethical appeal. The only workable technique is a kind of definition argument: You place the situation in an ethical category that your audience *will* react to.

Suppose you are proposing a replacement for quota systems in medical school admissions. You have to convince your audience that the present situation, the quota system, is bad and should be removed. You can point out its bad consequences, but you may also want to argue that a quota system is simply wrong in itself. Because your audience will probably not recognize quota systems as ethically wrong, you have to place quota systems into a class that the audience will have an immediate response to. You can do that by defining a quota system as a form of discrimination. Chances are your audience will immediately recognize discrimination as ethically wrong. Similarly, you might argue that factory farming is a form of cruelty to animals, that collecting unemployment compensation is a form of fraud, that turning off a presidential address on television is unpatriotic. In each of these examples you are trying to place a subject into a category your audience will judge in a predictable way.

Here is the ethical assessment section of our continuing sample proposal. What appeals are being made?

> I often have to remind myself why I and 30,000 other people are here. Supposedly we came to get an education, to learn about things we never heard of before and to prepare ourselves for a career. Of course, most of us agree that there is more to college life than studying. That's why I'm in the band, and I enjoy an occasional party. But sometimes two nights every weekend are too much socializing for some of us. Surely students in a dorm should be given a chance to study if they want to.

Every term my parents pay my dorm bill. I have a loan to cover tuition, and everything I earn in the summer goes to pay for books and incidental expenses. And many people have a harder time financially than I do. It isn't fair to pay that much money every term and not get in return the facilities to do what I came here to do—learn. The university has a responsibility to provide not only instruction in the classroom but also support outside it. Since the university requires students to live on campus their first year in overcrowded dorms, they should at least make quiet places available, even on weekends, for those who want them. It really seems ludicrous that the hardest thing a college student should have to go through is finding a place to study.

EXERCISE

Write a paragraph addressed to an audience that is unaware, demonstrating that a problem exists in the following areas:

1. In your college or university
   a. a safety problem
   b. a housing problem
   c. a problem relating to student recreation facilities
   d. an administrative problem
   e. a course-availability problem
2. In your town or city
   a. a parking problem
   b. a zoning problem
   c. a transportation problem
   d. an education problem
   e. a tax problem
3. In a course you are studying
   a. a problem with a text
   b. a problem with the instructor
   c. a problem with the organization of the material
   d. a problem with the amount of work in a course
   e. a problem with the grading

Causal Analysis of the Situation to Be Corrected

Once we have convinced our audience that an undesirable situation exists, they might naturally ask, "How did it get that way?" To answer that question is to find causes, and often to find causes is to find a clue to a solution. It makes sense that one way to correct a situation is to attack the causes that have produced it. Our proposal may be designed to alter or eliminate the causes and therefore to alter or eliminate the effect.

If we are convinced, for example, that violence on TV causes violence in children, we can work to reduce the violence on TV; if we know that mosquitoes carry malaria, then we can work to control mosquito populations; if we have evidence that a poor translation caused diplomatic friction, we can fire the incompetent translator.

We may have to convince our audience that we have identified plausible causes of a problem. Otherwise, they won't accept the solution designed to change those causes. The proposal argument will have to incorporate causal argument here as well, using any of the techniques described earlier. The purpose of your causal argument here will be to identify necessary and sufficient causes without which the effect cannot occur, or blocking causes, the kind that will stop the effect. The following example will help you see the place of causal analysis in a proposal argument.

Suppose you are confronted with and affronted by a polluted river. As a reformer, you can propose two types of solutions. First, you can apply remedies to the effect itself by proposing that a filtration plant be built to purify the waters continually or that an effort be organized to dredge the muck. But notice that remedies that attack only the effect often require continuous application: The filtration plant will never be turned off, and the dredging will have to go on indefinitely.

Second, you may take a trip upstream and see the enormous industrial complex dumping waste into the river. You may decide to attack this *cause* of pollution instead of or as well as the pollution itself. You may propose that each factory be required to install its own filtration system or that all the factories dispose of their wastes in another way.

As you can see, in some situations a proposal that attacks causes of a problem is more convincing than one that attacks effects alone. Attacking causes, when you can get at them, can produce a permanent solution. However, in other situations, the causes are unreachable. An audience in the United States cannot change the entire political structure of North Africa to prevent famine, and no audience on earth can stop sun storms to improve radio transmission.

Our continuing proposal now turns to causal analysis.

Why is it so difficult to study on the weekend at this university? There are many reasons. First of all, the dorms are crowded. No single rooms are available, and many small rooms that used to be singles are now doubles, crammed with bunkbeds. Put hundreds of us in overcrowded conditions and we are bound to be noisy and trip over one another. Add to that the fact that almost everyone has a stereo, many of them with 100-watt-per-channel amplifiers that would fill a gymnasium with sound, let alone a 10-foot by 10-foot dorm room.

Now not even the world's worst grind would want to study every weekend.

We all need to release tension, and Friday and Saturday nights are the natural times to do so. But even a few students partying, let alone most, are enough to make the dorm temporarily uninhabitable for anyone who needs silence. Since the minority of students have no right to silence the majority who want to party, the minority must go elsewhere. But on this campus there is no elsewhere. The few places that are open are crowded. Most of us cannot go home every weekend. Worst of all, the one safe centrally located place to study—the library—is closed. After 5:00 on Fridays and Saturdays, the doors are locked, the long tables bare, hundreds of chairs empty, and thousands of books inaccessible.

EXERCISE

If you did the previous exercise, you have demonstrated the existence of a problem. Now build on that by adding a causal analysis of the situation. You should, if possible, identify a dominant cause or one that can be changed. Look in particular for responsible agents or the absence of blocking causes. A factor contributing to the problem may even be the failure of other proposals to solve it.

PROPOSAL STATEMENT

General Proposals

After you have roused your audience to the awareness of a situation, its bad consequences, its ethical wrongness, and its causes, the next step is to suggest what should be done about it. In some cases you may not know exactly what should be done, or you may think it is not your place to propose the solution. So you may end after your preliminary argument, which is actually a negative evaluation, with a vague proposal such as: "Why doesn't somebody do something about this?" "Let's form a committee to study the matter and come up with a proposal." "The people responsible should be informed so they can correct the situation."

Some of these vague suggestions might be called passing the buck, although it is only fair to say that such general proposals have many legitimate uses. A general call to action is one way for an individual with no power to arouse conviction and emotion in an audience, which can in turn demand action from those with power. Exposés of election corruption, sawdust in sausage, birds poisoned by pesticides eventually have aroused appropriate responses from those in a position to do something.

The Specific Proposal

Of course there is a continuum from the very general to the very specific proposal, but usually the specific proposal provides an exact description of what action should be taken to correct a situation and sometimes offers elaborate supporting arguments for that precise solution. A specific proposal statement can be wedged into one sentence, while some rather intricate proposals may take considerable space simply to explain. A proposal that the Defense Department develop a new ICBM will itself be very elaborate and detailed. A proposal that "refrigerators should be permitted in dorm rooms" may be just that, complete in one sentence.

Although we all like to sit around and propose schemes for a better world, we do not usually bother to argue for a specific proposal unless we are addressing an audience that can take action. A student who is prevented from studying by the noise in the dorm, for example, might complain vaguely to his roommate that something should be done about the stereos, shouts, carousing, and water fights. But as a member of the dorm committee that had the power to make and enforce regulations, the student might urge the adoption of specific rules for quiet hours.

The path to authority may be relatively short and direct in a dorm. But in our tangled bureaucratic society, we often have trouble finding our way to the people who have the authority to act on our specific proposals. With whom do you argue if you think the electric company should read your meter every month instead of every other month (that is, who is hired not just to listen to complaints, but actually to change things)? Who can implement your proposal that realistic guns be removed from toy stores or that the United States adopt a new policy toward the Middle East? If you want to argue for any specific proposal, you have to find out who can change things.

Two Paths to the Same End

In real-life situations, actually moving people to take action on a specific proposal can require different appeals to different audiences. When you want to move different groups of people to different actions that are, nevertheless, means to the same end, you must carefully adapt arguments to these groups. Suppose, for example, that the president of a tenants' union, outraged by a recent 30 percent rent hike, proposes to her landlord that he hold to a lower ceiling on rent increases (not an easy line to take with a landlord). To put pressure on the landlord, the angered tenant may, at the same time, propose at a tenants' meeting that her fellow residents organize a rent strike. These two proposals, although they are both strategies to the same end, are aimed at different audiences and would obviously have to be different. The appeals and language that would arouse tenants to the unfairness of their situation would not persuade the landlord.

But sometimes you can use the same appeals with two different audiences, leading to two different actions. Many such dual-purpose proposals appear in newspapers and magazines every day. These are specific proposals that argue fully for a desired change, but one that no single individual or group could bring about alone. Such proposals are often put where the public can see them, as well as those who have the power to bring them about. For example, we might read in the newspaper a detailed argument urging that the United States extend diplomatic recognition to Cuba. Such a proposal is legitimately addressed to the people in government who have the constitutional authority to bring such an action about. But the average citizen, who is not in Congress or the State Department, cannot individually go out and recognize Cuba. So why is the argument aimed at newspaper readers? Obviously, some action is desired from the public. That action, at the very least, may be our awareness or at the most, an expression of that awareness in the form of telegrams, letters, phone calls, and votes.

The publicly aired proposal has still another function. Making public a proposal that could be sent directly to Congress, the FDA, the CIA, wherever, is a way of putting pressure on the powerful. In our society, officials feel a duty to respond to issues that have been brought before the public. And we as citizens have a corresponding duty to express our views, if we can do so rationally and responsibly. Our continuing sample has two audiences: the student body and the university administration. Now that its preliminary arguments are completed, here is the specific proposal:

> The solution is obvious. If the university were genuinely interested in the welfare of its students as students, it would unlock the doors of the library on Friday and Saturday nights. A library open twelve more hours a week would be a place for the hundreds who want to study to get away from the thousands who don't.

EXERCISE

You have already demonstrated the existence of a problem and identified its cause or causes. For what audience would only a general proposal be appropriate? What audience could legitimately have a specific proposal addressed to them? Write at least two possible proposal statements for different audiences.

SUPPORTING ARGUMENTS

The Good Consequences That Will Flow from the Proposal

No one argues for a proposal that would bring about bad consequences. Every proposal, even one to do nothing or to undo something, promises good things to come: A proposed new sewer system will give better drainage; brushing with brand X will whiten teeth. Such promises must be substantiated with causal arguments that predict how the proposal will bring about good things. Here we see again how crucial causal argument is, especially prediction arguments, in a proposal.

To make these predictions of good things to come from your proposal seem inevitable, two causal techniques are particularly helpful. These are the chain of causes and analogy. Let's demonstrate these supporting techniques in the following two examples. Suppose you make a do-nothing proposal: "Alaska should not be carved up into any more National Parks." In your "good consequence" section, you will come up with a mini-argument for the following prediction: "If the government refrains from creating parks, the Alaskan wilderness will be preserved." This prediction can be supported with a chain of causes:

No parks ———→ No roads ———→ No vehicles ———→ No people ———→
No disturbance ———→ Preserve the wilderness

(This argument assumes that there is no other source of roads and all the things that follow from roads.)

A basic technique for supporting a prediction is to zero in on agency itself, to find a chain, as it were, with one link in it. You are more familiar with this technique than you may think because you hear it all the time in commercials: Toothpaste X has a *whitening agent* to give you brighter teeth; bathroom cleaner Y has *scrubbing bubbles* to make your sink sparkle; shampoo Z has *protein* to make your hair thicker. Advertisers often claim that *agents* (that is, *agency*) are present, producing wonderful results and supporting the unstated proposal that "the customer should buy."

A prediction can also be supported by an analogy if you can find another case where the same policy you are proposing has led to the very same effect you are predicting. In other words, you argue that if proposal-led-to-result "there and then," proposal-will-lead-to-result "here and in the future." Suppose, for example, you are proposing a job training program for welfare mothers in your area and you want to support the prediction that "Job training for welfare mothers will cost taxpayers less than supporting them at home." You could cite the result of job-training programs versus straight welfare in comparable cities. To support your prediction, you will present evidence that X city, with a training program, spent fewer tax dollars per welfare mother over a certain period of time than Y city, which simply paid welfare mothers who stayed at home. When you can find such an analogous case, it is as though an experiment with your proposal had been performed in another laboratory; you simply predict the same results from your similar set of givens.

Here is the next section supporting the specific proposal in our continuing argument:

> An open library is a benefit not only to students who carry texts, notebooks, and calculators around looking for a place to put them down and study. It is also a benefit to students who have work that can be done only in the library. One of the girls I talked to when I surveyed my chemistry class was a nursing major who said she had several papers to do this term, all of which required a considerable amount of research. She would welcome access to the periodicals in her field, even on Friday and Saturday night, and so would many others who have to write papers requiring extensive use of library materials. And let's not forget the students who work to put themselves through school. Their study hours are pared to a minimum and they may need library services at odd hours. One business major in my English class complained bitterly about the library's weekend hours. He works twenty hours, several evenings a week, and must make maximum use of his weekends for studying. If the library were open, he would have access five extra hours a week to the documents and reference materials he needs. Undergraduates are not the only ones who would use the library on weekend nights. Our campus has five thousand graduate students whose academic interests are demanding. No doubt they would appreciate the extra hours to work on their theses, as would some faculty members to work on their books and articles.

The Bad Consequences That Will Be Avoided If the Proposal Is Adopted

Remember that a proposal is designed to correct a situation that has led to undesirable consequences. You probably demonstrated the existence of this bad situation and traced its bad consequences earlier, before you made your full proposal. The desire to eliminate a situation and its bad consequences provided a strong motive for change to begin with, when your purpose was simply to make your audience receptive to change. Now, after you have disclosed your specific proposal, you may want to remind your audience of all the evils that will be avoided if your solution is adopted. For example, when the government recalls defective radial tires, the number of accidents caused by blowouts will decrease. When processed meats are eliminated from the diet, nitrate levels in the blood will go down.

You can do this "reminding" briefly, by simply mentioning again what the world will be better off without. Or you may want to go into a fuller discussion, even if it is repetitive, just for the sake of emphasizing this appeal. Of course, if you have not already traced the bad consequences to be avoided in your preliminary arguments, you might want to do it now. But if you have done it, and done it thoroughly, and do not think that repeating it will lend any persuasive force to your argument, this whole section need not exist.

What kind of claim do you have to support here? Again, a causal one. If you want to argue that certain bad consequences will be avoided, you are, in effect, claiming that a chain of causes will be broken or a sufficient cause removed or blocked. Since the bad consequences follow inevitably from the cause that you want to replace, you will simply argue that once a critical cause is removed or blocked, bad consequences will disappear and good ones take their place.

Let's look at a proposal whose effect will be simply the elimination of bad consequences. Arson destroys lives and property and ultimately raises insurance rates and the cost of police and fire protection for all of us. If you propose that insurance companies pool their resources to form arson-investigating squads, you will want to show that once these squads have caused the number of cases of arson to decrease, the bad effects of large-scale arson on the average citizen will also decrease.

Here are some of the bad consequences that a library open on weekends might eliminate. Notice the fringe benefit, the avoidance of quite a different bad consequence.

> A library open on Friday and Saturday nights would also help some students, me especially, avoid those occasional all-nighters, when, with the help of too much coffee, I produce something far less than my best work. And if I had someplace else to go, I might not cringe at the sight of my roommate's boyfriend on campus for yet another football weekend.
>
> A further benefit might result from longer library hours. Right now, the library has a problem with the theft of material. Articles are razored out of journals, and, despite security precautions worthy of the Pentagon, those precious readings on the reserve shelf—readings that your very survival in certain courses depends on—do disappear. Perhaps these problems would diminish if heavily used or reserved materials were available extra hours each week.

The Ethical Appeal for the Proposal

In the first half of your proposal, when all the attention was focused on a problem, you may have appealed to your audience's sense of what was wrong. Now you may want to appeal to their sense of what is right. If slavery is wrong, then freedom is right. If child abuse is wrong, then fostering care is right. Again, if you think you can count on your audience's immediate response to an ethical appeal, you simply make the appeal. But if you cannot count on it, once again you must place your subject in a category your audience will respond to immediately.

You can also argue that not only is the situation brought about by your proposal ethically right, but that the person or institution that acts to bring it about fulfills an ethical obligation. Because institutions have obligations and people have duties, showing how action on your proposal fulfills such a responsibility or a duty can be a strong ethical appeal. The passerby who intervenes to prevent a mugging not only produces a result that is good, but also lives up to the responsibility of a concerned citizen.

Our sample proposal makes an ethical appeal to the ideal definition of a university, claiming that if the proposal is followed, the university will be living up to its responsibilities.

> Carved in stone over the door of the library are the words "A true university is a collection of books." According to this definition, the library *is* the university. Of course a university is also an administration, a student body, and a complex physical plant. But it fulfills its function as a holder and disperser of knowledge more truly when it unlocks the library than when it sponsors a pep rally.

EXERCISE

If you have done the exercises so far, you have written the first two parts of a full proposal: the preliminary arguments and the specific thesis. Now try your hand at supporting arguments. But do not overdo it. You will almost certainly not need all three types of supporting arguments we have just outlined. Choose the one or two that will be appropriate for the audience you are keeping in mind.

FEASIBILITY: "IT CAN BE DONE"

If you are making a specific proposal, if you want a certain action taken, if you want people to get out of their chairs, then you must convince them "it can be done." Feasibility means workability, showing your audience that you are not proposing ice palaces in the desert, making your own black hole, or feeding hungry nations with fried earthworms. It is one thing to dream up pie-in-the-sky proposals and quite another to argue that they are actually doable. Arguing feasibility is often a matter of anticipating the questions a skeptical reader is likely to ask. A specific proposal usually requires detailed consideration of feasibility. The following sections show how to answer the kinds of questions audiences usually have about feasibility.

Can We Afford It?

Action costs money, so it is not surprising that for most people feasibility means economics. How fully you answer this most predictable of all questions, "How much?" depends on your proposal and audience. If you are applying to the government for a research grant, you must submit an itemized budget. If you propose that the School Board open the high school in the evening for adult education, you show that tuition will offset the increased operating costs (teachers' salaries, electricity, and janitor). Even if you cannot predict costs down to the last penny, you should still show readers that you have considered money by giving a generally correct assurance: "We can afford it." "It won't cost too much." "It's not expensive."

And, of course, if you are actually proposing something that will save more than it costs, make a big point of that as a good consequence. If your proposal to recycle glass, wood chips, used motor oil, cocoa bean hulls, or autumn leaves will create income where there was once only waste, that is a benefit too great to be overlooked.

Does It Take Too Long?

People tend to be as thrifty of their time as of their money. They will resist a proposal that takes too much time either to prepare or to perform. The exercise routine of a ballet dancer may keep the body in perfect physical shape, but if it takes eight hours and the body works in an office all day, it is hardly feasible. And sometimes not the process but the goal of a proposal can seem to take too long, in some eyes, to come to fruition. As a society, for example, we are eager to open professions and influential positions to women and minorities because doing so is fair. But we have been impatient with solutions that ask us to wait fifteen years for improved education to work wonders on today's kindergartners.

You can try to answer the time question the same way you answered the money question, with arguments that amount to assurances: "No, it won't take too much time." "Anyone can spare ten minutes a day." "By this time next week we'll have results." And of course if your proposal can actually save time, adding minutes to the day or hours to the week, you have a strong selling point. Microwave ovens take seven minutes to cook a potato, the computerized turnstiles in the Washington Metro process passengers quickly, and the supersonic Concorde crosses the Atlantic in about three hours. This kind of time saving has strong appeal for most audiences.

Can We Get People To Do This?

"It's a fine idea," your reader says, "but how are you going to get people to go along with you?" Human nature hangs back; it resists change, newness, progress, innovation, and disturbance of the status quo. If your proposal involves getting people to move, to act, to change, you have to convince your audience that you can get people moving. Let's imagine that you are proposing to the managers of your company that the secretaries be trained to use a multiple word processing, spreadsheet, and data base program. You point out to them all the time that will eventually be saved once the switchover is accomplished. Nevertheless, they want to know how you will get the secretaries to commit themselves to the training period for this demanding new procedure. You answer that the secretaries should be eager to upgrade their skills for higher salaries, but any secretary who refuses to go along will be transferred to the word processing pool. Your audience is convinced when they see how you will convince those who must act.

Suppose your proposal involves moving the general public or a large, varied group of people to action? Such general appeals are common: The governor asks Californians to conserve water; the Surgeon General campaigns against smoking; and doctors urge most of us to lose weight, shape up, and eat wholesome food. Common sense tells us that we can never convince *everyone* to stop smoking, drinking, overeating, or wasting water. When defending your public proposal, you may have to concede that the entire populace will not go along with it, but that a significant number will respond when good and bad consequences, ethical rightness and wrongness are pointed out to them. We can imagine the Governor of California defending a conservation appeal to advisers by arguing that though some people will be too selfish to cut back on water consumption, most Californians will respond to an appeal to the public good if they can see that it is also in their self-interest.

The question "Can we get people to do it?" can have a second meaning. In the examples above, it means "Can we motivate them?" It can also mean "Do we have the personnel? Can we find them? Can we hire them?" You may feel like the playwright who has a great role for an elderly woman who can tap-dance and sing opera, but can the part be filled? No doubt the originators of the manned space flight program must have defended the feasibility of finding astronaut candidates who combined technical training, stable personalities, perfect physical condition, and the daredevil recklessness of test pilots. When money is not an object, personnel may be easier to find or train, but in more ordinary situations, the question becomes "Can we get the people at our price?"

Trade-offs

In any particular proposal a separate, satisfactory answer to each of the above questions may not be possible. Your answer to one of the questions might dismay your audience: Your proposal will be expensive, take time, and meet with great resistance. How do you get around such stumbling blocks? Imagine how an excellent salesperson would get someone to buy a car that leaks oil. The seller admits it does leak a little oil, but points out its rust-free body, its custom upholstery, and its low mileage. In other words, an arguer whose proposal has problems engages in trade-offs. You persuade your audience to accept the defect in your proposal because of its greater overall benefits. Yes, canning your own vegetables takes time, but it saves money; and yes, frozen spinach soufflé is expensive, but convenience foods save time in the kitchen. Yes, your plan to convert the old train station into a recreation center will take hours of volunteer work, but once they see the benefits, enough townspeople will turn out to help.

How Can We Do It?

Even if you have the time, money, and people, your audience may still withhold assent until you show them exactly how your proposal will be accomplished. The end looks great, but far off. Your audience asks, "What steps, what parts, what processes must we go through to get there?" You can anticipate such predictable questions by going into the details of your proposal in an orderly, sequential fashion. Just showing your audience that you have thought your proposal through, that you have a fully worked-out plan in mind, is in itself persuasive.

Suppose you send a letter to the parents of nursery-school children in your town, proposing piano, violin, and cello lessons for three- and four-year-olds. Time, money, teachers, and equipment are all available. But you have to persuade the parents that teaching such tiny children to play an instrument is possible. The only way to do it is to explain the process, the sequential teaching method you will use. First, the children learn basic rhythms, which they then combine into longer patterns. Next, they are introduced to the instrument, and finally they put all their skills together into a simple song like "Twinkle, Twinkle Little Star." Once they've mastered one song, they are taught another that recombines the same elements and introduces some new ones. In this way the children build up a repertoire of songs. When parents can see the steps for bringing a four-year-old from clapping to mastering a song, they are more likely to be convinced to the point of enrolling their children. (We have just described the famous Suzuki method of teaching children violin, cello, or piano.)

What's the First Step?

Your audience can acknowledge your proposal's merit, agree that it is feasible, and understand the steps to bring it about, yet still be unmoved to action because they do not clearly see the first step to take. You cannot overcome human inertia, even when your audience is willing to act, without very precise instructions for an initial action. Without specific guidance into that first step, their commitment will fade away. You may have filled your nursery-school parents' heads with visions of little Jessica as the next Heifitz or Rubinstein, but unless you specify the first organizational meeting for next Thursday night at 8:00 at the church, the visions will evaporate.

Not only should the first move be clear, it should also be easy. Wise businessmen know this when they send you a post-paid addressed card as a first step in taking action on their ads; all you have to do is check the appropriate box, drop it in the mail, and in three weeks a crew arrives to dig up your back yard and put in a swimming pool. That first step was *so* easy.

Has It Been Done Before?

One of the most convincing ways to show that something can be done is to show that it has been done. If your proposal has been tried elsewhere and worked successfully, you have a case history of its feasibility to bring in as support, an analogy to predict its workability. Your main challenge will be to show that "elsewhere" is similar to "here" in all essential ways. If another community the same size mounted a successful antivandalism campaign, if a museum in another city put in a "living science" exhibit, if another supermarket installed a computerized check-out system, then why not your community, your museum, your supermarket? This appeal is even stronger when you have more time, more money, or better facilities than your model.

Our continuing sample proposal argues for the feasibility of opening the library on weekends. This part of the proposal is aimed at the administrators who could act on it.

According to the head librarian, Dr. Murray, a skeleton staff of ten or twelve could run the library on Friday or Saturday nights. The university would have no trouble hiring student help for most of these positions. Students work for the minimum wage, and many are available and even eager to work at odd hours; those contributing to their own financial support would gladly trade the luxury of weekend socializing for a chance to earn extra money. In fact, right now, the Student Employment Office has several hundred more names on file than it has jobs to give out. And certainly working in the library will be more attractive to many people than raking leaves or baby sitting or moving pianos. Only two or three professional librarians would be needed to supervise, answer questions in the reference room, and take care of documents. Microfilms, periodicals, and the reserve reading room could be staffed by students. None of the special services like inter-library loan would have to be available; they are always closed on week nights anyway.

Of course even a skeleton staff does not work for free, and it costs something to heat and light the building. The staff and maintenance could bring the cost of keeping the library open up to $600 a night, $1,200 a weekend, or $12,000 a ten-week term. That sounds like a lot of money to spend on a service that will probably be used by only a few hundred students at any one time. But according to last year's Annual Fiscal Report, published by the Board of Trustees, maintaining the university's recreational facilities on weekends costs considerably more than $600 a day, yet the heated swimming pool, the lighted tennis courts, the ice-skating rink, and the bowling alleys with automatic pinsetters, all expensive luxuries, are used by only a few hundred students any weekend night. Even if the university insisted on transferring the cost of the extra library hours to the students, tuition would have to rise by only $1.00 per student per year. The chance of two extra evenings in the library is a bargain at that price.

Surely our university, one of the largest state universities in the country, can bring together the planning and money and personnel for this project. After all, comparable universities like Mammoth State, Gargantuan Polytech, and Northeast Enormous all open their libraries Friday and Saturday nights. Even little Old Diminutive College, sixty miles away, keeps its collection of 100,000 books available on weekend evenings with the help of two part-time librarians.

As a first step for our school, the administration could open the library for two weekends three or four weeks into the next term. That way, they could discover whether or not there is sufficient demand to warrant the extra hours. If fewer than a hundred students appear, there would be no point in continuing the experiment. But I believe that at that point in the term, with work piling up, many of us—hundreds I imagine—would find the library a welcome refuge.

Anticipating Difficult Questions

Anyone who makes plans for other people, and that is exactly what you do when you make a proposal, should anticipate some hostile questions:

"Who asked you?" "What business is it of yours?" "Who are you working for?" But if you know what to expect from your audience, you can prevent hostile questions from forming in their minds. Some of the techniques used to forestall such questions are the accommodation tactics that work with all arguments (see Chapter 15), but here we will look at a few objections that proposal makers are particularly vulnerable to.

If Your Idea Is So Good, Why Hasn't Anyone Done It Before?

This question has two roots. First, it can come from a suspicion that you have overlooked something that has kept others from your solution. In other words, no one else has seriously proposed your idea before because they have seen the folly of it. No one is building Corvairs these days, or transmuting base metals into gold, or proposing one simple cure for everything from the common cold to cancer. If your proposal has never been tried or even suggested before, the best defense against suspicion is a very thorough feasibility section, showing that you have not overlooked anything vital.

Second, this question may reflect honest puzzlement as to why such a good solution never occurred to anyone else working on the problem. You may want to answer, "Because no one else was smart enough to think of it before." But that statement is too boastful and blunt. A better defense here could take one of the following forms:

New Circumstances

You may argue that the situation has changed so that now a solution like yours is possible. For example, your cure for inflation may work only when it goes over 10 percent; when inflation is that serious, public motivation will work for you.

A Blocking Cause Removed

One special new circumstance is the disappearance of something that had previously prevented a solution to a problem. The old boss has retired, so now you can finally propose revamping the outdated procedures of the complaint department. Or now that the union is no longer opposed to computerized check-outs, you can propose installing a new system in your store. Or now that the old bridge has rotted away, you can think of building a safe new one.

New Knowledge

You can argue that a new technology, a new approach, a new technique is now available to tackle a previously insoluble problem. Computer technology has been our number-one new solver of problems everywhere from the supermarket to outer space. Advances in medical technology, like the CAT scanner, new management techniques such as MBO (Management by Objectives), the copying machine, the laser, and polyurethane roller-skate wheels have inspired solutions never before possible. The appeal to new knowledge may well be your strongest defense against impertinent objections.

Not Really a New Idea

It may be possible for you to forestall the lethal question by attacking it head on. You may argue that your proposal is not really a new, harebrained idea at all. It's an old idea applied in a new way, or one that was proposed before but never had a fair hearing. Anything that gives your proposal a history can give it authority. For example, your proposal to use bean derivatives as a protein source to improve school lunches may not be as far-fetched as it sounds. The supermarkets already sell hamburgers enriched with soy protein, and Japanese and Chinese cuisines feature bean curd.

What's in It for You?

That is a very impolite question, but even people who don't ask it might think it. The motives of do-gooders are always suspect. If no one has authorized you to come up with a proposal, if the problem is not in your domain of responsibility, if you apparently have nothing to gain, then people will wonder why you went to all the trouble. They will suspect that you are going to profit in some hidden way—a job for your brother-in-law, a contract for your construction firm, a future favor from the candidate you are supporting.

How do you forestall this suspicion? First, if you are going to benefit, you should admit it, as long as what benefits you helps others as well. Although you could not effectively support a proposal that would benefit only yourself, people accept honest and open self-interest. Benjamin Franklin's many proposals for Philadelphia provide us with models of what has been called "enlightened self-interest" in action. The free public library he proposed certainly was in Franklin's interest; he was an avid reader and found it hard to get books in colonial America. But the public library also benefited everyone else. So did his fire company, bifocals, stove, plan for a militia, lightning rod, the American Philosophical Society, and the University of Pennsylvania.

What if there really is nothing in it for you? Say you are a graduating senior proposing an improvement in a high school you will never attend again, or a math student who got an A in calculus suggesting that the course's multiple-choice tests be replaced by "show-all-work" exams. In situations like these, the benefits of your proposal are for others, not for you. Should you point out what a good person you are? You may be but no one wants to hear about it; it is best not to include a long passage in praise of your own unselfishness.

Yet some justification is necessary when you have been neither authorized to make a proposal nor led to it naturally by self-interest. Most audiences will accept proposal making from certain ethical motives. The graduating senior could bring up school loyalty as a motive, since most people are attached to the schools they attended and want to see them prosper. The math student could not convincingly claim loyalty to the math department, but could identify with the student body, which will benefit from the proposal. And both the graduating senior and the math student can boost their credibility by identifying their unique positions as "one who has been through it all and lived to testify." It is as though they looked around and said, "No one else is in a better position to make this proposal than I am, so I do it."

What's Wrong with the Other Proposal?

Unless you are the only one making a proposal, you are in competition with others, and in a competition it is unwise to ignore the existence of your opponents. Better to acknowledge them and take them on, to be aware of the other proposals and refute them where logically possible. Suppose your county is considering what to do with abandoned railway tunnels. Your rival has proposed that they be turned into mausoleums; bodies can be deposited behind the large paving bricks, which can then be replaced and suitably inscribed. You, on the other hand, have come up with the brilliant idea of leasing the cool, damp tunnels to mushroom producers. When you present your proposal before the county commissioners, you may want to point out that while your rival's idea is certainly original, you wonder how many folk will want to bury their loved ones in an abandoned railway tunnel. (By the way, mushrooms are grown in abandoned railway tunnels in Pennsylvania.)

Of course, an idea like tunnel mausoleums is easy to ridicule; you are far more likely to have to defend your proposal against others that are not very different and that seem on the surface just as plausible as yours. If you find yourself working in a large corporation or research institution,

you may have to evaluate competing proposals. Here is where your knowledge of the parts of the full proposal will be useful. By comparing part to
part you can uncover your competitor's deficiencies—weak ethical appeal,
unforeseen consequences, poor feasibility.

Our library argument concludes by forestalling some objections:

> I have heard the argument that opening the library on weekend nights is
> dangerous; women walking home at midnight are risking attack. If that's so,
> then it's true from Sunday through Thursday nights as well when the library
> is open. The university does not close the library out of concern for student
> safety those nights. Women who are out at that hour have learned to stay in
> groups on lighted walkways. In fact, weekend nights are probably even less
> dangerous than week nights because more people and more police are around.
>
> My proposal is not really a new idea. The senior reference librarian told me
> that up until six years ago the library was open till twelve every Friday and
> Saturday night. Then six years ago, when the budget was being trimmed every-
> where, the library hours were cut back as a temporary economy; full service was
> never resumed even though the library's operating budget was restored. Yet
> today, six years later, we are still living with a short-term economy. Maybe that
> economy is too expensive when we consider that the percentage of students
> who finish four years here has dropped from 71 percent to 54 percent. Perhaps
> if the university improved the academic environment, more students would
> make it through four years.

HOW PROPOSALS CAN GO WRONG

Since proposals are made up of arguments about the nature of things and
arguments about causes, often combined in evaluations, they can go wrong
in all the ways discussed in the three preceding sections. Three spots,
however, are particularly vulnerable in proposal arguments whose distinctive feature is actually encouraging an audience to do something. First, an
audience unconvinced that a situation is a problem cannot be moved to act;
they perceive neither bad consequences nor ethical wrongness in a situation and therefore will not vote or contribute money or take on a committee assignment or whatever. Or an audience may indeed recognize the
problem, but find it quite tolerable, especially if it is an old familiar problem: "It is a bit hard on pedestrians, but we've lived without sidewalks here
for thirty years." "We'd like to keep every student we admit, but some
always drop out." "A few guys get shaken up now and then, but we have
always played without helmets." If you cannot give your audience that
first push into the water, they will not swim with your proposal.

Second, if you have competition from other proposals, your argument
must refute in order to win. Oddly enough, an easy time with the "we have

a problem" section may spell trouble from rival proposals. What everyone perceives as a problem, many try to solve, and you cannot hope to attract an investment of resources in your solution unless you carefully establish its superiority. If only one road can be built from Lhasa to Kathmandu, then it should pass your magnificent roadside stand and bypass your rival's diner.

Third, the most vulnerable part of a specific proposal argument is usually its feasibility section, the section that explains exactly how the proposal will come about in the real world. Readers have a right to expect a proposal arguer to hold out a reachable goal and show a plausible first step. So imagine yourself answering questions about money, time, and the availability of resources like the following: "Granting the desirability of the goal, can we expect the university to abolish grades before the end of the term?" or "Yes, it would be nice if Centreville had a domed stadium like Houston, but can a town of 30,000 afford a $100 million project?" or "If our school district can hire only one person, is it likely we can find a football coach who can also teach sewing?"

FOR YOU TO ANALYZE

Examine the following proposal arguments. Each of them modifies the full proposal outline by eliminating or rearranging some parts. Identify the parts and explain why the selection or arrangement works or does not work.

I propose an end to neckties! They are uncomfortable, unnatural, and a superficial pretense to importance. Males should not have to suffer this archaic hang-up so their peers will approve their "well dressed" look. Women dress as they please. I think men should too.

—Ray "Anti-Necktie" Giger

PUT THIAMINE IN LIQUOR

Brandon Centerwall

The man wanders from ward to ward, unable to remember where he is. A sign is taped on the back of his hospital robe:

My name is Green
I am probably lost
Please return me to Ward 6W

Such signs are sometimes useful to help the elderly senile. Mr. Green is 40 years old. He has a disease called Wernicke-Korsakoff syndrome. It could have been prevented.

Wernicke-Korsakoff syndrome is the partial destruction of the brain resulting from a lack of thiamine (vitamin B-1). It usually occurs among the severely malnourished. During World War II, an epidemic of Wernicke-Korsakoff syndrome broke out at the Singapore prisoner-of-war camp, killing 21 soldiers. Small amounts of thiamine in their diet could have saved them.

Like Mr. Green (this is not his real name), most victims of this disease in the United States today are severe alcoholics who don't eat nutritious food. They frequently die of the disease. If they don't, many end up in nursing homes because of brain damage.

The disease can begin over a period of weeks. Ocular muscles become weak or paralyzed. The sense of balance is affected, sometimes so badly that it is impossible to walk. Amnesia and general confusion take over. Finally, the victim may lapse into a coma and die.

Treatment with thiamine reverses most of the syndrome, but the ability to remember events as they happen is often lost forever.

Yet the disease can be prevented—simply by adding thiamine to all liquor, wine and beer.

The idea is not new. After the first synthesis of thiamine in 1936, prevention on a mass scale became possible. Soon it was publicly advocated that thiamine be added to alcoholic beverages to prevent the thiamine-deficiency diseases of alcoholics.

By 1940, the alcoholic-beverage industry was experimentally adding thiamine to its products. Seagram & Sons found it was stable in their whiskey. The California Wine Institute found it was stable in their wines. Anheuser-Busch found it was stable in their beer.

Nor were the drug companies idle. Both Abbott Laboratories and Smith-Dorsey Company piloted thiamine-fortified wines.

But a chill descended. By law, all food additives must be listed on the label. In 1940, a Federal ruling prohibited listing the vitamin content of alcoholic beverages on the label as this would imply that drinking alcohol is healthy—an improper inducement; thus, added vitamins cannot be listed on the label. However, this would violate the first law concerning food additives in general: Therefore, vitamins cannot be added to alcoholic beverages. The American Medical Association declared the drug company wines "unacceptable" for similar reasons. With these barriers, interest in fortification waned.

Recent research that I conducted shows that not only would adding thiamine to alcoholic beverages save lives and minds but also it would actually save public money as well.

Since the public pays for the care of many alcoholics suffering from this disease, adding thiamine would save us millions of dollars. Each dollar's worth of thiamine, or one of its derivatives, added would save up to $7 in nursing-home costs—a good return on an investment.

Technical issues remain to be solved. It is already known that thiamine is sufficiently stable in alcoholic beverages, but how does it taste? When thiamine is added to whiskey, wine and beer in the proposed concentrations, it has been observed that there is little or no effect on flavor. However, these are only the anecdotal observations of a few individuals; more formal taste tests will be undertaken.

Finally, to obtain the approval of the Food and Drug Administration, routine screening studies must be performed to make absolutely certain that the combination will not give rise to any noxious substances.

On the legal front, the 1940 ruling should be changed to permit the addition of vitamins to alcoholic beverages without listing them on the label.

Of course, the ideal way to prevent Wernicke-Korsakoff syndrome is to prevent alcoholism.

Indeed, during Prohibition rates of Wernicke-Korsakoff syndrome dropped by 90 percent. Considering the terrible destruction it causes, our main effort should be against alcoholism.

Purists will ask, "So why prevent this rare disease in alcoholics when we should be preventing alcoholism?" To demand fair trials for criminals is not to condone crime. To demand proper health care for alcoholics is not to condone alcoholism. Apart from economic gains, there is a moral imperative.

SAMPLE ANALYSIS

The proposal thesis of this article, which appeared in a large-circulation newspaper aimed at the general public, is a specific one, requiring a rather full argument. The preliminaries are, however, condensed, though the argument does open with the usual demonstration of a problem. The reader is given a single, pathetic example of a forty-year-old man wandering in senility. Because the loss of a human being to such premature mental decay is so evidently a bad consequence, so obviously against the ethical values of almost any audience, the author, Brandon Centerwall, need not fill in these potential sections in the full proposal outline. He can and does go right to causal analysis.

The wandering man has Wernicke-Korsakoff syndrome, whose immediate cause is brain destruction due to thiamine deficiency; an example from the past supports this causal connection, an example that adds to the pathos associated with the disease. The cause of such a deficiency in these days of food additives and vitamin consciousness is inadequate diet due to alcoholism. Alcoholism is thus a remote cause of Wernicke-Korsakoff syndrome in the following chain: Alcoholism → deficient diet → thiamine deprivation → brain damage → Wernicke-Korsakoff syndrome. This chain could be cut at its lethal end and the causal process reversed by putting thiamine in the one form of sustenance alcoholics do take. Thus the proposal that comes in paragraph 7.

Since Mr. Centerwall's proposal is so simple, he feels compelled to answer the unspoken question "If your idea is so good why hasn't anyone thought of it before?" by admitting that it is not new; it has been proposed ever since thiamine was first artificially synthesized. In giving evidence of this early advocacy, the author also gives evidence of the feasibility of his scheme: Thiamine has proved stable in whiskey, wine, and beer. His proposal can be done because it has been done.

A blocking cause, however, currently prevents thiamine additives in alcohol. The government both requires that all food additives be listed on labels and specifically prohibits labeling alcoholic beverages as vitamin fortified. Paragraph 16 refers to the removal of this blocking cause as the first step required to facilitate the author's proposal.

Mr. Centerwall makes a further strong supporting argument for his proposal when he asserts that it could save money as well as prevent a deplorable disease; if the disease were eliminated, as it so easily could be, taxpayers would no longer have to support the institutionalized senile like Mr. Green. Creating himself as an authority (in his only use of "I"), Mr. Centerwall claims that the savings will be sevenfold on any investment in his proposal. In paragraphs 14 and 15, Mr. Centerwall shows moderation by conceding the need for further research into the effects of thiamine additives on taste and their long-term stability in alcoholic beverages. These concessions do not really weaken his argument; rather, they show his reasonableness.

Mr. Centerwall did not have to point out the ethical wrongness or undesirable consequences of the problem he demonstrates in his preliminary arguments, but in the conclusion he attempts to forestall an ethical objection to his proposal. Rather than putting this objection into the mind of his reader, he invents a character, "the purist," who has ethical reservations. The purist would argue that the greater evil, alcoholism itself, should receive attention rather than a very rare disease that strikes a few alcoholics. The answer to this objection (a bit of a straw man as he has worded it) is self-evident: To prevent Wernicke-Korsakoff syndrome in a few is not to ignore or even excuse alcoholism.

CONTINUING ED FOR JOCKS

Steve Robinson

All across the country freshly minted college graduates are setting out in search of jobs. Unfortunately, many of their classmates—those who spent four or five years as scholarship athletes—are making the search at a distinct disadvantage. About 1% of them, the outstanding athletes, will play their sports professionally; the other 99% are job hunting, and more than half of those who played at the Division I level are brandishing only their varsity letters, not diplomas.

With the demands placed upon Division I football and basketball players, it's a wonder that they have time to master their playbooks, much less to study diligently enough to graduate. In fact, in the lower divisions, in which sports are more integrated into other aspects of college life, athletes tend to perform better academically than the student body as a whole. But playing for a big-time athletic power is a full-time job. As a result, the contract between athlete and school is shamefully one-sided. In return for four (or five, if the athlete has been redshirted) years of attending practices, lifting weights, watching films and, oh yes, playing games, the athlete is given the opportunity to receive a college education. But it doesn't always work out very well. While the university gets its 250 pounds of flesh, the athlete is often not much better prepared for a career than he was after high school.

In an era in which a bachelor's degree usually is required even for entry-level jobs, the contract needs to be rewritten. If an athlete upholds his end of the bargain—that is, if he practices and plays for four years—he ought to be entitled to work toward his degree at the university's expense for as long as it takes him to get it. This is not to encourage shirkers; the scholarship would remain in force only as long as the former varsity athlete has a declared major and is working toward a degree.

But if the athlete could spare only three nights a week away from a job, and therefore had to attend class for another four years to earn a degree, so be it. And what if our student-athlete played his ball at Oklahoma but found himself living in Florida? He should be allowed to complete his education in a comparable academic program at a school near his home, with the tuition paid for by Oklahoma. We're talking only tuition here, not room and board.

Sounds like a lot for schools to cope with, especially in these days of rising costs. All the more reason why the proposed contract makes sense. If colleges shudder at the thought of footing the bill for their former athletes for years on end, then let them educate their athletes properly the first time around, while they are full-time students.

True, the new contract would have a varied impact on NCAA member schools. The graduation rate for athletes now ranges from almost nil at some schools to 100% for Duke basketball players, every one of whom, since 1975, has earned a degree.

What are the perils in this plan? None that are insurmountable. To prevent somebody from goofing off during his playing years, knowing that his education would be paid for indefinitely, I propose that an athlete must have studied hard enough to have remained academically eligible during his athletic career. And what if a fellow takes a shine to the halls of academia and prolongs his education deliberately? Highly unlikely. Our scholar still has to make a living after his eligibility runs out, and therefore has every reason to hustle toward his degree and a better job.

Will universities respond to the new pact by automatically bestowing degrees upon athletes who have completed their tenure on the field or the court? Again, not likely. Even schools that are not known for academic excellence would be loath to further cheapen their reputations and diminish the value of their degrees by dispensing them like candy.

On a small scale, a consortium of 31 colleges and universities organized by Richard Lapchick, director of Northeastern University's Center for the Study of Sport in Society, has already agreed to finance former scholarship athletes who wish to return to the campus to earn their degrees. In exchange the athletes participate in outreach programs promoting education. The program is in its infancy, and not all of the schools play Division I basketball or football, but the addition last month of Penn State to the group represents an enormous vote of confidence.

Why should universities finance the education of former athletes? Simple, says Lapchick. As the public becomes more aware of scandals and abuses in college sports, schools become increasingly sensitive about their credibility. According to Lapchick, the schools in the Northeastern consortium "saw a problem and wanted to be part of the solution." The NCAA should endorse those good intentions by making open-ended scholarships mandatory.

THE GREENHOUSE EFFECT? REAL ENOUGH.

A fierce drought is shriveling crops from Texas to North Dakota and has shrunk the Mississippi to its lowest levels on record. Dry years are part of nature's cycle. Still, it's time to take seriously another possible influence—the warming of the atmosphere by waste gases from a century of industrial activity. Whether or not the feared greenhouse effect is real, there are several preventive measures worth taking in their own right.

The greenhouse theory holds that certain waste gases let in sunlight but trap heat, which otherwise would escape into space. Carbon dioxide has been steadily building up through the burning of coal and oil—and because forests, which absorb the gas, are fast being destroyed. There is no clear proof that the gases have yet begun to warm the atmosphere. But there's circumstantial evidence, and some experts think it is getting stronger.

For example, four of the last eight years—1980, 1981, 1983 and 1987—have been the warmest since measurements of global surface temperatures began a century ago, and 1988 may be another record hot year. Still, there have been hot spells before, followed by a cooling.

According to computer simulations of the world's climate, there should be more rain in a greenhouse-heated globe. The rain falls in different places: more at the poles and the equator, less in the mid-latitudes. The drought in the Middle West falls in with these projections. But it stops far short of proving that the greenhouse effect has begun. "As far as we can tell, this is a tough summer well within the normal range of variability," says Donald Gilman, the Weather Service's long-range forecaster.

That's the nub of the problem: It's hard to identify a small, gradual sign of global warming amid wide natural fluctuations in climate. Even over the long term, the evidence is merely indicative. The world has warmed half a degree centigrade over the last century. But the warming is less than some computer models predict, forcing defenders of the greenhouse theory to argue that the extra heat is disappearing into the oceans.

With the greenhouse effect still uncertain, why take preventive steps, especially since the main one, burning less coal, would be enormously expensive? One answer is that it may take years to acquire positive proof of greenhouse-induced climate change, and the longer society waits, the larger a warming it will have to adapt to if the greenhouse theory turns out to be valid. Even a small warming could produce violent changes in climate. At worst, the Gulf Stream might shift course, failing to warm Europe. Sea level could rise 20 feet if the West Antarctic Ice Cap melts, flooding coastal cities from New York to New Orleans.

Several measures to slow the greenhouse warming are worth taking for other reasons:

- Cut production of freons, chemicals used as solvents and refrigerants. Important greenhouse gases, they destroy the life-protecting ozone layer.
- Protect tropical forests, which not only absorb carbon dioxide but also nourish a rich variety of animal and plant life.
- Encourage conservation of energy and use of natural gas, which produces half as much carbon dioxide as does coal.
- Develop cheaper, safer nuclear power; nuclear plants produce no carbon dioxide or acid rain.

Many climatologists expect that the greenhouse theory will eventually prove true, but fear to issue alarmist warnings ahead of time. Their caution is justified. But there's an ample case for taking these initial preventive measures when the cost of such insurance is so low and the discomforts of abrupt climate change, as the drought demonstrates, so high.

THE ONLY FAIR WAY FOR ELITE COLLEGES TO CHOOSE THEIR FRESHMAN CLASSES IS BY RANDOM SELECTION

James W. Jump

Every spring, thousands of high-school seniors across the country anxiously watch the mail for a letter from the admission office of one or more of the so-called selective colleges and universities, the contents of which will profoundly affect the course of the recipient's life. The fortunate minority receive a thick letter of acceptance, opening the door to an exclusive club and all the privileges of membership. The rest receive a thin letter of rejection and, along with it, a lesson in the disappointments of adulthood.

It can be a hard lesson to swallow. As a college-admission counselor at a high school I spend a lot of time trying to console talented young people who have suddenly discovered, after four years of outstanding performance in their school work and extracurricular activities, that they are not good enough. I try to persuade them not to take the rejection personally, to convince them that they are simply victims of a process that is essentially unfair. To understand that, they have to know about how college admission works and what it is that makes an institution "selective."

For all colleges, I tell them, admission is first and foremost a numbers game. Each institution seeks to enroll a certain number of freshmen. To reach that goal, admission offices must send out more acceptances than there are places, since not every accepted applicant will enroll. For the selective colleges the difference between the two numbers is relatively small.

An institution is defined as "selective" if qualified applicants always outnumber the spaces it has available and it routinely has to reject some candidates who fully meet its standards for admission. The competition for admission to the 50 or so truly selective institutions in this country is intense; a handful of those colleges admit fewer than a quarter of the students who apply.

Most applicants for admission at selective institutions are not just qualified; they are superbly qualified, with high-school grades and Scholastic Aptitude Test scores at the top of the scale. In 1982, Princeton accepted only one-third of the high-school valedictorians who applied, and barely half of the applicants with S.A.T. scores in the 750-800 range. In 1984, the mean score on the verbal section of the S.A.T. for the 2,492 students accepted at Georgetown was 628. Last year, Stanford turned down 60 per cent of the applicants who had all A's on their high-school transcripts, and 70 per cent of those whose S.A.T. scores were above 700.

To choose a freshman class from a large group of exceptional applicants, admission committees must subject them all to rigorous and exhaustive scrutiny. At most selective colleges, anywhere from two to five people read each application and evaluate the candidate's grades, courses, activities, test scores, essays, and recommendations. Being a superb student isn't enough. Personal qualities are also considered, and applicants are given both academic and non-academic ratings.

In putting together a class, the committee gives major consideration to "diversity," not only to assure students a broad educational experience but also to achieve other goals, ranging from increasing minority enrollment to satisfying the demands of alumni. No one can deny that the process is thorough, but is it fair? The huge gap between the number of highly qualified applicants and the spaces available forces admission committees to make fine (and usually subjective) distinctions among applicants with almost identical credentials.

It is part of admissions mythology that individual merit is the yardstick by which candidates are judged. The problem is that little agreement exists on what constitutes merit, how it can be measured, or how to compare applicants of diverse background and interests. The admission process should be an exercise in just distribution, in finding a fair means of allocating a scarce resource— places at an elite institution—among too many qualified candidates.

To be fair, selection must be based on clearly defined objectives and relevant, easily measured criteria, and the judges must accord due process and equal consideration to each applicant. By those standards, the process as presently conducted is far from fair—institutions rarely, if ever, spell out their objectives; special preference is customarily given to certain candidates; and the judgments underlying admission decisions are mostly subjective and arbitrary.

Is the purpose of the process to identify and select the applicants most likely to succeed academically, or those most likely to benefit from the educational opportunity? Or is it simply to reward past performance? The answer is None of the above. The real purpose is to admit the candidates who can best help a particular institution achieve the goals (which in most cases are more political than educational) hidden behind the concept of diversity. To reach those goals, the committee may give candidates in certain categories special preference, with the effect that those candidates compete only among themselves rather than with all applicants. For example, if the institution's goal is a champion football team, and a fullback is the missing link, the fullbacks will compete for admission only against other fullbacks. If the goal is to maintain balanced proportions of men and women in the student body, then candidates of the sex that predominates will find it more difficult than the rest to gain admission. If the goal is to increase the number of students from certain minority groups, then applicants from those groups will have the edge. And because all institutions have fundraising goals, children of alumni and of the rich and famous will usually get preference.

Diversity is clearly a laudable objective, particularly given the history of minorities' limited access to higher education, but should it be achieved at the expense of fair, equal consideration for all applicants? In the name of diversity, the likes of Brooke Shields, Patrick Ewing, and the Kennedy kids get the chance to receive their education at elite universities, while other talented young people, with equal or superior credentials, do not.

The way in which selective colleges guarantee the diverse make-up of their entering classes is only one of the factors compromising the fairness of the process. Another is the unlimited discretion the colleges exercise in deciding whom to admit. Obviously, the more subjective and arbitrary the decision, the less fair it is.

One reason for such subjectivity is that grades and test scores, the objective measurements most commonly used to predict success in college, are of little use in making close distinctions among the superior students who apply to selective institutions. Their grades and test scores predict success for all of them. Unfortunately, not all can be admitted, and, because the differences are statistically insignificant, it is impossible to predict which applicants will be most successful.

Another reason is the committees' lack of accountability. Selective colleges have far more qualified applicants than they can admit. Without objective information with which to make fine distinctions, the committee is free to decide arbitrarily. It has the luxury of knowing it will choose a superb freshman class, no matter how it decides. The undeniable fact that there are always too many applicants for too few places provides immunity from criticism of its choices.

The excess of qualified candidates also distorts the way in which applications are evaluated. Because many well-qualified applicants must be turned down, admission committees are put in the position of looking not for reasons to admit but rather for reasons to exclude. Numbers are of overriding importance. Every year, quite a few applicants on the accepted list end up being cut, because of concern that more on the list will enroll than there is room for. They are rejected at the last minute, never knowing how close they came to getting in.

The only fair way to choose a freshman class from among too many qualified applicants is by some type of random selection. One way would be to have the qualified applicants draw lots. Another would be to accept candidates when their credentials are complete and they are judged qualified, until the class is full. A third, which an admission officer of my acquaintance has long recommended, would be to put every qualified applicant on a "waiting list" and admit the ones who respond first.

Random selection has several clear advantages. It would guarantee equal consideration, and it would make rejection easier to take, since not getting in would be due to bad luck rather than to personal failure. It would also be easier on admission committees. Not only would it save a great deal of the time and money currently spent splitting hairs to select a freshman class, but it would also restore the committees to their proper function of determining who is qualified, rather than who among the qualified should be admitted.

Despite the advantages, however, random selection is probably not an idea whose time has come. The benefit to selective colleges of being able to use discretion in choosing a freshman class is too great. Also, many admission professionals actually believe it's possible to make informed choices among equally qualified candidates and, ironically, so do some students.

It can be argued, of course, that admission to a selective college has nothing to do with just distribution, because higher education is not a scarce resource. There are over 3,000 colleges and universities in the United States, the argument goes, and no one who wants a higher education is denied the opportunity to get it. That being the case, selective colleges, particularly those that are privately owned, should be free to admit whomever they wish.

Such reasoning ignores the fact that the elite institutions occupy a special place in American society. Therefore, they have a special obligation to uphold the national ideals of fairness, equality of opportunity, and due process in allotting the coveted places in their freshman classes. Unless they do so by instituting a means for just distribution of places, the qualified candidates who get thin envelopes will have to continue either to accept the rejection as an authoritative judgment of their worth (and perhaps allow it to ruin their lives) or take it as a challenge to go out and prove through their accomplishments that the admission committees blew it.

FOR YOU TO WRITE

No one makes specific proposals unless in a position to do so. Therefore, rather than suggesting theses in various areas of knowledge, we offer roles you, as a proposal maker, might plausibly assume: student, citizen, consumer, employee, fan, and viewer. Under each role we have suggested very specific topics, which may meet your interests or may stimulate you to think of others. Each role and topic also suggest several possible audiences. Of course, we cannot anticipate every stance you might legitimately assume, so in thinking of proposal topics, consider other roles (such as club member, church-goer, hospital patient, or member of an organization) and potential audiences.

The proposal maker as student.

1. Tuition at state universities should be free to state residents.
2. Physical education courses should be graded on effort rather than performance.
3. Campus police should not carry guns.
4. The dorm meal plan should be changed so that students pay only for what they eat.
5. No lecture classes should have more than fifty students.
6. Fall semester should start after Labor Day.
7. The math department should give show-all-work rather than multiple-choice exams.
8. Twenty percent of the desks in every classroom and lecture hall should be left-handed and not in the back row.
9. The sexist institution of Homecoming Queen should be abolished, or we should have a Homecoming King too.
10. Students should be able to regulate the heat in their own dorm rooms.
11. No classes should be held on Saturday.
12. Outside doors to dormitories should be locked and residents issued keys.
13. All colleges should have a twelve-credit foreign language requirement toward graduation.
14. Teaching assistants who are nonnative speakers should pass a spoken-language competency test.

The proposal maker as citizen of a local, state, or national community.

1. The state should retest all drivers under sixty-five every ten years and all drivers over sixty-five every three years.
2. Our national anthem should be changed to "America the Beautiful."
3. Pay toilets should be outlawed.
4. Cats should be required to have licenses just as dogs do.
5. Bicyclists who break traffic laws should receive the same fines motorists do.
6. The United States should have a law against spanking children, just as Sweden does.
7. Our town should have a civic center for conventions and the performing arts.
8. This state should not control liquor sales.
9. Immigration should be more carefully restricted than it is.
10. Our community needs an ordinance banning the hanging of laundry outside.

The proposal maker as consumer.

1. The size of cars should be controlled by federal law.
2. Travel agents should guarantee that any airline ticket they sell is at the lowest possible price.
3. The actual manufacturer of any generic brand product should be accessible public information.
4. Kick stands should be standard equipment on ten-speed bicycles.
5. All stores should provide free gift-wrapping service.
6. Packaged produce should be dated.
7. Alterations on women's clothing should be free.
8. Renters should get a tax rebate.
9. Book and record clubs should have no minimum purchase requirements.
10. The ingredients of all fancy drinks should be listed on the menu.
11. Advertising of beer and wine should be banned from television.

The proposal maker as employee.

1. The amount of money a student earns in summer employment should not affect his tuition aid.
2. All employees should receive at least three weeks of vacation during their first year of employment.
3. Full-time students who work should not have to pay any social security tax.
4. Workers in fast-food chains should unionize.
5. Waiters and waitresses should receive the minimum wage, regardless of their income from tips.
6. Large corporations should offer more summer internships to college students who are prospective employees.
7. Engineering firms should have apprenticeships for undergraduate engineering majors.
8. The college placement office should offer job search seminars to seniors.
9. The federal government should hire young people in a Summer Youth Employment Corps.
10. The tax laws should encourage young people to set up their own small corporations.
11. Large employers should offer day-care facilities for the children of employees.

The proposal maker as sports fan or participant.

1. NCAA football should have a play-off to determine a national champion.
2. The NFL should not use instant replay to help referees on critical calls.
3. The baseball season should be shortened.

4. High-school football should be banned.
5. Professional hockey should impose stiff fines to curb violence.
6. The college's racquetball and squash courts should operate on a telephone rather than in-person reservation system.
7. The gym should install Nautilus equipment.
8. All elementary-school physical education programs should include gymnastics.
9. Tennis scoring should penalize uncivilized behavior.
10. Our community should have an annual bike race.

The proposal maker as viewer and reader.

1. Movies should not be rated, or should be rated separately for violence, sexual explicitness, and profanity.
2. Network evening news broadcasts should be expanded to one hour.
3. TV should have more programs for and featuring senior citizens.
4. It's time to bring back radio drama.
5. We should pass a law prohibiting the display of adult magazines in drug and grocery stores.
6. Newspapers should include daily science coverage.
7. Our local newspaper should include a weekly listing of new books, with a brief description of their content.
8. Presidential addresses should not be followed by rebuttal from the opposite political party.
9. Local high-school sports events should be televised.
10. This country needs a history magazine with a format similar to *National Geographic*.

Part Five

WHAT EVERY ARGUMENT NEEDS

14 The Indispensable Refutation

REFUTATION

The refutation of opposing positions is not a mere afterthought in argument. Discussion of refutation has been built into every chapter of this book because refutation is an indispensable part of all positive argument. To begin with, refutation affects your first consideration of audience; you have nothing more than an easy demonstration argument (like "Running is popular") unless you see at least the possibility of an opposition. In fact, if no one has expressed an argument against yours, you should go through the mental exercise of inventing opposing premises yourself, just to articulate other ways your subject might be approached.

Second, refutation influences the content and structure of almost any argument. If you are arguing to characterize something in a certain way and your opponent defines a key word differently, you will have to spend more time on your counterdefinition than you would if you were unchallenged. Similarly, if your opponent emphasizes one cause and you emphasize another, you must refute that other cause and show why yours is the more likely candidate. And if your proposal faces objections or a rival, you must show how your idea is more feasible, practical, fair, or sensible and your opponent's less so. All of this is refutation, a necessary part of the support for any proposition, especially one likely to meet resistance from its audience.

BUILDING ARGUMENTS WITH REFUTATION IN MIND

Writing in *On Liberty* in 1859, John Stuart Mill described the ideal arguer as one who can imagine and articulate all the possible arguments against a position.

> He who knows only his own side of the case knows little of that. His reasons may be good, and no one may have been able to refute them. But if he is equally unable to refute the reasons on the opposite side, if he does not so much as know what they are, he has no ground for preferring either opinion. . . . Nor is it enough that he should hear the arguments of adversaries from his own teachers, presented as they state them, and accompanied by what they offer as refutations. . . . He must be able to hear them from persons who actually believe them, who defend them in earnest and do their very utmost for them. . . . So essential is this discipline to a real understanding of moral and human subjects that, if opponents of all-important truths do not exist, it is indispensable to imagine them and supply them with the strongest arguments which the most skillful devil's advocate can conjure up.

One device that can help you achieve Mill's goal of fairness and fullness is listing the pro and con arguments on an issue. Such a list can be generated in many ways. You might put down all your own points first and then think of opposing ones. Or you might do the reverse and imagine all the points in a strong argument against yours. Either way, you will eventually come up with some arguments that are directly opposed to each other and some that have no counterparts. Here is an example of such a list of pro and con arguments on the subject of colorizing old movies.

Colorizing Rejuvenates Old Movies	*Colorizing Ruins Old Movies*
1. The technology of computer colorization is good and getting better.	1. The colors imposed on movies look unnatural and bleed into one another.
2. Colorization improves the TV and VCR markets for old movies.	

3. The original directors would have used color had it been available.

3. Black-and-white film is an aesthetic medium in its own right.

4. Colorizing makes movies accessible to audiences that would otherwise not see them.

4. These audiences are not seeing the movies as they were meant to be seen.

5. Colorization makes movies appear less dated.

5. Colorization distorts film history.

6. Prominent directors, actors, and critics object to colorization.

7. You can always turn the color off.

8. These movies are in the public domain.

Suppose you are developing the con argument on this issue, trying to convince readers of the entertainment section of your local newspaper that colorization ruins old movies. Some of your arguments are directly refuted by the other side; others on both sides cannot be contradicted directly. In supporting any argument for which the opposition does have a counterpoint, you will inevitably try to refute your opponent. A paragraph on contested point 3 above might look like the following:

> Colorizers often claim that directors of the 1930s and '40s would have used more color had it been available or less expensive. Perhaps some directors might have preferred color, but the fact remains that their achievement is in black and white, that they mastered the medium available to them and created great effects with it. Color is not an inherently superior medium for film. As all photographers know, black-and-white film offers unique opportunities for the composition of light, shadow, and line. Movies like *Citizen Kane*, *Mildred Pierce*, *Spellbound*, and *The Maltese Falcon* exploit the graininess and high contrast of the black-and-white medium. Even after color was widely available, many filmmakers still chose black and white as the best vehicle for certain kinds of movies: Bergman's *The Seventh Seal*, Wilder's *Some Like It Hot*, Frankenheimer's *The Manchurian Candidate*, Hitchcock's *Psycho*, Allen's *Manhattan*, and Scorsese's *Raging Bull*.

Some points on each side go unmatched. However, you can refute your opponent's point even without a direct rebuttal from a matched point of your own, and you can of course develop your own independent line of argument.

In our colorization example, the pro side cannot muster the authorities to counterbalance the objections of all the directors, actors, and critics who have been appalled by colorization. On the other hand, the con side may have no rejoinder to the suggestion that people offended by colorization can simply adjust their TV sets, but still that argument need not pass without comment.

> Colorizers claim that the rest of us can simply adjust our dials to get rid of the unwanted tint. But that is not the real issue. Anyone who respects film and its creative history resents any tampering with the integrity of artifacts from the past. Colorizing films is like painting the Washington Monument or modernizing Shakespeare's language.
>
> Certainly most directors, actors, and critics agree that movies should be left in their original state. Siskel and Ebert of *At the Movies* fame have registered their disdain for the practice, and an outraged Woody Allen even sought legal means to prevent colorizations. The only ones supporting colorizations are those who stand to make a profit from the practice.

Even though one side may generate more supporting points than the other in an initial list of pro and con arguments, the side with more points is not necessarily the better case. One strongly weighted reason can seem more compelling to an audience than any number of lesser ones. In our colorization example, the con side might rest its whole case on the aesthetic merits of black-and-white film, dismissing all appeals to wider audiences or the feasibility of colorizing technology.

HOW EXPLICIT SHOULD REFUTATION BE?

Although an awareness of opposing views is necessary to help an arguer construct a more convincing case, it does not follow that all the opposing views should be articulated in one's own argument. Actually there are dangers in including either too much or too little refutation. How much of a voice you should give opponents in your own argument depends on your audience's initial resistance to your view and their awareness of opposing views. If a neutral or uncommitted audience hears your meticulous elaboration and heroic refutation of all possible objections to your thesis, they may begin to doubt the force of your case. You may have planted in their minds objections that would never have occurred to them; they will begin to have an "argument with your argument." At the other extreme, it can be strategically unwise to ignore the objections your audience knows and will raise, if not aloud then in their minds. Once again the arguer has no simple recipe to follow, only sensitive choices to make.

EXERCISE

The following is a list of controversial issues. Make a table of at least three points on each side (that is, definition, causal, comparative, evaluative propositions). Match up any that directly oppose each other, and put the unmatched ones at the bottom of each list.

1. The United States should/should not reinstitute the draft.
2. Employers should/should not assign specific vacation times.
3. Private secondary schools are better/worse preparation for college than public high schools.
4. Soccer will/will never be really popular in the United States.
5. Senior citizens are an asset/liability to the economic health of the country.
6. Smoking should/should not be banned in public places.

Take two matched points under any issue and write a paragraph refuting one side and making a counterpoint on the other.

Repeat the above, taking the other side.

Take one of the unmatched points on either side and try to dismiss it.

THE ARGUMENT THAT IS WHOLLY REFUTATION

It sometimes happens that you have no sustained argument you want to make yourself, but you have a great deal to say against another argument or position that you have heard of or read. Admittedly, arguments against one position can often be flipped over into arguments for another, as the discussion above reveals. But still, your main purpose in writing may be to show the inadequacy of another argument. For example, you are angered by the stupidity of an editorial or column in the newspaper, so you write a letter to the editor listing all the things wrong with it. Or someone in your company has come up with a proposal and your boss asks you for a written critique; that is, you are expected to find every flaw. Or your seminar professor hands you a book or article to review and you have only negative things to say about it. All of these situations call for refutation. They do not ask you to come up with or defend any position of your own.

You may think that refutation is an impolite or even a dirty business, an attack that results in hurt feelings and bitter enemies, but it doesn't have to be if you keep the following principles of refutation in mind.

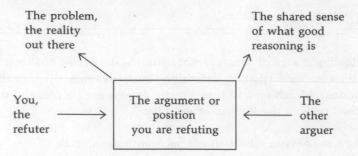

Refuters need not attack the other arguer at all. You can define your activity as that of comparing the other argument or position against two possible standards. The first is the audience's sense of facts and assumptions that give rise to the issue the argument addresses. The second is the audience's sense of what good reasoning is, the ways we agree to draw conclusions from evidence. You can fault an argument on either ground or both, and you can even indicate which standard you are referring to: "The information is incorrect." "The argument overlooks these important facts." "The conclusion does not follow." "The reasoning in this article is confused." Such criticisms need never directly attack the personality of the other arguer.

Imagine yourself framing the refutation to an argument you have just read criticizing the students of today for being politically inactive. The magazine article uses three extended examples of undergraduates, one from a prestigious private university, one from a large state university, and one from a small college. It points out the dwindling membership in politically activist groups and even in the Young Democrats and the Young Republicans, and it claims that no new student political groups have been formed in the last several years. As further, if less direct evidence, it also points to the increasing enrollments in vocational majors, especially business.

You may not be in a position to support the counterargument that students are politically active. You don't have the information, and you're not even honestly convinced it is so. Still, you are convinced that this article's characterization of students is too extreme, that its author has not earned the right to make such a large claim on the basis of such small evidence. So although you cannot uproot this argument and plant your own, you can prune it back.

First, you might take up the reasoning. The arguer has cited dwindling student membership in political organizations as a sign of apathy. You cannot deny that fact; enrollment in such organizations certainly has declined. But perhaps you can criticize the significance of that fact. You might argue, "Of course the membership in activist organizations like SDS (Students for a Democratic Society) has declined. But that was always a fringe movement designed to meet the needs of a particular political situation, America's involvement in Vietnam. Once the war ended, SDS was inevitably defunct. Therefore, the decline in SDS membership is no sign of political apathy."

You can also criticize the reasoning that increased enrollment in business courses and other vocational majors is a sign of political apathy. Again, you are not denying the fact, only questioning its significance. You might point out that what students major in reflects the job market more than their political commitment. And who is to say that a business or engineering student cannot be politically committed and active? Imagine further that one statement in this argument falsifies the reality you know, the statement about no new student political organizations forming lately. You know of two on your campus alone, one that organized to campaign for a professor running for the city council and another nonpartisan group, SBG (Students for Better Government), which organized to encourage good people to go into politics. You will certainly emphasize these exceptions because the argument you are refuting seems to be making a very general claim. If the argument does not mention any exceptions or qualify its thesis in any way with a "basically," "largely," or "generally" (that is, "Students are generally politically inactive"), you certainly can criticize it for exaggeration.

To summarize: You have found several ways to refute the argument supporting the proposition "Students are politically inactive." When you compared the argument to what you knew, you found that it overlooked some facts. And when you examined its reasoning, you found that the arguer failed to qualify the thesis and jumped to conclusions from facts about declining memberships and increasing vocational enrollments. Thus, your refutation has pruned back the thesis from "[All] students are politically inactive" to "most" or "many," and after digging around in the roots, left it with less certain support.

PARTS OF A REFUTATION

Every refutation can begin by identifying the type of argument being refuted, for each type has its inherent weaknesses. In earlier chapters we have already indicated what can go wrong in definition, comparison, causal, evaluation, and proposal arguments. A full refutation can also consist of the following elements:

1. What is the issue?
   Summarize the controversy, the events, whatever reality the argument responds to.

2. What does the other argument have to say about the issue?
   Summarize the argument you are going to refute or state the position you are calling into question.

3. Does this argument have all the relevant and accurate information?
   Test the argument against reality; ask for verification of the facts given.

4. Does this argument violate a standard of good reasoning your audience should hold?
   Consider the type of argument and question whether the arguer uses inapplicable or insufficient support.

5. Are there any flaws in accommodation?
   Look for imprecisions in word choice, meretricious emotional appeals, mistakes in emphasis or ordering, and offensive audience manipulation.

Like the ideal proposal outline, this list is a full format you can select from. Which parts you choose to put in or leave out will depend on your audience, their state of knowledge or ignorance of the position or argument you are refuting, and of course their attitude toward it.

What Is the Issue?

If your audience is unfamiliar with the issue behind the argument you are refuting, you will have to inform them right at the start. Suppose you are refuting an argument in favor of mainstreaming retarded and handicapped children. Suppose further that you cannot count on your audience being aware that this policy has been mandated by law in many school districts, let alone that much controversy has arisen over the wisdom of it. So a little background information is called for. The information you give can take at least two forms. You can answer the question "What events have brought about this controversy?" or the question "What positions have people taken on it?" or both.

What Does the Other Argument Have to Say About the Issue?

A refutation has to take off from something. It makes no sense to go on the attack without an object to attack, and that object can be anything from a one-sentence restatement of an argument or position on an issue to a paragraph or longer summary of the other arguer's whole line of thought. Once again, how much summary or quotation is necessary depends on your readers' awareness.

Very often you may be refuting not a specific written argument but a general position held by many people. So long as your audience does not include the people you are refuting, you can open your refutation by stating what others believe and then go on to tell why they are wrong. This tactic is not quite the same as simply using an opponent's view as a springboard to your own. In that case you have a positive argument to make. Here you are only refuting.

If you are refuting a written argument that your readers do not have in front of them, then you must do them the favor of summarizing or quoting from it. And you must summarize fairly; you don't help your side by misrepresenting the other or by presenting their position as one only fools could hold. You might put this constraint on yourself: "My readers have not seen the argument I am summarizing, but if they did, would they think my summary fair?"

Letters to an editor and editorials that refute other editorials often omit this opening summary because they assume that readers of the paper have been following current controversies and remember the piece being refuted. Therefore it is always difficult to pick up cold a refutation in a newspaper.

Does This Argument Have All the Relevant and Accurate Information?

Now you are getting to the meat of refutation. Any argument that has its facts wrong, or not enough of them, or does not verify where necessary deserves severe criticism. Of course, you can recognize errors in fact only if you have greater knowledge yourself, and if you don't have that knowledge to begin with, you must patiently try to verify the facts in the argument you want to refute. You probably would not even try to refute an argument on a subject you knew nothing about, but you may still need to check out specific pieces of information. For example, "Opponent"—the arguer you are refuting—claims that no one ever scored a perfect ten in international gymnastics competition; you check that fact in a book of sports statistics. "Opponent" says that Alexander Hamilton was once a candidate for the presidency; you find a biography of Hamilton and look that up. "Opponent" says that the FDA regulates the use of dyes in cosmetics and has banned some; you can try to verify that statement by finding the government publication that gives FDA regulations on cosmetics. Checking out facts is not terribly difficult if the writer has provided sufficient documentation or mentioned necessary sources. If not, you may have something else to complain about. It is less likely that facts will be wrong than that they will be stated in an imprecise way, in a way that you believe gives them more or less significance than they deserve.

You might also consider if there are facts the writer has ignored. It is possible for an argument to have all the facts it does give straight, yet to have left out important information. Suppose that "Opponent" is arguing that there is no unemployment problem today because more people are working than ever before. You must agree with that fact—yes, in sheer numbers, more people are working. But you point out that the population is also larger now, and therefore the percentage of employed in the whole population is less than before. How do you know when facts are missing or inadequate? There is no magic test. We recommend a "show-me" attitude, a little common sense and skepticism, as well as background reading on the issue.

Does This Argument Violate a Standard of Reasoning the Audience Should Hold?

From the point of view of rhetoric, if you are going to refute an arguer for poor reasoning, you can judge that reasoning only in relation to the argument's audience and situation. Different audiences and situations call for different standards of reasoning. Whole textbooks are devoted to detecting presumably absolute flaws in reasoning called fallacies. But what is a fallacious argument to one audience may be persuasive to another. So to criticize or refute the reasoning in an argument really amounts to arguing that it fails to meet a standard of reasoning its audience has or ought to have. The refuter tries, in effect, to convince an audience that they are "too good" for an argument.

An article in a checkout counter tabloid once claimed in screaming headlines "Elvis Lives!" The evidence cited to support this claim consisted of a tape-recorded voice of unknown origin and authenticity (though supposedly recent and supposedly of Elvis), a film clip of a shadowy figure behind a screen door at Graceland during Elvis's funeral, and, most important, the fact that Elvis's middle name (Aron) is misspelled (Aaron) on his tombstone. Just to seize on this last item, a refuter might ask by what chain of "good reasoning" a misspelled name on a tombstone could signify that the person allegedly buried under it is not really dead. Perhaps the tabloid writer's reasoning went something like the following: "It is highly unlikely that a person's name will be misspelled on a tombstone. Therefore if it is misspelled, the misspelling is probably intentional and highly significant. Knowing he is alive, Elvis's family probably did not want his real name on his tombstone, so they had it deliberately misspelled. Therefore Elvis is not dead."

Needless to say, most people would find this leap from physical evidence to subsequent inference unreasonable. A few people, however, will still be persuaded, especially those who want to believe Elvis lives. For them the reasoning in this article is acceptable, so we could say that this argument meets the standards of reasoning demanded by tabloid readers. If we refute this argument on the basis of its reasoning, we are really trying to convince an audience that they ought to have a different or higher standard of reasoning than the one it offers.

Are There Any Flaws in Accommodation?

Aside from errors in the reasoning and inaccuracies in the facts, minor matters of format, word choice, and correctness may offend you and deserve mention in your refutation. For example, does the author consistently misspell important names like "Michael Anjello," "Minnieapplis," or the "Midevil Period"? Does the writer misuse pretentious foreign words or phrases, saying *faux pas* instead of *coup d'état*? Does she make grammatical errors? Or any slips in taste or accommodation such as dwelling too long on the gory details of some example or insulting the intelligence of the audience by belaboring an obvious point? Professional reviewers in magazines and newspapers love to pick on these ants at the picnic.

You should never make such cavils the entire substance of your refutation. Then the reader could turn criticism on you for being picky, instead of on the piece you are refuting. Nevertheless, a writer's credibility is certainly undermined by signs of carelessness or insensitivity.

FOR YOU TO ANALYZE OR WRITE ABOUT

Here are paired pro and con arguments; you may support a counterargument to either side or refute one side or the other. Remember that you can agree with the overall thesis, but still find flaws in the argument for it. If none of these arguments engages your criticism, find one that does. Good places to look are the editorial and letters-to-the-editor pages of newspapers and magazines, the signed columns of your campus newspaper, and the articles in special-interest magazines such as *Ms., Psychology Today, Mother Jones, Sports Illustrated, The New Republic,* and *The National Review.*

EXCERPTS FROM JUSTICES' OPINIONS ON SEARCHES OF CURBSIDE TRASH BY POLICE

Following are excerpts from the opinions in the Supreme Court's decision . . . that the police may freely search through garbage left outside homes for collection. Justice Byron R. White wrote the majority opinion, joined by Chief Justice William H. Rehnquist and Justices Harry A.

Blackman, John Paul Stevens, Sandra Day O'Connor and Antonin Scalia. Justice William J. Brennan Jr. dissented, joined by Justice Thurgood Marshall. Justice Anthony M. Kennedy did not participate.

FROM THE MAJORITY OPINION
Justice White

The issue here is whether the Fourth Amendment prohibits the warrantless search and seizure of garbage left for collection outside the curtilage of a home. We conclude, in accordance with the vast majority of lower courts that have addressed the issue, that it does not.

In early 1984, Investigator Jenny Stracner of the Laguna Beach Police Department received information indicating that respondent Greenwood might be engaged in narcotics trafficking. Stracner learned that a criminal suspect had informed a Federal drug-enforcement agent in February 1984 that a truck filled with illegal drugs was en route to the Laguna Beach address at which Greenwood resided. In addition, a neighbor complained of heavy vehicular traffic late at night in front of Greenwood's single-family home. The neighbor reported that the vehicles remained at Greenwood's house for only a few minutes.

Stracner sought to investigate this information by conducting a surveillance of Greenwood's home. She observed several vehicles make brief stops at the house during the late-night and early-morning hours, and she followed a truck from the house to a residence that had previously been under investigation as a narcotics trafficking location.

Request to Trash Collector

On April 6, 1984, Stracner asked the neighborhood's regular trash collector to pick up the plastic garbage bags that Greenwood had left on the curb in front of his house and to turn the bags over to her without mixing their contents with garbage from other houses. The trash collector cleaned his truck bin of other refuse, collected the garbage bags from the street in front of Greenwood's house, and turned the bags over to Stracner. The officer searched through the rubbish and found items indicative of narcotics use. She recited the information that she had gleaned from the trash search in an affidavit in support of a warrant to search Greenwood's home.

Police officers encountered both respondents at the house later that day when they arrived to execute the warrant. The police discovered quantities of cocaine and hashish during their search of the house. Respondents were arrested on felony narcotics charges. They subsequently posted bail.

The police continued to receive reports of many late-night visitors to the Greenwood house. On May 4, Investigator Robert Rahaeuser obtained Greenwood's garbage from the regular trash collector in the same manner as had Stracner. The garbage again contained evidence of narcotics use.

Rahaeuser secured another search warrant for Greenwood's home based on the information from the second trash search. The police found more narcotics and evidence of narcotics trafficking when they executed the warrant. Greenwood was again arrested.

The Superior Court dismissed the charges against respondents on the authority of People v. Krivda, which held that warrantless trash searches violate the Fourth Amendment and the California Constitution. The court found that the police would not have had probable cause to search the Greenwood home without the evidence obtained from the trash searches.

The California Supreme Court denied the State's petition for review of the Court of Appeal's decision. We granted certiorari, and now reverse.

The warrantless search and seizure of the garbage bags left at the curb outside the Greenwood house would violate the Fourth Amendment only if respondents manifested a subjective expectation of privacy in their garbage that society accepts as objectively reasonable. Respondents do not disagree with this standard.

They assert, however, that they had, and exhibited, an expectation of privacy with respect to the trash that was searched by the police: The trash, which was placed on the street for collection at a fixed time, was contained in opaque plastic bags, which the garbage collector was expected to pick up, mingle with the trash of others, and deposit at the garbage dump. The trash was only temporarily on the street, and there was little likelihood that it would be inspected by anyone.

It may well be that respondents did not expect that the contents of their garbage bags would become known to the police or other members of the public. An expectation of privacy does not give rise to the Fourth Amendment protection, however, unless society is prepared to accept that expectation as objectively reasonable.

"Public Inspection"

Here, we conclude that respondents exposed their garbage to the public sufficiently to defeat their claim to Fourth Amendment protection. It is common knowledge that plastic garbage bags left on or at the side of a public street are readily accessible to animals, children, scavenger, snoop, and other members of the public.

Moreover, respondents placed their refuse at the curb for the express purpose of conveying it to a third party, the trash collector, who might himself have sorted through respondents' trash or permitted others, such as the police, to do so. Accordingly, having deposited their garbage "in an area particularly suited for public inspection and, in a manner of speaking, public consumption, for the express purpose of having strangers take it," respondents could have had no reasonable expectation of privacy in the inculpatory items that they discarded.

Furthermore, as we have held, the police cannot reasonably be expected to avert their eyes from evidence of criminal activity that could have been observed by any member of the public. Hence, "what a person knowingly exposes to the public, even in his own home or office, is not a subject of Fourth Amendment protection." We held in Smith v. Maryland (1979), for example, that the police did not violate the Fourth Amendment by causing a pen register to be installed at the telephone company's offices to record the telephone numbers dialed by a criminal suspect. An individual has no legitimate expectation of privacy in the numbers dialed on his telephone, we reasoned, because he voluntarily conveys those numbers to the telephone company when he uses the telephone.

Backyard Surveillance

Similarly, we held in California v. Ciraolo that the police were not required by the Fourth Amendment to obtain a warrant before conducting surveillance of the respondent's fenced backyard from a private plane flying at an altitude of 1,000 feet. We concluded that the respondent's expectation that his yard was protected from such surveillance was unreasonable because "any member of the public flying in this airspace who glanced down could have seen everything that these officers observed."

Our conclusion that society would not accept as reasonable respondents' claim to an expectation of privacy in trash left for collection in an area accessible to the public is reinforced by the unanimous rejection of similar claims by the Federal Courts of Appeals. In addition, of those state appellate courts that have considered the issue, the vast majority have held that the police may conduct warrantless search and seizures of garbage discarded in public areas.

The judgment of the California Court of Appeal is therefore reversed, and this case is remanded for further proceedings not inconsistent with this opinion.

FROM THE DISSENTING OPINION
Justice Brennan

Every week for two months, and at least once more a month later, the Laguna Beach police clawed through the trash that respondent Greenwood left in opaque, sealed bags on the curb outside his home. Complete strangers minutely scrutinized their bounty, undoubtedly dredging up intimate details of Greenwood's private life and habits. The intrusions proceeded without a warrant, and no court before or since has concluded that the police acted on probable cause to believe Greenwood was engaged in any criminal activity.

Scrutiny of another's trash is contrary to commonly accepted notions of civilized behavior. I suspect, therefore, that members of our society will be shocked to learn that the Court, the ultimate guarantor of liberty, deems unreasonable our expectation that the aspects of our private lives that are concealed safely in a trash bag will not become public.

"A container which can support a reasonable expectation of privacy may not be searched, even on probable cause, without a warrant."

Carrying Personal Effects

Our precedent leaves no room to doubt that had respondents been carrying their personal effects in opaque, sealed plastic bags—identical to the ones they placed on the curb—their privacy would have been protected from warrantless police intrusion.

Respondents deserve no less protection just because Greenwood used the bags to discard rather than to transport his personal effects. Their contents are not inherently any less private, and Greenwood's decision to discard them, at least in the manner in which he did, does not diminish his expectation of privacy. . . .

Had Greenwood flaunted his intimated activity by strewing his trash all over the curb for all to see, or had some nongovernmental intruder invaded his privacy and done the same, I could accept the Court's conclusion that an expectation of privacy would have been unreasonable. Similarly, had police searching the city dump run across incriminating evidence that, despite commingling with the trash of others, still retained its identity as Greenwood's, we would have a different case. But all that Greenwood "exposed . . . to the public" were the exteriors of several opaque, sealed containers. . . .

"Grim Picture" of Society

In holding that the warrantless search of Greenwood's trash was consistent with the Fourth Amendment, the Court paints a grim picture of our society. It depicts a society in which local authorities may command their citizens to dispose of their personal effects in the manner least protective of "the sanctity of the home and the privacies of life," and then monitor them arbitrarily and without judicial oversight—a society that is not prepared to recognize as reasonable an individual's expectation of privacy in the most private of personal effects sealed in an opaque container and disposed of in a manner designed to commingle it imminently and inextricably with the trash of others. The American society with which I am familiar "chooses to dwell in reasonable security and freedom from surveillance," and is more dedicated to individual liberty and more sensitive to intrusions on the sanctity of the home than the Court is willing to acknowledge.

I dissent.

ENDURING INTEREST PUTS A TRUE CLASSIC ON THE LIST

Wayne C. Booth

As someone who has had a lifelong love affair with various works that appear on various "canonical" lists, I might be expected to get upset when anticanonists offer their rival substitutes.

But the truth is that like most other lovers of Homer and Shakespeare (to name only the two most canonical of all canonic authors), I have never embraced a fixed canon of works that everybody ought to love.

My "list," never since adolescence formally written out, changes every year, every month, as some new work offers me that special radiance that turns works into classics (at the moment I am "nominating" Toni Morrison's *Beloved*). Though some old loves have lasted, others have simply been dropped: I haven't reread *Tristram Shandy* for 20 years, though it must still be on my list somewhere. What's more, some of the works that other people would go to the stake for have always left me cold: I've never reached the end of *The Faerie Queene*.

So part of what the rebels insist on is surely sound: Frozen lists of "classics" are not what we need, and such lists *can,* in the hands of martinets, lead readers to hate "culture."

But there's another reason the rebels don't scare me: They obviously don't believe their own more extreme claims. Some of them claim that it doesn't matter what we read, that to study *any* work is as valuable as to study any other work—and therefore (the logic goes awry here) what we should really study are such-and-such works, which are more valuable than those traditionally canonized.

I don't worry much about this kind of illogic, because the works the rebels tout, while claiming that no works *really* deserve to be touted, will either earn widespread admiration, and thus endure, or not; one good definition of a classic is a work that is sure to hold its own in a fair fight.

And the works they attack will either drop from sight, or not, depending on whether they continue to feed us. There has never been a fixed canon of the kind that Education Secretary William J. Bennett and others sometimes seem to believe in. What's more, we could lose half of anyone's current canonic list and suffer no drastic consequences, *provided our engagement with other works were passionate and critical.*

Others claim that the age of bourgeois aesthetic and ethical culture, buttressed by canonical lists and the illusion of a common human nature, is at an end; as David Lloyd puts it, "the emergent literature of minorities . . . will dissolve the canonical form of Man back into the different bodies which it has sought to absorb." Well, maybe. Who can tell?

Meanwhile, such confident prophets of the demise of my loved ones write to me, their reader, clearly expecting me to understand and embrace *their* (tacitly) canonical list of minor writers who are now, in their view, truly major. And they write, at least some of the time, in our shared language, using forms of argument that we share. Most comforting of all, they praise literary virtues and effects that most "bourgeois" literature has praised for something like the past 200 years: daring, originality, freedom from authority, and an embrace of a revolutionary new epoch that only a few rebels can see for what it is.

What does scare me a bit is that while all this ill-defined debate goes on, a large proportion of our graduates remains innocent of another "canon" entirely: the range of reading, writing, and thinking skills that enable anyone to deal critically with *any* text, classical or modern. The making and breaking of canonical lists leaves our major educational problems untouched.

A CANON MUST INCLUDE WORKS OF MANY CULTURES

David Lloyd

Recent debates on literary canons, courses in "Western civilization," and core curricula have focused on the *content* of syllabuses as indicating the values they express. While it would be foolish to underestimate the urgency of the need to expand the canon, focusing solely on the list of canonical works obscures what is really at issue. The inclusion of third-world or minority writings in the present canon is a primary act of intellectual affirmative action, and thus far more valuable, but in itself is limited to a minimal reparation for past ignorance. For the canon expresses more than its immediate content. It is founded on certain principles to fulfill specific functions.

Liberal, and even conservative, upholders of the canon frequently emphasize its expansive and assimilative capacities. The literary canon, they say, has successively incorporated American writers, Irish writers, lower-class writers, women writers, even a few Afro-American writers. Someday even some Asian-American or Chicano writers may be absorbed. They forget that the assimilative function of the canon has always been its essence and that this assimilation takes place according to a quite determinate model of human development. Individual works or the literary productions of whole peoples become canonized insofar as they seem to represent the attainment of an ethical selfhood defined in terms of disinterest and universality.

All that is excluded from the canon is defined as primitive, uncultivated, underdeveloped, or political. Only after the excluded classes, whether racially, sexually, or politically defined, have undergone ethical cultivation and traded their identity for identification with dominant models of culture can they be canonized.

This is the tale told in the founding texts of cultural education, from Schiller's *Letters on Aesthetic Education* to Arnold's *Culture and Anarchy*. It has not been significantly modified by modernism. The tale is intrinsically political and imperialist and intimately linked, as the vocabulary of assimilation and development indicates, to the imperialist logic it legitimates.

Since the moment of its emergence, more or less in time with the American and French Revolutions, the primary function of aesthetic culture has been to give a developmental form to the manifest contradiction between the universal claims of Western bourgeois states and their systematic exclusion of certain classes of humans. According to this scheme, all will be included in time, but in time with their assimilation to a singular model of ethical subjectivity not so improperly characterized as a white, bourgeois, and masculine ideal. A more generous version of this canon has little consequence, serving only to confirm the absorptive capacities of a culture to which all difference is subordinated.

In the meantime, cultural education will continue to legitimate the most insidious myth of Western civilization, that it represents the apex of a preordained scheme of human development.

Paradoxically, the famous claim that culture transcends politics turns out to be its most political moment. For the problem with the values traditionally expressed by cultural education—universality, disinterest, freedom—lies not in those values so much as in the fact that culture itself functions to prevent their genuine realization. The various representative works of the canon substitute for any approach to cultural diversity, while purely formal rehearsals of ethical disinterest and autonomy indefinitely defer the struggle to forge a society in which self-determination at all levels might be achieved. That deferral, founded on a premature declaration of human reconciliation, is the political function of culture.

Any revision of the processes of cultural education must take seriously Walter Benjamin's famous remark that every document of civilization is at one and the same time a document of barbarity. Teaching the canon must give way to a critical history of the exclusions and oppressions on which the "civilizing process" 'has depended. If we would really know Western civilization, we should know the terms and costs on which it has come to dominate and not merely the catalog of fetishized cultural commodities which PR men of neo-conservatism extend to us.

DAVID LLOYD RESPONDS TO WAYNE BOOTH . . .

What Wayne Booth writes of his reading habits is generous, liberal minded, a little Utopian even. Unfortunately, it misses the point. The issue concerning the canon has little to do with anyone's informal list of preferred reading matter. It is not a question of love, but one of power, though in a Utopian scheme of things one would like to believe that love would displace power.

Missing the point, however, and in the name of private delectation, is right now a political act of a precisely *aesthetic* nature. The formation of taste is private only in its immediate appearance, and the liberal appeal to private experience masks the social mediation of taste through institutions for which the individual is a primary ideological category and of which any given canonical "list" is no more than a symptom. Private acts of love have little directly to do with the apparatus of pedagogy, though they may be and are intended to be reproduced as one of the ends of a normalizing education.

Opponents of the canon are its opponents not in order to establish their preferences in some alternative list of essential works, but in order to dismantle the universal normative claims disseminated through canons of however variable a content. That certain writers whose experience is that of minorities have produced works that contribute to this critique does not imply that they are to be reevaluated for a new canon. Rather, the facts of marginalization and exclusion which their works explore and the resoluteness of their rhetoric of negation give us grounds and means to move outside the educational and hegemonic assumptions that the canon represents.

In the meantime, if the discussion has an academic flavor, it is as well to remember that the issues more widely broached here are not irrelevant to the continuing business of "daily life." Much of the pathos surrounding the defense of the canon may come, not from the viciousness of attacks on a cherished institution, but from the fact that the ideological function of high culture has been largely superseded by the mass cultural institutions that carry on its hegemonic work. In conjunction with the critique of the canon, its opponents will have to concern themselves with what already has gone beyond it, though in not so different forms, namely, the formation of "private" subjects through the most powerful assimilatory media of our time.

. . . WAYNE BOOTH RESPONDS TO DAVID LLOYD

Every writer should stand before the class and repeat aloud, 100 times, the worst sentence in that day's essay, explaining it clause by clause. Short of that, will David Lloyd please come forward and explain just one of his sentences:

"Since the moment of its [modernism's] emergence, more or less in time with the American and French Revolutions, the primary function of aesthetic culture has been to give a developmental form to the manifest contradiction between the universal claims of Western bourgeois states and their systematic exclusion of certain classes of humans."

What these piled abstractions seem to mean is that there was a vast though unconscious conspiracy among "modernists," American and French revolutionaries, bourgeois political leaders, and "aesthetic culture"—among all the writers, composers, painters, and readers, listeners, and viewers, since the late 18th century. In preferring *these* works over *those* works, they all expressed the same "primary function": to exclude "certain classes." These works embodied an inescapable contradiction between *everybody's* claims to speak for everybody and *everybody's* rejection of everyone outside the center.

Can anyone really claim to have evidence for such a melting down of all "differences" but one? Does my skepticism about Lloyd's wild conceptual lumpings spring simply from a blindness imposed by having lived with some monstrous "canon," from being one of those "white, bourgeois, masculine" folks Lloyd deplores? Naturally I prefer to think that it springs from a respect for "difference," a "palpable, resistant, cultural diversity" that contrasts sharply with his monolithic abstraction, aesthetic-bourgeois-Western-white-civilization-culture. My skepticism springs in part from reading Marx (surely part of *Lloyd's* canon), with his profound deconstruction of words like "self." It springs from reading Montaigne, who cast a cold eye on universalist claims. It springs from reading Hume and Voltaire, Fielding and Jane Austen, Derrida and Foucault and finding that *I can't put them all together as any kind of monolithic cultural inheritance.* They contradict each other, in me.

In short, "the canon"—works now widely studied—teaches us that there is no canon and that what we must fear most is the imposition, from cultural right or left, of some universalist dogma.

TEACH THE DEBATE ABOUT THE CANON

Gerald Graff

To teach or not to teach the Great Books? There is a solution to the recent heated debate over this question that is so obvious, hardly anybody has offered it: Teach the debate itself.

When I say "teach the debate itself," I don't mean that teaching the controversies over books should replace teaching the books themselves. I mean that these controversies can be used to make books more interesting and intelligible to students.

Our mistake has been to assume that we have to *resolve* the dispute between David Lloyd and Wayne Booth in order to teach the humanities effectively, that without a consensus on what to teach and why, the curriculum must be chaotic and confused. Social and demographic changes since World War II have knocked the stuffing out of the past consensus on these questions and expanded the range of cultures, subcultures, and traditions asking to be represented.

At the same time, the so-called knowledge explosion has so diversified the ways of thinking about intellectual inquiry that once agreed-on definitions of the academic fields have been called into question. So, instead of a single shared tradition there are competing traditions, and, where knowledge is under constant redefinition, the belief that educators have to get a consensus on what to teach is a prescription for paralysis.

The most familiar symptom of this paralysis is the chaotic "cafeteria counter" curriculum, which responds to the difficulty of choosing among conflicting interests by including essentially everything. Conservatives are right in complaining that this kind of curriculum lacks coherence. But their only remedy. is for everyone to line up behind the conservatives' brand of coherence. When you point out that their brand differs from that of other groups, they have no answer except to cry "relativism," which doesn't usefully address the problem.

A more practical and democratic alternative to the cafeteria-counter curriculum would be to see that you don't necessarily have to get consensus to get coherence. That is, disagreements and conflicts, if they can be clarified, can themselves be a source of coherence. We could use the disputes over texts, canons, and traditions (and their interesting history) to make the curriculum less disconnected and help students make sense of their reading.

The point of recent attempts to broaden the canon of texts being taught is not to substitute "Westerns as Lit" for "Western Lit," as an ill-informed writer recently complained in the Wall Street Journal. The point is not to scrap the classics (which are still very widely taught, contrary to belief), but to teach the classics in relation to the challenges that have been posed to them. This means teaching various kinds of texts from Plato to popular culture, from Western to third-world cultures. The best way to kill the classics has always been to set them on a pedestal, protected from hostile criticism and competing traditions.

Nor is it necessarily just "relativism" to recognize that standards that were formerly taken for granted are now controversial and have to be defended by argument. Here, I'm afraid, is what really enrages many critics about the changes now taking place in the teaching of literature: Whereas these critics could once assume that their view of what counts as good literature was the official one, they now have to *fight for* their view.

This is what the Right refuses to understand and what the media coverage of the controversy over the humanities has failed to bring out. It is in the interests of all ideological factions to recognize that there are legitimate reasons for disagreement about what should be taught in universities, and that rival positions cannot always be reduced to a distinction between trendy relativist nonsense and sound wisdom.

Objectors will say that you can't hope to engage students in a cultural debate when they don't possess elementary "cultural literacy," the knowledge of who Napoleon was or the century of the Civil War. Seductive though it seems, this line of argument ignores the motivations and incentives—or the lack of them—that make students want to acquire information. Students will start acquiring cultural literacy when they see the point of doing so, when it comes as a byproduct of doing something else that seems worthwhile and coherent. Feeding them lists of meaningless factoids, like those E. D. Hirsch would evidently foist on schoolchildren, is no substitute.

Which is why, to come back to my point, "teaching the debate" over culture and education should be the response to the current Great Books controversy. Students will take an interest in the Great Books when those books are presented in clear and interesting contexts. But this will be hard to do when books are set apart from the rest of culture and from the debates that give life to culture. The only way to save the Great Books is to put them into relation to the forces that are challenging them.

15 | Accommodation

Everything done to an argument from its earliest stages to shape it for its particular audience is called *accommodation.* So far this book has dealt entirely with the various kinds of arguments and their essential components. You already know that certain claims suggest certain kinds of supporting arguments and that they may even require several types of smaller arguments as the proposal combines definition, comparison, evaluation, and causal arguments. But if argument involved only putting premises and conclusions in sequence, the best argument would be an outline—logical, orderly, and explicit. An outline, however, is hardly persuasive; argument needs the flesh of accommodation to come alive and dance for the audience.

Perhaps our point about accommodation would be clearer if we did not use the word *argument* all the time. It suggests hostility, conflict, disagreement, even raised voices, red faces, and dilated nostrils. The word *persuasion* is not much better. It often suggests an attempt to convince by using tricks that bypass good reasons. So we stick with *argument* because at least it suggests the proper emphasis on rational appeals. If we could invent a new word, it would keep the emphasis on reason but add suggestions of respect, of civility, of a dancer reaching out for a partner. All these added suggestions define what we mean by accommodation.

When you accommodate an argument to a particular audience, you have to ask yourself two questions.

1. What am I telling the audience about itself?
2. What picture of myself am I projecting to my readers?

Both of these considerations should affect everything from individual word choice to the entire structure of the argument. You will have to decide whether a single word is too loaded (like *persuasion* above), whether your audience needs extensive background information or already knows enough, whether you want to start with your thesis or wait until you have prepared your audience with some preliminary arguments.

Making such choices because you are considering the effect of what you write is not a form of dishonesty. Suppose, for example, you are advocating a rehabilitation program for former prison inmates. You are not lying if you refer to this group of people as "parolees" rather than "former prisoners" because you want to emphasize their present state of freedom rather than their former state of confinement. You are making a word choice that favors your thesis, as well as one that may even be more precise.

Some people think they achieve moral grandeur by "telling it like it is," "not mincing words," "being very up front." People who use these clichés think any consideration of audience is selling out. All we can say of such people is—they are all ignorant fools! Now there is an example of lack of accommodation. We want to make a case for the moral respectability of accommodation. Do we help our argument by accusing our audience of ignorance and immorality?

Accommodation is based on the assumption that other people—in written argument our readers—deserve respect whether or not they agree with us, whether or not they are powerful. This same assumption has given us kindness, civility, compromise, and the politeness to greet a stranger not with a raised club but with an outstretched hand. That kind of respect for others requires no betrayal of principle, no lessening of ardor for a cause. In fact, when we hold our own positions most clearly and precisely, we often have the least trouble finding ways to convince others. Because we know our own minds, we can know our audience's as well—where they are farthest apart, where they are closest together. Therefore, we can choose the best words, the best emphases, the best arrangement. By accommodating to our audience we have not lessened our conviction; our conviction has made conscious choices.

TELLING THE AUDIENCE ABOUT ITSELF

Identifying Your Audience

Before you can make fine adjustments for the sake of your audience, you have to know who that audience is. In the world outside the classroom, people seldom set pen to paper without knowing, at least generally, who their audience is. Letters of application, proposals for grants, reports to a boss, even letters to the editor—the occasion for writing and the identification of audience are often simultaneous. In a writing course, the situation is somewhat different, since every paper is to some extent directed at the instructor. But in every discipline, the sense of audience will differ, and many writing assignments will ask you to address audiences with widely varied attitudes and levels of awareness. Still, however, the writer may need to articulate what is knowable about the attitudes and assumptions of that audience.

Are the members of your audience all alike in any significant respect? For example, is your audience young, middle-aged, old, or mixed? Or are they homogeneous in any of the following ways: sex; occupation; education level; area of residence, from "this block" to the "eastern seaboard"; economic status; religion; politics; nationality; or ethnic group? Do they have an interest in common such as hang gliding or rug hooking? What is their predictable response to your argument? Are they likely to be hostile, neutral, indifferent, lukewarm, wholeheartedly in favor? How much do they already know about the issue? Are they well informed, ignorant, or at any point between those extremes? And most important, how do they think? What kinds of arguments are they likely to find convincing?

You will not be able to answer all of these questions if your audience is larger than any small, intimate group. But you ought to ask them anyway, and you *must* assess your audience's position on any issue that touches your argument. You would rarely, for instance, launch into a political argument without knowing the political loyalties of your audience, or address an argument for estate planning to eighteen-year-olds, or advise welfare recipients on how to invest in the stock market.

The Audience That Is Everyone but No One in Particular

At this point you might ask, "What if I am not writing for any particular audience? What if I just have *any* reader, the general public in mind?" Though it is perfectly possible to have such a vague audience in mind when you write, even that general audience has characteristics. Writers often think of their arguments appearing in mass-circulation magazines and newspapers like *Time, Newsweek, The New York Times,* or *The Christian Science Monitor.* Yet even these publications have readerships that can be precisely characterized.

First of all, what kind of reader would even bother to read an argument on your issue? You say, "Everyone could read it," but in fact not everyone would. Think how many times you have flipped through a magazine, passing over many articles intended for a general audience which have not caught your attention. So to begin with, the topic selects its own audience. Some people will never read anything about Central America, conversion to the metric system, sports, or the latest births, deaths, and marriages. Others will read nothing but. (At this point we are talking only about the kind of interest that will get a member of the so-called general audience to *start* reading an argument. Once readers start, it becomes the author's responsibility to pull them through to the end.)

Second, writing for a general reader does not make accommodation unnecessary. Think about the characteristics of the so-called general American reader. It would be fair to say that the average American reader understands references to "end zone," "Babe Ruth," or "Elvis Presley"; would think that calling an action "unconstitutional" was saying something bad about it; and would not blaspheme the name of George Washington. That same general reader would probably need most technical terms explained, would know relatively little about the culture and history of other countries, and would be unfamiliar with any but the most famous works in art, literature, and music. The general audience has these permanent characteristics as well as many temporary ones. You can count on familiarity with the major news stories of the day, but not memory of them one year later. Of course, no particular person fits this profile exactly, but these are the kinds of characteristics you have to take into account in accommodating to a general audience.

You may also want to get your general audience to cast itself in a certain role. Perhaps your argument appeals to them as if they were more generous, more public spirited, more intellectually alert than they may be in actuality. Some arguments successfully address us as we might be; others, unfortunately, appeal to our less admirable potentials. Even a general audience is not static or predictable in its attitudes. It can be ennobled or debased by the appeals made to it.

BUILDING AUTHOR CREDIBILITY: PROJECTING A GOOD PICTURE OF YOURSELF

Everything you write is stamped with your personality. That's true of your shopping lists and even more true of any extended argument you write. If you lost all the signed pages of your friends' letters, you would still know who wrote each one; their word choices, their turns of phrase, their content would give them away as written by a particular friend. Similarly, though perhaps less obviously, the writing you do at work and at school reflects your character and personality.

Since you inevitably convey your personality in your written arguments, you should project the aspects of it that work for you rather than against you. Over two thousand years ago Aristotle recommended that an arguer should convey a positive *ethos,* an impression of a "good person arguing well." This advice has two elements. First, you must argue well; this whole book is about that. Second, your audience must not only understand your arguments, but also perceive that "you" behind the words as a good person, someone who is intellectually honest as well as courageous, moderate, just, generous, prudent, and wise. No book on argument can teach you how to be a good person, and conveying an impression of goodness without substance behind it is difficult. Unfortunately, it is not impossible. Many a bad person has posed as good and won conviction to catastrophic ends. We recommend no such dishonesty. But given what good is in your position and in you, this book can offer you some tactics to help bring out both.

CHOOSING A VOICE

In written argument you can to some extent create a personality by the voice you choose. You are immediately present to your reader in your words when you use the pronoun of self-reference, *I.* You create a sense of closeness with your audience when you use *you* (as in this sentence), and still another effect when you choose *we.* Finally, you can diminish the presence of your personality (though never eliminate it) by writing in an objective voice. You can and should move in and out of these voices in different parts of your argument. The following discussion of their relative merits will help you make effective choices, depending on your audience and purpose.

Using *I* or Not Using *I*

Pick up a newspaper and read the articles on the front page. Is there an *I* in any of them? Probably not. Do you have a sense of a distinctive individual talking to you in any of those "*I*-less" articles, or do they sound like a disembodied voice coming out of a box? Turn to the signed columns and find one that does use *I.* Suddenly the voice has a personality that can project anything from the stern wisdom of the political commentator to the racy wit of an advice columnist.

Of course, the news is conventionally presented in the voice of objective authority. When a journalist wants to convey an impression of fact not influenced by personal experience or point of view, then it is most effective to write impersonally, to leave out the *I.* Indeed, the conventions of news reporting forbid the *I.* But in other situations certain effects can be achieved only by writing in your own voice, by appearing in your own writing as *I*.

The I of Personal Experience

Some writers avoid references to personal experience in written argument because they think using the pronoun *I* is improper. Somewhere they have heard that "one" doesn't refer to "oneself" as "I" in anything more formal than a letter home. There is some truth to this belief because in many writing situations (in history papers or lab reports for example) no personal experience is significant. You wouldn't write, ". . . and then I turned on the Bunsen burner" or "I feel that World War II was an unfortunate occurrence."

But in other, less formal writing situations, if a personal experience was in any way the origin of your argument—something that happened to you or put you on the track of a conclusion—it need not be left out. Although it may have only a small place in your argument, it can have a large effect on your audience.

The following is the opening of a proposal that Vietnam veterans speak out about their experiences. You know that a proposal needs a demonstration section to convince its audience that a problem exists. The author, Mr. Broderich, demonstrates that a problem exists by telling of his own experiences in his own voice. After this personal example Mr. Broderich returns to an objective voice.

> When I first was on my way to the Vietnam war, it was difficult for me to pick up the check. Even in the vast unknowns of New York, people wanted to show their appreciation and to hold close for a moment a piece of their past. Less than three years later in the City of Brotherly Love subway system, a whole new world was shown to me.
>
> I was on my first three-day convalescent leave from the hospital. I was going home to surprise the folks. I was thin, weak, glad to be alive and in military dress. They offered cheaper rates on the railroad to people in uniform, a policy left over from the past. The money wasn't worth having my cane deliberately knocked away and being shoved to the cement where I received a torrent of verbal abuse and spit. An hour later at the train station a different group of people would simply not allow me to pay for a treat. I know it was the uniform, not me; it was just a symbolic gesture.
>
> —*The Christian Science Monitor*

We as readers sympathize with the author for what he has suffered personally, and that sympathy is likely to be extended to his thesis.

The I of Authority

I can be used even when you are not talking about your personal experiences. You can also bring yourself into an argument as an authority who believes, thinks, claims, or asserts. Columnists who write week after week on politics, economics, sports, or the arts have authoritative personal voices that go easily into *I*. The language expert William Safire boldly proclaims a change in grammar on his own:

> I don't like the idea of claiming "It is I" is right for writing and "It is me" is acceptable for speaking. The colloquial form has taken over. The subjective form (I, they) should be used only when the word looks and sounds like the subject. But when it looks like the object (as in "It's them"), use the objective (me, them). If anybody demands to know who told you to do this horrible deed, tell them it was me.
>
> —William Safire, "On Language," *The New York Times Magazine*

Notice how the biologist E. O. Wilson puts his personal authority behind the assessment of evidence: "The question of interest is no longer whether human social behavior is genetically determined; it is to what extent. The accumulated evidence for a large heredity component is more detailed and compelling than most persons, including even geneticists, realize. *I will go further* [italics added]: it already is decisive" *(On Human Nature)*.

If you are a student you are probably thinking, "That's fine for the expert who can use *I* anytime, but what about me?" The *I* of authority does come at a great price, and few things sound worse than an unjustified claim to it. Yet anyone who engages in an argument should acquire at least a modest authority on that subject, should have conscientiously read much on the topic, interviewed the people concerned, or collected fresh evidence. The authority that honestly comes from background work can give the arguer an *I* to stand on.

Authority can come not only from recognized expertise or research in a discipline, but also from bringing to an issue a unique point of view. The management expert who proposes a new scheme for running a family efficiently, the psychoanalyst who brings to a new field such as literature or history the constructs of his or her own, or the classical musician who evaluates jazz—all of these bring a kind of authority from a fresh point of view. And this authority comes across well when claimed by a vigorous *I*.

The Ordinary I

You can sometimes accommodate to your audience most effectively by *not* claiming authority. If your point of view on an issue is that of an *average* citizen, a *typical* college student, a *representative* suburbanite, an *ordinary* American, you can identify yourself in that role. Here is an example from a letter to an editor:

I'm a rather ordinary woman, rational rather than radical, one whose femininity has never been doubted. But having seen sex discrimination first hand both in my schooling and in my work life, I do support ratification of the Equal Rights Amendment.

—*The Christian Science Monitor*

The reasoning behind the appeal of the "ordinary *I*" is something like this: "If an average person like me can hold this position, so can an average person like you. If something is good for or appealing to ordinary me, it's good for you too." The effect here is to put the writer on the same level as the audience, not on a platform looking down at them.

The I of Method

You can also speak in your own voice in order to let your reader know what the method of your argument is. In other words, you can guide your readers through your own argument, stopping now and then to give directions or encouragement or to explain your method of investigation. You can say things like "First I will trace the history of the Shakers," "I found such austerity difficult to understand until I had seen a Shaker house," and so on.

What do you gain by using *I* to convey information that could be written impersonally? You can gain several things. First, you highlight the organization of your argument if your argument is at all extended or complicated or difficult. Structuring sentences can be written without *I*, but they gain emphasis when *I* speaks them. Second, you add the sense of a person going through a process and inviting readers to join in. "If *I* went through these steps and came to a conclusion, so can *you*." Finally, there are sometimes spots in your argument where you might lose, confuse, or alienate your readers. You want to carry them over such spots so they will continue reading, and you can do that by having *I* tell them of the trouble to come. Here is an example of such a warning worded in different ways.

Impersonal   1. This is a difficult concept to grasp until the Russian meaning of *science* is understood.

You   2. You will find this concept difficult to grasp until you understand what the Russians mean by *science*.

I   3. I found this concept difficult to grasp until I understood what the Russians mean by *science*.

Nothing is wrong with version 1, and it might be the preferred choice in some circumstances, but it doesn't call attention to itself as dramatically as 2 or 3. Version 2 is certainly emphatic, but it also risks insulting the reader's intelligence, quite the opposite of what you want to do in argument. Number 3 gets attention without talking down. *I* admits to the difficulty, thereby making the author seem more human and the reader smarter. The writing situation will determine which choice is most effective.

The Dangers of I

Every choice you make in accommodation is a double-edged sword. It can work for you, but it can also hurt you. The advantages of using the *I* of personal experience, of authority, of method have corresponding disadvantages.

1. The personal experience of *I* can sometimes be set aside by readers as untypical. Your readers could easily say, "This incident might have happened to you, but you can't draw any general conclusions from it." The more personal the experience seems, the less it seems to represent a large number of similar experiences.

2. Your reader might find your claims to authority—your "I think" and "I believe"—arrogant. It is one thing for a seasoned diplomat to make statements about United States foreign policy beginning "I think" or "I believe," but quite another for someone with no obvious credentials.

3. The *I* of method is emphatic, but that emphasis can work against you. If, for instance, *I* points out all the procedures gone through, the reader can more easily criticize what was or was not done. "I take my figures from a newly published study," brags the writer. "You mean you didn't check them out yourself?" replies the reader.

4. In some situations, calling attention to *I* is inappropriate or foolish. If the use of *I* gives your audience an opening to question your objectivity, then be very cautious. Of course you must admit anything that if found out would damage you, but don't harp on the problems for *I* or the benefits either. Or if your argument includes a very severe criticism, even a denunciation, of someone else's actions or arguments, such an attack should never seem as personal (it should not *be* personal) as the use of *I* would make it.

5. A letter or signed article is often a legitimate occasion for the author's *I.* But if you are writing as the representative of a group, as the chairman of a committee, and if what you write is not going to appear under your own name, the unexplained presence of *I* may dismay your reader. Can you imagine an official report from the FDA including a sentence like this: "I have done some research, and, although my results were ambiguous, I still think nitrates are harmful"?

We have given you two kinds of advice: some of it urging you to use *I* and some of it warning you against it. We have not given you a rule to follow; instead you have to choose for yourself, taking into account your audience, your subject, and yourself. The benefit of *I* is that it can human-ize your argument. The danger of *I* is that it can work against the very basis of argument by suggesting too personal a point of view. We have no argument without interpersonal grounds of support.

Using *You* or Not Using *You*

If you want to get the attention of someone near you, you call her name or put your hand on his shoulder. Keeping the attention of a listener who is within reach is fairly easy in face-to-face interaction, and even when you are speaking before a large audience, you can pull their attention toward you by maintaining eye contact and addressing them collectively as *you*. But it is much more difficult to get and keep the attention of a reader who can drop your pages without the slightest twinge of conscience.

One way is to use the written equivalent of the hand on the shoulder or the eye contact. Address your audience as *you*. Unless you are writing an argument in a letter to one person, your audience will be many people, not one. Yet, paradoxically, the act of reading is solitary and any written argument is taken in by only one person at a time. So the indefinite *you* can be an efficient way of addressing the entire audience as though you meant only that one person.

The purpose of accommodation is to bring your argument to your audience, and direct address accommodates by bringing an argument to an audience in two ways. First, it helps capture and keep attention. Just as we perk up when we hear our own names, so also do we respond with extra attention when addressed directly. Second, using the *you* of direct address makes it easier to apply an argument to your audience. When *you* have seen how difficult the problem is, when *your* future is involved, when *you* will profit, the *you* being addressed, actually any reader of the argument, will feel the impact of its appeals more forcefully. Readers will not have to work to imagine themselves in the situation of the argument; you, the writer, can do that for them.

Opening with an Attention-Getting *You*

Many experienced writers begin arguments with a direct address or invita-tion to *you*. These attention-getting *you*'s appear even when the subject of the argument is far removed from the reader's experience; the professional writer knows how to draw a reader to a subject not normally interesting, so the writer dangles a hook for *you*. The direct address is usually dropped after a few paragraphs once the writer gets down to business. Here is an example of a *you* opening in an otherwise impersonal argument.

> Would you rather have botulism or cancer?
> That's essentially the question federal regulators are asking in formulating policy on the hazard of sodium nitrite in cured meats, fish and poultry.
> —Jean Carper, "Stop Playing Politics With the Nitrite Issue," *The Washington Post*

After that collar-grabbing opening, the author never uses *you* again.

Audience Creation

That opening *you* can be more than just a hook to grab the uninterested. It can also single out just those to whom your argument is directed and define or create the audience you are aiming at. Of course, this very specific audience creation may also drive away those unconcerned with your argument, but that may be no loss. Those who are concerned will feel they are being given special treatment and will read more attentively.

Here is an example of audience creation from the opening of a proposal on how to prepare a preschool child for kindergarten.

> If you have a 4-year-old who will begin school in September, what can you do *now*—every day—to help the child get a good start? You can do what the kindergarten teachers do—recognize that learning comes through experience and that all experiences come through the senses.
> —Bernard Ryan, Jr., "Helping Your Child Get a Start in School," *The New York Times*

This argument speaks directly to the parents of four-year-olds. Others might read this little proposal, but they are overhearers rather than the target audience.

A Scene Starring You

The next step up from identifying the role of *you* is having *you* act that role out. A writer can not only talk to a reader, but also imagine that reader into a scene. *You* then becomes more than just a reader; *you* is a doer involved in some action that pulls *you* into the argument. Victor B. Scheffer used this technique in the opening lines of an argument against killing seals for their fur.

> You pause for a moment in a shop where a sealskin coat is on display. You admire its rich and perfect texture. Expensive, yes; but oh, so handsome. Then

a troubling thought: Is it right to want luxury at the cost of wildlife? You remember the ads and articles and television shows that deplore the killing of seals. You hesitate—then drift on. Maybe you'll return, but for the moment, you're overwhelmed by an odd sense of guilt.

The writer takes *you* on a shopping trip and imagines even *your* unspoken thoughts. Here Scheffer skillfully (though perhaps to some tastes excessively) identifies the points of contact between the average reader's life and the subject of his argument. Most of us have nothing whatever to do with seals, but we have heard of the controversy about killing them in ads and articles and television shows, as the author reminds us, and we can choose whether or not to buy a sealskin coat.

Giving Directions to You

This whole book is an example of speaking to the reader as *you* in order to give directions. We are constantly suggesting that you consider this point and you avoid that tactic. We hope we have avoided the dangers of sounding either too tentative or too dictatorial. How can those dangers be avoided? Perhaps the best way is not to give a direction without including the reasons for giving it or the consequences of following or not following it. That is, never say boldly to your reader, "Don't you ever buy a sealskin coat" without giving a reason like "If you do, you will be contributing to the deaths of innocent animals." And now that we have given you that direction we will give *you* a reason for it. People prefer to move themselves by the force of their own conviction rather than to be moved by the force of external authority. No one responds well to a list of unexplained dos and don'ts.

Directions appear naturally in the supporting arguments for a proposal, particularly in the description of the first step. These directions are often addressed to *you,* as in the following excerpt from a time-management expert's advice on how to begin using time efficiently:

> It may seem trite to say so, but perhaps you've never stopped to take stock. The basic resource that each person starts with is his lifetime—all the minutes, hours, days, and years that he is alive. It's only within this total framework that good time planning is possible. Which is why I recommend you start by defining your lifetime goals.
>
> I'll soon get down to your minute-by-minute problems of today. But right now a written Lifetime Goals Statement will help you to discover what you really want to do, help motivate you to do it and give meaning to the way you spend your time. It will give a direction to your life. It will help you feel in control of your destiny. And it will provide a measuring stick against which to gauge alternate activities as they come along. You'll be better able to balance

the many aspects of your life. And you'll reduce unnecessary conflict over how to use your time.

—Alan Lakein, *How to Get Control of Your Time and Your Life*

Talking to You About the Argument

Throughout Parts I to IV we have talked about the value of imagining your reader's responses to your argument. When you define a key word, for example, you must anticipate how your reader might confuse that term with another. When you single out one cause, you have to be aware of what other causes might occur to your reader, and when you propose a course of action, you must overcome your reader's inertia and forestall any objections. In these and in many other places, you are putting yourself in your reader's mind.

Putting yourself in your reader's mind is one thing; it is quite another to *show* your reader that you have done so. One way, as we have demonstrated, is to use direct address. In effect, you articulate the thoughts in your reader's mind and use those thoughts as structuring devices in your argument. Here are some examples of this use of direct address from Martin Luther King, Jr.'s "Letter from Birmingham Jail." We are quoting only the first sentences from several different paragraphs:

> You may well ask, "Why direct action?" [The answer to this anticipated question follows.]
> You express a great deal of anxiety over our willingness to break the law. [In this case, King is about to answer a verbalized objection rather than an imagined one.]
> I hope you are able to see the distinction I am trying to point out. [Here King senses that his point is a difficult one for his audience to comprehend, and he warns them to give it special attention.]

The Pitfalls of Using You

You is a very powerful audience grabber, sometimes too powerful. If readers feel that they are being grabbed by the collar and forcibly detained, their reaction will be negative. They may not fling your pages across the room, but they will feel uncomfortable, as though someone with bad breath were standing too close.

Here is an example of excessive use of *you* from a brochure soliciting subscriptions to a magazine.

> I have reason to believe that you are part of an important minority in this country . . . that you are politically alert, independent and more than a wee bit suspicious of power . . . that you won't be lured by high-sounding but meaningless political rhetoric . . . that you are concerned about trends in government that

threaten certain inalienable rights like liberty and the pursuit of happiness
. . . that you cherish old-fashioned liberal ideals but are suspicious of mounting
government intervention in our lives . . . that you try to read between the
headlines of newspapers . . . that you don't want your issues spoon-fed and
predigested . . . that you don't want other people to do your thinking for you
. . . that bungling bureaucracy in government angers you . . . that you believe
well-informed, responsible, involved citizens can bring about much-needed
changes in our system . . . that you inquire.

If you can say, "Yes, that's me," allow me to say thank you. It's people like
you who helped create and build this nation. And we need more of you if our
democratic system is to survive.

That's why I urge you to stand up and be counted—to make your voice heard
on important matters—to keep yourself continually informed about the issues—to keep your mind open without losing sight of your principles.

This kind of "hard sell" probably repels more than it convinces. The crude
repetition of *you, you, you* is too aggressive and too manipulative. The writer
who uses too many *you's,* one after the other, seems to be bullying or
flattering an audience rather than allowing them freely to make up their
own minds.

The *you* of direct address can also work against accommodation if it is
used to characterize an audience negatively. To accuse your audience, to
make them feel guilty, lazy, stupid, fat, inadequate, bigoted, uninformed,
immoral, or insensitive is no way to bring them around to your side. Some
arguments do require that people criticize themselves or see their own
shortcomings, but that does not mean that the writer should address them
about their failures. Unless the circumstances were exceptional, a writer
trying to persuade an adult audience to enroll in the community night
school could not motivate them with insults: "You are stupid and lazy. You
sit in front of the television set, drinking beer, while your mind rots away."
Bringing them to some state of self-criticism in order to motivate them
might be done in one of the following ways instead:

1. The arguer can include himself in the accusations, using *we* instead
   of *you:* "We all spend too much time in front of the television set
   while the exciting world of new knowledge and ideas passes us by."
2. Or the arguer can be impersonal, creating a group to which neither
   she nor the readers necessarily belong. Then the readers have the
   freedom to decide whether they fit into this group: "Most Americans
   think their education is over when they finish school. They settle in
   front of the television set and allow their minds to go idle, losing
   what learning they once had."

Either of these tactics might work better than an insulting direct address
that is in effect a direct attack. Direct address is most effective when it
attracts readers into an argument and guides them through it, not when

it pulls them by the hair. Notice how Lance Trusty, author of the following advice for college students, avoids direct address when he characterizes students negatively, but switches to *you* when he offers them positive suggestions.

Few students recognize the importance of self-conditioning in their examination attitudes (remember Dr. Pavlov, who was trained by his dogs to ring a bell whenever they salivated?). One who prepares thoroughly for tests is usually relaxed and confident. Luck has little to do with his or her performance. This student quickly becomes "test-wise."

The poor student relies heavily on cramming and luck and hopes for the "right questions." Despite his surface bravado, he senses the dangers ahead, and "psyched out," does poorly. Each "blown" exam makes the next one more important and the student more tense and forgetful. By the end of the semester, when the low grades arrive, he has conditioned himself to be a poor test taker.

The sense of well-being conferred by good grades makes it easier and more rewarding to maintain them, while failure breeds an avoidance pattern. So a good start in college is vital for the conditioning process. Pulling up low grades is a powerful test of self-discipline, and one that many fail.

Learn [*you* understood] the required material through scheduled reviews. Your first college crisis will be midterm week, when every professor seems to assign a major exam simultaneously, so plan your reviews carefully. Avoid or minimize [*you* understood] cramming, a common but poor study technique.

If the test in a given subject covers, for example, the notes from three weeks' classes, and you need five reviews, space them equidistantly over the study period. Do [*you* understood] the final review just before the test.

Check [*you* understood] previous examinations, often available from student organization files, the library, or friends who have taken the course. Evaluate [*you* understood] their overall format and the kinds of questions asked. What are the professor's thought patterns? Which elements of the course does he emphasize? The answers should shape your preparations.

—Lance Trusty, "College Students: Test-Taking Advice for the Wise," *The Christian Science Monitor*

Dialogue Building with Questions

Questions are another excellent device to bring your readers into dialogue with you. When you are interested in what you are reading, don't questions about the material occur to you? And when someone asks you a question, don't you have a natural impulse to answer it? (Didn't you have a natural impulse to answer that question?) When you write arguments, you should take advantage of your readers' instinct to ask and answer questions.

QUESTIONS THAT YOU ANSWER   Suppose you work up a proposal in favor of changing the parking regulations where you work. In the course of doing your research, you asked many questions: "What are the legal ordinances governing parking near a building with a certain occupancy? What inconveniences do the current regulations create?" After investigating the issue, you have answered these questions for yourself.

When you write up your argument remember that your readers will most likely be asking the same questions. If you want to accommodate your argument to their mental processes and pull them into dialogue with you, *ask the questions for them.* Anticipate the questions, articulate them, and then answer them. If you include these structuring questions, readers may follow your argument more easily because it duplicates their own reasoning process.

Asking and answering questions can help you to structure your argument, to decide what parts come in what order. Suppose, for instance, you think of an objection or a question that readers are likely to raise at a particular point. If you ask that question and then answer it satisfactorily, you effectively forestall that objection and strengthen your argument. Carl Sagan uses this technique in an argument on the nature and causes of sleep.

> It makes sense that today, when sleep is highly evolved, the stupid animals are less frequently immobilized by deep sleep than the smart ones. But why should they sleep deeply at all? Why should a state of such deep immobilization ever have evolved?
>
> —Carl Sagan, *The Dragons of Eden*

The questions that Sagan asks here are those that any intelligent reader would ask at this point in the discussion. And once readers have been drawn into the discussion this way and their reasonable questions satisfactorily answered, they are more likely to become your allies than your opponents.

RHETORICAL QUESTIONS: QUESTIONS THAT YOU DON'T ANSWER Unlike the structuring question that you ask and answer for your readers, the *rhetorical question* is one you ask but don't answer. In a sense, your readers answer it themselves, in their own heads; thus, rhetorical questions are an excellent device for involving readers in a dialogue with you. When they find themselves mentally answering your questions, they are in effect talking with you.

Since a rhetorical question is really a way of making a statement your audience will agree with, it should be worded so that it requires only a short predictable answer. You ask, "Do we want our school to have a bad reputation?" The readers feel compelled to answer, "No." You ask, "What kind of parent allows her ten-year-old child to be out until 2:00 in the morning?" Your readers quickly reply, "A bad one." They may not even consciously verbalize the short answer that is required; the question itself seems to provide it. However, any question requiring a lengthy, complicated answer—"Why is bubble gum so popular in the United States?" "What are the qualities of a good high-school principal?"—should not be left unanswered by the writer. The questions that have to be answered at length are the kind of structuring questions we talked about above.

Of course, the rhetorical question works only if readers answer it in exactly the way that will support your argument. If they answer it in the opposite way, it is working against you. So the rhetorical question must be framed and asked in such a way that just the right answer, just the one word, is the only one that occurs to your readers. The writer of the following (from a proposal that drug addicts receive free drugs) knows exactly what answer to expect from the final rhetorical question in the paragraph:

> In planning what to do right now, we have to start with the fact that addicts as a rule can't shake the habit, and that nothing we know how to do is much help to most of them. The psychiatrists have quit on the problem. One of them, Dr. Joost A. M. Meerloo, recently put their belief in his own kind of language: "Drug addiction is much more related to the pusher and the existence of criminal seduction and the hypocritical laws than to circumscribed pathology within the individual." Do you eliminate the pushers and criminal seduction and hypocritical laws by ordering people into hospitals?
> —Jonah J. Goldstein, "Give Drugs to Addicts So We Can Be Safe," *The Saturday Evening Post*

The readers are supposed to answer the last question with a resounding "No!" A contradictory "Yes" would be disastrous and even a doubtful "Maybe" would be damaging. But with a no in mind, the readers will be more receptive to the proposal that follows. The unanswered rhetorical question is also a vehicle or outlet for some of the emotion you feel about your topic and want to convey. It is especially effective for communicating anger or defiance or the exasperation the author feels, as in the preceding example.

A rhetorical question is an effective accommodation device when you feel confident that your readers will answer it the way you want and comprehend just the shade of emotion you want to convey. But use the rhetorical question sparingly. An argument that is merely one question after another, that keeps readers answering "Yes," "No," "No," "Yes," will simply bewilder or irritate them.

Using *We* or Not Using *We*

We have already discussed the advantages and disadvantages of speaking of yourself as *I* and to your reader as *you* in an argument. Another possible voice is *we*. When *we* is used as the voice speaking in an argument, it can have one of several different meanings.

The Genuine Plural We: I + I = We

The least common *we* in written argument is the *we* that stands literally for two or more writers. That is the *we* that we (Fahnestock and Secor) use occasionally in this book. It is the voice of two or more authors who have produced one work and therefore sensibly refer to themselves as we. This *we* is simply the plural of *I*. It has all the same benefits of *I* (personality and informality in the writing) as well as the same drawbacks. If you look at the introduction to this book, you will find the *we* of plural authors. Elsewhere, *we* occasionally means ourselves, the writers of the book, but more often means the *we* of the next category.

The We That Unites Reader and Writer: I + You = We

A commonly used *we* is simply a combination of *I* and *you*, writer and reader. This *we* is a particularly accommodating choice. When *we* talks in an argument, writer and reader get together in a friendly way. The egotism of *I* and the finger-pointing at *you* are replaced by the comradeship of *we*. Can you sense the difference pronoun choice makes in the following statements?

> I believe in the Bill of Rights and I assume you do too.
> We believe in the Bill of Rights.

Both sentences say basically the same thing, but the first version seems to build a barrier between the writer and reader and at worst even challenges the reader. The second, however, unites writer and reader in agreement and suggests that the two are joined in a larger group.

We is a wise choice when your argument builds on values and assumptions that reader and writer share. Speaking as *we*, you can remind your reader of things you have in common. Notice how the noted cancer researcher Lewis Thomas uses *we* to engulf himself and his reader in a common failing and a mutual plea for improvement:

> We like to think of ourselves as the most special things on earth, uniquely endowed with intelligence and awareness, the owners and operators in charge of the place. But this is a notion we will probably have to outgrow. If we try to hang on to the view too long we run the risk of not outliving it. We cannot

survive indefinitely thinking of the earth as a kind of combination domestic animal and kitchen-garden placed, by luck or providence, at our disposal for consumption. We are obliged, like all other living beings, to pay our way.

—Lewis Thomas, "On Ants and Us,"
Discover

Here the *we* includes the writer, the reader, and by extension everyone else who acknowledges the self-evidence of what the writer asserts.

The amorphous *we* stands for the writer and any member of the audience who would plausibly be reading the argument. That audience always has characteristics, even if it is as large and vague a group as the American public. After all, the American public does not include the Chinese public, the Belgian public, the Costa Rican public. The *we* used in the Thomas quotation does not really include everyone; it conveys the values of an audience of Americans with some environmental awareness.

The Position Speaks as We

Legend has it that when someone commented on how short Queen Victoria was, she drew herself up to her full 4 feet and 11 inches and replied frostily, "We are rather small for a Queen." Queen Victoria quite properly used the "royal we" to refer to herself, because even as a small queen she was more than a single person. She represented a ruling house, a church, a country.

In much the same way, when the pope speaks for the entire Roman Catholic Church, he speaks as *we.* Anyone who speaks or writes with authority as the representative of a group, an organization, a team, a corporation, an institution, can speak as *we.* He or she has been chosen, as it were, to speak for many, not simply to represent a personal point of view. Not "I, the president of the corporation," but "We at Universal Motors." Not "I, the editor of the *Daily Sentinel,*" but the editorial *we.*

The official *we* can be used only in sanctioned situations. It sounds arrogant if its authority is not earned and if the position it is taking does not represent the position of its audience. We all resent the politician of the other party who claims to speak for "we, the American people" when representing only partisan views.

The We of Well-Defined Groups

No clear line separates the *we* that stands for a large, amorphous group and the *we* that stands for a well-defined group, such as all people who have visited Iceland. It is difficult to say exactly where a *we* that *includes* any plausible reader of an argument turns into a *we* that *excludes* other readers. But when that zone is crossed, when *we* excludes as well as includes, a significantly different tactic of accommodation is being used.

This new tactic is the creation of a group to which writer and readers can belong but from which others are eliminated. The writer wants the reader to join in a little circle of insiders who all have an interest, an occupation, a something in common. This appeal to group identity can be effective when the group legitimately has something to do with the argument. Suppose, for instance, you are writing a letter to the newspaper to create support for a cooperative nursery school. Although others may glance at your letter, the group you are really addressing is the parents of three- and four-year-olds. Because they have common experiences and share common concerns, the language of your argument can reinforce that cohesiveness by helping them think of themselves as a group. If you belong to the group too, you can appropriately talk about the experiences *we* share: "We parents of four-year-olds know how easily our children get bored and how much stimulation they need during the day." Readers who fit the group will nod agreement and realize that the writer understands their concerns and has something worthwhile to say to them. Perhaps you can see the strength of such a group appeal if you try to imagine its opposite: "Although I have no children of my own and have never been around them much, let me tell you what your four-year-old needs."

In the following example, the author uses *we* to announce her community with Chicanos, the well-defined group she addresses:

> We are as heterogeneous as our history. Without that background of history, it is difficult to understand us. *No somos Mexicanos.* [We are not Mexicans.] We are citizens of the United States with cultural ties to Mexico and in some instances to Spain, but, within our ties of language and culture, we have developed a culture that is neither Spanish nor Mexican.
> —Lydia R. Aguirre, "The Meaning of the Chicano Movement," *Social Casework*

Since arguments generally aim to make writer and reader identify with each other, to agree as though they were members of the same group, it may seem that *we* is always the wisest choice. But not always. *We* has pitfalls just as *I* and *you* have, and once again knowledge of your audience helps you determine the right choice. Some audiences will resist the arm-around-the-shoulder chumminess of *we*. It may be presumptuous to think that people will identify with your cause or your values.

Other Ways of Creating and Appealing to Groups

"Everybody," "Anyone," "Everyone," "People"

The pronoun *we* is not the only way of creating a group for your reader to join. The *we* that forcefully unites writer and reader is sometimes inappropriately personal. *Anybody* and *everybody*, however, can create groups that do not necessarily include reader and writer, but do not exclude them either. The group seems open for the reader's self-election. If, for instance, the writer talks about "everyone who is concerned about higher education," any readers can nominate themselves for membership in that group. Of course, no reader would want to join a group that sounded undesirable—"anyone who has lice," "everyone of below-average intelligence," "anyone who never reads a book." A skillful arguer mentions an undesirable group only as one to be avoided.

Naming the Group

You can also create desirable groups for your readers to join by naming them and giving them attractive attributes. "The sensitive person," "high-minded individuals," "people in the know," "successful young professionals"—all these labels describe ingroups most people want to belong to. Advertisements bombard us with glitzy images of attractive groups we desperately want to belong to, if only we buy the right breath mint.

Putting the Opposition in a Group

Another way to pull your readers toward you is to push the opposition away. This effect can be accomplished by identifying the opposition with or putting them into groups that you define as undesirable. We are *not* talking about creating scapegoats or calling names or pigeonholing people in stereotypes. Such labeling is always unethical. Rather, we are talking about characterizing groups by the *positions* they hold on a certain issue or the *consequences of those positions.*

Suppose that you are arguing against price controls on milk with a largely uncommitted audience. You can talk with your audience about the opposition as "those who support price controls on milk," as though they were not present among your readers. That identification is merely neutral, but it still has the effect of separating your opposition from you and your readers. They become "those out there." Of course, your argument cannot stop with merely identifying "them" as the opposition; you must honestly refute their position.

You can also characterize your opposition or their position in negative ways. Those who haven't thought about the consequences of a policy you are critical of may be "short-sighted" or "impractical." Those whose ethical assumptions disagree with your own might become "insensitive" or "unfair." Those who don't know what they should know can be called "poorly informed." Do not apply these labels unless you can support them rationally. They should come from your considered evaluation of your opponent's position, not from an emotional rejection of your opponent.

Using or Not Using the Objective Voice

Any sentence without a pronoun or any other reference to writer or reader is written in an objective voice. Most sentences in an argument are written in this background voice; the other voices of *I, you,* and *we* are used for special effects, mainly in the opening passages, where writers introduce themselves, and in the closing passages, where they take leave and perhaps exhort their readers to action. But this other, transparent voice, which fixes points in impersonal Lucite, predominates in written argument, and understandably so.

The objective voice creates certain effects or impressions on the reader. First, it offers no competition to the content of the argument, but allows the subject matter to claim all the reader's attention. Second, it diffuses, though it does not eliminate, the emotional appeal of an argument. And third, it downplays any egotism in the argument and replaces it with a voice the audience is more likely to perceive as authoritative. Since argument by its very nature requires premises that more than one person could hold, the objective voice goes a step further and presents premises for anyone to hold. Thus, this impersonal, unemotional, authoritative voice speaks powerfully in argument.

The dominance of the objective voice is in direct proportion to the verifiability of the argument's content. In other words, the more information, the more impersonal the writing is likely to be. The objective voice writes the textbooks, most scholarly articles, and in fact much of what students read for courses. It certainly dominates in science, where the criteria of verification are most precise and where the personality of whoever performed the experiment, programmed the computer, interpreted the data, or wrote the paper should be of no importance.

When to use the objective voice is a function of the writer's authority, the argument's content, and the audience. Some disciplines and writing situations demand an impersonal voice; others allow more variation. When well-established scientists write on matters of current research for their colleagues, they use an objective voice. But when they turn to address the general public on scientific issues, they often let their personalities show.

Many inexperienced writers mistakenly believe that the exclusive use of the objective voice is a mark of mature writing, but in fact accomplished writers alternate voices. A more personal voice is appropriate when thought processes are demonstrated, when the territory of a definition is staked out, when the audience is drawn in, and is a must when personal experience is narrated. The objective voice can take over when verifiable information is being presented or when an evaluation, especially a negative one, is set out.

FOR YOU TO ANALYZE

For what audiences were the following passages written? (You may not be able to answer this question precisely, but at least you can eliminate certain audiences.) Examine the use of voice in each. When has the author used *I, you, we,* or the objective voice and to what effect? Do you think other choices would have been more appropriate?

Since this is a study of human fantasies, it may be useful to begin it by considering that official fantasy which in the mid-nineteenth century went by the name of scientific knowledge. I use the word "fantasy" not in a belittling or deprecatory sense but to describe the quality of thinking or of mind that one meets with in scientific or medical accounts of human sexuality in the English nineteenth century. This thinking, one soon learns, rests upon a mass of unargued, unexamined and largely unconscious assumptions; its logical proceedings are loose and associative rather than rigorous and sequential; and one of its chief impulses is to confirm what is already held as belief rather than to adapt belief to new and probably disturbing knowledge. And as we shall see it shares all these qualities in common with pornography itself. No doubt most people think this way about most things most of the time—that is to say, a good deal of our thinking consists of fantasy cast in the form of opinion or assertion; or, in another context, such thinking has the characteristics of what in the social sciences is called "ideology." Furthermore, no subject has had anything like the power to elicit such prepared responses as the subject of sexuality.
—Steven Marcus, *The Other Victorians*

About a year has elapsed since Pattee Library instituted an automated, computerized lending service. By and large it's quite nice. It's pleasant not to have to fill out cards, etc. It's great to bring search questions to the operators at the terminals and to get prompt answers. Service is speedy. By and large, the new system constitutes an improvement.

There is one aspect of the new lending service policy which needs re-evaluation. That is the policy limiting "outsiders" to the University to four books at a time. The semantics of the word "outside" are questionable in the extreme.

I am an alumna of the University, and had the tacit, but obviously erroneous idea that during my four years of undergraduate work and several terms of graduate study I had just scratched the surface, vis-à-vis reading lists, human development in various areas, continuing education and research in my major area, and that Pattee would be available as a major resource for work in my specialty as long as I lived in the area. I am now classified as an "outsider." The four book limit curtails my personal research and enrichment role as a parent considerably.

Now, despite my receiving nauseatingly frequent and insipid letters begging for my contributions as an alumna from various moneygrabbing offices in Old Main, I find my favorite connection with Penn State being seriously weakened. I don't give a damn about football, but I love the library. I do not think alumni should have the kind of problems getting books that they have getting football tickets. I do not see our local public library putting any exceptional restrictions on University faculty and students who use its facilities. I do not understand why Pattee should curtail its services to a group potentially capable of gaining more support for its services, if only via the mechanism of letters to our local Assemblyman!

Folks, many of you will relinquish your student status before long. Your chances at staff status are slim. You are in for a rude awakening when you want to follow up into the bibliographies you were given in your 400s, etc. No doubt you hadn't time to develop expertise in many areas during the 12-term rat race. You'll find that many books cited are unavailable at your local public library, and that the librarians there will tire early on of your requests for interlibrary loans. An unfettered access to Pattee should be a lifetime benefit for holders of degrees from Penn State. It should not be a "privilege" reserved only for membership in the "Alumni Association" or "Friends of X, Y, or Z" or the faculty.
—Martha Evans, *The Daily Collegian*

FOR YOU TO WRITE

Practice your ability to move in and out of different voices.

1. The letter to the editor of the *Daily Collegian* in the For You to Analyze section was written for the readers of a college newspaper. Try rewriting the same argument for the Dean of the Library. What changes in voice would you make?

2. Write four versions of a one-paragraph evaluation of a movie you have seen recently: one with *I,* for an audience that has seen the movie; one with *you,* for an audience that has not; one with *we,* for an audience that has; and one entirely in the objective voice for an audience that has not.

VIRTUE IN ARGUMENT

The Intellectual Virtue of Reasonableness

So far we have been concerned with how you address your readers and how they perceive your presence and your relationship with them in a written argument. Now we are concerned with how they sense the qualities of mind you as a good arguer should have. We can call these qualities intellectual virtues, as Aristotle did over two thousand years ago. We usually think of "virtues" as habits of good behavior, but we can also speak of virtues of the mind, habits of good thought. Like all virtues, they are resolutions of extremes, midpoints between opposite tendencies. Perhaps the greatest intellectual virtue in argument is *reasonableness,* a moderation of the mind that sits between the extremes of stubbornness and spinelessness. Reasonable people are open to reason; they are neither so intransigent that they will not listen to the other side, nor so weak-minded that they refuse to take a stand at all. Reasonableness in argument can take many forms, and for convenience we have represented these forms in the following imaginary self-declarations.

I Am Not an Extremist

Most people walk a wide way around any wild orator on a soapbox or discard without reading any polemical pamphlet thrust into their hands. We instinctively cringe from extremism and like to think of ourselves as moderate, sane, and balanced. Given this predisposition, the appearance of moderation is an effective accommodation device in an argument. But it is not something you can fake for your audience. You must really have identified other positions as too extreme, too strained, or too far-fetched. If you can locate your position between two more extreme ones, then it may be convincing to point out its moderateness to your audience.

I Know the Other Side and They Are Wrong

In most issues involving action and value, there are several competing points of view. As we pointed out in Chapter 14, arguing *for* your own position is usually not enough; you may also need to argue *against* competing positions. You cannot argue against them unless you understand them first, no matter whether you see them as extreme, completely wrong, or so close to your own as to be almost correct. And your reader must *know* that you understand them, so you should present the other position or positions in your argument.

The very least you can do is mention competing positions without giving them any credit at all. This is the minimum requirement of reasonableness. You say, in effect, "I know my opposition, and they are wrong." That is exactly what the English zoologist Richard Dawkins does in the following excerpt from his book-length argument on the true nature of evolution.

> My purpose is to examine the biology of selfishness and altruism. Apart from its academic interest, the human importance of this subject is obvious. It touches every aspect of our social lives, our loving and hating, fighting and cooperating, giving and stealing, our greed and our generosity. These are claims which could have been made for Lorenz's *On Aggression,* Ardrey's *The Social Contract,* and

Eibl-Eibesfeldt's *Love and Hate*. The trouble with these books is that their authors got it totally and utterly wrong. They got it wrong because they misunderstood how evolution works. They made the erroneous assumption that the important thing in evolution is the good of the *species* (or the group) rather than the good of the *individual* (or the gene).

—Richard Dawkins, *The Selfish Gene*

Dawkins does not give an inch to the other side. But he cannot be accused of not knowing what the other side represents, even though he disagrees with it.

I See Merit in the Other Side

You can do more than just acknowledge the existence of the other position: You can be sympathetic toward it. Without going so far as to concede that your opposition is right, you can display to your audience that you treat other points of view with respect and even kindness. You can compliment the opposition on their reasoning, acknowledge their good faith, appreciate their point of view—anything short of conceding that they are right and you wrong.

Seeing merit in the other position is a middle road between cold acknowledgment and concession. It is the only civilized position left to you when your opposition is strong and your audience will not allow you to rebuff them. Here is an example from a science writer arguing that concern for the environment is an important part of contemporary ethics.

> Many intelligent, articulate and powerful people disagree violently with my views. To them, the environmental movement seems a passing fad—
> —Ian C. T. Nisbet, "Who Are Those Environmentalists, Anyway?" *Technology Review*

To call your opposition intelligent is certainly to see merit in them, though such a compliment is not the same as agreeing with them.

I Concede One or More Points to the Other Side

Very rarely is any issue so clear that right is all on one side and wrong all on the other. Of course, you must be convinced that your side has better arguments, or you would not bother to defend it. But your opponents may be right about a few things; they may even be right about all but one. You do not have to show them totally wrong in order to show yourself right.

When right and wrong are mixed on your opponent's side, the indispensable gesture from your side is *concession*. Concession is the graceful acknowledgment that "on this point" or "in that matter" your opponent's argument has merit. Intellectually, concession is a sign of honesty, precision, moderation, and thoroughness. It is also a valuable accommodation device. At the same time that you are being intellectually honest, your audience perceives you as gracious and reasonable. The following arguer, who is attacking Senator Proxmire's "golden fleece" awards given for outstanding examples of government waste, concedes some value in the senator's actions with compliments and great respect.

> Senator Proxmire, to be sure, is performing a useful public service with his awards. Without such men on Capitol Hill, those of us who work in Washington shudder to think of what would happen to public funds, over which lobbyists and special-interest groups hover like vultures. Proxmire serves as a stone in the Congressional shoe, a built-in ego deflater for Washington bureaucrats who begin to believe their own press releases.
> —*Psychology Today*

Conceding so gracefully shows intellectual honesty and moderation. But you cannot allow a concession to stand alone. It has to be answered, downplayed, or discounted in some way. After all, if Senator Proxmire is the conscience of Washington, why is our arguer criticizing him?

An arguer must "come back" from a concession. The paragraph of compliments to Senator Proxmire is immediately followed with this retort:

> But Proxmire is sometimes wrong, and sometimes becomes often when he moves into areas about which he knows nothing.
> —*Psychology Today*

The indispensable accompaniment of a concession, then, is a *but*.

I May Be Wrong, But . . .

Another way to show moderation is to admit openly the potential problems of your own position. To do so is not necessarily a confession of weakness or incompetence. Not every position can or should be held as though it were the one correct view, the only perfect solution. Nor can you as an arguer be sure that you know everything or that you will never change your mind. Arguing from a temporary or tentative position is often the best anyone can do in specific circumstances. When you honestly find yourself somewhat uncertain on an issue, though you have thought through some arguments, you can shift into lower gear. You can admit your own uncertainty, the tentative nature of some of your conclusions, your openness to new ideas. Notice how paleontologist and science writer Stephen Jay Gould qualifies his indictment of anthropologist and theologian Teilhard de Chardin:

Perhaps I am now too blinded by my own attraction to the hypothesis of Teilhard's complicity. Perhaps all these points are minor and unrelated, testifying only to the faulty memory of an aging man. But they do form an undeniable pattern. Still, I would not now come forward with my case were it not for a second argument, more circumstantial to be sure, but somehow more compelling in its persistent pattern of forty years—the record of Teilhard's letters and publications.

> —Stephen Jay Gould, "The Piltdown
> Conspiracy," *Natural History*

The modesty of this opening admission is appealing, and in the face of strong opposition, such tentativeness may be the only sensible stance, just to get a hearing.

Gould's problem was using circumstantial evidence to make a case against a legendary authority. The writer of the following passage has a different problem, a proposition that is so difficult to support he must *admit* that difficulty.

I have claimed that a concern for environmental quality is part of the late twentieth century ethic. I believe that our rights to a high-quality environment have been permanently incorporated into the value system of modern Western society, in just the way that workers' rights have taken hold in the past hundred years. This opinion, however, is not stated without twinges of uncertainty. How can I be sure that my finger is on the pulse of Western culture? Perhaps I merely hear my minority opinion reflected in my association with likeminded people. When challenged for evidence of widespread popular support for environmental protection, I find little to cite but the record of the U.S. government (and those of other Western nations) in enacting radical environmental legislation. However, this evidence by itself is far from persuasive: the idea that the U.S. Congress reflects the will of the people is contested by almost everyone. . . .

But how do we know whose values are twisted? I have to admit that I may be wrong. Perhaps the leaders of the oil industry, the Chamber of Commerce, the *Wall Street Journal,* the Governor of Massachusetts, the Council on Wage and Price Stability, and the Council of Economic Advisors are all in the mainstream of American thought, and my colleagues and I are not.

> —Ian C. T. Nisbet, "Who Are Those
> Environmentalists, Anyway?" *Technology
> Review*

Of course, the argument did not end here. Although Nisbet could not defend his own side fully, he could attack the other.

We are not recommending that you disguise strong conviction as modest tentativeness, that you say "I may be wrong" when you are sure you have powerful arguments on your side. Nor are we suggesting that arguing from weakness or incomplete evidence is wise. A claim of modesty is no excuse for not having done the research, not having thought the issues through, not having listened to the arguments on all sides. Yet even after we have done all the work that an honest conscience demands, most of us still have much to be modest about.

The Overall Effects of Conviction and Moderation

In accommodation, every gain has a corresponding loss. The stronger the conviction you convey, the less moderation. When an audience senses your intransigence, your stubbornness, they naturally perceive you as less moderate. And when you open your arms to every point of view, your fidelity to your own becomes questionable. Striking a balance is possible if the arguer, poised in the middle, is thoroughly convinced of his or her own position while understanding and acknowledging the other side.

We do not want to suggest that a middle-of-the-road position is at all times and in all circumstances the best. Tipping the balance in one direction or the other is often legitimate. With some audiences and some topics, strong conviction may wisely dominate moderation, as when, for instance, you have a strong argument on your side or a willing audience. On the other hand, a moderate stance may be preferable when your audience has doubts about you or your argument. Imagine yourself arguing a proposal for coed dorms with two different audiences and see how your natural sense of accommodation would favor an impression of conviction or one of moderation. To an audience of students, predisposed to favor coed dorms, conviction will ride high and may proclaim itself in statements like this: "Certainly we have a right to have coed dorms. We are mature, responsible adults. We don't need babysitters anymore. We need to interact freely with our peers. Those fuddy-duddies on the board of trustees with their antiquated morality don't know that times have changed." But to an audience of parents, a tone of moderation ought to prevail: "Coed dorms do require greater maturity and responsibility from their residents, but that is exactly why they are a good idea. All major universities now have them, and they are optional. No one has to live in a coed dorm against his or her will." Note that all these reasons for coed dorms are really answers to objections against them. We expect this kind of response from a moderate position; it anticipates the objections of its audience, treats them respectfully, and replies to them reasonably.

Our best advice, then, is that you should be aware of the connected effects of moderation and conviction. Since you gain an excess of one only at the expense of the other, you should know what you are sacrificing.

Disclaimers: Don't Get the Wrong Idea About Me or My Argument

What would people think of you if you proposed cross-country travel by pneumatic tube? Or mile-high skyscrapers? Or mandatory vegetarianism? They would think you a dreamer or a fool, and if you ever wanted to argue seriously for such fanciful proposals, you would have to begin by convincing your audience, "No, I am not a fool."

A claim that anticipates and answers an audience's negative reaction is a *disclaimer*—a denial, a repudiation of what your audience is likely to think. Disclaimers are useful in far more moderate arguments than the fanciful proposals above. Any time your audience would be likely to think ill of you, slap a label on you, put you in a box or category you do not want to be in, you may need to deny before being accused.

Disclaimers are not very different from concessions. A concession anticipates a reader's assumption that you differ in every way from your opposition. Similarly, a disclaimer disassociates you from a predictable position, but it is usually personal, like the following from the author of an extended criticism of the 1980 census who nevertheless feels called on to disclaim a thoroughly negative attitude.

> I have been one of the Bureau's most loyal fans. I have written two books and numerous articles based on Census materials, for which I will be forever grateful. Not only that, I find that its reports make splendid bedtime reading.
> —Andrew Hacker, "The No-Account
> Census," *Harper's*

Hacker does not want to be accused of crankiness. Rather, he wants to show that though he chastens the Census Bureau, he has warm feelings toward it.

Is there danger in making a disclaimer? Yes, if you disclaim an accusation that your audience would never have thought of. You would not deny being an embezzler when you applied for a job as a bank teller if your prospective employer had no reason to suspect you. You would not disclaim that your proposal is unrealistic if your audience is not likely to think it so. Making a disclaimer, then, requires a very accurate sense of audience.

EMOTION IN ARGUMENT

The reasonableness we have been advocating need not be a cold virtue. The good person who argues well may also be the sensitive person who has emotional conviction, who feels anger, pity, fear, or warmth over an issue. Such emotion can be conveyed to the reader as an aid to, though never a substitute for, rational conviction. As servant of the premises, emotion is conveyed in carefully chosen words and examples.

Careful Word Choice

Many words are bristly. They have a core of meaning and a surface that produces feelings or sensations in the reader. A simple term like *ice cream* refers to a frozen confection of cream, sugar, and flavoring and for most of us evokes pleasant memories and happy anticipations. A word like *cancer,* on the other hand, produces as much fear as meaning. In argument you should make the good and bad associations of words work for you to transfer appropriate emotions to your audience.

When you have a choice among a set of words that have approximately the same meaning but different associations, choose the one with appropriate associations for your audience and argument. If, for example, you are arguing with adults for kinder treatment of teenagers who break the law, you would not refer to them as "juvenile delinquents" or "young criminals," terms with harsh associations. You would do better to call them "youthful offenders" or "problem teenagers," words with more neutral associations, or even "disturbed children," a term that calls for sympathy.

If you want to avoid a certain word, you can directly substitute for it a more neutral or more attractive word. The substitution word is called a *euphemism.* Or you can use a different word or phrase that is at the same time more precise and less offensive. Another possibility is to avoid a label or single term altogether, and take the long way around in several sentences. Thus, word choice is not only a matter of substituting one synonym for another; it can also affect the content or length of your argument.

Euphemism

A euphemism is a substitution, a word that takes the place of one that has unpleasant or unacceptable associations. Euphemisms abound whenever the subject is war, politics, human categorization, death, or private bodily functions. Direct or embarrassing reference to these topics can hurt. Consideration for an audience often means that a reference must be sweetened; the reader eats it anyway, but it tastes better.

When is it legitimate to use a euphemism and when is it not? It all depends on the situation, the purpose, and the audience. Euphemisms often replace words that an audience would find crude or socially taboo. For example, unless you want to shock or offend in order to serve some more important purpose, you would never say consolingly to a friend,

"Your father died last week, didn't he?" Your sense of decency would lead you to make some less direct statement like "Sorry to hear about your father." When, on the other hand, the situation is impersonal, it may be more appropriate to use the direct word. You would not, for instance, write, "Thomas Jefferson and John Adams both passed away to the great beyond on July 4, 1826." No audience's sensitivities need be considered; no eyes will fill with tears if you simply say that both men died. The topic of death is a twentieth-century taboo, while other ages and places had or have their own undiscussable subjects. For example, the Victorians never referred to a woman as "pregnant"; she was, instead, "soon to be confined." We laugh at them now while we respect our own taboos.

Similarly, certain euphemisms for classes of human beings have come into use to replace labels that had offensive suggestions. For example, we now prefer to call people over sixty-five "senior citizens" rather than "the aged." "Senior citizens" has desirable suggestions of activity, respect, and responsibility. Likewise, a "retarded" child is often called an "exceptional" or "special" child, a garbage collector is a "sanitary worker," a janitor becomes a "custodian," and an undertaker is a "mortician" or a "funeral director." Because language changes over time, a term that is merely descriptive to one generation becomes offensive to the next. Some of the newer labels may sound strained or stilted to you right now. Time will either bring them into common usage or discard them.

However, euphemisms that conceal the ugly realities of oppression or the underhanded dealings of any group are immoral. It is inexcusable to call concentration camps "temporary detainment centers," when innocent civilians are forcibly incarcerated for undefined periods of time. And politicians should not call their vacations at taxpayer expense "fact-finding missions" or claim "franking privileges" that they dare not call free mail. If you are engaged in an argument that requires hiding ugly realities or moral shadiness of any kind, then you are engaged in an argument you should not be making.

Perhaps this advice sounds excessively idealistic. You may agree that individuals, responsible to their own conscience alone, can take high moral stands. But, you might ask, what about someone who is speaking not for one but for a nation? Wouldn't such a spokesperson be justified in concealing ugly realities for the sake of a higher aim such as national security? In time of war, for example, wouldn't it be wiser to call a lost battle "strategic withdrawal" rather than "defeat"?

No, it would not be wiser. Let's consider this example, which is the toughest, and explore why even a government at war, and by extension any arguer, should tell the truth. A "strategic withdrawal" implies an intentional retreat or a planned regrouping of forces rather than a military loss. Of course, a government that has to admit a lost battle is in a difficult position. It is torn between giving accurate information and sustaining the wartime morale of its people. Yet it can do both with careful word choice. The lost battle might honestly be called a "temporary setback," a phrase that admits defeat but not its finality. We are here getting into ethical matters that require patient untangling. Nevertheless, we maintain that a euphemism that actually lies is wrong. Avoiding it with carefully chosen words that do not lie is always possible and in the long run always wiser. A well-informed nation can make wiser choices, engage in better public debate, and have more confidence in its government than one that is kept in the dark. And a government can be honest without giving away details of national security. A public that knows, for example, that its government has strategic missiles in place need not know exactly where they are. What holds true for the government spokesperson, weighted down by moral responsibility, certainly holds true for any arguer.

More Particular Substitutions

At times it may be possible to replace an undesirable word with an equivalent that is both more precise and less offensive to an audience. This kind of substitution, still a euphemism really, accomplishes two good ends—avoiding the word with bad associations and conveying more information.

Suppose you are a teacher explaining the causes of a child's failure to a parent. Would you call the child "dumb" or "stupid"? Not only would you avoid hurting the parent with such a harsh word, you would also try to inform the parent more precisely what the problem is. You would say that the child has trouble paying attention, that he learns slowly, even that he has a learning disability if he does—anything but the vague, unhelpful label. Similarly, no one likes to be called "lower class." Class distinctions are not supposed to exist in this country, so we replace this insulting term with more precise descriptive labels, referring instead to "unskilled labor," "welfare recipients," "the unemployed," "the underemployed," or the "working poor." All these terms make more precise distinctions on the basis of income; they help us avoid permanent stereotyping into class. It is, after all, possible to stop being a "welfare recipient," but less possible to stop being "lower class."

Periphrasis or Circumlocution: Taking the Long Way Around

Sometimes when you are trying to avoid a sensitive word or phrase or issue in an argument, no direct substitution will help. Instead, you must take the long way around the matter in a series of sentences. The Greek word *periphrasis* and the Latin word *circumlocution* both mean taking many words to say what could be said in few. Such wordiness, as long as it does not obscure, is not dishonest. Meaning is not hidden, but lengthened and softened. Periphrasis can be pompous and long-winded, but it can also be useful at times when any single word or short phrase would work against you.

Imagine yourself as a personnel director in the awkward situation of having evaluated a good friend's qualifications for a job and found them wanting. You have bad news to deliver and there is no euphemism for *no*. You could just blurt out "no job" and get it over with, but another choice is available. You can let the message emerge from a lengthy sequence in which you explain the qualifications of other candidates, the budget constraints you are working with, your plans for the future, and how much your friend has always meant to you. This tactic is periphrasis.

Emotion in Example Choice

You already know from the sections on generalizations and causal arguments that examples can be part of the structure of your argument. Examples tie your thesis to reality, but they can have another function as well. They are the best place to make a direct appeal to your audience's emotions, and these invitations to the audience's fear, pity, anger, love, disgust, pride, and laughter are ways of accommodating, of bringing an argument to an audience.

Examples are effective magnets for the various emotions, pulling sympathetic responses out of readers and drawing them toward your argument, because people all respond with the most immediacy to anything made present to their sight, hearing, touch, smell, and taste. Let us go back to our favorite old thesis, "My roommate is a slob," to illustrate our point here. Suppose you are going to support this thesis with the example of your roommate's bed. You could simply say, "Her bed is a mess," or you could develop the example in more detail:

> The gray sheets are rumpled and the edges trailing on the floor are brown; if you happen to touch a sheet it feels gritty from sand and ancient cracker crumbs. The pillow smells gamy as though the chicken feathers in it were not quite clean, and when I venture on her side of the room, a stale, acidic smell reaches me.

This example, rendered in concrete imagery, should arouse disgust in any reader. Just as most people respond with revulsion to unclean beds, you can similarly count on the general effectiveness of some emotional appeals. Images of starving refugees cast adrift in frail boats in the ocean arouse pity for them and anger at those who caused their plight. Examples of homeless children and lonely old people upset anyone who reads about them, and many of those hard to move about their own species respond to bedraggled kittens, loyal dogs, and noble horses. On the positive side, you can count on consistent human delight with chortling babies, sunshine, flowers, plentiful food, and warm homes.

Whenever you use an example with emotional appeal, you aim not only for your audience's mental assent to your argument, but also for their emotional conviction. This "yes" of the heart is no replacement for the "yes" of the head, but it is a powerful stimulus to agreement, and to action if your argument is a proposal. So by all means use examples when you can be sure that the emotion they evoke will work for you.

But be sure. Aside from some obvious and often stale examples, such as those listed above, many will not have universal emotional appeal. You might produce not the emotion that will reinforce your argument, but its opposite instead. If, for example, you tried to persuade hunters that their sport was evil and should be prohibited, they would probably be unmoved by any examples of deer shot down and dying, bleeding in the snow, and not at all disgusted by graphic descriptions of field dressing. And farmers who raise thousands of chickens would laugh at examples that elevate them to the level of feeling creatures in order to serve an argument against factory farming. Chickens just don't move them that way.

Whenever you use examples of less extreme forms of human suffering, some audiences may remain unmoved by the emotional appeal. Veteran teachers feel little pity when bleary-eyed students tell them they have studied all night for this exam or that paper. Professionals who treat or work with the mentally ill, the sick, or the severely retarded have learned to resist painful emotional involvement, although one such case brought to the attention of an uninitiated audience might bring tears to the eyes.

Now think of the positive reactions inspired by examples with emotional appeal. Here responses are even less predictable. You know what it is like to have a joke fall flat, to have a pleasant story shrugged off, to have a double meaning taken singly. A proposal often hinges on creating a pleasant image of future good results, a positive evaluation of the picture you paint in words. Suppose you are evaluating different kinds of classrooms, the traditional and the open. If you are arguing that the traditional classroom is best, you will describe the orderly rows of desks, the quiet of children absorbed in work, the way the children lift their heads and all look at the teacher when she is talking, and the A papers tacked up neatly on bulletin boards. You hope that your readers will find this example pleasant and agree with your evaluation. But many prefer the kind of classroom where children are moving around, where the noise level is many decibels above silence, where the teacher is not easy to find, and the room is a bit cluttered, supposedly a sign of creativity. Your example of the traditional classroom might strike them as authoritarian and cold.

Try to choose examples whose emotional appeal you can count on for a particular audience, but remember that many audiences are mixed, presenting a wide range of attitudes toward your issue. Some readers will be ready to agree before you start, and others will be far, far away. But because those who disagree are hardest to convince, it is best to aim your examples at them. Those who agree will come along anyway.

If you are at all unsure, if you have any suspicion that an example might work against you, two options are open to you. First, you can simply take it out. Second, you can leave it in but "frame" it. Anticipate the possible negative response to your example, raise it yourself, and refute it. In the case of classroom evaluation, you might follow the description of the traditional setting with a sentence like this: "Many people find a quiet, orderly classroom too cold and structured." After raising this objection you might continue immediately with a refutation: "But warmth does not come from pink walls, clutter, and the kind of noise that keeps the easily distracted child from learning."

Other Places Emotion Can Appear

Emotion is contained not only in examples but also in individual words. To describe someone else's proposal as "heartless" and your own as "humane" is to make a play for your readers' emotions. You can choose direct emotional labels, adding words like *unfair, disgusting, cruel, pitiful, joyous,* or *pleasant* to shape an emotional reaction to what the words describe. Readers will sense a large difference between a "policeman," a "jolly policeman," and a "menacing policeman." It makes a difference whether you describe a meeting as just a meeting, or as "angry," "tense," or "friendly."

Or you can choose words that do not describe an emotion directly but are nonetheless charged with emotional associations. For some audiences *fascist, communist, atheist, left/right wing, mother, home,* and *school* are as emotional as *pain* and *joy.* We are not, however, recommending that you sprinkle your argument with meaningless emotional salt.

When Is an Emotional Appeal Legitimate in Argument?

Let's begin with a reminder: No argument should depend entirely on emotional appeal. If it were possible to put into words an attempt to convince an audience that was nothing but emotional manipulation, the result would not really be an argument. The very nature of argument is appeal to reason. It is not illegitimate to appeal to your reader's emotions, but appeals to the emotions can only supplement appeals to reason; they cannot replace them. Even when the emotional appeal reaches the reader first and is quite strong, the mind should also be engaged.

FOR YOU TO ANALYZE

The following passage uses emotional appeals in a variety of ways. Locate the words and examples in which emotion resides. Given the type of argument, to what extent do the emotional appeals seem legitimate?

From a letter to a state senator proposing a change in adoption laws:

I am writing on behalf of a minority of people who are quietly struggling to achieve what they, and I too believe is a basic human right, yet which present legislation denies them. The minority I speak of are the millions of people in this country who were adopted as children, and now, as adults, find the attitudes and policies surrounding adoption to be discriminatory and detrimental to their well-being.

I was not adopted, nor do I even know many people who were, but as a student who has done research on the subject of adoption for a class, I can empathize with anyone who feels that existing adoption laws should be modified, if not radically changed.

The formation of adoptees' liberation groups (such as ALMA) within the past decade has brought adoption laws and practices to the public eye. Under attack, especially by adoptees and activists, is the practice of sealing the original birth records at the time an adoption is finalized. This procedure has not been altered since the early 1940's. It has been a widely held belief that all parties involved in an adoption—the typically unwed mother, the usually illegitimate child, and the adoptive parents—need the protection of lifelong secrecy to start successful new lives. This assurance of secrecy may seem like a great idea for a scared and pregnant teenager, a hopeful adoptive couple, and an illegitimate baby, but what about this "baby" who is now eighteen or twenty and feels as though a piece of himself is missing—the piece called "heritage" or "identity"?

An adoptee may simply desire information concerning his nationality, origins, or pertinent medical history. This information is basic to identity formation, yet it would be denied to him by almost any adoption agency in this country. In an effort to gain knowledge about their pasts, some adoptees begin seeking their natural parents and embark on what has come to be called "The Search." Long thought of by social workers and adoption agencies as an indication of emotional problems or the couple's failure as parents, the search is really a need for identity and not a neurotic hunt for love.

FOR YOU TO WRITE

1. Visit your local SPCA and investigate the conditions and treatment of animals available for adoption. Write a positive or negative evaluation of the

conditions there for one of the following audiences: the director of the SPCA, or a letter to the editor of your local newspaper. If your evaluation is negative, write an argument addressed to students urging them not to abandon pets carelessly at the end of the school year. Or write what would be, in effect, an advertising brochure, urging people to adopt one or more of the particular animals in the shelter.

2. Visit a nursery school, day-care center, nursing home, or hospital and write an argument characterizing it, based on your impressions. Remember that your evidence will be incomplete, so your characterization will be carefully qualified. However, if you know any of these institutions intimately, perhaps from working in one, you might attempt a full-scale evaluation.

3. Imagine that you are ultimately proposing some improvement in the financial support of students to an audience of university or state officials. Your opening demonstration section will have to support the thesis that "some students live difficult, financially strained lives." Write that section using specific examples to evoke your audience's sympathy.

4. Try to convince an audience that differs from you in age, education, or life style that some activity you enjoy is fun. Remember that your aim is to convince that audience of your evaluation and perhaps encourage them to participate, not just to expose your personal taste.

VARIATION IN ARRANGEMENT

The Size of the Argumentative Unit

We are about to discuss how to move around the parts of an argument in order to accommodate it to an audience. Questions of arrangement and rearrangement often come up in the revision process, after the necessary parts of an argument have been created. First, we need to define the size of the parts we are moving around. Are we moving bricks, walls, or whole houses—sentences, paragraphs, or chapters in a book? After all, an argument for a proposition can vary in length from a paragraph to a volume (although an argument that requires a volume of support sits on top of a pyramid of smaller arguments).

For convenience we are going to frame our advice about arrangement for arguments of about 1,000 words. This is about the size of a substantial student theme, a short article in a magazine, or a newspaper column—long enough to support a single thesis convincingly and short enough to be read all at once. But this advice will tend to hold for major term papers, long reports, chapters in books, and even whole books, because any piece of writing that exists as a discrete unit ultimately serves one thesis. The parts may be bigger, but you move them around for the same reasons.

Where to Put the Thesis

A major organizational concern for you as an arguer is where to reveal to your reader the main point you are trying to support, the thesis of your argument. Where the thesis actually appears is an accommodation choice; the actual substance of your argument is determined by the kind of thesis you are supporting. Your first thought might be that the thesis always belongs in the beginning; you may even have learned somewhere that in a five-paragraph essay it should be the last sentence of the first paragraph. But any advice that allows only one way to arrange a piece of writing is not taking audience into account. Actually, you can put your thesis any-where—up front, at the end, somewhere in the middle—or even nowhere at all, depending on how your audience will probably respond to your topic.

Thesis "Up Front"

"Up front" means in the first paragraph of a 1,000-word argument, if not in the title of the piece itself. Once again, this early position seems to be the natural place to put the thesis, and it often is. You announce to your reader what you are arguing for, mention the major points of your argu-ment, and then go ahead with detailed support. Now let's think about the value of that "spill the beans" approach and in what situations it is appro-priate.

The basic effect of thesis "up front" is to give your audience a frame-work on which to hang all subsequent arguments. If readers know what thesis is being supported right from the beginning, then everything else they go on to read is placed in relation to that thesis. It is as though the readers were doing a puzzle in a frame ready-made to contain all the pieces with the shape of each stamped on the cardboard bottom.

Our metaphor describes the way children learn to do puzzles. We can continue the metaphor to help characterize the audience of an argument with its thesis up front. Children who have never done puzzles need an outline or frame so that they can see the goal of their task. An audience that is uninformed on a topic or one that takes no stand on an issue may want the purpose of the whole argument, the thesis, set out in the begin-ning. Otherwise they may be impatient with a heap of pieces or parts and no way to relate them. For instance, what do you make of these two paragraphs rich in detail?

> French fried potatoes, for example, may also be restructured. Processors take whole raw potatoes apart, cell by cell, and blend them with other ingredients. The mixture, reshaped into uniform pieces, is then frozen and shipped to feed-ing institutions, especially fast-food chains and schools. The produce is de-

scribed as uniform in flavor, texture, color, and appearance 12 months a year, for all the variations have been controlled. The rationale for using this process is that ascorbic acid, added to the blend, is retained sufficiently to meet requirements for the school lunch program. The possible losses of other nutrients in the potato, owing to this harsh treatment, are ignored.

Onion rings may also be restructured—from inexpensive dehydrated onion, first reconstituted in water and then added to a matrix mix that acts as a "skin setting" bath. The blend, pumped into an extruding machine, forms uniform onion ring-shaped products.

—*The Christian Science Monitor*

You don't know whether to pay attention to the process of restructuring food, the ascorbic acid, the school lunch program, or the nutrition. You are given plenty of information, but no frame to place it in. Actually, these two paragraphs are the second and third in an argument. Now read the following paragraph, the first, which gives the claim that the examples support:

The restructuring of potato chips, made from dehydrated potatoes, was a well-publicized technological feat. What is unknown by many consumers is that numerous other foods are being restructured without being recognized as different from their traditional counterparts.

If you go back and reread what are actually the second and third paragraphs, the details will no longer confuse you. They fit under the umbrella of the general statement that "foods are being restructured without being recognized as different."

Not only does the thesis up front give coherence to the supporting points that follow, it can also grab the interest of an indifferent audience. Any piece of writing has to begin with a hook to catch a reader, and the thesis of an argument, given all at once, can do the grabbing, especially if there is something daring about it. Most of us would want to read about something that has been hidden from us, like the restructuring of food.

In general, then, putting the thesis first is wise when your readers need the help of a frame to make sense of the points in an argument that is either very detailed or very complicated. Also, if you think your thesis will intrigue uninformed or neutral readers, put it up front.

Thesis at the Very End

Some writers wait until the very end of an argument to disclose its thesis. They may even set up a tentative thesis in the beginning and then replace it at the conclusion with a better one. This tactic may seem odd. Why keep the reader in doubt about the claim that is being supported? After all, you lose the advantage of that frame to fit pieces into, and you may even try your readers' patience. Instead, to pick up our puzzle metaphor again, you give readers a pile of pieces with no indication of the shape or size of the final picture they are to complete. They must patiently fit piece to piece until all at once the final picture emerges.

But that creation of the final picture may be just the effect you want. The "thesis at the end" dramatizes the compelling order and nature of the support for an argument and the inevitability of its conclusion. This technique can work well with a hostile or resistant audience who will not bother to read an argument if they know from the first it is for a thesis they reject. But if they can be led to pick up the pieces one by one, they are made to complete the puzzle almost without realizing it. They themselves put the final piece in place and may come close to accepting your argument.

The catch in this method is that the pieces have to be so well shaped that they fit together in only one way to form only one picture. That is, the parts of the argument had better lead to one and only one conclusion, or else your readers, who have been forming tentative theses all along, may come to the end with one in mind that is quite different from yours.

Certain kinds of arguments do well with the thesis at the end. A truncated proposal, for instance, comes sensibly at the end of an argument giving all the reasons why "something" should be done. Readers won't acknowledge the need for action until they know what the problem is. Similarly, a causal argument can sometimes hold back its thesis the way a detective mystery holds back both the identity of the murderer and his motives. This postponing works because causal argument, like a detective story, can take readers through the reasoning or discovery process that the author has gone through. Readers are compelled to track down the common factor or the single difference, to eliminate one by one the rival causes or to pull in every link in a chain until the important cause is identified. Holding back the thesis and emphasizing the process makes the conclusion of a causal argument seem all the more inevitable.

It is also possible, though not common except in short arguments, to save for the end the generalization that draws together a number of examples. Such a conclusion must strike readers as the sum of all the parts or examples that have preceded it, not one that requires careful definition. It must be as self-evident as the 6 at the end of $2 + 2 + 2$.

Thesis Somewhere Along the Way

Actually, you can put your thesis anywhere you want. The only requirements are that you know why you put it where you put it, and that the *why* be the result of consideration of audience and purpose. Just as there are reasons for beginning or ending with the thesis, there are also good reasons for postponing it a bit in order to prepare the readers. Often the thesis can wait a paragraph or two while you make a play for your readers' attention or appeal overtly to their emotion. You open with an example, a clever quotation, a witty paradox, a knotty problem to be solved, or an emotional appeal. You can begin by spending some time talking about yourself, establishing your authority to be making the argument in the first place, or by characterizing and refuting your opposition. All these tactics are good fanfare before the thesis appears front and center stage.

Another reason to postpone the thesis a paragraph or two in the 1,000-word argument is to take time to define crucial terms. Suppose you are arguing that "the rich are different from the rest of us." Before springing that thesis on your audience, you might want to stake out what you mean by "the rich." Everyone knows that someone who is rich has lots of money, but how much? Is someone "rich" who earns over $50,000, over $100,000, or over $500,000 a year? If you define *rich* before declaring your thesis, you may have a much easier time making your thesis acceptable.

You may also find it necessary to put off your thesis for a while, if not to the end, in order to disarm the predictable hostility it will arouse in your readers. You may talk directly to readers for a paragraph or two, saying in effect, "Yes, I know that you have strong opinions on this subject, but wait and hear me out." Or you can try to find some common ground, some matter on which you and your hostile audience do agree, in order to draw them toward you in the beginning of your argument. If, for instance, your hostile readers are Republicans and you are a Democrat, you can at least remind them that you are all Americans. Or if your audience is for Medicare and you are against it, you can remind them that you are both concerned with the welfare of the aged.

No Thesis at All

Strange as it may sound, you can argue vehemently for a thesis precisely formulated in your mind that never appears explicitly in your argument. Of course, it must appear eventually in your readers' minds as well (if you have argued well), but for various reasons you have kept it off the page. Perhaps putting it in would seem like an overstatement, for the evidence is so strong readers can frame it for themselves. Perhaps the actual bald statement of the thesis would shock the readers. A series of very vivid examples, even one extended example, can yield a thesis even though that thesis is never written down. A writer provides a list of examples like the following:

A restaurant in New England serves what the menu calls "Maine lobster." But the lobster had actually been a resident of the New Jersey shore. Another restaurant advertises "home made apple pies," but the chef does not live in the kitchen where he baked them. Often the "butter" on the menu is margarine, the "freshly whipped cream" a vegetable substitute, and the "scrambled eggs" are made from powdered eggs.

Readers could formulate to themselves the generalization that emerges from these examples: Some restaurant menus misrepresent the food actually served.

The thesis that might shock a particular audience is sometimes wisely withheld; instead, the readers are guided by a carefully structured argument to verbalize the suppressed thesis to themselves. Some ideas look too extreme and are too easy to reject when a hostile audience sees them in writing. If you face an accommodation struggle that would be like climbing a perpendicular rock face, you might give up altogether the appearance of argument and simply present your reasons as though they were a series of gentle observations. Suppose, for instance, you really want to argue with the super-successful football coach and his staff that the football program is worthless, even detrimental. Want to try it? The ink would congeal in your pen. The most you could come up with would be a series of milder theses about the program's waste of money, time, and effort. You might hope that your readers would extend the implications of your argument, or extrapolate from your milder points to a stronger thesis. But that thesis itself, "The football program should be abolished," might remain unwritable for the audience that enjoys or makes its living from football.

FOR YOU TO ANALYZE

Here are some short arguments. Identify the thesis in each and, taking audience into account, explain the accommodation devices used by the author.

WHAT NEXT FOR THE BOOMERS? THE NEW SERIOUSNESS!

P. J. O'Rourke

Ever since the stock market went to the bathroom last fall, a lot of us have been pretty busy—talking our broker pals down from window ledges and convincing friends in the junk bond business to shut off the Porsche and open the garage door. We've been so busy that we may not have noticed Black Monday, Blue Tuesday, Black and Blue Wednesday, etc. marked the end of an era. Neopoverty means curtains for the Yuppies, a.k.a. the Me Generation, a.k.a. the Now Generation, a.k.a. the Dr. Spock Brats. Everybody born between WWII and the early '60s is finally going to have to grow up. It's all over now, Baby Boom.

Of course, the collapse of the Reagan Pig-Out wasn't the only thing that did us Boomers in. There was massive drug-taking, which turned out to be a bad idea. Maybe drugs make you a better person, but only if you believe in heaven and think John Belushi could get past the doorman. And having sex with everyone we could think of—this broke up our first two marriages and gave most of us chronic venereal diseases and the rest of us obituaries. And then there was us, just being ourselves—"finding out who we are," "getting in touch with our feelings," "fulfilling our true inner potential"—frightening stuff. You'll notice that now we're all running out to see *Fatal Attraction* so we can moon over a nuclear family and cheer for traditional morals. It seems like that boring middle-class suburbia where we grew up was swell after all. The problem is, we've spent all our money on cocaine and Reeboks and we can't afford it.

What went wrong? We were the generation of hope; the generation that was going to change the world; the biggest, richest, best-educated generation in the history of America—the biggest, richest, best-educated spot in this or any other galaxy. Nothing was too good for us. It took thousands of doctors and psychiatrists to decide whether we should suck our thumbs or all our toes, too. Our every childhood fad had global implications. One smile at Davy Crockett and the forests of the temperate zone were denuded in the search for raccoon-tail hats. When we took up Hula Hoops, the planet bobbled in its orbit. Our transistor radios drowned out the music of the spheres. A sniffle from us and *Life* magazine was sick in bed for a month. All we had to do was hold a sit-in and governments were toppled from the Peking of Mao Tse-tung to the Cleveland of Dennis Kucinich. "We are the world," we shouted just a couple of years ago. And just a couple of years ago we were. How did we wind up so old? So fat? So confused? So *broke?*

The truth is our generation was spoiled rotten from the start. We spent the entire 1950s on our butts in front of the television while mom fed us Twinkies and Ring-Dings through strawberry Flavor Straws and dad ransacked the toy stores looking for 100 mph streamlined Schwinns, Daisy air howitzers, Lionel train sets larger than the New York Central system, and other novelties to keep us amused during the few hours when Pinky Lee and *My Friend Flicka* weren't on the air.

When we came of age in the 1960s, we found the world wasn't as perfect as Mr. Greenjeans and Mrs. Cleaver said it would be, and we threw a decade-long temper tantrum. We screamed at our parents, our teachers, the police, the president, Congress and the Pentagon. We threatened to hold our breath (as long as the reefer stayed lit) and not to cut our hair until poverty, war and injustice were stopped.

That didn't work. So we whiled away the '70s in an orgy of hedonism and self-absorption, bouncing from ashram to bedroom to disco to gym at a speed made possible only by ingesting vast quantities of Inca Scratch-N-Sniff.

Even this proved unsatisfying, so we elected President Reagan and tried our hand at naked greed. We could have it all—career, marriage, job, children, BMW, Rolex, compact disc player, another marriage, more children, and a high-growth, high-yield, no-load mutual fund. Actually, for a while, it looked like we *could* have it all. As long as we didn't mind also having a national debt the size of the Crab Nebula, an enormous underclass making its living from 5-cent beverage can deposits and currency that the Japanese use to blow their nose. But now our economy has the willi-waws, and our Youth Culture has arthritis, Alzheimer's and gout. Life's big Visa card bill has come due at last.

The Baby Boom has reached middle age. It's time for us to pause, time to reflect, time to . . . OH, GOD, DARLING DON'T DO IT WITH A GUN—WE JUST REDECORATED THE BATHROOM!!! . . . time to evaluate the contributions that we, as a generation, have made to a world which presented us with so many unique advantages. Contributions such as . . . uh . . . um . . . BZZZZ77777, Time's Up! Well, some of the Beatles' songs are really great. (Although, technically, the Beatles aren't part of the Baby Boom.) And there's the first Tom Robbins novel, "Another Roadside Attraction." That was good, I think. I mean I was very stoned when I read it. And . . . and . . . New Coke?

Wait a minute, I hear dissenting noises. Civil rights, you say? But the civil rights movement was founded by people a lot older than us. Harriet Tubman, for instance. We Boomers *did* start the Peace Movement. That was a big success. The Vietnam War only lasted another eight or 10 years, once we got the Peace Movement going. Then, darn it, the Communists took over South Vietmam, Laos and Cambodia and killed everybody they could get their hands on just like Gen. Westmoreland, that pig, said they would. So I don't think we can count the Peace Movement as a major contribution, especially not as far as the former citizens of Phnom Penh are concerned. Our political commitment, however, really changed things. You can tell by the quality of the presidents we used to have, such as Truman and Eisenhower, compared with the quality of the presidents we got as soon as the Baby Boom was old enough to vote, such as Carter and Reagan. And our idealism has made a difference. Ever since Live-Aid, all the Ethiopians have had to do the Jane Fonda work-out to keep from larding up around the middle.

It is true that our generation was the first to take feminism seriously. That's because old-timey feminists used to worry about boring things like voting rights and legal status. But Boomer Women put some real life in the issues by emphasizing upscale grabbiness, pointless careerism and insane arguments about pronoun antecedents. Fitness is another trend pioneered by the Boom. Millions of us are leading empty, useless, pitiful lives and lifting weights and eating fiber to make those lives last longer. Also, the computer revolution—we invented a brilliant matrix of complex and intricate software programs which allow us to compile, cross-reference and instantly access all the nothing that we know. Finally, there's our creativity—our wild, innovative, original artistic gifts—surely a legacy to the ages. Huh? Huh? Sorry, I couldn't hear you. I had the new L. L. Cool J "Bigger and Deffer" tape turned all the way up on my Walkman.

Let's face it, our much-vaunted rebellion against bourgeois values meant we didn't want to clean the bathroom. All our mystical enlightenments are now printed in Hallmark greeting cards with pictures of unicorns on them. Our intellectual insights led to a school system that hasn't taught anybody how to read in 15 years. All we've done for the disadvantaged is gentrify the crap out of their neighborhoods. And now we're about to lose our jobs.

Do we have any skills or anything? No. Complain, play Donkey Kong, and roll joints with E-Z Wider papers are the only things this generation has ever been able to do. Will anyone feel sorry for us? No. We've been making pests of ourselves for four decades, hogging the limelight, making everybody feel un-hip and out of it. The Earth has had a belly-ful of us. We'll be selling kiwi fruit on the street and rattling microchips in a tin cup and people will *laugh*.

We're the generation whose heroes were Howdy Doody, Jerry Rubin, Big Bird and Ivan Boesky. We deserve the stock market crash, and herpes and the Betty Ford Clinic, besides. We're jerks. We're clowns. We're 40 and still wearing jeans. Nobody takes us seriously . . .

Wait a minute. *Serious.* That's it. Oh, man, this will really bug the squares! What we do is we all start wearing dumpy corduroy sport coats and cheap, shiny navy-blue wash pants and Hush Puppies. We get those stupid half-glasses and wear them way down on the end of our nose. We read Schopenhauer, Wittgenstein, Kant—all those guys. We call it *The New Seriousness.* The media will wig out. We'll be all over network TV again.

Dig this—we start going to church, not Moonie church or born-again church but real Episcopalian church, every Sunday. We invite each other over to afternoon teas and discuss the novels of Thomas Mann. We take up the cello. We do the London Times crossword puzzle in ink. We admire Woody Allen's *recent* movies. We vote in local elections.

We'll be *crazy* serious—international superstars of, like, heavy, pensive eggheadery. We fire David Letterman and replace him with Jean-Paul Sartre. (Is he still alive? Well, somebody like that.) Shoot MTV videos for Handel and Rimsky-Korsakov. Do a feature movie about the life of Euripides with the sound track in ancient Greek. There are 76 million of us. Everybody's going to want a books-on-tape cassette of Bertrand Russell and A. N. Whitehead's *Principia Mathematica* for their car. We'll make a fortune! We'll be famous! And we'll change the world!

The New Seriousness—it's bitchin', it's far-out, it's rad to the max, it's *us.* Gotta go now. Gotta call Merrill Lynch and buy stock in the Cleveland Symphony Orchestra.

A PLEA FOR THE CHIMPANZEES

Jane Goodall

The chimpanzee is more like us, genetically, than any other animal. It is because of similarities in physiology, in biochemistry, and in the immune system that medical science makes use of the living bodies of chimpanzees in its search for cures and vaccines for a variety of human diseases.

There are also behavioral, psychological, and emotional similarities between chimpanzees and humans, resemblances so striking that they raise a serious ethical question: Are we justified in using an animal so close to us—an animal, moreover, that is highly endangered in its African forest home—as a human substitute in medical experimentation?

In the long run, we can hope that scientists will find ways of exploring human physiology and disease, and of testing cures and vaccines, that do not depend on the use of living animals of any sort. A number of steps in this direction already have been taken, prompted in large part by a growing public awareness of the suffering that is being inflicted on millions of animals. More and more people are beginning to realize that nonhuman animals—even rats and guinea pigs—are not just unfeeling machines but are capable of enjoying their lives, and of feeling fear, pain, and despair.

But until alternatives have been found, medical science will continue to use animals in the battle against human disease and suffering. And some of those animals will continue to be chimpanzees.

Because they share with us 99 percent of their genetic material, chimpanzees can be infected with some human diseases that do not infect other animals. They are currently being used in research on the nature of hepatitis non-A non-B, for example, and they continue to play a major role in the development of vaccines against hepatitis B.

Many biomedical laboratories are looking to the chimpanzee to help them in the race to find a vaccine against acquired immune deficiency syndrome. Chimpanzees are not good models for AIDS research; although the AIDS virus stays alive and replicates within the chimpanzee's bloodstream, no chimp has yet come down with the disease itself. Nevertheless, many of the scientists involved argue that only by using chimpanzees can potential vaccines be safely tested.

Given the scientists' professed need for animals in research, let us turn aside from the sensitive ethical issue of whether chimpanzees *should* be used in medical research, and consider a more immediate issue: How are we treating the chimpanzees that are actually being used?

Just after Christmas I watched, with shock, anger, and anguish, a videotape—made by an animal rights group during a raid—revealing the conditions in a large biomedical research laboratory, under contract to the National Institutes of Health, in which various primates, including chimpanzees, are maintained. In late March, I was given permission to visit the facility.

It was a visit I shall never forget. Room after room was lined with small, bare cages, stacked one above the other, in which monkeys circled round and round and chimpanzees sat huddled, far gone in depression and despair.

Young chimpanzees, three or four years old, were crammed, two together, into tiny cages measuring 57 cm by 57 cm and only 61 cm high. They could hardly turn around. Not yet part of any experiment, they had been confined in these cages for more than three months.

The chimps had each other for comfort, but they would not remain together for long. Once they are infected, probably with hepatitis, they will be separated and placed in another cage. And there they will remain, living in conditions of severe sensory deprivation, for the next several years. During that time, they will become insane.

A juvenile female rocked from side to side, sealed off from the outside world behind the glass doors of her metal isolation chamber. She was in semidarkness. All she could hear was the incessant roar of air rushing through vents into her prison.

In order to demonstrate the "good" relationship the lab's caretaker had with this chimpanzee, one of the scientists told him to lift her from the cage. The caretaker opened the door. She sat, unmoving. He reached in. She did not greet him—nor did he greet her. As if drugged, she allowed him to take her out. She sat motionless in his arms. He did not speak to her, she did not look at him. He touched her lips briefly. He returned her to her cage. She sat again on the bars of the floor. The door closed.

I shall be haunted forever by her eyes, and by the eyes of the other infant chimpanzees I saw that day. Have you ever looked into the eyes of a person who, stressed beyond endurance, has given up, succumbed utterly to the crippling helplessness of despair? I once saw a little African boy whose whole family had been killed during the fighting in Burundi. He too looked out at the world, unseeing, from dull, blank eyes.

Though this particular laboratory may be one of the worst, from what I have learned, most of the other biomedical animal-research facilities are not much better. Yet only when one has some understanding of the true nature of the chimpanzee can the cruelty of these captive conditions be fully understood.

An Isolating Cage

Chimpanzees are very social by nature. Bonds between individuals, particularly between family members and close friends, can be affectionate and supportive, and can endure throughout their lives. The accidental separation of two friendly individuals can cause them intense distress. Indeed, the death of a mother may be such a psychological blow to her child that even if the child is five years old and no longer dependent on its mother's milk, it may pine away and die.

It is impossible to overemphasize the importance of friendly physical contact for the well-being of the chimpanzee. Again and again one can watch a frightened or tense individual relax if she is patted, kissed, or embraced reassuringly by a companion. Social grooming, which provides hours of close contact, is undoubtedly the single most important social activity.

Chimpanzees in their natural habitat are active for much of the day. They travel extensively within their territory, which can be as large as 50 km^2 for a community of about 50 individuals. If they hear other chimpanzees calling as they move through the forest, or anticipate arriving at a good food source, they typically break into excited charging displays, racing along the ground, hurling sticks and rocks and shaking the vegetation. Youngsters, particularly, are full of energy, and spend long hours playing with one another or by themselves, leaping through the branches and gamboling along the ground. Adults sometimes join these games. Bunches of fruit, twigs, and rocks may be used as toys.

Chimpanzees enjoy comfort. They construct sleeping platforms each night, using a multitude of leafy twigs to make their beds soft. Often, too, they make little "pillows" on which to rest during a midday siesta.

Chimps are highly intelligent. They display cognitive abilities that were, until recently, thought to be unique to humans. They are capable of cross-modal transfer of information—that is, they can identify by touch an object they have previously only seen, and vice versa. They are capable of reasoned thought, generalization, abstraction, and symbolic representation. They have some concept of self. They have excellent memories and can, to some extent, plan for the future. They show a capacity for intentional communication that depends, in part, on their ability to understand the motives of the individuals with whom they are communicating.

Chimpanzees are capable of empathy and altruistic behavior. They show emotions that are undoubtedly similar, if not identical, to human emotions—joy, pleasure, contentment, anxiety, fear, and rage. They even have a sense of humor.

The chimpanzee child and the human child are alike in many ways: in their capacity for endless romping and fun; their curiosity; their ability to learn by observation, imitation, and practice; and, above all, their need for reassurance and love. When young chimpanzees are brought up in a human home and treated like human children, they learn to eat at table, to help themselves to snacks from the refrigerator, to sort and put away cutlery, to brush their teeth, to play with dolls, to switch on the television and select a program that interests them and watch it.

Young chimpanzees can easily learn over 200 signs of the American language of the deaf and use these signs to communicate meaningfully with humans and with one another. One youngster in the laboratory of Roger S. Fouts, a psychologist at Central Washington University, has picked up 68 signs from four older signing chimpanzee companions, with no coaching from humans. The chimp uses the signs in communication with other chimpanzees and with humans.

The chimpanzee facilities in most biomedical research laboratories allow for the expression of almost none of these activities and behaviors. They provide little—if anything—more than the warmth, food and water, and veterinary care required to sustain life. The psychological and emotional needs of these creatures are rarely catered to, and often not even acknowledged.

In most labs the chimpanzees are housed individually, one chimp to a cage, unless they are part of a breeding program. The standard size of each cage is about 7.6 m² and about 1.8 m high. In one facility, a cage described in the catalogue as "large," designed for a chimpanzee of up to 25 kg, measures 0.76 by 1.1 m, with a height of 1.6 m. Federal requirements for cage size are dependent on body size; infant chimpanzees, who are the most active, are often imprisoned in the smallest cages.

In most labs, the chimpanzees cannot even lie with their arms and legs outstretched. They are not let out to exercise. There is seldom anything for them to do other than eat, and then only when food is brought. The caretakers are usually too busy to pay attention to individual chimpanzees. The cages are bleak and sterile, with bars above, bars below, bars on every side. There is no comfort in them, no bedding. The chimps, infected with human diseases, will often feel sick and miserable.

A Harmful System

What of the human beings who administer these facilities—the caretakers, veterinarians, and scientists who work at them? If they are decent, compassionate people, how can they condone, or even tolerate, the kind of conditions I have described?

They are, I believe, victims of a system that was set up long before the cognitive abilities and emotional needs of chimpanzees were understood. Newly employed staff members, equipped with a normal measure of compassion, may well be sickened by what they see. And, in fact, many of them do quit their jobs, unable to endure the suffering they see inflicted on the animals yet feeling powerless to help.

But others stay on and gradually come to accept the cruelty, believing (or forcing themselves to believe) that it is an inevitable part of the struggle to reduce human suffering. Some become hard and callous in the process, in Shakespeare's words, "all pity choked with custom of fell deeds."

A handful of compassionate and dedicated caretakers and veterinarians are fighting to improve the lot of the animals in their care. Veterinarians are often in a particularly difficult position, for if they stand firm and try to uphold high standards of humane care, they will not always be welcome in the lab.

Many of the scientists believe that a bleak, sterile, and restricting environment is necessary for their research. The cages must be small, the scientists maintain, because otherwise it is too difficult to treat the chimpanzees—to inject them, to draw their blood, or to anesthetize them. Moreover, they are less likely to hurt themselves in small cages.

The cages must also be barren, with no bedding or toys, say the scientists. This way, the chimpanzees are less likely to pick up diseases or parasites. Also, if things are lying about, the cages are harder to clean.

And the chimpanzees must be kept in isolation, the scientists believe, to avoid the risk of cross-infection, particularly in hepatitis research.

Finally, of course, bigger cages, social groups, and elaborate furnishings require more space, more caretakers—and more money. Perhaps, then, if we are to believe these researchers, it is not possible to improve conditions for chimpanzees imprisoned in biomedical research laboratories.

I believe not only that it *is* possible, but that improvements are absolutely necessary. If we do not do something to help these creatures, we make a mockery of the whole concept of justice.

Quality of Life in the Laboratory

Perhaps the most important way we can improve the quality of life for the laboratory chimps is to increase the number of carefully trained caretakers. These people should be selected for their understanding of animal behavior and their compassion and respect for, and dedication to, their charges. Each caretaker, having established a relationship of trust with the chimpanzees in his care, should be allowed to spend time with the animals over and above that required for cleaning the cages and providing the animals with food and water.

It has been shown that a chimpanzee who has a good relationship with his caretaker will cooperate calmly during experimental procedures, rather than react with fear or anger. At the Dutch Primate Center in Rijswijk, for example, some chimpanzees have been trained to leave their group cage on command and move into small, single cages for treatment. At the Stanford Primate Center in California, a number of chimpanzees were taught to extend their arms for the drawing of blood. In return they were given a food reward.

Much can be done to alleviate the pain and distress felt by younger chimpanzees during experimental procedures. A youngster, for example, can be treated when in the presence of a trusted human friend. Experiments have shown that young chimps react with high levels of distress if subjected to mild electric shocks when alone, but show almost no fear or pain when held by a sympathetic caretaker.

What about cage size? Here we should emulate the animal-protection regulations that already exist in Switzerland. These laws stipulate that a cage must be, at minimum, about 20 m² and 3 m high for pairs of chimpanzees.

The chimpanzees should never be housed alone unless this is an essential part of the experimental procedure. For chimps in solitary confinement, particularly youngsters, three to four hours of friendly interaction with a caretaker should be mandatory. A chimp taking part in hepatitis research, in which the risk of cross-infection is, I am told, great, can be provided with a companion of a compatible species if it doesn't infringe on existing regulations—a rhesus monkey, for example, which cannot catch or pass on the disease.

For healthy chimpanzees there should be little risk of infection from bedding and toys. Stress and depression, however, can have deleterious effects on their health. It is known that clinically depressed humans are more prone to a variety of physiological disorders, and heightened stress can interfere with immune function. Given the chimpanzee's similarities to humans, it is not surprising that the chimp in a typical laboratory, alone in his bleak cage, is an easy prey to infections and parasites.

Thus, the chimpanzees also should be provided with a rich and stimulating environment. Climbing apparatus should be obligatory. There should be many objects for them to play with or otherwise manipulate. A variety of simple devices designed to alleviate boredom could be produced quite cheaply. Unexpected food items will elicit great pleasure. If a few simple buttons in each cage were connected to a computer terminal, it would be possible for the chimpanzees to feel they at least have some control over their world—if one button produced a grape when pressed, another a drink, another a video picture. (The Canadian Council on Animal Care recommends the provision of television for primates in solitary confinement, or other means of enriching their environment.)

Without doubt, it will be considerably more costly to maintain chimpanzees in the manner I have outlined. Should we begrudge them the extra dollars? We take from them their freedom, their health, and often their lives. Surely, the least we can do is try to provide them with some of the things that could make their imprisonment more bearable.

There are hopeful signs. I was immensely grateful to officials of the National Institutes of Health for allowing me to visit the primate facility, enabling me to see the conditions there and judge them for myself. And I was even more grateful for the fact that they gave me a great deal of time for serious discussions of the problem. Doors were opened and a dialogue begun. All who were present at the meetings agreed that, in light of present knowledge, it is indeed necessary to give chimpanzees a better deal in the labs.

I have had the privilege of working among wild, free chimpanzees for more than 26 years. I have gained a deep understanding of chimpanzee nature. Chimpanzees have given me so much in my life. The least I can do is to speak out for the hundreds of chimpanzees who, right now, sit hunched, miserable and without hope, staring out with dead eyes from their metal prisons. They cannot speak for themselves.

FOR YOU TO WRITE

Write an argument of about 1,000 words and put it together in several different ways.

1. For an audience who is uninformed and unbiased on the topic.
2. For a slightly resistant audience or one to whom you must establish your authority to make this particular argument.
3. For a very resistant audience, one that holds the opposite thesis.

You may take any subject suggested in previous sections or one of the following specific suggestions.

1. Characterize a person, either real or fictional, living or historical, as belonging to a category, class, or type. You must avoid offensive stereotyping.
2. Evaluate the clothing and appearance of a group or an individual. The challenge in this argument is to make it impersonal.
3. Make a causal argument for one person's responsibility as the main cause of another person's success or failure.
4. Propose that your college replace its current grading system with another (from letter grades to pass/fail or from numerical average to letter grade or some other system).

Index